THE ENGINE OF ENTERPRISE

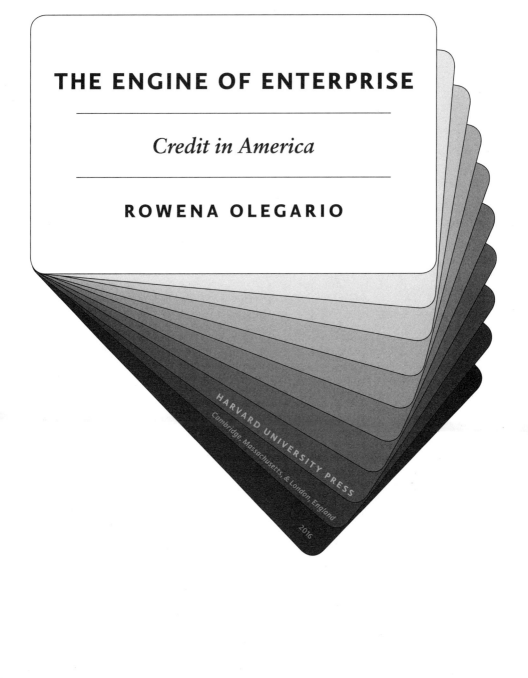

THE ENGINE OF ENTERPRISE

Credit in America

ROWENA OLEGARIO

HARVARD UNIVERSITY PRESS
Cambridge, Massachusetts, & London, England
2016

Library of Congress Cataloging-in-Publication Data

Olegario, Rowena.
The engine of enterprise : credit in America / Rowena Olegario.
pages cm
Includes bibliographical references and index.
ISBN 978-0-674-05114-0 (hardcover : alk. paper)
1. Commercial credit—United States—History. 2. Mercantile
system—United States—History. 3. Finance—United States—History.
4. Economic development—United States—History. 5. United States—
Economic conditions. I. Title.
HG3754.5.U6O443 2015
332.7'420973—dc23   2015013113

To my family

and

To the memory of Thomas K. McCraw (1940–2012)
Historian, mentor, friend

CONTENTS

THE ENGINE OF ENTERPRISE

INTRODUCTION

In 2010, Americans had total debt outstanding of $52.4 trillion, more than three-and-a-half times the country's gross domestic product (GDP). The household sector represented one-quarter of the debt, or $13.2 trillion. Businesses, including the financial sector, bore nearly half, at $24.5 trillion. Government at all levels accounted for another $12.4 trillion, or 24 percent, with the federal government bearing the bulk of the debt.[1] Americans now (in 2008–2010) used more credit, in absolute terms, than at any other time in their history. If the outstanding debt were divided up among the population, every person would have been responsible for nearly $170,000.

Although these numbers seem staggering, the high use of credit was in itself unremarkable. Americans now borrowed more to consume more. But from the beginning, they had used credit productively to increase assets and to conduct commerce. Credit, not savings, funded the Revolution and then propelled the infant republic's economy. It is no exaggeration to say that the United States was built on credit.

Alexander Hamilton foresaw credit's potential. He called credit "the invigorating principle" and "among the principal engines of useful enterprise."[2] As the first secretary of the Treasury, Hamilton strove to put the finances of the United States on a stable footing. But he also wanted to stimulate more private credit for business activities. For this reason, he erected new structures of public finance that included a national bank.[3] The bank put Hamilton on a collision course with his colleague in the Cabinet, Thomas Jefferson, the first secretary of state. Jefferson had approved

1

of the colonial governments' printing of paper money (a form of credit creation) during wartime. But he drew the line at bank credit, believing that it benefited a financial class whose interests were inimical to the well-being of small producers and farmers. A longtime debtor himself, Jefferson saw in credit the potential for self-enslavement. The tensions embodied by Hamilton and Jefferson—between those who considered credit a productive force and those who warned against its destructive tendencies—have existed since the nation's founding.

Problems with credit recurred in every stage of the nation's history. In addition to reconciling people's differing attitudes about credit, Americans struggled with how to improve (or control) credit availability, how to assess creditworthiness, and how to accommodate (rather than simply eliminate) the risks associated with credit. These were the enduring concerns of the nation's lenders, businesses, regulators, political and religious leaders, and households. They form the themes of this book.

The Debates about Credit

People were of two minds about lending and borrowing. In the colonial period, advice books and almanacs became popular, and nearly all of them warned about the dangers of debt. "Rather go to bed supperless, than run in debt for a breakfast," goes one of the sayings in *Poor Richard's Almanack,* the most famous collection of aphorisms about lending and borrowing in American literature. But author Benjamin Franklin also took for granted that credit was essential to commerce. In his "Advice to a Young Tradesman," Franklin urged ambitious young men to cultivate and display the character traits of honesty, frugality, and a good work ethic in order to inspire confidence in their creditors.[4] The ability to command credit was a skill that no tradesman could afford to neglect.

Alexander Hamilton went further. As the first secretary of the Treasury, he had the power to create the institutions that mediated between those who had money to lend and those who needed it. Of all the founders, Hamilton was the most attuned to the potential of a well-ordered regime of public credit: so long as it was properly administered, public credit would benefit both the national government and private businesses. But first Hamilton had to counter the ambivalence that many Americans felt about the public debt. Credit had established the American republic. Loans from France and Holland and the fledgling country's own citizens had enabled the newly independent states to continue fighting the costly eight-year War of Independence. Hamilton called these debt obligations the "price of liberty."[5] But now their sheer volume threatened the viability of the new national government and caused political disaffection within the indebted states. Failure to place the new republic on a stable financial footing made it vulnerable to threats from abroad, from a hostile Britain in particular. Amid objections from Thomas Jefferson and James Madison, Hamilton fought for a program to refinance the federal and state debts into a series of federal securities, in essence replacing the chaos of state issues with the credit of the new U.S. government. The resulting U.S. debt ended up being forty-six times greater than the federal revenues, so large that Hamilton feared the nearly bankrupt republic would disintegrate before it had properly begun. To his relief, the bonds found a ready market among speculators and prudent investors alike in the United States and abroad. By the time Hamilton left office in January 1795, the U.S. financial system stood on a much sounder footing, making possible the surge in business activities that followed. (Even so, for the first twenty years of its existence, most of the United States' federal revenues went to pay off its revolutionary war debts.)[6]

In January 1795, after five years in office, Hamilton presented a valedictory to Congress, stressing again the importance of the public credit. Like his first report on the same topic in 1790, it urged the federal government to sustain the credit of the United States by keeping faith with all who invested in the country's securities, whether they were foreign or domestic investors. The most urgent reason for maintaining the new republic's creditworthiness—which by 1795 had become among the best in the world—was the need to defend itself against mature combatants such as Britain and France. (Hamilton knew that imposing taxes would not be popular, even for a defensive campaign. Instead, the United States would rely mostly on bonds and customs duties.)

The power to command credit went beyond the need to ensure the public safety. At the end of the report, Hamilton offered an argument for the importance of credit in an underdeveloped country. It was, he wrote, "the invigorating principle" that underpinned the country's economic development: "No well-informed man can cast a retrospective eye over the progress of the United States, from their infancy to the present period, without being convinced that they owe, in a great degree, to the fostering influence of credit, their present mature growth." Hamilton listed the different kinds of credit, "mercantile and public, foreign and domestic," that had galvanized the country's development. The colonial governments' emissions of bills of credit (discussed in Chapter 1) had supplemented the mercantile credit coming from abroad by providing the colonists with a form of currency. "Their united force," Hamilton noted, "quickening the energies and bringing into action the capacities for improvement of a new country, was highly instrumental in accelerating its growth."

Hamilton stressed repeatedly that credit was "among the principal engines of useful enterprise and internal improvement." It was "a substitute for capital . . . in agriculture, in commerce, in the manufacturing and mechanic arts." The secretary drew from the everyday observations of his audience—the congressmen and senators of the United States, many of whom were or had been farmers, artisans, and merchants—to illustrate his point:

> One man wishes to take up and cultivate a piece of land; he purchases upon *credit,* and, in time, pays the purchase money out of the produce of the soil improved by his labor. Another sets up in trade; in the credit founded upon a fair character, he seeks, and often finds, the means of becoming, at length, a wealthy merchant. A third commences business as manufacturer or mechanic, with skill, but without money. It is by credit that he is enabled to procure the tools, the materials, and even the subsistence of which he stands in need, until his industry has supplied him with capital; and, even then, he derives, from an established and increased credit, the means of extending his undertakings.

Without means, but possessed of a willingness to work, a fair character, skill, and industry, the citizens of the new republic would use credit to flourish, and their individual prosperity would be the foundation for national wealth and power. Hamilton ended his report by observing that public and private credit were unavoidably intertwined. "There is, perhaps, no example of the one being in a flourishing, where the other was in a bad state. A shock to public credit would, therefore, not only take away the additional means which it has furnished, but by the derangements, disorders, distrusts, and false principles which it would engender and disseminate, would diminish the antecedent resources of private credit."[7]

Alexander Hamilton and Benjamin Franklin thought hard about how best to encourage credit's productive potential while ensuring that its destructive capacity remained under control. Neither man would have considered his own ideas revolutionary. For Hamilton, the fact of credit's productive power was just a "matter of daily experience in the most familiar pursuits." Both founders had worked in trade as young men and taken a youthful interest in the workings of credit and paper money. (In 1729, the twenty-three-year-old Franklin published an essay on how to align Pennsylvania's supply of paper money with the growth rate of its economy.)[8] But although Franklin's Poor Richard still exercises a hold on Americans' moral imaginations, it is Hamilton's institutional legacy that has had the greater effect on their behaviors. Plentiful U.S. Treasury bonds, a vibrant securities market, and banks (including, eventually, a permanent central bank) were all part of the first Treasury secretary's sweeping vision. Underlying it were the assumptions, which Franklin shared, that credit was necessary to fund productive enterprises, and that honesty and a willingness to work were sufficient collateral to secure credit.

Franklin and Hamilton lived much of their lives in port cities, in an Atlantic world held together by commerce. The benefits of credit shaped their worldviews and that of their near-contemporaries in Britain, including the pamphleteer and novelist Daniel Defoe. In 1726 Defoe celebrated the English merchants' wide use of credit, by which "the flock of the kingdom in trade is doubled, or trebled, or more."[9] (As a boy, Franklin had read Defoe's writings and admired them. He later printed and distributed *The Complete English Tradesman* in the American colonies.)[10] Adam Smith devoted several chapters to banking and credit in *The Wealth of Nations,* published in 1776. Like many economic thinkers of the time, Smith saw credit as a means to activate assets that would otherwise lie idle. Merchants' bank balances, for example, could be lent to other merchants to fund short-term capital needs. Banks could discount merchants' paper, turning the debt instruments into bank notes for commercial use to increase the volume of transactions within the economy. Smith could draw on the example of the Scottish banking system, perhaps the most innovative and stable of its time. Scottish banks had many of the features of modern commercial banks, including branches, interest-bearing deposits, overdrafts, and a clearinghouse for notes.[11]

But Smith's view of credit differed from that of Franklin and Hamilton in a fundamental way: Smith in no way supported the idea that credit could be extended to people who had little more than good character and a demonstrated capacity for hard work. In his view, legitimate credit had only one purpose—to prevent *already existing* assets from lying idle and unproductive. Bank notes, being underpinned by merchants' IOUs, were thereby always tied to the level of business actually being conducted in the economy. Credit, in other words, could fuel business activity but not outrun it. "It is not by augmenting the capital of the country, but by rendering a greater part of that capital active and productive than would otherwise be so, that the most judicious operations of banking can increase the industry of the country," Smith argued. Banks could not print money or create credit; the only way a country could augment its capital stock was through the increased savings of its citizens.[12] "Parsimony, and not industry, is the immediate cause of the increase of capital," he wrote. "Whatever industry might acquire, if parsimony did not save and store up, the capital would never be greater."[13]

Saving and storing up were precisely what impatient American entrepreneurs declined to do. Shortly after establishing the constitutional foundations of their new nation, Americans began chartering banks, some twenty-eight in 1800 and far more than that afterwards. The early banks were not mainly for deposits because few people had surplus money. Rather, the banks did what Adam Smith thought banks ought not to do: they printed money and made loans for things that did not yet exist.

Americans discovered that creating credit through banks was relatively easy, given the lax regulatory environment in most states. Many people could not resist the temptation to speculate heavily with borrowed money. In the 1930s Joseph Schumpeter, the great theorist of innovation and capitalism, pointed out that the "reckless banking" of the first decades of the nineteenth century was "the only method available" for creating the credit that funded innovation. According to Schumpeter, capitalism "is that form of private property economy in which innovations are carried out by means of borrowed money, which in general, though not by logical necessity, implies credit creation."[14] Schumpeter insisted on the central role of credit in enterprise. "The headquarters of the capitalist system," he wrote, was the money markets, where investors and lenders made decisions about which entrepreneurial projects to fund. "All kinds of credit requirements come to this market; all kinds of economic projects are first brought into relation with one another, and contend for their realization in it." Crucially, Schumpeter believed that the available funds were the result not just of saving but of credit creation by bankers, who generate "new purchasing power out of nothing."[15]

Exactly who could set up banks, the creators of credit and sources of the country's circulating currency, quickly politicized the new institutions.

It was not simply the case that people distrusted banks, although many did. Entrepreneurs and artisans who had limited access to the banks' resources, or who had no opportunities to establish their own lending institutions, complained bitterly about the "privileges" of the existing banks, including the branches of the Bank of the United States. Solid banks benefited their communities, but when they malfunctioned, it seemed that nearly everyone found something to dislike about the institution of banking. These sentiments shaped the politics of the early nationalist period and—in even more dramatic fashion—the Jacksonian era, roughly the 1820s to the 1840s. When President Andrew Jackson began hinting that he would oppose the recharter of the Second Bank of the United States, he launched the so-called Bank War. It galvanized his opponents, the Whigs, who for the next decade and a half countered the Jacksonians with speeches, essays, and pamphlets setting out the case for rechartering the national bank and for more bank credit generally.

Collectively, the speeches and writings of Henry Clay, Daniel Webster, and other Whigs represented a new view of credit. Henry C. Carey, the most notable economist of the time, argued that the circumstances of the United States made the country's credit system markedly different from that of France and even Great Britain. In an essay that anticipated the new institutional economics by a century and a half, Carey listed the advantages that the United States possessed: secure property rights and a banking system that was less unstable (he claimed) than most people believed it to be. Together, the existence of these healthy institutions inspired a mutual confidence among individuals, which was a great advantage in a large country. "There are few circumstances connected with the American Union more worthy of remark than the credit system, which extends itself over the whole of their vast territory," Carey wrote. "Where property is most secure labour will be most productively applied—the power to accumulate capital will be greatest—and the tendency to moral and physical improvement will be most rapid. Where such is the case, confidence will be most universal, and the existence of that confidence may be taken as evidence of a general disposition to comply with engagements . . . Such is the case in the United States."[16] Americans, according to Carey, showed an unusual willingness to enter into credit contracts with one another because they had confidence in the country's institutions. Carey is today mostly forgotten, and his writings about credit form no part of Americans' intellectual legacy. The pronouncements on credit by national political figures Clay and Webster are remembered only within the context of how the country's modern political party system came into existence in the 1820s and 1830s. The Whig arguments that the American republic needed plentiful credit to be prosperous and that credit was a distinctive feature of advanced societies have disappeared in the historical shadow cast by Andrew Jackson's campaign against the Bank of the United States.

In England, the political philosopher John Stuart Mill expressed ideas that accorded with those of the Whigs. In *Principles of Political Economy* (1848), Mill wrote extensively about banking, credit, and the currency.[17] Like Adam Smith, Mill believed that although credit "cannot make something out of nothing," it could make idle assets productive. But Mill also thought that credit was "generally, and naturally, a transfer to hands more competent to employ the capital efficiently in production." Credit could do more than just animate the assets that already existed. When extended to people of few resources but good character, credit could direct their energies to productive ends. "While credit is thus indispensable for rendering the whole capital of the country productive," Mill wrote, "it is also a means by which the industrial talent of the country is turned to better account for purposes of production. Many a person who has either no capital of his own, or very little, but who has qualifications for business which are known and appreciated by some possessors of capital, is enabled to obtain either advances in money, or more frequently goods on credit, by which his industrial capacities are made instrumental to the increase of the public wealth." For this process to work, a society's educational levels, laws, and morals must have reached a stage "that personal character can be accepted as a sufficient guarantee."[18]

The worldview shared by Defoe, Franklin, Smith, Hamilton, Mill, and the American Whigs gave a legitimate role to credit, and all except Smith allowed for the possibility that credit could be extended on the basis of good character.[19] Their writings, however, existed alongside a steady stream of diatribes against credit and banking not just in the United States, but in every advanced economy of the time. Most people's conceptions about lending and borrowing remained closer to the mindset of the middle ages: they distrusted moneylenders, including banks. Among the founders, we need look no further than Thomas Jefferson, an adherent of Enlightenment and other advanced ideas but a fierce opponent of banks. Jefferson's objections were ideological; he denounced the privileges that banks gave to their stockholders and directors, and the power that banks had over the circulating currency. Rather than heralds of modern finance, banks in his view were instruments of political tyranny. His views could not have been further from those of Hamilton, who admired the Bank of England for "unit[ing] public authority and faith with private credit," and allowing the latter to flourish.[20] Banks, Hamilton argued, "have proved to be the happiest engines that ever were invented for advancing trade."[21] The political fights over banks and the currency began with the founding of the United States, and for two generations these subjects dominated the political stage. People were using credit to build the nation; yet in Congress and the popular press, credit was blamed for the ills that now afflicted people and their communities.

Plenty of Americans today believe that things were different in the past—that somehow their forebears were wiser about keeping out of debt and paying for things only when they could afford them. As we will see, this depiction of the past was never true. Credit was present from the beginning. It evolved and expanded along with the American economy, enabling the creation of productive enterprises and increased consumption. Throughout the nation's history, credit provided opportunities and imposed hardships that shaped how Americans viewed their world.

The Phases of Credit

The story of credit can be divided into four phases:

First phase (1790–1850): A new credit culture emerges. At the nation's founding, credit was confined to networks of people who knew one another, or who had mutual acquaintances. There were only three commercial banks, and paper money was scarce. Creditors had the right to bring an act of bankruptcy against debtors, but debtors had no corresponding right to seek discharge from their debts. By 1850, wholesalers were extending credit based on the reports issued by the new credit reporting agencies. More than 800 commercial banks were issuing hundreds of different currencies and creating credit for all manner of enterprises. A new national bankruptcy law had, briefly, given debtors the right to walk away from their debts and make a fresh start. Along with European observers such as Alexis de Tocqueville and Gustave de Beaumont, Americans sensed that the attitudes, institutions, and politics surrounding credit were shifting. When President Andrew Jackson declared war on the Bank of the United States, members of the new Whig party took up their pens to defend credit as a positive force in society. Credit, they said, was the hallmark of an advanced civilization and a distinctly American device. The dual impulse to monitor debtors closely while showing them leniency when they got into trouble was born during these decades. It was a distinctive feature of American commerce.

Second phase (1865–1910s): The inequities of credit intensify. The disruptions caused by the Civil War slowed the integration of regional credit markets. The South, formerly the richest section of the country, lost much of its wealth. Southern banks that were integral players in the export economy before the war mostly disappeared. The lack of credit and the end of slavery gave rise to sharecropping arrangements that kept tenant farmers, both black and white, in debt to local merchants, who were themselves dependent on outside creditors. The North's victory destroyed the immoral system of slavery, but it also intensified the inequities among different groups. Northern industry and Wall Street had adequate access to credit and money, whereas the expanding agricultural and business sectors in the South and West struggled to get their "fair" share. State laws against branch banking, moreover, protected local bankers from competition. The banking system was highly fragmented and had no lender of last resort, leading some historians to argue that the United States was less able than other countries (such as Britain and Canada) to withstand panics. The seasonal needs of agriculture also placed great strain on the system.

Inadequate money and credit, along with a fragile banking system that struggled to meet the needs of agriculture, disproportionately affected people who lacked influence with the government and Wall Street. Bitter political debates erupted about what should be the basis of money and credit—gold only, gold and silver, or even agricultural commodities. Fears grew that the Wall Street bankers were monopolists, just like the railroad, oil, and steel barons. Reformers called on the federal government to do something, but the national political parties were themselves split over the issues. Finally, in 1916 Congress passed the Federal Farm Loan Act. The legislation created federally supervised cooperative and land banks to increase lending to the agricultural sector. The Federal Reserve, established in 1913 to stabilize the banking system and to make credit availability fairer among regions and interest groups, was born out of the frustrations of the post–Civil War era.

Third phase (1920–1970s): Credit for households expands. At the beginning of the twentieth century, the amount of credit that was available

10

to households was small by modern standards. Very little capital moved between regions to fund home buying. Individuals, home builders, building and loan societies, savings banks, and insurance companies (with some important exceptions) made the bulk of their loans to people living in the same locality. Consumer credit was not too plentiful either. Grocery retailers tried to cut back their credit sales (but they could not eliminate all of them). Installment buying was confined to a few durable goods like farm machinery, sewing machines, and pianos. Personal loan companies had spread, but most people still thought of them as little better than loan sharks.

By the 1970s, this scenario had changed almost beyond recognition. The spread of automobile purchases and the onset of the Great Depression were the key transformative events. To sustain the mass market for durable goods, especially cars, business leaders such as General Motors' Alfred Sloan endorsed installment finance. GM and other industrial corporations even set up their own finance companies to help consumers afford their products. During the Great Depression, the federal government quickly stepped in to stem the mortgage foreclosures and to help the construction industry. The government created secondary markets for home mortgages—markets that the private sector at the time could not create—enabling the banks to lend even more. After the Second World War, veterans could access mortgage financing through the GI Bill. Americans' attitudes about debt shifted. Owning a home was now linked to good citizenship, a worthy goal that eased the government's involvement in the mortgage markets. Buying on installment and having a mortgage became normal components of household budgets, like saving and investing. Consumer credit became an engine of enterprise for the construction industry, the producers of consumer goods, and the purveyors of vacations and other luxuries. Banks went from ignoring home buyers and consumers to being their biggest source of credit. The formerly conservative banks came up with new ways of making money through consumer lending, including the Visa and MasterCard payment systems. People could now carry balances from one month to the next, and many chose to do so even at relatively high interest rates. The credit cards helped to turn Americans into the world's most prodigious users of consumer credit.

Fourth phase (1980–early 2000s): The standards of creditworthiness change. For most of U.S. history, nearly everyone agreed on what constituted a good credit risk. Creditors scrutinized a combination of factors that included good character, a record of prompt payments, and sound collateral. Around 1980, the old way of assessing creditworthiness began to change as a result of many simultaneous developments: technological innovations, globalization, debt securitization, and the ideological shift to freer markets and greater federal support of home ownership. The changes accelerated the "democratization" of household credit that had begun in the 1920s. Credit cards, an unsecured form of lending, spread even to low-income households. Wall Street securitized home mortgages (turned them into bonds) to sell to eager investors. Lenders searched constantly for more borrowers, both to absorb the exploding supply of credit and to provide the mortgages for securitization. Regulatory agencies such as the Securities and Exchange Commission (SEC) and the private credit rating agencies did little to ensure the quality of the debt instruments. Securitization relieved lenders of responsibility until they had no reason to care any more about whether people could afford their loans, and still less about what earlier generations called borrowers' "moral character." (In fact, inquiring too closely about people's behaviors and lifestyles was now illegal.) For a time, some banks were granting mortgages based solely on the applicants' own testimonies about their employment and assets.

The United States evolved through these four phases, from having too little credit to having too much. But the narrative was not simply linear. Cyclical booms and busts meant that even in the early nineteenth century people worried about easy credit. And in the latest phase, when credit was plentiful, reformers continued to tackle the challenge of providing emergency credit to the poor. How much credit should be available, and to whom, were among the questions that recurred in every phase.

Chapter One

"THE SOUND OF YOUR HAMMER"

The Foundations of Credit in the New Republic

The history of credit practices in America has two starting points: overseas trade, primarily in the area known as the Atlantic world; and the informal credits that local storekeepers granted to their customers. The first can be termed mercantile, or business, credit because it was extended from one merchant to another; the second was retail credit. Although it is tempting to label the first as "productive" and the second as "consumer" credit, the line between the two was far less firm than it would later become. Retail credit made consumption possible, as it does today, but it also helped people to establish farms, workshops, and other productive household enterprises.

Of the two types of credit, the one used by overseas merchants was more significant from the viewpoint of economic growth and the evolution of modern business practices. Merchants who dealt over long distances had to overcome several problems: obtaining good information about trading partners, ensuring that contracts with distant merchants were honored, and making certain that agents did what was in the merchant's best interests rather than their own. These difficulties also dogged storekeepers, but they had better access to local sources of information, and they conducted business in a more personal fashion that enhanced their ability to monitor business partners and collect from debtors. Long-distance merchants had no such advantages. For them, the attempts to solve the problems of information, enforcement, and what economists call the principal-agent issue resulted in certain ways of thinking. Shared experiences and habits formed an ethos about how merchants ought to behave toward one another and a general agreement about what made such men (and they were almost exclusively men) worthy of trust. Manuals aimed at young traders reiterated the same basic tenets for success.[1] Personal reputation, created and maintained through networks of fellow merchants, was paramount.

By the eighteenth century, the precepts that governed the conduct of trade were well entrenched, to the point of being uncontroversial: to be successful, a merchant had to behave in ways that signaled his trustworthiness to the mercantile fraternity. In his *Autobiography*, Franklin recalled that he was able "to secure my Credit and Character as a Tradesman" not only by being "in *Reality* Industrious and frugal" but also by avoiding "all *Appearances* of the Contrary." He counseled young tradesmen to signal (literally) their virtues to their lenders: "The Sound of your Hammer at Five in the Morning or Nine at Night, heard by the Creditor makes him easy Six Months longer."[2] Successful tradesmen built reputations for dependability and predictability, based on a record of timely payments and the perception that they were prudent, honest, and willing to work hard.[3] Merchants and their champions labelled these behaviors "virtues," but the mercantile community was probably no more virtuous than the individuals outside it. Instead, the values were adaptations to the demands of the economic environment.[4] These mercantile virtues were broadly compatible with the Protestant system of beliefs and to a large extent came to define Protestantism itself. It is not surprising that this highly effective ethos expanded into areas of life beyond the commercial and that advice on how to succeed in trade came to be regarded as sound counsel on how to succeed in life.

Trust would have been far less of an issue if long-distance trade had been done on a cash basis. But in the American colonies, as in the Atlantic world generally, the shortage of gold and silver coin and the perils involved in transporting them made credit important. So did the fact that merchants had to first sell the goods before they could pay their suppliers. By the mid-eighteenth century, British merchants sold about 80 percent of their goods on credit.[5] Whether the "goods" in motion were human beings from Africa or cloth and buttons from England's manufacturing cities, their journeys were fueled by the willingness of merchants to trust that their counterparties in other parts of the empire were willing and able to pay.[6]

Direct and indirect knowledge of markets, goods, and people underpinned commercial trust in circumstances where transactions could take years to complete. The exchange of Caribbean slaves for East Indian tex-

14

tiles, to take just one example, required complex coordination among a number of markets where there was no established infrastructure.[7] Credit transactions, and the coordination across time and space that they required, were a powerful force that helped to integrate the British trading empire in the eighteenth century.[8] When America's inland trade grew in scale and momentum during the nineteenth century, the experiences of generations of overseas traders provided the "handbook" for answering the critical questions of long-distance exchange: What makes for a sound credit risk? How does one distinguish those who are worthy of credit from those who are not? Understanding the evolution of the beliefs and practices of overseas trade is, therefore, critical to understanding the business culture of the early republic and beyond.

Mercantile Credit and Economic Development

Business credit came primarily from merchants, not banks. Instruments such as bonds, notes, bills of exchange, and book credit predated the existence of a commercial banking network. According to Atlantic trade historian Jacob Price, when the network of banks developed, it merely "made more efficient a system whose key elements were already in place and working."[9] The English novelist and pamphleteer Daniel Defoe celebrated the paradoxical idea that mercantile indebtedness was a necessary condition of economic growth. In *The Complete English Tradesman* (1726), he wrote that credit led to "infinitely more business carried on."[10] Later historical research confirmed Defoe's reports that English merchants used credit widely. Their ability to borrow enabled British and American traders to conduct business far beyond what their current resources allowed.

The large urban merchants of England—the drapers, ironmongers, and warehousemen—were the hubs of the networks. Their capital resources enabled them to acquire goods on short or medium credit and export on terms of up to two years. Farther down the distribution chain, the importers and domestic dealers in American ports gave their own customers credit on slightly shorter terms; and link by link it went, ending with the modest storekeepers who sold the goods to the final consumers.[11] Credit terms depended on the goods. Woolens for export, to take one important example, had commanded a year's worth of credit since the late 1600s, and the terms became entrenched through long usage.[12] Credit terms also reflected economic conditions. When the business cycle turned negative, creditors became less liberal and insisted on getting paid sooner. But during normal trading conditions (which, by definition, was most of the time), merchants sought to attract and keep customers by offering generous credit facilities. Buyers paid careful attention to credit terms. Often, they were the single most important determinant in choosing whether to initiate a trade relationship.[13]

For the American colonies, long on natural resources and entrepreneurial energy but short on capital, the willingness of British merchants to extend credit was a valuable advantage. Occasionally, even religious writers such as Cotton Mather acknowledged the productive role of credit: "It would strangely Cramp the Trade of a People," he wrote in 1716, "if it might be no more than the Cash that is running among them."[14] By the eve of the American Revolution, the British had pumped an estimated £9 million of credit into their trade with west Africa, North America, and the Caribbean, including the slave trade.[15] In Virginia alone, around 35,000 planters were recipients of credit.[16]

Scottish merchants became important intermediaries in the colonial tobacco trade beginning in the 1730s.[17] They set up stores along the Chesapeake River and its tributaries, both to collect the tobacco crops and to sell imported goods to farmers and their families. Aware that they could not replace the relationships between the large colonial planters and London merchants, the Scots focused instead on smaller producers.[18] Unlike sugar and rice, tobacco could be grown profitably by people with modest landholdings. Many colonists took the opportunity to participate in the international market, aided by the willingness of Scottish merchants to take risks on newcomers.[19] As one Glasgow trader operating in the Chesapeake observed, young men in that area "must have some household furniture and working tools. With these, they are supplied upon Credit, by some Factor or Storekeeper." Competition and the desire to enlarge their sources of supply made the Scots liberal in extending credit. According to the Glasgow trader, credit was granted on the basis of the young men's "labour, industry, and honesty" rather than on their "real property."[20] One Scottish exporter, mirroring the attitude of his peers, instructed his colonial representative to base his judgments on character and to extend credit generously to gain market share: "If a man be good it is not material if he cannot pay you any thing next year. By selling goods to such men you no doubt increase your debts, but at the same time, you will extend your influence."[21]

16

In the long term, the enlarged trade in tobacco pushed down prices. Occasional price rises spurred planters to borrow to invest in more land and slaves, but the additional loans only worsened their exposure when prices dipped. During the Stamp Act hearings in Parliament in 1766, the Committee of Merchants of London Trading to North America estimated that the colonists owed a total of £4.45 million, with the bulk of the debts held in the tobacco states of Virginia and Maryland. In the early 1770s, at least fifty-five members of the Virginia assembly had debts to British creditors exceeding £500. The scale of colonial obligations has led some historians to argue that chronic indebtedness was an important reason why the colonists in the Chesapeake region sought independence from Britain.[22] Not until the following century, in 1811, were these American debts finally settled.

Extending credit was never free of risk. Parliament periodically required debtors to issue bonds to secure their debts or expanded the kinds of property that could be seized to satisfy unpaid obligations.[23] Additionally, if their American debtors could not pay on the agreed date, the British trade creditors charged explicit or concealed interest. Large merchants with a reputation for deep pockets could ride out the downturns in the business cycle because they could issue medium-term bonds. British investors were drawn to the securities, which provided higher returns than government bonds and were considered reasonably safe. Substantial wholesalers with strong credit could also issue notes that then circulated as money.[24] Traders with smaller capital resources were not so fortunate. During economic downturns, these smaller operators found that credit had rendered them vulnerable, and that a blessing during good times became a burden when times turned hard.

The critical element that made this extensive system of mercantile credit work was information—good, accurate information on business conditions, products, and trading partners. Merchants had their channels of trade gossip that included family, friends, agents, and other business associates. Members of religious groups such as the Quakers and Jews, who were well represented in the Atlantic trade, benefited from the information that circulated within their communities. The Philadelphia Quaker Jabez Fisher took any opportunity to acquire information on potential trading partners. On a trip around Britain during the late 1770s, Fisher made detailed assessments of British merchants, including their credit standing.[25]

From around 1750, competition for customers drove overseas merchants to offer more liberal credits.[26] At times, the easy availability of credit resulted in goods lying unpurchased in warehouses and stores. One such period occurred in the 1760s following the Seven Years' War; another took place in the early 1770s in the tobacco trade, and yet another transpired in the mid-1780s following the end of the War of Independence.[27] When these credit bubbles burst, distressed debtors implored their lenders to wait for payment. But competition increased, regardless, causing alarm among the established colonial merchants. English hopefuls continued to arrive in port cities such as Philadelphia, financed with commercial credit from the large English mercantile houses. Colonial merchants formed trade associations that attempted to exclude the newcomers. But the maneuvers failed because the British exporters were willing to deal with anyone who seemed like a good prospect.[28] A large London firm could supply as many as 150 businesses in a single urban port city.[29] Royal Governor of Massachusetts Francis Bernard reported that "for the sake of advancing their Profits," the London merchant houses bypassed their traditional customers, the large American importers and wholesalers, and solicited the small colonial retailers directly. Not even armed conflict could shut out the British suppliers for long. After the War for Independence ended in 1783 they returned, drawn by pent-up demand from American consumers. According to one estimate, the number of merchants in Philadelphia was 50 percent higher than before the hostilities began.[30]

Competitive pressures drove merchants to offer liberal credit terms, but the difficulty of obtaining good information on their trading partners also compelled them to be cautious. These conflicting impulses later prompted institutional innovations, especially for solving the problem of "information asymmetry" where creditors have less information than debtors about the debtors' willingness and ability to pay. Sometimes, creditors had only informal knowledge, such as assurances from other merchants that someone was a good risk, or rumors about a person's past behavior. Later, banks and mercantile associations pioneered the use of more impersonal ways of judging creditworthiness. But in the eighteenth century, there were few such practices. Society was small, and personal reputations and relationships were the basis for transactions. When things went sour people attributed the bad incidents to specific personal actions and defects in character. At the end of the eighteenth century, the seeds of impersonal institutions for the control, administration, and monitoring of credit and creditworthiness began appearing. In London, for example, merchants formed a mutual protection society against fraudulent debtors (described later in this chapter), while in the United States, newspapers began to carry advertisements for debt collection services.

The founding of the Bank of North America in 1781; the establishment of banks in the commercial centers of Boston, New York, and Philadelphia; and growing interest by European investors led some American merchants to predict that their heavy reliance on British credit would soon end. The prediction came true, but not for another century.[31] In contrast to England, which could support hundreds of "country banks" operating outside London, the new republic barely had enough bank capital to supply short-term credit to its growing export trade.[32] Britain's far more advanced capital markets remained an important source of financing for American merchants. In London, the private "goldsmith" banks and money market and brokerage businesses numbered some one thousand firms and individuals. Many of these firms were already carrying out the multiple functions that would characterize the great merchant banks of the future.[33] At the end of the eighteenth century, the United States was very much a debtor country, but its businesses benefited from the availability of capital from the large merchants, bankers, and brokers across the Atlantic.

Debt as the Basis for Money

Debt was important for another reason: it was the basis for paper money in the colonies. In the mercantile community the most important debt instrument was the bill of exchange. Italian merchants had used it since the thirteenth century, and English merchants since the mid-1400s, but its popularity soared two centuries later when the Atlantic trade expanded.[34] By the seventeenth century, the bills functioned as currency among overseas merchants. They became widely used in the slave trade between the Caribbean and South Carolina, where credit terms ranged from between three to sixteen months.[35]

Unlike precious metals, which became scarce during times of heavy economic activity, the supply of bills of exchange expanded precisely when they were most needed. Merchants issued them in large amounts before and after the harvest season for staples such as tobacco, rice, and sugar. An infrastructure of services sprang up in Britain, mostly in London, to facilitate the use of the bills. Along with merchants, they included goldsmiths (a kind of private banker) and full-time brokers. Commercial trust and reputation underpinned the infrastructure; for a fee, well-known merchant houses guaranteed the bills of their correspondents. Evidence that the bills of exchange worked well could be seen in the way South Carolina's slave factors preferred to be paid in bills rather than rice.[36]

Overseas traders used bills of exchange routinely, but the bills were less useful for domestic traders. Small-denominated gold or silver coin would have been more appropriate for storekeepers and other petty traders, but this kind of specie was scarce. To make up for the shortfall, the colonists relied on a number of arrangements.[37] They used commodity money such as sugar, tobacco, and deerskins, whose precise values were determined by local and colonial authorities.[38] In addition, the colonists resorted to paper money from two sources. First, private groups and colonial governments established land banks, which were not banks in the modern sense but an issuance of paper currency that was given out as loans. A typical loan term was repayment of one-fifth of the principal each year with interest at five percent per annum, but some loans were renewed again and again. One loan ran for more than thirty years.[39] (Parliament, wanting to protect the advantages it had granted to the Bank of England and other British banks, and responding to British merchants' dislike of colonial money, prohibited the colonists from establishing joint-stock commercial banks.[40] The first, the Bank of North America, was founded during the War of Independence in 1781.) Land banks enabled the colonists to use their most plentiful asset as the basis for money and credit. Even farmers with modest assets could get loans for as little as 5 percent.[41] In nearly every colony, land banks made loans in the form of bills of credit that then circulated as money.[42] Tiny Rhode Island issued a "bank" of loans nine times between 1711 and 1750.[43] Public land banks were popular in the middle colonies of New York, Pennsylvania, New Jersey, and Delaware partly because the interest on the loans substituted for taxes. Pennsylvania operated a land bank almost continuously after 1723. According to John Adams, the Currency Act of 1751, which prohibited private land banks in New England, "raised a greater ferment" in Massachusetts "than the Stamp-Act did."[44]

The second type of paper money consisted of the bills of credit issued by colonial governments to pay for wartime expenditures. Massachusetts issued the first of these in 1690 to pay for military expenses in aiding the British against French Canada.[45] Other colonies followed suit. Rather than levying additional taxes that would have been unpopular with voters, the colonial governments issued bills of credit to pay for supplies. The bills were later retired—that is, taken out of circulation—when the governments accepted them as payment for taxes. This method was often the only way that colonial governments could get people to pay for public expenditures.[46]

Before the War of Independence, the paper money issued by colonial governments and land banks generally worked well, especially in the middle colonies. But paper money was among the many irritants that inflamed tensions between the colonists and the mother country. Colonial creditors and British traders complained whenever the bills of credit lost their value, as they sometimes did in New England and the southern colonies, when the bills were insufficiently backed by land or taxes. Parliament passed the Currency Act of 1751, which ordered the New England colonies to retire their bills of credit within two years after they had been issued and prohibiting the use of paper money in the settlement of private debts.[47] When in 1758 the Virginia assembly authorized the issuance of notes that would circulate as legal tender, the London merchants complained.[48] In 1764 Parliament prohibited the colonies from using paper money to pay any kind of debt, public or private. Both the 1751 and 1764 acts caused great resentment among the colonists, and they often broke the law. In 1773, Parliament relented and allowed paper money to be used for paying taxes.

A few colonists argued that paper currencies were good for the economy so long as they were carefully monitored by the colonial authorities.[49] Among the most consistent supporters was Benjamin Franklin, who printed some of the bills issued by his home colony of Pennsylvania. Franklin believed that land was the best basis for paper money. The market value of land, he argued, was a good indication of the current state of the local economy and would balance the supply of paper currency with the legitimate demands of trade and other economic activities. Franklin first published these arguments in 1729 at the age of twenty-three, and he returned to them several times during his long life whenever paper money became a political issue.[50] Thomas Jefferson was another founder who approved of government-issued bills of credit. If hard money was unavailable, he supported the idea that governments could print money, so long as the bills were taken out of circulation as soon as possible. Jefferson vehemently opposed notes issued by banks, however, because he believed that they were "only the ghost of money, and not money itself." In his view bankers grew rich by trading an insubstantial commodity and abusing the unearned privilege of government-issued bank charters.[51]

Most colonists regarded government bills of credit as a wartime expedient rather than a tool to increase trade.[52] Their confidence in paper money was severely tried by the War of Independence (1775–1783) when the new state governments and the Continental Congress had no choice but to issue large amounts of bills of credit to pay for supplies and war materiel.[53] Demand for these items sparked an entrepreneurial surge in some areas. In the midst of the war, Henry Laurens, the South Carolina planter and statesman, claimed that "the demand for money" had "spread over a surface of 1,600 miles in length, and 300 broad."[54] But the bills dramatically lost their value as the conflict wore on, giving the populace its first and most severe taste of hyperinflation. Americans would not experience anything similar until the latter years of the Confederacy during the American Civil War (1861–1865), when the value of the money issued by the rebel government plunged along with the fortunes of the Confederate army. But even so, the War of Independence accelerated commerce in the nascent republic by making debt-based currencies more widely available.[55] By war's end, Congress and the states had issued some $400 million worth of paper money. An additional $60–70 million of loan certificates issued by Congress were held by investors in the United States and abroad.[56]

After the war, the need for money and credit grew more urgent as increasing numbers of people became involved in producing for the domestic and international markets. Farmers, storekeepers, craftsmen, and artisans needed the equivalent of the overseas merchants' bills of exchange—some instrument that would allow them to more easily engage in trade.[57] People set up banks to provide credit, and the resulting notes circulated as money. The citizens of the world's newest and largest republic believed that the future would be better than the present, and they borrowed accordingly. Thomas Jefferson and his closest followers feared the existence of banks within the new republic, but after 1790 they were unable to stop the spread of these establishments. As commercial activities increased, more and more people advocated the chartering of banks that would issue notes to serve as currency. (The Constitution forbade the state governments from issuing currency, but they could do so indirectly, by chartering banks.) Banking establishments became most numerous in Philadelphia, and their discounting services enlarged the amount of paper currency there. In contrast to the Bank of North America, the new banks were meant not just to serve the needs of governments and merchants but also tradesmen, farmers, and manufacturers. Pennsylvania's Omnibus Banking Act of 1814

In 1690 the Massachusetts Bay Colony issued the first bills of credit. The act helped to fund what turned out to be an abortive attack on Canada. The bills were America's earliest paper money. This particular specimen survived because it had been fraudulently altered. Genuine bills were destroyed upon acceptance for tax payments. *Source:* Indented Bill of twenty shillings, issued by the Massachusetts Bay Colony, February 3, 1690. Collection of the Massachusetts Historical Society.

stated that 20 percent of the banks' capital had to be loaned to people in these occupations.[58]

The hundreds of new banks, along with the Bank of the United States (chartered in 1791) and its branches, issued the paper money that an entrepreneurial society desired. War also drove the supply of bank notes higher. During the War of 1812, the government was forced to borrow from banks, which further swelled the amount of paper money in circulation. Bank notes became so widely used that in 1819 Alexander Baring, the head of the prominent British mercantile house and a member of Parliament, told a committee in the House of Commons that "the system of a paper currency has been carried to a greater extent in America than in any other part of the world."[59]

Bank creation itself became an entrepreneurial venture, and the new institutions became the primary means for ambitious people to acquire money and credit. The banks sometimes issued paper money recklessly. Lacking a strong central authority that had the exclusive right to issue a national currency, as the Federal Reserve does today, Americans found themselves living in an entrepreneurial society underpinned by bank notes that were vulnerable to external shocks. The new banks backed their note issues with specie, government bonds, and land. Prudent bankers and states made sure that they had adequate capital reserves to back their notes, but others did not. And no matter how careful and conservative individual banks may have been, all banks were vulnerable to political manipulation. During the first decades of the new republic, the disagreements over the "system" of banking and bank notes became intensely politicized.

The Moral Economy

Alongside the growing calls for economic expansion—expansion that was based on borrowing and paper money—there persisted older ways of thinking about debt. These attitudes were expressed in the way that local retailers administered book credit: they noted the value of purchased goods in a day book or ledger without issuing formal instruments like notes or bills of exchange. Storekeepers often did not charge interest, although it could be reflected in the higher price of goods.[60] The accounts were settled after six months, a year, or sometimes much longer. Book credit was commonplace, leading some economists to argue that it should be included in any analysis of the money supply. (Unfortunately, book credit is very difficult if not impossible to quantify.)[61] Barter, too, played an important role in local economies.[62] Farm women traded eggs and butter for store goods. Households bartered produce, game, and animal skins to obtain the services of blacksmiths, coopers, and other artisans. These transactions were sometimes notated in rough ledgers using monetary values even though no actual cash changed hands. Sometimes they were not recorded at all but were instead treated as informal exchanges among neighbors that would be settled at some unspecified future date.[63]

Retailers used a wide variety of payment arrangements. Sarah Kemble Knight, observing the activities in a Connecticut store in the early 1700s, noted that the storekeeper accepted "Pay, money, pay as money, and trusting. *Pay* is grain, pork, beef, &c. at the prices set by the General Court that year. *Money* is pieces of eight, rials, or Boston or Bay shillings (as they call them) or good hard money, as sometimes silver coin is termed by them; also wampum, viz. Indian beads, which serve for change. *Pay as money* is provisions, as aforesaid one-third cheaper than the Assembly or General Court sets it. And *Trust* as they and the merchant agree for time."[64] As Knight discovered, payment options could be complicated. So were the webs of credits and debts that existed among households in a community. Unlike the impersonal transactions that characterize a cash economy, credit forced the mingling of business and social relationships at a time when many small traders did not strictly separate their business and domestic accounts.[65] A state of semipermanent indebtedness among neighbors that mixed sociability with market exchange may well have been the norm in many smaller communities.[66] Debt carried an implication of social, not just monetary obligation. The wish to maintain stable and friendly relationships with other people living in the same community balanced, and at times outweighed, the desire for profit.[67]

Because there were few institutional sources of credit, private loans between family members, friends, and neighbors were more important than they are today. Such loans reinforced the noncommercial morality that governed ideas about borrowing and lending. Among family and friends, lenders sacrificed or minimized interest charges, and debtors struggling to repay would likely have been treated leniently by creditors motivated by affection or obligation. Wealthy merchants and planters, whom John Adams termed "men of fortune, who live upon their income," made interest-bearing loans in the hope of securing a profit, and their manner of lending was more impersonal than would have been the case among family members and friends.[68] For these entrepreneurs, money lending provided a more stable income than trade, agriculture, or land speculation, the activities that had made them wealthy in the first place. A few, like the seventeenth-century Boston trader John Hull, came to rely on lending as their largest source of income. Hull even began calling himself "goldsmith," after the London guild composed of gold craftsmen, bullion merchants, and moneylenders.[69] Charles Carroll of Annapolis, the wealthy planter who later signed the Declaration of Independence, at one point had £24,000 loaned out to his neighbors.[70]

But few people in this position sought to publicize that they were primarily in the business of lending money. The profit-seeking moneylender was a disreputable figure, and most people who loaned their excess capital preferred instead to be known as merchants, planters, and landowners. Moreover, even wealthy John Hull and Charles Carroll were *individuals* who made loans to other individuals. The loans were still of a personal nature and so were governed by an ethos of obligation imposed by the communities in which these lenders lived and worked. At the very least, wealthy individuals felt restrained from making harsh demands for repayment when times were hard. Although falling short of full-fledged paternalism (except in the case of some large southern planters who saw themselves as the benefactors of their less wealthy neighbors), such attitudes were markedly different from the impersonal demands for payment that later came to characterize banking institutions.[71] Britons on both sides of the Atlantic were entrepreneurial, but they did not admire ruthless individualism and naked self-interest.

As internal trade and commercial borrowing increased, the personal bonds between borrowers and lenders weakened. In Massachusetts, debt disputes in the courts were numerous even in the late 1600s. By the middle of the next century, traders everywhere relied more on formal signed instruments like promissory notes and bills of exchange. Litigation involving such instruments rose, too; in the Connecticut country courts, they comprised the vast majority of all debt litigation by the middle of the eighteenth century.[72] The instruments made debt collections more routine and eliminated the need to call large numbers of witnesses to testify.[73] Their more intensive use did not change the emphasis on maintaining creditworthiness, however. Formalizing contracts clarified the terms of engagement and made litigation easier, but it did not remove the creditors' biggest concern: who among potential borrowers could be trusted to repay loans, at the time agreed, and on the terms specified? Legal instruments may have encouraged compliance, but a reputation for trustworthiness was considered a much better assurance of good future conduct. Behaviors that signaled reliability and commercial ability therefore continued to be vitally important to maintaining the confidence of lenders and the flow of credit.

Borrowing for Consumption

Colonial Americans accepted that credit was a necessary feature of trade. "Credit is to Trade, what the Blood is to the Body," a Rhode Island debtor wrote from his jail cell. "If credit fails, Trade stagnates."[74] Borrowing for consumption, however, was another matter entirely. The colonists were in agreement about the deleterious moral effects of buying too many unnecessary products, especially before one had earned the money to pay for them. It is nearly impossible to find anyone who argued otherwise.

From the mid-1700s onward, however, the sheer bounty of consumer goods imported from Britain began to chip away at the older norms. These value systems had been formed in societies that were poorer, more static, and hierarchical compared to the more egalitarian societies now prospering on the American mainland. The availability of tempting merchandise and the rhythms of the agricultural economy encouraged people to rely on retail credit even though their incomes were higher than ever. Surviving records indicate that storekeepers in the Chesapeake, the middle colonies, and New England sometimes sold 80 percent of their merchandise on credit.[75]

Between 1720 and 1770, imports per capita rose by about 50 percent. Much of the rise was in goods that people considered luxuries, or what Franklin described as "superfluities" and "mere conveniences."[76] It was not just the urban sophisticates who bought them; modern archaeological research has revealed that farm families bought such goods as well. Newspaper advertisements changed accordingly. Formerly terse announcements now spread to two-column descriptions of newly arrived goods. By 1760, advertising took up more than half the pages of many colonial newspapers, evidence that people were as interested in goods as they were in news.[77]

The ability to acquire superfluous goods before one had earned the money to buy them offended the sensibilities of the colonies' moral spokesmen. They warned that credit from shopkeepers tempted the weak to buy more than they needed. "'Tis well known," according to one typical writer, "how Credit is a mighty inducement with many People to purchase this and the other Thing which they may well enough do without."[78] Another writer calling himself "Incultus Americanus," observed that shopkeepers seduced "people to purchase their commodities, with a promise of long credit, insinuating that payment would be easily made."[79] The

27

most famous of the moralists, Franklin, warned against the perils of over-indebtedness in works such as *The Way to Wealth* (1757). Franklin was merely the latest in a line of commentators on consumer credit that stretched back at least a generation in America, when newspaper advertisements in cities such as New York and Philadelphia began hawking a multitude of goods that were available on short credit.[80]

For the people who came of age in the middle of the eighteenth century, the consumption of items that had previously been deemed luxuries was a defining experience that separated them from their forebears. Franklin, already in his fifties when he published *The Way to Wealth,* appeared skeptical that his mostly younger readers would heed his warnings. At the end of the book, the crowd of listeners turns away from Father Abraham's lecture on thrift in order to attend a nearby auction, the colonial equivalent of a liquidation sale or an outlet mall. Other writers voiced concern that the easy access to luxury goods made people lose the incentive to work. They proposed passing sumptuary laws, a traditional form of regulation that forced people to live according to their rank—and therefore within their means.[81] (In 1574 Queen Elizabeth I had expressed similar concerns when she passed a sumptuary law condemning people "seeking by show of apparel to be esteemed as gentlemen, who, allured by the vain show of those things, do not only consume themselves, their goods, and lands which their parents left unto them, but also run into such debts and shifts as they cannot live out of danger of laws without attempting unlawful acts.")[82] Paradoxically, the relative egalitarianism of colonial life prodded some people to pay closer attention to outward distinctions.[83] A lingering belief in social hierarchies made credit seem destabilizing because it gave the humbler orders a means to emulate their wealthier neighbors.[84]

Usury Laws

The lack of consumer lending institutions, combined with traditional fears about overindebtedness, restrained the volume of credit that was available to ordinary people. So, too, did usury laws, although historians are not in full agreement about how stringently they were enforced.[85] Colonial usury laws did not prohibit interest but instead restricted it to moderate rates of around 6 to 8 percent, with 6 percent being dominant. (Massachusetts was the first to adopt a usury law, in 1641. The law exempted the bills of exchange used in overseas trade.)[86] The regulations were a holdover from ancient times, when authorities tried to control money lending by capping interest rates. During the middle ages, European monarchs and the Catholic Church broke with their predecessors in ancient Babylonia, Greece, and Rome and prohibited interest altogether.[87] Charlemagne, whose reign lasted from 800 to 814, outlawed it throughout his realm, and by the middle of the century, Church law made usurers subject to excommunication. In eleventh-century England the taking of any interest at all was equated with robbery, punishable with confiscation of the lender's land and chattels. The Second Lateran Council, a general meeting of the Catholic Church that was held in Rome in 1139, prohibited all usury.[88]

Over time, the Church came to tolerate interest on loans for productive uses. As trade increased, Church theologians found exceptions to the usury laws, including premiums on loans that were made in one currency and repaid in another to cover the exchange risk. Creditors could also demand compensation for late payments, on the principle that they were prevented from investing the money in some other venture.[89] The Church allowed Jews to lend money at interest; it was a convenient ploy for Christian borrowers and opened up a profitable niche for Jews, who were prohibited from practicing many other occupations. But the exemption also contributed to the hostility against them when Christian writers, artists, and politicians portrayed Jews as unethical profit-mongers who were immune to the effects of Christian charity.

By the twelfth century, moneylenders from Northern Italy (called Lombards) and the French town of Cahors began to outnumber the Jewish moneylenders, driving the Church to tighten its regulation of usury. In 1179 the Church once again declared that usurers would be excommunicated. But even monasteries found ways around the prohibitions, and bankers employed a variety of schemes to offer interest on savings deposits—for example, by giving depositors shares of the profits earned when the bank invested the money.[90] By the early seventeenth century, the charitable pawnbrokers (*monti di pieta*), initially created by Italian cities to help the indigent, were accepting deposits at interest.[91] The *monti di pieta* became large credit institutions that served both the wealthy and people of more moderate means. (In time, they became part of the public financial regime of cities such as Bologna, and survived into the twenty-first century as one of Italy's largest banks.)[92] In France during the late eighteenth century, charitable pawnbrokers were instrumental in reducing interest rates from 30 percent to 18 percent.[93]

Under Queen Elizabeth I, Parliament in 1571 reversed its prohibition of all interest and imposed a maximum legal rate of 10 percent, a law that lasted until 1854. Parliament's reversal was in line with the thinking of the French theologian John Calvin, who had died in 1564. Calvin broke with both the Catholic Church and the Protestant reformer, Martin Luther, by proclaiming that money was not sterile, as Aristotle had taught, and that interest could be charged on commercial loans. (Calvin was adamant, however, that loans to the needy could not carry interest.) By the middle of the seventeenth century, nearly all Protestant denominations tolerated interest rates of around 5 percent. By then, interest rates for business and other creditworthy borrowers had fallen in western Europe: they were 8 percent in England after 1624, and 6 percent after 1651. In 1713, they fell another percentage point, to 5 percent.[94] The Catholic Church never rescinded the papal edicts against usury, but its resistance moderated in the nineteenth century, around the same time that many American states loosened their strictures on interest rates.[95] Until then, people in Europe and the colonies could evade the law by charging a late payment fee in place of interest, a practice that may have been so widespread that it rarely elicited much comment.[96]

In New England, attitudes about usury began to shift at the end of the 1600s. Boston pastor Cotton Mather stated in 1699 that only Catholics continued to equate all usury with sin. Other New England ministers, however, continued to stand firmly against usury.[97] Their collective ambivalence set a pattern that would continue in the wider American society for generations to come.

In addition to the religious prohibitions, a number of secular writers defended the usury laws. Adam Smith maintained that rates should be kept as low as possible. He reasoned that minimal rates would make credit more widely available to prudent borrowers because lenders would not have to rely on the two groups who were willing to pay more for credit: the "prodigals," who consumed heavily, and the "projectors," who sought funding for grandiose schemes. In Smith's lifetime, however, the most devastating arguments against the usury laws appeared from Utilitarian philosopher Jeremy Bentham. In the provocatively titled *Defense of Usury* (1787), Bentham presented arguments that are held by free-marketers today: that anti-usury laws drove interest rates higher than in a competitive market, and that the laws did not work anyway because lenders could so easily evade them. Worse, the usury laws forced desperate people to rely on questionable or criminal lenders.[98]

Usury laws were an early form of consumer protection, similar to concepts such as the just price, which had attempted to safeguard people from vendors who charged substantially more than was deemed fair.[99] Such regulations of credit and prices served societies that were hierarchical, where the desired goal was to maintain security and stability rather than encourage entrepreneurialism. In the United States, where settlers in the newer regions of the country demanded capital for their various undertakings, state usury laws became more liberalized beginning in the nineteenth century.[100] Yet the stricter laws were later reinstated. Their continued existence spoke of a lingering tendency to view unregulated interest rates as a potential threat to social harmony and stability.

Bankruptcy and Insolvency

Before the 1700s, people in the colonies did not perceive a need for bankruptcy laws. Although they participated in the Atlantic trade and bought and sold goods on credit among themselves, the transactions were small and local.[101] Things changed in the eighteenth century when the colonists became more enmeshed in Atlantic commerce as sellers, buyers, and brokers of goods. Their experiences in handling credit and paper money exposed them to the riskiness inherent in trade. More and more people saw their commercial ventures end in failure, with all of the legal and social complications that accompanied it. The moral framework of lending and borrowing shifted: older attitudes that saw defaulting on one's debts as a sin began to co-exist with a greater acceptance of insolvency as part and parcel of commercial risk.[102] In a society that took both religion (or at least morality) and commerce seriously, these contradictory ideas lived together uneasily. The ambivalence created by these tensions would continue until the modern age.

Bankruptcy laws, in the rare instances when they were passed, reflected the assumptions of English and European law. The laws held that creditors were the party in need of support because debtors' actions, such as hiding and lying about their financial condition, prevented the just recovery of debts. Once a debtor exhibited such behavior, the law regarded him as having committed an "act of bankruptcy"; the creditor, therefore, was justified in bringing a bankruptcy proceeding against him. This state of affairs constituted an involuntary bankruptcy, and until 1841, it was the only form that was available in the United States. Subsequent laws would chip away at the idea that debtors were always morally culpable or criminal, but the assumption that bankruptcy was brought about by the debtor's misconduct turned out to have a very long life; it was not until the Bankruptcy Reform Act of 1978 that this legal presumption was put to rest.[103]

As in Europe, bankruptcy was confined to commercial people because it was thought that only merchants, traders, and brokers had the means to delay payments and defraud creditors. Other people, including artisans and landowners, could only become "insolvent," a condition that was based on mere fact (they owed more than they could repay) rather than on an action brought by a creditor as was the case with bankruptcy. On very rare occasions, and in certain circumstances, insolvency laws allowed for release from prison or relief from debt.[104] But neither the insolvency nor bankruptcy laws were driven by the philosophy of giving debtors a fresh start. To the contrary, the laws were designed to deter people from stealing from their creditors, or attempting to move above their stations by illegally using other people's money.[105]

By the eighteenth century, the idea that some bankrupts were the victims of circumstance had become established in a few commercialized areas of Europe. In Germany, for example, legal handbooks distinguished between innocent and fraudulent bankruptcies.[106] The distinction existed as well in commercial Amsterdam and Antwerp. Local governments tried to minimize the disruptions to trade, and in the process, bankruptcy became an inevitable part of commercial activities. Regulatory bodies tried to help business lenders and borrowers reach solutions rather than simply throwing the debtors in jail (although they continued to do that, too). But their ultimate goal was negotiation, not imprisonment.[107]

English law, reflecting the increase in commerce during the previous century, distinguished between honest and dishonest debtors. Opposition to debt imprisonment began to circulate. Still, a dual attitude toward insolvency was reflected in the Statute of Anne (1705), which for the first time granted a discharge to cooperative debtors but simultaneously imposed the death penalty on fraudsters. (The penalty was almost never used.) Like its predecessors, the law was meant to assist creditors, not debtors. The following year creditor consent was added to the statute as a prerequisite to the granting of a discharge.[108] The statute was passed not out of a new compassion for debtors, but because an economic crisis in the 1690s had landed a large number of merchants in debtors' prison. Among the incarcerated was Daniel Defoe, who afterwards argued that honest insolvents should be permitted to settle with their creditors and obtain a discharge from their debts.[109]

Several American colonies began passing laws providing for discharge. But most were short-lived, and the provisions differed widely: some colonies developed more liberal debtor relief measures than were available in England; others did not. Heavily commercial Rhode Island passed the most significant provisions for the relief of insolvents, including allowing them to shield future earnings, and came closest to having a routine process of dealing with bankruptcy. Wars and other shocks prodded legislatures to act, as when the Seven Years' War (1756–1763) destabilized markets, giving opportunities to some enterprising colonists but also ruining others. New York, Rhode Island, and Massachusetts responded by enacting bankruptcy systems that discharged insolvent debtors from further liability once their assets had been distributed among their creditors. Connecticut did the same in 1763 and also passed a general relief act for insolvent debtors. It was repealed the following year, and the colony passed another in 1765, this one lasting for two years.[110]

One of the most vexing problems was how to apportion debtors' assets among creditors. A few colonies made early, desultory attempts to resolve the issue. Maryland in 1639 required insolvent debtors to assign their property to their creditors in proportion to their debts. In the 1670s Rhode Island mandated proportionate distribution of debtors' estates, but it repealed the law only six weeks later. At the end of the century, Massachusetts law stated that a debtor who took the poor debtors' oath triggered the convening of his creditors to decide what to do. In 1714 the colony permitted two or more creditors to file against a fraudulent debtor and seize his property, but the law expired after just three years. Massachusetts did not enact another bankruptcy law until the one in 1757 during the Seven Years' War. These haphazard laws hardly provided a systematic and routine means of dealing with failure. In the absence of clear legal guidance and procedures, insolvents resorted to other means, including applying to the colonial legislatures for relief. In the early 1770s, when tensions intensified between the colonists and the mother country, these acts gave some protection from British creditors, prompting Britain's Privy Council to disallow them.[111]

Opposition to imprisonment for debt began appearing in the colonies by the 1750s, a further indication that attitudes were softening. Pennsylvania had earlier replaced imprisonment with a procedure that allowed some debtors to assign their property to creditors and exempt certain items. A parallel shift occurred in England, where pamphlets and broadsides condemning the imprisonment of debtors who were trying to repay their creditors circulated beginning in the mid-1600s. A century later attitudes about bankruptcy had shifted sufficiently to allow the great English jurist and judge William Blackstone to claim that the laws were calculated for the benefit of trade and founded on principles of humanity and justice.[112]

The revolutionary sentiments that began stirring in the colonies during the 1760s further shifted the way Americans thought about debt and bankruptcy. Their beliefs were shaped by their day-to-day experiences. Of all the shocks to the early American economy, none was greater than the disruptions brought about by the War of Independence. To pay for supplies and materiel, the Continental Congress and the newly formed states issued paper currency that became unstable, causing hardship among the populace. Various states responded by enacting stay laws that prevented or delayed creditors from claiming the property of debtors. The economic difficulties continued into the postwar period, when American merchants struggled to find markets abroad, resulting in a serious trade deficit for the new country.[113]

A number of state constitutions now included provisions opposing the imprisonment of honest debtors. Only Pennsylvania passed a true bankruptcy act that offered to commercial debtors a discharge of their debts. (The law was passed in 1785 and lasted just a few years, expiring in 1793.) In Massachusetts, merchants allied with lawmakers to force harsh terms on debtors, many of them farmers. Finding no relief from the legislatures and courts, the hard-pressed borrowers turned violent, precipitating a movement that became known as Shays's Rebellion. They directed their rage not just against the state's legal and political institutions but also at the retailers who had extended them easy credit and then pressed hard for payments. The rebels asked not for outright debt relief, but for less onerous conditions for repaying their loans.[114]

Bankruptcy was among the many political and commercial issues that the framers tackled during the Constitutional Convention that met in Philadelphia in the summer of 1787. Because of the paucity of contemporary reports detailing the framers' thinking, we will probably never know why Article I, Section 8 of the Constitution, which calls for uniform bankruptcy laws, was adopted with so little discussion. It may well have stemmed from the framers' awareness of the problems caused by the diverse state laws, including the difficulties faced by creditors trying to recover debts from borrowers living in another state. Memories of the economic hardships imposed by the war and of the alarming debtors' rebellion in Massachusetts were still fresh and no doubt influenced the proceedings.

According to James Madison's *Notes of Debates in the Federal Constitution,* it was South Carolina delegate Charles Pinckney who, on August 29, 1787, moved to add the language "to establish uniform laws upon the subject of bankruptcies and respecting the damages arising on the protest of foreign bills of exchange." The first part of the phrase "to establish uniform laws on the subject of bankruptcies" was adopted a few days later, on September 3.[115] The framers probably did not mean for the bankruptcy laws to extend to nontrade creditors and debtors. At any rate, the New York constitutional convention in 1788 urged an amendment ensuring that the law would apply only to individuals involved in commerce, and that it would leave the regulation of other types of insolvents to the states. Several months later, Madison expounded on the issue in the *Federalist:* "The power of establishing uniform laws of bankruptcy is so intimately connected with the regulation of commerce, and will prevent so many frauds where the parties or their property may lie or be removed into different states, that the expediency of it seems not likely to be drawn into question."[116] In the opening session of the new Congress, a committee of the House was named to prepare a bankruptcy bill.

The complicated politics that pitted "Republicans" against "Federalists" in the 1790s impeded any progress in implementing uniform bankruptcy laws. Of course, the issue of problematic debtors did not disappear. In 1792, just a few years after the Constitution was ratified, the first serious financial panic began when the speculator William Duer ran into trouble. Duer had been secretary of the Board of Treasury during the war and was a signer of the Articles of Confederation. He served in Washington's administration as the first assistant secretary of the Treasury under Alexander Hamilton. Duer's insider perspective likely drove him to speculate on bank stock and on depreciated government warrants and certificates; in effect, he bet that the new national government would redeem them at prices higher than what their desperate holders had sold them for.[117] Some "jobbers" even went beyond the new nation's borders and peddled the securities to individuals and syndicates in Europe.[118]

Duer's schemes resembled England's South Sea Bubble earlier in the century. Such schemes were a pyramid, in which ordinary people were told that they would be paid an annual interest of up to 60 percent on "safe" promissory notes.[119] New commercial banks in New York and Philadelphia provided loans to some of the speculators.[120] All went well so long as prices continued to rise. In one scheme involving Bank of New York stock, Duer found himself on the opposite side of New York's influential Livingston family; each side tried to manipulate the price of the stock, Duer trying to force it up while the Livingstons drove it down. Depositors tried to withdraw their money, and the bank called in its loans, which precipitated a decline in stock prices.[121] Finally, too many of Duer's schemes failed, and he and his associates found themselves unable to honor their notes. They were insolvent—and so, too, were many of the people who had trusted them. (Duer was imprisoned for seven years for failing to pay his creditors. He died outside the prison while still serving out his sentence.) The Panic of 1792 was the new republic's first full-blown financial crisis. It was contained by the actions of Secretary of the Treasury Alexander Hamilton, who organized purchases of government securities by the Treasury and the Bank of New York. He also launched a scheme to keep panicked securities dealers from dumping their securities at distressed prices. They were able to get bank loans, using their securities as collateral.[122]

William Duer was disgraced, but the speculation continued, especially in land. To pay their debts, the states had thrown millions of acres of their holdings on the market, sparking a wave of buying. One of the epicenters of the mania was Philadelphia. The city's three largest banks made loans to people who were "flipping" land—buying it only to sell to the next speculator.[123] The most prominent land buyer, Robert Morris, was the well-respected Philadelphia merchant and founder of the Bank of North America. His skill as the superintendent of finance had helped to secure desperately needed funding for the War of Independence. Morris and his partners bought land in the new national capital, as well as in Pennsylvania, Virginia, and other states. They had some impressive successes, including Morris's lucrative sales to two European investor groups, the Holland Land Company and Pulteney Associates.[124] But malfeasance by one of Morris's partners, slower-than-anticipated sales, the misguided cross-endorsing of one another's notes, problematic land titles, and scarce credit resulting from yet another outbreak of war in Europe seriously weakened their business. The partners consolidated six million acres of their holdings, some of it heavily encumbered by debt, into a diversified entity that they called the North American Land Company. The plan was to sell shares in the company to European investors. But interest in

Europe was tepid, and the company survived by issuing notes backed by little more than Morris's reputation.[125]

During the 1790s, the failure of Britain's banks drove its merchants to expand their investments in American trade. The Dutch soon followed, and the increased capital fueled an export boom. Between 1792 and 1797, U.S. exports increased threefold, from $19 million to $59 million, or six times the value of the colonies' trade with the mother country at the start of the War of Independence twenty years earlier. But then a financial panic hit, and it highlighted the extent of U.S. dependence on British trade credit. The Bank of England suspended specie payments, severely curtailing trade credit. As trade stagnated, the new American banks tightened their lending and note issues.[126] Coastal areas saw the effects first, but big land speculators such as Robert Morris and his partners soon lost any takers for their depreciated notes.[127] Like Duer before him, Morris and a number of people who held his paper became insolvent. The financier of the Revolution ended up in Philadelphia's Prune Street prison when one of his small creditors initiated an act of bankruptcy against him. Other prominent revolutionaries who saw their land speculations end in bankruptcy included Henry Knox, secretary of war in Washington's administration, and James Wilson, a justice of the Supreme Court.[128]

The financial crises in 1792 and 1797 and the resulting insolvency of some of the republic's most prominent men fueled a national debate about bankruptcy legislation. At the time, insolvent debtors were permitted discharges in just three states—Rhode Island, Connecticut, and Maryland—and only by submitting a special petition to those legislatures.[129] After several unsuccessful bills, a national bankruptcy act finally passed in 1800. Mirroring the beliefs of previous generations and of the English common law, the legislation was intended to aid creditors, who retained the exclusive right to initiate bankruptcy proceedings. The law was restricted to commercial people, specifically to debtors owing a minimum of $1,000 and who had exhibited "intent unlawfully to delay or defraud his or their creditors."[130] A limited amount of debtor discharge was allowed, subject to certification by the bankruptcy commissioner that the debtor had cooperated, and contingent on two-thirds of creditors consenting to the discharge. Among the beneficiaries of the new law was Robert Morris, who was released from prison in 1801.[131]

The Bankruptcy Act of 1800 was a compromise. It failed to garner wide support, and lawmakers limited its duration to five years. Among its strongest opponents were southern senators who feared the law's effects on their rural communities. Southerners attempted to confine the act to merchants, and to exempt farmers, tavern keepers, and small manufacturers from being placed within its purview. Disagreements about the national bankruptcy law were sometimes technical in nature, but the issue became part of the larger ideological debates about federal versus state power, the nature of democracy, and the republican experiment. In 1803, even before it was scheduled to expire, Congress repealed the law by a vote of ninety-nine to thirteen. By then, enterprising men had begun acting as debt collectors, and a few had businesses large enough to justify using printed forms.[132]

Jefferson in Debt: The Ordeals of Independence

Alexander Hamilton's defense of credit and paper money brought him into open conflict with Thomas Jefferson, his rival in the Cabinet. Jefferson was a complex figure, a man of refined tastes and advanced ideas, whose unyielding dedication to human liberty placed him among the most radical thinkers of the age. It would be unjust to present Jefferson simply as the foil to Hamilton's modern vision of finance; and yet, more than any of the founders, Jefferson embodied the uneasiness that Americans felt about borrowing and lending. The writer of the Declaration of Independence had a fraught relationship with debt; he was preoccupied by it, on a personal, political, and philosophical level. Jefferson's absorption by the subject lay behind his famous dictum "'that the earth belongs in usufruct to the living' . . . the dead have neither powers nor rights over it," an idea he expressed in a letter to James Madison. The letter's larger question, "whether one generation of men has a right to bind another," was rhetorical; Jefferson, it was clear, was on the side of liberty against the oppression of the past.[133] His radical stance accorded with the doctrines of the Enlightenment. Some historians, however, speculate that it was influenced equally by prosaic matters, and in particular Jefferson's own intergenerational predicament, in the form of the very large debt he had inherited from his father-in-law. There is, writes Jefferson biographer Joseph J. Ellis, "precious little in the way of evidence to document Jefferson's personal anguish over slavery. There is, on the other hand, a great deal of evidence that he was tormented by his mounting debt, which he tended to describe as his own enslavement."[134]

In 1774, a year before the War of Independence began, Jefferson and his wife's family had decided to divide her father's estate among the heirs. The plan was not unwise; like most planter families, the Jefferson-Wayles clan were cash-constrained and continually in need of working capital. Having immediate use of their inheritance made financial sense. But British creditors had claims on the estate, and in apportioning it before these creditors were paid, the heirs became personally liable for its debts. Like many Virginia debtors, the family struggled to free themselves of the burden.[135]

A dozen years later, Jefferson wrote to Jean Nicholas Démeunier, author of *Economie politique et diplomatique,* that British merchants had profited so handsomely from tobacco consignments that they had contrived to keep the colonial planters dependent. "A powerful engine for this purpose," Jefferson explained, "was the giving of good prices and credit to the planter till they got him more immersed in debt than he could pay without selling his land or slaves. They then reduced the prices given for his tobacco, so that, let his shipments be ever so great, and his demand of necessaries ever so economical, they never permitted him to clear off his debt." Historians often quote Jefferson's bitter next lines: "These debts had become hereditary from father to son for many generations, so that the planters were a species of property, annexed to certain mercantile houses in London."[136] He repeated these sentiments in a letter to the wife of a young planter: "Long experience," he cautioned her, "has proved to us that there never was an instance of a man's getting out of debt who was once in the hands of a tobacco merchant."[137] (A century later, tenant farmers and sharecroppers in the cotton-growing South would feel the same sense of injustice against the "furnishing merchants," whose loans against their crops kept the growers in a permanent state of indebtedness.)

The burden of his personal debts may have been especially galling because independence worsened Jefferson's position with his British creditors; it did not free him from their demands. The Treaty of Paris ended the war but did not provide for a discharge of Americans' debts to their former imperial trading partners, nor did it suspend the interest on those debts. There is plenty of evidence that Jefferson was not inclined to dodge his responsibilities: he intended to pay his debts in full. And so he found himself in a decades-long dance with creditors both in Britain and in the United States that ended only when he died, insolvent. Jefferson spent too much on his beloved Monticello. He never managed to make his various projects profitable enough to clear his mounting debts, and he cosigned a large loan for a friend who later ran into trouble. His plight was not untypical of a man in his position. Still, it may not have escaped the radical revolutionary that, had the country remained within the British empire, his family may well have worked their way into the clear. But war and independence had dismantled the intricate trans-Atlantic apparatus for marketing the exports of the Chesapeake. And in a final irony, British creditors were able to use the new nation's federal courts to press their suits against their American debtors.[138]

The prospect of being in thrall to creditors, whether as an individual or nation, was hateful; but unfortunately for Jefferson neither he nor the young republic could escape the need to borrow. In his official capacities, first as ambassador to France and later as secretary of state, Jefferson was forced to deal with the debts incurred by the states and the national government in fighting the War of Independence. The obligations were substantial: about $67 million owed to Americans and $12 million to foreigners. Jefferson's energetic colleague Alexander Hamilton, as secretary of the Treasury, conceived of a scheme for managing the debts that would at the same time accomplish a number of other objectives: put the new republic's finances on a secure footing, provide support to the nation's businesses, and establish the United States as a first-class investment. Hamilton put forth the plan in his First Report on the Public Credit, delivered to Congress in 1790 during the first months of the Washington administration. The newly established national government would assume the states' debts and offer to redeem all of the various IOUs, bonds, and bills at face value.[139] All would be consolidated into a permanent national debt whose interest charges would be paid for by import duties and special excise taxes.

In effect, Hamilton proposed to securitize the debts and turn them into investment vehicles—"U.S. Treasuries," as Americans of the future would know them. The new securities, he hoped, would provide a safe investment and serve as a liquid storehouse of value, the better to meet the needs of business. To safeguard the value of the securities, and thereby the credit of the United States government, Hamilton proposed to establish a sinking fund to buy up the securities whenever they dipped below par. For this and other purposes, he put forward the establishment of a Bank of the United States. It would be a permanent body within the federal government, which would own the bank along with private investors in the United States and abroad. The bank would issue loans in the form of bank notes that were backed by gold and silver. Hamilton had as his model the Bank of England, which had been instrumental in the prosecution of Britain's wars with France and Spain, and which now stood at the center of Atlantic commerce.[140] In return for financing the government's wars by purchasing its debts, Parliament gave to the Bank of England valuable advantages, including the exclusive right to operate as a joint-stock (limited liability) bank. All other banks had to be structured as unlimited liability partnerships, with a maximum of six partners. These rules enabled the bank to grow much larger than its competitors. The bank issued notes that functioned as paper money, accepted deposits, and discounted merchants' bills.[141]

At first Jefferson agreed, reluctantly, to let the national government assume the states' debts. His native Virginia had already paid most of what it owed, so its citizens would now be taxed to pay interest on the debts of other states.[142] Jefferson's price for going along with the scheme was an agreement to move the proposed national capital farther south—from New York or Philadelphia, where it might naturally have been placed, to an undeveloped area along the Potomac River. This agreement was accomplished, informally, at a dinner attended by Jefferson, Madison, and Hamilton. (To placate Pennsylvania, they agreed that Philadelphia would for ten years replace New York as the nation's capital.)[143] In the ensuing months, as the full implications of Hamilton's plan became clear to him, Jefferson began to feel uneasy. He abhorred the idea of a permanent national debt because it contravened his firm belief, as he had earlier put it to Madison, that no generation had the right to bind future ones. Like many of the founders, Jefferson thought the plan to pay all obligations at face value would benefit speculators who had bought them at steep discounts from their original holders, some of whom were veterans of the war. He grew to regret the taxing of citizens to support an investment vehicle that would benefit the wealthy of the United States and other countries. In a letter to Washington, Jefferson claimed, "I was duped . . . by the Secretary of the treasury, and made a tool for forwarding his schemes not then sufficiently understood by me; and of all the errors of my political life, this has occasioned me the deepest regret."[144]

Most emphatically, Jefferson opposed the Bank of the United States. His antipathy seems extreme to modern Americans long used to the workings of the Federal Reserve and the necessity of central banks. But for Jefferson, the bank was the epitome of everything he hated about banking: he was convinced that it would subvert the very character of the republic because the bank would benefit speculators, stockjobbers, and financiers, not his beloved farmers and small traders. Jefferson had good reason to fear that a few wealthy individuals would benefit disproportionately from banks. In 1786 almost one-half of the Bank of North America's shares were held by just five men, one of them Robert Morris.[145] The paper money issued by the Bank of the United States would not be retired but remain in permanent circulation, egging on the speculators. (Hamilton, in contrast, believed that the paper currency would stimulate enterprise.) Jefferson clung to his views regarding paper money in the decades that followed, through eight years as president (1801–1809), and then in retirement at Monticello. When the War of 1812 caused an overissuance of bank notes, and nearly all banks outside of New England stopped redeeming their notes for specie, Jefferson likened it to "an act of bankruptcy" and complained that "by the dupery of our citizens, and tame acquiescence of our legislators, the nation is plundered."[146] When calls to charter a Second Bank of the United States began circulating, Jefferson, then in his seventies, used his political capital to try to stop it. But again, he was unsuccessful. This time even his staunch ally who was now president of the United States, James Madison, broke with him and signed the bill for the bank's recharter. Madison's difficulties in fighting the British without the support of a national bank now inclined him to support it.

Throughout his political career the well-being of the yeoman farmers and artisans of his imagined republic served as Jefferson's guiding principle. They were foremost in his mind during the debates about a national bankruptcy law in the 1790s. Unlike the English law, the proposed American statute would not exempt such occupations, meaning that creditors could bring an involuntary act of bankruptcy against the very people whom Jefferson considered to be the backbone of the republic. The law would empower creditors to seize debtors' lands, an alarming specter for residents in the southern states for whom land constituted a large share of assets.[147] When Jefferson became president his secretary of the Treasury, Albert Gallatin, delivered the argument against the national bankruptcy law: "Go into the country, and you will scarcely find a farmer who is not, in some degree, a trader. In a grazing part of the country, you will find them buying and selling cattle; in other parts you will find them distillers, tanners, or brick-makers. So that, from one end of the United States to the other, the people are generally traders." Because it was involuntary only, creditors could bring the act against these rural folk, forcing them to part with their land at sacrifice prices.[148] The law was passed that year, when the growing economic divergence between the sections of the country was already becoming apparent. In time, the issue of a national bankruptcy law would become embroiled in the growing tensions between the northern and southern states.

In his privileged positions as a member of the Virginia gentry and holder of the republic's highest offices, Thomas Jefferson embodied the paradoxes of his country's experiences with credit. Like many of his class, he lived like a gentleman thanks in part to the liberal credit extended to him and his family by British and American merchants. Unlike his fellow Revolutionaries, Jefferson never made his peace with banks and bank notes or the securitization of the national debt. He continued to believe that those who worked the land were God's chosen people, while those who made a living dealing in money and securities were most assuredly not. More than any of his contemporaries, Jefferson remained true to the radical ideas of the Revolution's earliest years, and he tried longer than they to keep the ideals alive within the machinery of the federal government. His notions became fanciful even in his own lifetime, leading some historians to brand him as deluded, naïve, and even tragic.[149] But his opposition to the financial elites, the men who attained their position through government-endowed privileges and the manipulation of money, would continue to resonate with Americans.

Chapter Two

"TO BE A BANKRUPT IS NOTHING"

Credit, Enterprise, and Risk in the Antebellum Era

In 1841, Congress and entrepreneurs responded to economic depression by introducing two institutional changes. The first, the National Bankruptcy Act, was hotly anticipated; the other, Lewis Tappan's Mercantile Agency, went largely unremarked. Both the law and the agency were designed to manage the risks of a credit economy. Those risks were now very much in view. Four years earlier, in 1837, a short-lived financial panic had roiled the country's financial markets; then, in 1839, a more serious disturbance led to an economic depression that was deeper and broader than any the country had faced before. Americans had never experienced anything quite like the turbulent years from 1837 to 1843.

The causes of the panics and depression were complex, but the lessons were clear: credit lured gullible people to take extreme financial risks. As the writer of an early bankruptcy manual observed in the 1830s, "In every commercial country there is necessarily a system of credit, and in no country has personal enterprize . . . pushed this system to a greater extent, than has been witnessed in the United States."[1] Borrowing enabled people to achieve material well-being, but an impatient few used credit to speculate on land and other assets. When the bubbles burst everyone suffered: during the worst years of the economic contraction, the unemployment rate in some localities reached 25 percent. Prices fell dramatically between 1839 and 1843, almost as much as in the period 1929 to 1933, the worst years of the Great Depression.[2] Stunned by the shortage of employment and the drop in asset prices, debtors turned for relief to their state legislatures. The elected politicians obliged them by granting stay laws and other restrictions on the sale of debtors' property.

The dire economy hastened passage of a national bankruptcy law that was designed both to assist lenders and to alleviate the suffering of debtors. Lewis Tappan's new Mercantile Agency, meanwhile, promised to help merchants to judge the creditworthiness of businesses. Both the law and the agency were institutional solutions to problems that could not be solved by moral suasion alone. Yet neither institution attempted to discourage lending and borrowing. Instead, they helped Americans to adjust to a risky business environment.

The Spread of Financial Institutions

Banks and insurance companies became more numerous in the American republic, transforming the way people thought about capital. Some Americans still preferred to keep their surplus capital in the form of buildings and livestock, workshops, and farm equipment. But even rural residents showed a willingness to entrust their surplus money to institutions, which pooled the savings of communities and loaned the funds to businesses and local and state governments. Many Americans clearly shared Alexander Hamilton's intuition that credit was the "invigorating principle" in the economy.

Property and casualty insurance companies were especially important. They were among the country's earliest lenders on property. The Philadelphia Contributionship for the Insurance of Houses from Loss of Fire made its first loan—$500 secured by a corner house and lot, plus the ground rent—in 1752, just four months after it was established. Thirty-three state charters to incorporate insurance companies were issued by 1800.[3] Entrepreneurs also set up institutions to encourage saving, which generated capital for productive use. Most of the institutions already existed in Europe, including the building and loan (B&L) societies, the forerunners of savings and loans. In a B&L, members were required to make regular payments, or dues, for their shares in the association. The B&L loaned out the accumulated capital to members to buy or to build homes, simultaneously encouraging both saving and borrowing. The first American B&L, the Oxford Provident Building Association, was established in Philadelphia in 1831. Its first loan was to a lamplighter living in what was then the village of Frankford outside of Philadelphia. Most members, however, were textile workers.[4] Mutual savings banks, institutions that

45

Comly Rich House, 4276 Orchard Street, Philadelphia, PA. Comly Rich, a lamplighter and comb maker, bought this modest frame house in 1831 for $500. The newly organized Oxford Provident Building Association loaned him $375. It was the first time a building and loan society financed a house purchase in the United States. The house, located in the Frankford neighborhood of Philadelphia, still stands. Photo by Jack E. Boucher, 1977. Historic American Buildings Survey/Library of Congress Prints and Photographs Division Washington, D.C.

are jointly owned by their depositors, were another European import. They first appeared in 1816, with the establishment of both the Provident Savings Institution in Boston and the Philadelphia Saving Fund Society. The banks' expenses were borne by philanthropic-minded individuals, and their costs were kept minimal by offering very limited opening hours.[5] By 1860, mutual savings banks would become among the largest businesses in the country.[6]

The directors and trustees of insurance companies, building and loan societies, and savings banks placed their capital in safe investments or loaned it to one another.[7] The strict rules that prohibited insider lending did not yet exist. Lending to insiders made sense because it circumvented the creditors' problem of obtaining information on borrowers. Sometimes the directors and trustees took chances on riskier ventures such as out-of-state mortgages. At any rate, more money was now available in Boston, New York, and Philadelphia for farms and other enterprises.

Commercial banks played an increasingly critical role in the economy. Parliament had prohibited the colonists from establishing joint-stock banks, but after the War of Independence, and especially after the Constitution's ratification in 1789, entrepreneurs and states began establishing banks to fund entrepreneurial ventures of all kinds. It is difficult today to imagine how unfamiliar the business of banking was, even to experienced merchants. The six men who chartered the Massachusetts Bank in 1784 wrote to Thomas Willing, president of the Bank of North America, asking his advice on how to establish and run a bank. Willing replied at length and even gave the would-be bankers suggestions for "Laws" and "Rules and Regulations." The bank's main activity was discounting merchants' notes, bills, and acceptances, for a fee of 6 percent. (Banks gave their own notes in exchange for merchants' paper. The bank notes then entered circulation.) The Massachusetts Bank accepted only deposits over $300 and prohibited withdrawals of less than $100. Rather than pay interest on deposits, the bank charged a fee for the service; like all banks of this period, its capital came from shareholders, not depositors. (Even in 1841, the 784 commercial banks then in existence reported outstanding loans and discounts of $386.5 million but just $64.9 million in deposits. By contrast, the capital provided by the banks' investors totaled $313.6 million.)[8]

By 1810, the United States had 102 state-chartered banks, and then more than double that number just five years later. In 1835, more than 80 percent of banks were located in the northeast.[9] There was no universal model for banking; instead, banking activities were idiosyncratic and experimental, reflecting the new republic's varied local economies and political cultures.[10] New England's unit (one-office) banks were closely held, made loans to a small group of insiders, and were lightly regulated by their state governments. By contrast, the southern states were home to some of the country's largest banks, some with several branches. In a few states, banks served as the government's financial arms. The Bank of Pennsylvania was one; it held the state's deposits, and about half of its directors were state appointed.[11] Legislators sometimes chartered banks to provide economic relief, as happened in Kentucky, Tennessee, and Illinois during the Panic of 1819.[12]

In the South, where export crops like cotton dominated the economy, large banks became part of the export infrastructure. Southern states issued bonds to establish banks. The ones that were backed by prime agricultural land of stockholders had reputations for being among the country's safest investments.[13] As in the North, southern banks performed a number of functions. In the 1820s and 1830s, Virginia chartered banks to help fund new ports and roads to compete with rival Baltimore's. South Carolina had a state-owned bank that helped planters and farmers to compete with the state's merchants for credit. Louisiana, buoyed by New Orleans' position in the growing international cotton trade, chartered banks that specialized in particular activities: mercantile and manufacturing, internal improvements, and long-term mortgages.[14] Georgia established the Central Bank to serve as its fiscal agent.[15] Foreign investors considered southern banks to be good investments. In 1832, the House of Barings encouraged Louisiana to form a state bank, whose entire bond issue Barings bought at a premium. In total, British investors held about half of the bonds of the South's "planter's banks."[16]

Banks played a significant fiscal role in many states. State governments invested in the stocks of the banks they chartered (sometimes buying the stocks with bank loans), or extracted bonus payments from banks in return for granting or renewing their charters.[17] Pennsylvania obtained about half of its revenues this way during the period 1801–1805.[18] Beginning with Massachusetts, states began taxing bank capital, adding still more money to state treasuries and diminishing the need to impose levies on the general populace.[19] From 1810 to 1830, up to one-third of some states' revenues consisted of bank dividends and taxes. Legislatures could also require banks to hold state debts as the collateral for their note issues.[20]

All banks were founded by people with entrepreneurial, pragmatic mindsets, the qualities that have led historians to dub this period of banking as an age of experimentation. As with all wide-ranging experiments, the spectrum of outcomes ranged from very successful to dismal. People understood that well-run banks benefited their communities. So long as the economy was healthy, most Americans did not object to the multiplication of banks or to the involvement of governments in creating and sustaining them. The objections to chartering new banks or to the establishment of unincorporated banks often came from incumbents who feared competition. Alexander Hamilton founded one of the earliest unincorporated banks, the Merchants Bank, in 1803, sparking a negative reaction from the incorporated banks of New York. As a result, New York passed legislation mandating that anyone entering the banking business had first to obtain a corporate charter.[21] States that invested in banks, however, had an incentive to limit the number of charters in order to discourage competition, and thus protect the dividends the states earned from their investments.[22] The clashing incentives of entrepreneurs who wanted more credit and the governments of some states that tried to limit the number of banks added to the heated arguments about credit.

The Jeffersonians voiced their distrust of banks, especially during times of distress, and against the Bank of the United States (BUS) in particular. But the growing entrepreneurial portion of the populace, regardless of which political parties they identified with, demanded more banks and more circulating currency. Their desire was not to limit the number of banks, but rather to make the banks accountable and free of elite control. Entrepreneurs needed funders who were willing to bet on riskier projects, as some banks were willing to do. Banks themselves sometimes engaged in speculation—on cotton and railroads, for example.[23] By contrast, the Bank of the United States (in existence from 1791 to 1811, and again from 1816 to 1836) was a conservative institution. It disciplined its correspondent banks, and as a result, BUS notes were trusted throughout the country. But the bank did not directly fund ventures such as speculation in western lands, which attracted risk-taking entrepreneurs.[24]

By 1800 the United States had roughly the same amount of bank capital as England and Wales, on a per capita basis. Twenty-five years later, bank capital in the United States was nearly two-and-a-half times that of England and Wales. Wide use of the corporate form allowed for limited liability and dispersed ownership of banks, unlike in England, which still required banks to be structured as small partnerships with unlimited liability.[25] In the period 1820–1860, bank credit in the United States increased at an annual average rate of 6.3 percent, significantly greater than the increase in the country's gross domestic product (GDP), estimated at 4.3 percent.[26] Historians find it difficult to determine just how effectively the banks allocated capital, so we may never know what percentage of GDP growth can be attributed to banks.[27] But when we consider the explosion in bank credit—especially when compared to the amount of bank credit in other countries—and the wide variety of enterprises that banks funded, the United States was clearly a nation that was built on credit.[28]

Then, too, the securities markets of the United States developed quickly. They were boosted by the federal debt securities created by Alexander Hamilton, and once established, the securities markets enabled entrepreneurs to found more banks. At this time, banks were more dependent on shareholders than depositors for their capital. Most banks were established as corporations, and in the early years of the stock market, bank stocks made up the largest share of traded securities. Savings institutions, insurance companies, private individuals, and the banks themselves invested in the stocks.[29] As they did with the state governments, banks even helped investors by lending them the money to buy the securities. When the financial markets deepened, the public and private securities acquired a secondary value—they could serve as collateral for bank loans. Banks and the securities markets thus grew up together in the new republic, and their intertwined nature led to a distinctive feature of American economic life.[30]

Booms and Busts

The entrepreneurial mindset of Americans had a terrible downside: too many people were tempted to speculate using borrowed capital. Land was a popular investment, but credit sometimes poured freely into all manner of business schemes. During the booms, creditors lowered their lending standards and made loans to the "projectors" Adam Smith had warned against.[31] Almost no institutions were in place that might have dampened these speculative fevers. Credit reporting was in its infancy, and there was little in the way of bond credit ratings. Nothing in the Bank of the United States' charter authorized it to intervene in the economy, and it had no power to set national interest rates. Apart from state usury laws and some (usually ineffective) state regulation of banks, restrictions on credit were fairly lax. At any rate, there was no guarantee that these institutions or more stringent regulations could have stopped a speculative binge once it began.

When a credit boom occurred, the prices of assets such as land and securities rose very quickly.[32] But then a spike in interest rates in London or an event that fanned a panic would result in tighter credit. A rash of insolvencies followed, causing asset prices to drop as fast as they had risen. Then a period of depressed economic activity usually followed, although the length of the downturns varied. From the ratification of the Constitution to the beginning of the Civil War, Americans experienced four major panics whose effects were felt by a broad section of the population: in 1792, 1819, 1837, and 1857.

The panics of 1819 and 1837 were especially serious. The 1819 panic and the depression that followed were the first to affect every region of the country. Banks proliferated in the years just before 1819, providing easy credit especially for new settlements in the West and the South. Americans faced a novel problem—there were now too many banks, extending what seemed like an extravagant amount of credit. When European demand for American food and cotton waned, and the prices of these commodities fell, everyone—northern merchants, southern planters, western farmers—felt the effects. Banks called in their loans, and an unprecedented number of borrowers faced foreclosures, business failures, and unemployment.[33] The defaults were so widespread that the federal government changed its policies regarding land sales. Formerly, it had allowed buyers to make a down payment of one-quarter of the purchase price within forty days of signing the contract. The rest was payable in three installments, with the last one due four years after the purchase at an interest rate of 6 percent.[34] In 1820 the government stopped extending credit and required all purchases to be made in cash.

The Panic of 1837 and the severe downturn that occurred in 1839 posed even more significant political and cultural challenges. These events followed the protracted "war" that President Andrew Jackson had waged on the Bank of the United States, from 1829 to the end of his tenure in 1836. The ideological disputes helped to create the two-party system of Democrats and Whigs that lasted until the late 1850s. After vetoing the recharter of the Bank of the United States in 1832, Jackson the following year ordered the Treasury to transfer the government's deposits from the BUS to a number of state banks. The transfers coincided with a series of economic events that together fueled a rise in speculative activities: first, a greater amount of Mexican silver entered the United States and became the backing for more bank loans; second, British demand for cotton raised the price of the commodity; and finally, the British invested heavily in state bonds, fueling a boom in internal improvements. In addition, the federal government had a surplus for the first time in its history; it distributed the $37 million among the states to spend as they saw fit. Many states planned new infrastructure projects that raised the price of real estate.[35]

Ironically, by the time Jackson's presidency reached its end, the country was enmeshed in the kind of feverish speculation that he had condemned. Jackson tried to dampen the boom by pushing for an all-metallic currency, which he framed as democratic alternative to paper money: gold and silver, he argued, would take away the power of bankers and politicians to manipulate paper currencies. His Specie Circular of 1836 required the buyers of large land parcels to pay with gold or silver. (The Circular proved very unpopular, and Congress tried to repeal it, but Jackson vetoed the repeal.) In his farewell address, Jackson widened his criticisms to include "the money power" and the "paper system" of currency.[36]

The economic bubble of President Jackson's last months in office eventually burst. With the British economy suffering a recession, the British merchants and manufacturers curtailed their lending to U.S. cotton growers.[37] Crop failures in England increased that country's importation of foodstuffs. When the Bank of England raised interest rates, the credit-dependent American cotton market was hit hard. The first failures occurred in March 1837, just when Martin Van Buren, Jackson's successor and a fellow Democrat, took office. Banks foreclosed on properties; firms failed in the South and in New York. When some banks suspended their redemption of notes, they sparked a full-blown panic, and a serious but temporary recession occurred. Then, in 1839, the economy slowed again. This time it slipped into a deep depression, one of the worst in the country's history—not until 1845 would the country see a substantial business recovery.[38] The depression drove many Americans to try their luck further west, or to find meaning in the hardship by joining religious and social reform movements.[39]

During the course of the protracted bank war, writers all over the country from different walks of life and political persuasions analyzed the causes of the economic instability and offered remedies.[40] Underlying the debates was a common theme that combined the political and economic concerns of the era: how should a democratic republic balance the release of entrepreneurial energies with restraints—the moral censure and formal regulations that would prevent social chaos and mitigate unfairness? A few budding theorists spoke about the larger forces at work within the country's political economy, but most people understood negative events as the result of personal actions and moral failings. Someone, somewhere was to blame.

Banks, with some justification, became a focal point of people's anger. Even well-run banks could malfunction when the economy was hit by events like poor harvests or when the Bank of England raised its rates, making credit harder to obtain. Without a robust central bank, there was no mechanism to guarantee that money would keep flowing or to allocate it to the places that needed it most. Nor was there a uniform, safe paper currency. When banks failed, the notes they had issued lost their value, imposing hardships on the unlucky people holding them. The Bank of the United States had played the role of a central bank to a degree, but there was as yet no theory of central banking and therefore no way for people to make a competent judgment of the bank's actions.[41]

Rather than seeing banks as fragile players in an underdeveloped economy, many Americans considered them to be the causes of instability.[42] Banks issued too much paper money; they encouraged speculation and risk taking; they were run by people who were incompetent or criminally irresponsible. In some cases, these charges were true. And banks could exacerbate the problems; they were involved with other businesses, so when they malfunctioned they brought distress not just to their depositors and shareholders but to entire communities. And people continued to resent the way bank charters could make certain groups rich—when states and municipalities seemed to favor a privileged few who used the banks as vehicles to accumulate funds for their own business projects or benefited from insider knowledge in buying bank stock. In time, some states refused to charter any banks at all. On the eve of the Civil War, Arkansas, Mississippi, Florida, and Texas had only private banks.[43]

Bank directors and politicians across the country experimented with ways of stabilizing the banks. In 1819, New England's Suffolk Bank put together a consortium of city bankers who agreed to entrust Suffolk with redeeming the country bank notes that accumulated in their vaults. By redeeming on a regular basis the city banks prevented their country cousins from recklessly issuing notes. The system was so effective that the notes of all member banks, city and country, attained a reputation for being very safe to use. In New York, the legislature passed the Safety Fund Act in 1829, a novel experiment in bank insurance. The scheme worked well enough during ordinary times but proved inadequate during the Panic of 1837.[44]

New York also pioneered the concept of "free banking," where almost anyone could found a bank provided they met certain regulatory requirements.[45] These included having a minimum amount of capital in the form of specie or state and federal bonds, to guarantee that the banks could redeem their notes. By the eve of the Civil War, eighteen states out of thirty-three had adopted free banking laws. The laws were based on the idea that banking and note issue were businesses like any other and not special activities that required the privileges granted by state charters.[46]

Americans had ample evidence that bank credit and notes could function well. The highly commercialized states of Massachusetts and New York had made serious attempts to control note issues and protect bank depositors and shareholders. Nonetheless, in the 1830s and 1840s there were calls for a hard-money policy and for strict limits on the number of bank start-ups. Die-hard financial conservatives such as William Gouge, a Philadelphia editor and supporter of Andrew Jackson, argued that the United States had too many banks and that financial institutions should not enjoy the privileges of incorporation and limited liability.[47] There were calls for banks to be stripped of their abilities to issue paper money, or at the very least to be prohibited from issuing small-denominated notes to prevent people from using them in everyday transactions.[48] But, as in the colonial period, limiting the amount of paper money was controversial. Plentiful paper money, a form of credit creation, enabled enterprising people to overcome the strictures of specie, barter, and commodity money to achieve a living—and with it, independence. The disagreements about whether the money supply should be "easy" or strictly controlled became an important political issue in the nineteenth century. It would reemerge after the Civil War and culminate in the populist movement at century's end. But before the Civil War, the federal government never succeeded in prohibiting the private issuance of paper money. A Supreme Court decision of 1839 stated that "the right to issue bank notes was at common law an occupation open to all men."[49]

As the number of chartered and private banks rose, so did the number and variety of notes. The amount of counterfeit ones rose, too. In 1862, the notes of some fifteen hundred banks in twenty-nine states were in circulation, a total of about seven thousand different kinds of notes. In addition, at least five-and-a-half thousand fraudulent and otherwise problematic notes had been identified.[50] Such an abundance of bad money has led historian Stephen Mihm to dub the antebellum United States a "nation of counterfeiters."[51] Perhaps remarkably, the problem did not lead to a loss of confidence in paper money. The large supply of counterfeit notes may even have provided a solution to the problem of an inadequate circulating medium: if people believed that a medium of exchange was genuine, and used it as such, then for all intents and purposes it *was* genuine.

The supporters of bank credit and paper money faced a great deal of resistance throughout the 1830s, from Andrew Jackson and then from the heir to his hard-money policies, Martin Van Buren. Van Buren acknowledged that the "credit bestowed on probity and industry is the just reward of merit and an honourable incentive to further acquisition." But he also thought that bank credit and the paper currency were undermining the virtue of the citizenry. In a speech to Congress, Van Buren remarked on how American merchants and shopkeepers had grown cavalier about advancing goods and endorsing notes. When they could not pay their debts, they declared insolvency or sheltered their assets through legal dodges that forced their creditors to settle for a tiny fraction of the goods' value. Then the insolvents went into business again, ignored their previous obligations, and left their creditors to bear the consequences of their failure.[52]

The foreign holders of state bonds developed a similarly negative view of American borrowers. In 1803, Europeans held more than one-half of the U.S. public debt, including some $11 million that financed the Louisiana Purchase, and more than three-fifths of the stock of the Bank of the United States.[53] Then the state and municipal indebtedness exploded.[54] (A few railroads issued bonds in the 1830s, but the market for their bonds remained small until the 1850s. For Americans of this period, bonds meant federal, state, and municipal issues.)[55] Prominent marketers of state bonds included London's House of Baring and the American firm of Brown Brothers, the mercantile houses that had made their names in trans-Atlantic trade finance. The English branch of Rothschild, the international banking house, employed U.S. agent August Belmont to sell state bonds. (He went on to found a successful private Wall Street bank.)[56] As a result of the aggressive marketing, English investors came to hold $20 million, or more than half, of Pennsylvania's $35 million of outstanding bonds; the Dutch and French owned an additional $2.4 million.[57] In all, some two hundred million dollars worth of long-term American securities were held abroad in 1840.[58]

Boosters talked up their infrastructure and banking projects, convinced that their localities were destined to be the next gateway or commercial

The Second Bank of the United States issued this stock certificate for 25 shares on April 14, 1830, to the London merchant house Baring Brothers. The certificate had a street value of $3,125 and was probably issued to consolidate Baring's purchases of shares in the local secondary market. In his message vetoing the bank's recharter, President Andrew Jackson criticized the fact that "more than a fourth part of the stock is held by foreigners." *Source:* Museum of American Finance, New York City, NY.

hub. In retrospect, some of the projects seem foolhardy. Indiana, for example, had a state budget of $50,000 yet authorized its canal fund to borrow up to $10 million at interest rates of $500,000 per year. Underpinning this and other seemingly crazy schemes was the assumption shared by many state officials that land values were sure to rise. Better infrastructure would enhance the value of land, and rising property taxes (as well as dividends from the projects themselves) would pay for all the borrowing. The Swiss banker Alex Lombard was bullish on the projects, writing in the depression year of 1841 that "however overdone the simultaneous development of so large a number of projects may have been, and although some of them could actually be called insane, with a cost all out of proportion to their return, it is fair to say that they have all more or less contributed to that majestic pattern of business activity and growing prosperity that the United States represents."[59]

But as generations of Americans in the past had discovered, and many more would afterwards learn, relying on rising asset values to cover debt payments can easily go wrong. During the brutal economic depression of the early 1840s, eight states and the Florida territory defaulted on their bonds. Five of them—Michigan, Mississippi, Arkansas, Louisiana, and Florida—ended up permanently repudiating their debts.[60] The experience would have lasting consequences. In the wake of the defaults, most states amended their constitutions to alter the way they issued debt, especially for internal improvement projects.[61] In the South, the land banks were essentially private projects. When they collapsed, residents who had never anticipated any benefits from the banks voted to repudiate the bonds.[62]

Americans acquired a reputation for perfidy among the European financial establishment. The trans-Atlantic merchant banker (and later philanthropist) George Peabody, senior partner to Junius Morgan and mentor to Junius's son John Pierpont (J. P.), found himself barred from London's Reform Club for being "a citizen of a nation that did not pay its debts."[63] James de Rothschild, a member of Europe's most eminent banking family, declared to the representatives of the U.S. federal government in 1842 that they could not "borrow a dollar, not a dollar."[64] The majority of American states and municipalities eventually repaid part or all of their debts. When the economy began to recover in 1843, state and local governments (apart from the five states mentioned) paid interest on some $260 million of bonds.[65]

The Defense of Credit

The expanding democratic culture of the United States inspired Americans to try their luck in economic ventures. Gradually, the traditional attitudes about credit and risk shifted. Leading politicians voiced support for more bank credit. Albert Gallatin, the secretary of the Treasury under Thomas Jefferson and James Madison from 1801 to 1814, was one. Although a supporter of Jefferson, Gallatin had backed the Bank of the United States in the 1790s and fought for its recharter in 1811. His opposition to Alexander Hamilton's plan for the BUS stemmed not from a dislike of banks but rather from his belief that the BUS favored eastern speculators at the expense of western entrepreneurs. As secretary, Gallatin proposed a federal bank that would lend $2 million a year over ten years to promising manufacturing projects.[66] He returned to the subject in 1831, writing that the early manufacturers "would have been essentially relieved and some of them saved from ruin by moderate bank loans." Banks might have accelerated the "general progress of the country," which had been "extremely slow."[67] President Andrew Jackson's veto of the Second Bank of the United States filled him with worry.

For politicians such as U.S. senators Henry Clay of Kentucky and Daniel Webster of Massachusetts, President Jackson's war on the BUS was an opportunity to further their own political careers. Both were longtime supporters of the bank: after initially criticizing it for blocking opportunities for Kentucky bankers, Clay went on to serve as the bank's attorney; Webster argued its cases in the Supreme Court. Jackson's order to remove the government's deposits from the BUS galvanized Clay, Webster, and many of Jackson's other political opponents. In 1834, the former New Republicans began calling themselves Whigs, a reference to the English political party whose opposition to the Crown had inspired the colonial revolt against "tyranny." The intellectual defense of credit gained momentum within the febrile ideological environment of the Bank War.

Taken together, the arguments defending banks represented a formal shift from older attitudes that had viewed credit as a necessary but unfortunate component of trade. In early eighteenth-century Britain, Daniel Defoe had claimed for credit the capacity to produce national wealth, a viewpoint that Alexander Hamilton upheld in his two reports on the public credit. Now a number of lesser-known Americans came to the defense of bank credit and paper money. They included educators, lawyers, and businessmen, who aired their views in pamphlets and magazines. (Most were Whigs, but a few Democrats joined in defending the bank and the credit system.) They recast the country's heavy dependence on credit by arguing that credit was a distinctly American device that made opportunity possible.

From "the very first origin of this government," Webster declared, "credit and confidence have held a high and foremost rank. We owe more to credit and to commercial confidence than any nation which ever existed; and ten times more than any nation except England. Credit and confidence have been the life of our system, and powerfully productive causes of all our prosperity." The development of the West and South depended on the credit provided both by the BUS and lenders from outside these regions.[68] "It is to this system of a sound credit and currency, that, as a nation, we owe our unrivalled march of prosperity and wealth," wrote the Whig pamphleteer Calvin Colton.[69] Missouri lawyer Henry S. Geyer maintained that a banking system made usurious moneylenders unnecessary: "Solvent persons may borrow from the bank at six per cent., and by this means not only escape the necessity of resorting to usurers, but acquire capital to come in competition with those who have money, in all the business of trade."[70] Banks had a levelling effect, according to the former Whig congressman George Chambers. "The man of small means as well as the capitalist, may vest their money in this manner, in a corporation, so as to afford credit to a community that may want and be benefitted by it. . . . The citizen who applies for a loan does not humble himself, as many are obliged to do, who apply to an individual capitalist for a loan."[71] Credit was progressive, forward-looking, and possessed of the power to civilize. It "is the necessary system of society in an advanced state," wrote Abel Upshur, a Virginia judge and politician who served as secretary of state in the administration of John Tyler.[72] "To think of living without [credit]," wrote Colton, "is turning the eye and footsteps back to a state of barbarism. Credit is the moral peculiarity of civilisation."[73]

Henry C. Carey was the most systematic of the defenders. The son of Philadelphia publisher and prominent bank and tariff supporter Matthew Carey, Henry had successfully taken over the family business and retired a moderately wealthy man while still in his mid-thirties. After the Civil War, he became a prominent American political economist, second only to Henry George.[74] In between, Carey served as a consultant to Horace Greeley, editor of the *Herald Tribune*. In *The Credit System in France, Great Britain, and the United States* (1838), Carey argued that the essential characteristic that allowed the American merchant to operate on a larger scale than his European counterparts, given the same amount of capital, lay in the American's more highly developed attitude of trust and confidence in his fellows. Trust, wrote Carey, underlay the extensive reliance on contracts, negotiable credit instruments, and bank notes and allowed capital to migrate from the older to the newly settled regions.[75] Credit worked because America's republican culture encouraged people to trust one another.

Henry Carey and the other defenders of credit were not the dominant voices during this period—it was Andrew Jackson whose policies held sway. But the way they reframed credit, from being a necessary evil to being the critical aid to opportunity and democracy, was essential to America's evolving culture of credit. In the long run, their views outlived those of the Jacksonians.

Some historians have argued that the American experience with banks was not unique: other developing capitalist economies, too, endured some form of monetary chaos during their most dynamic periods of growth. From this perspective, the fact that nearly half of the twenty-five hundred banks that were founded in the United States between 1790 and 1860 closed within ten years of opening may not have been too significant. About one thousand of the remaining banks managed to last at least forty years. More than one-third of the banks founded prior to the War of 1812 survived at least one hundred years. And of the northeastern banks (which tended to be the most stable of all), nearly two-thirds endured for at least forty years.[76] Compared to the rate of failure among other contemporary businesses and given the volatility of the immature antebellum economy, these figures do not indicate a dismal performance. Moreover, the mild strictures on banks, particularly in the newer regions of the country, allowed them to create credit for entrepreneurial activities.

Credit, Reputation, and Expansion: The Role of Merchants

Underdeveloped banking, transportation, and communication facilities were hindrances to trade. But these shortcomings also provided plenty of opportunities for a variety of middlemen, all of whom worked with credit. These were the merchants, cotton factors, bank note dealers, gold bullion dealers, and brokers of all kinds who made up Adam Smith's "invisible hand," the agents who coordinated the antebellum economy and enabled it to function. In the retail sector, where the players were small and diffuse and the goods simple, networks of merchants formed to distribute the merchandise across the United States' large territory. A "merchant" could be a wholesaler, jobber, commission merchant, factor, broker, importer, auctioneer—almost any agent whose superior knowledge of particular markets and individuals allowed him to bring together sellers and buyers. Merchants sorted goods into lots, arranged for their transportation and storage, facilitated payments, and provided credit.[77]

The merchants' activities naturally led them to offer banking services. (Banking's origins lay in trade, as reflected in the English term "merchant banker.")[78] Merchants held money for clients, arranged access to credit, transmitted payments to distant places, and discounted other merchants' bills. The most successful, such as Philadelphia's Nathan Trotter, amassed capital that enabled them to move into banking or brokering full-time. An importer and metals dealer, Trotter also discounted other merchants' paper on the side. Toward the end of his working life, he left the importing business to his four sons and went into lending full-time. Trotter even withdrew substantial amounts from the firm to buy commercial paper from Philadelphia brokers, whose numbers had increased during the 1830s and 1840s. (Note and bill brokering became specialized in the United States because so many different kinds of bank notes and paper were in circulation. These included the bills of canal and road companies and "scrip" issued by local and state governments to fund their ongoing operations and special projects.) Unlike his earlier lending to friends and associates, Trotter's purchases of commercial paper were a form of indirect lending, in which he probably did not have direct knowledge of the borrowers.[79] Trotter's activities signified that Philadelphia's credit markets had by then become larger, more diverse, and impersonal.

As private bankers, merchants engaged in activities that paralleled those of state-chartered banks, including issuing notes that circulated as currency. Chicago's George Smith, active in that city from 1837 to the 1850s, issued certificates of deposit and checks through his Wisconsin Marine and Fire Insurance Company that at one point totaled nearly $1.5 million. The paper could be redeemed for specie at the company or its branches, agencies, and correspondents—just like the notes of a chartered bank.[80] Private bank notes were backed by the reputations of the bankers themselves. By 1860, more than a thousand were in business throughout the United States.[81]

Formal laws enhanced the informal trust among business associates. The states, and later the Supreme Court, established uniform principles governing the negotiability of bills of exchange, making them safer and easier to use.[82] The bills helped to connect the regional markets long before most banks had any branches at all and decades before there was a national market for commercial paper. This level of connectivity does not imply that Americans everywhere could get credit at the same interest rate. But thanks to the large networks of intermediaries (including, for a time, the Second Bank of the United States and its branches), capital flowed across regions without much impediment. Even people in the frontier areas were able to get credit from eastern lenders, although at a higher interest rate, at a time when good communication facilities were underdeveloped or lacking.[83] Interest rates in New England, the Mid-Atlantic, and the South tracked New York City's, suggesting that the different regions were well integrated, some as far back as the 1830s.[84] American laws enabled business people to pay one another with a wide array of instruments, including municipal and corporate bonds and chattel notes (promises to pay in goods rather than money). The principle of negotiability also made possible the use of long-term loans known as accommodations, which were extended by banks and merchants on the basis of the reputation of a third-party who agreed to act as a guarantor.[85] The notes were short-term, but it was a widespread practice to renew them at maturity several times, turning them into long-term loans.[86]

Most banks did not lend to very small enterprises.[87] Instead, mercantile (trade) credit, in the form of goods advanced by merchants, helped to meet the demand for start-up and working capital. Mercantile credit functioned as venture capital for thousands of businesses in the distribution chain, allowing thinly capitalized businesses to grasp opportunities whenever and wherever they happened to arise.[88] Credit accelerated the settlement of new areas and allowed ordinary people to make a living by setting up stores, workshops, and farms. Thousands of tiny businesses, from grocery stores to millinery (hat-making) establishments, run by individuals, married couples, families, and partnerships depended on the credit supplied by wholesalers in the country's large commercial centers. From the 1820s to the 1850s, the typical western trader operated on one to two years' supply of credit from eastern suppliers. One western merchant reported that the amounts owed to him at any one time by his customers was three times the value of the merchandise he had on hand.[89] Another trader wrote that on the eve of the Civil War, "the domestic goods commission houses were practically supplying capital for the jobbers, who, in turn, were to a great extent carrying the retailers."[90] The jobbers bought on six to eight months' credit and then extended it to the country retailers for a slightly shorter period of time. Six months' credit without interest followed by 6 to 10 percent interest for an additional six months was typical.[91] In 1858, the Mercantile Agency estimated that 157,394 village and country stores owed an average of $14,500 each to urban jobbers, an aggregate value of nearly $2.3 billion (out of a GDP of $4.1 billion).[92]

Competitive pressures increased the supply of trade credit. By the late 1850s, Cincinnati, St. Louis, and Chicago began to rival the eastern cities, whose merchants responded by offering larger amounts of credit to their customers. Their terms were so competitive that even southern storekeepers found it advantageous to make the long journey north. According to a resident of New Orleans, the city was losing out to northern suppliers, "not that their markets were better, as convenient, or really cheaper" but because the "wholesale jobbers of the northern cities could afford to extend . . . greater facilities in the way of long credits than could our jobbers and wholesale dealers."[93] New England just before the Civil

War marketed over $60 million worth of goods to the South and purchased over $55 million worth of that region's products, according to one estimate. Northern ports shipped to the South some $100 million worth of manufactured goods.[94]

Credit fueled the export trade, especially of cotton. The House of Baring was heavily involved in the cotton trade, as were Alexander Brown & Sons. The Browns had opened an office in Liverpool in 1810 to facilitate Atlantic transactions, and this put them in a privileged position when the international market for cotton began to grow a few years later.[95] New York merchants and their partners in the southern ports acted as go-betweens, or cotton "factors": they paid advances, transmitted information about creditworthiness, and acted as guarantors for cotton planters and buyers.[96] Factors gave advances for consignments, not just on the cotton that was ready for sale but also on crops that had yet to be planted. They provided supplies on credit, endorsed planters' notes, and arranged lines of credit for them when the planters traveled in Europe.[97] They also no doubt helped planters to buy slaves. (Smaller cotton producers did not use factors but instead relied on local storekeepers, who bought cotton from several small growers before selling it on. The system would continue after the Civil War, when sharecropping replaced slavery as the dominant form of labor.)[98]

Banks benefited from the factoring arrangements because they were spared the task of trying to determine the creditworthiness of hundreds of planters. Instead, they relied on a handful of factors to filter the good risks from the bad.[99] London buyers also came to depend on American factors. In 1833, Liverpool merchants bought three-quarters of American cotton on consignment from factors rather than directly from planters. The well-developed factorage system would be one of the casualties of the Civil War. But until then, factors gave cotton planters access to markets throughout the world.[100] In doing so, the factorage system may have helped to entrench the large, slave-based cotton plantations more firmly in the economy of the South.

The merchants' dominant positions in the economy also made them important funders of the industrial sector. Decades of experience with the intricacies of international finance gave them the know-how and the confidence to fund risky manufacturing ventures. Sometimes they themselves diversified into manufacturing. Or they discounted the paper of manufacturers, as Philadelphia's Nathan Trotter increasingly did, at high rates. Trotter's interest in the paper of canals, railroads, and textile mills reflected the growing industrialization of the Philadelphia area. His discounting activity included the notes of a steam sugar refiner, iron founder, manufacturer of nails and railroad iron, locomotive manufacturer, and brewers. Trotter also made loans to the Philadelphia & Reading Railway.[101]

Merchants were key figures in business networks that included banks and insurance companies, whose charters restricted their lending to locals. New England's textile mills, whose owners belonged to well-established networks of merchants and banks, benefited from the emphasis on local lending. Banks helped the mills to meet their operating expenses by discounting the IOUs the mills received from their customers. The close relationships allowed the mills' owners to borrow at relatively low rates.[102] When money was tight, the mills sought financing further afield, from whomever was willing to lend to them: retired merchants, trusts, other manufacturers, and even the companies that marketed the mills' output. They also turned to the New York money markets. These sources charged more interest, and the mercantile houses sometimes provided short-term credit only. But they were useful alternatives when credit was unavailable from local banks and insurance companies.[103]

How much risk banks were willing to take on manufacturing enterprises during this period is uncertain. To determine this, researchers would need to examine the different types of loans and borrowers of a wide range of banks across the country. But scattered evidence shows that at least some banks made short-term loans to industrial and transportation start-ups. And although almost no commercial banks made long-term loans to these enterprises, short-term loans to fund working capital (payrolls, inventory, and the like) were probably more important to these early industrial concerns, whose fixed assets (buildings and equipment) were on a much more modest scale than the industrial behemoths that appeared at the end of the nineteenth century.[104] Lenders like Nathan Trotter exploited the conservatism of commercial banks. He made loans to industrial companies on four to six months rather than sixty days and charged higher rates of interest.[105]

Usury Laws

Before the 1820s, Americans generally did not complain about usury laws. The rare exceptions included William Sheldon's *Cursory Remarks on the Laws Concerning Usury,* published in 1798. Money, Sheldon argued, "like every other article of exchange and merchandise, if left to its own simple operation, will find its own value"—therefore, usury laws unnecessarily restricted credit.[106] After 1825, however, pamphlets and books began questioning the moral, economic, and legal basis of the laws. States did not overturn their usury laws; at the start of the Civil War nearly all still had them. But by then the regulations had evolved to the point of ineffectiveness. The laws were stricter in the older regions of the country, but states with large frontier areas where credit was harder to obtain led the way in overturning the laws or rendering them powerless. (California did not even have a usury law.)[107] According to legal historian Morton Horwitz, it was possible "to arrange usurious transactions in such a way as to entirely avoid running afoul of the usury laws."[108] In Pennsylvania, for example, the legal rate of interest was 6 percent. Yet merchant Nathan Trotter found lending profitable because, as a legal manual of the time put it, state courts had decided that "a fair purchase may be made of a bond or note, even at twenty or thirty per cent. discount, without incurring the danger of usury."[109] Retailers resorted to the age-old technique of raising the price of items bought on credit, as one midwestern store did in the 1830s when it added between 20 and 30 percent to the sales price.[110]

To attract investment capital from eastern investors, midwestern states experimented with raising their usury rates. In 1852 Ohio raised its maximum rate to 10 percent. The experiment failed because eastern capitalists were unwilling to tie up their funds in long-term projects for what seemed a measly return.[111] Overall, there were significant differences between short- and long-term lending. The long-term market was dominated by institutional lenders like savings banks and trust companies that tended to hew more strictly to the laws. The short-term market consisted of lenders like individuals and mercantile houses, who were less likely to keep within the legal limits. Rates for short-term loans fluctuated widely, reflecting market conditions and the desperation of some borrowers, who were sometimes driven by the needs of their businesses to borrow at exorbitant rates.[112]

Toward the end of the nineteenth century, states began to enforce their usury laws more vigorously, partly in response to the new small-lending companies that were targeting households with offers of loans at sky-high interest rates.[113] State usury laws were one of the only forms of consumer protection until the latter half of the twentieth century, when the federal government became more active in this area.

Household Borrowing

After the Panic of 1819, the federal government ended its practice of selling land on installment credit. For the next several decades, it sold land to individuals and families for cash only. People could, of course, get credit from private lenders and investors; when land prices were rising, funds were available even to speculators. But generally, people who could not save the entire amount for a lot, house, or farm struggled to get mortgage loans. Banks saw these loans as risky because they were long-term and not very liquid.[114]

Entrepreneurs and social reformers developed (or imported) institutional solutions to ease access to mortgages for specific groups. The first building and loan society was the Oxford Provident Building Association, established in 1831 in Philadelphia. For a monthly payment of $7 to $11, or about the cost to rent, families of moderate means could own their homes within twelve to fifteen years. The association was designed to terminate once all the members had received and paid back their loans.[115] A few institutions enlarged the supply of mortgage financing by investing in mortgages. In 1834, New York's mutual savings banks were allowed to do so; despite the higher risks, many of the savings banks invested in mortgages to achieve higher returns for their shareholders.[116] By law or custom, many such institutions limited their loans to local properties and borrowers.

Institutions were not the dominant sources of mortgage lending, however. Would-be home owners also turned to land speculators, builders, brokers, local investors, relatives, and friends to lend them the money. The few mortgage loans that could be obtained from institutional lenders had terms that were not generous by modern standards. For example, the Massachusetts Hospital and Life Insurance Company (MHLIC) was set up in 1823 to invest the savings of Boston's moneyed elite. It provided mortgages to local farmers. The farmers paid interest annually, and then the entire principal was due in a lump sum after just a few years. One of the company's agents argued that allowing farmers to pay back the principal in installments would widen the company's pool of borrowers. But his ideas were rejected. The trustees believed that loans should be restricted to farmers who proved they could meet the stringent payment requirements.[117]

Households needed credit not just to buy large assets like real estate but also to pay for durable goods and everyday necessities. But banks did not provide credit for consumption purposes; they would not do so until the 1920s, and not on a mass scale until the invention of the bank credit card. Legitimate consumer credit came from local retailers who let their customers run tabs and settle periodically. The agricultural rhythms that dominated many Americans' lives demanded the use of store credit. Farmers had little cash and needed time to sell their crops before they could pay for the goods advanced to them by their local stores. The custom was of long standing, and although there was a move toward cash in the 1850s, retailers found it very difficult to abolish store credit.

Installment credit was available, but only for durable goods.[118] One of the earliest recorded instances (because a newspaper advertisement from 1807 survived) was Cowperthwait and Sons of New York, a furniture retailer. By the 1850s installment credit had become more available for items such as farm equipment, pianos, and sewing machines.[119] Cyrus McCormick, a manufacturer of farm equipment, instructed his sales agents to offer "liberal terms" to customers.[120] New York City piano dealers advertised monthly payment plans; Singer Sewing Machines introduced its installment plan in 1856.[121] Manufacturers had high fixed costs and had to ensure that their factories ran at close to full capacity. By enabling more people to afford their pricey goods, installment credit helped manufacturers to minimize downtimes. When Singer introduced its installment plan, its sales trebled in the very first year.[122] Improved legal protections helped to spread the practice. Conditional sales agreements made it easier for installment sellers to repossess the goods when customers could not pay. Sellers could require customers to sign "confessions of judgment" that empowered the sellers to garnish wages without having to file a suit. Many states eventually banned the practice because it violated due process, but not until the 1960s.[123] In the meantime, the legal protections encouraged more sellers to offer installment plans.

Chattel mortgages—loans taken out against household goods, livestock, and other non–real estate property—were widely used by farm families to pay for durable goods, or to tide the household over until the next infusion of cash.[124] For many households, however, running out of cash was a constant problem. Having a tab at the local grocery store was helpful; and stores in rural communities—such as Lewis, Adams & Company of Springfield—invited customers to pay with "gold and silver, bank notes, city scrip, Auditor's warrants, wheat, corn, oats, butter, eggs, rags, chickens, in short, your entire cash and produce."[125] But a household that was desperate for emergency cash and unable to turn to relatives or associates for help often had little choice but to use the services of pawn-brokers or illegal lenders. Reformers were aware that households ran out of money, but their preferred solution was not to provide more consumer credit. Instead, they organized savings banks to encourage thrift and hard work among laborers and artisans. Between 1810 and the 1840s, local savings banks spread in both Europe and America, especially in New England and the Mid-Atlantic states. Philanthropy was the main driving force behind savings banks, which were governed by unpaid boards of trustees.[126]

But the problem persisted, and Americans who needed cash were forced to turn to pawnbrokers and "loan sharks." The savings banks were no match for these lenders because savings accounts were not meant to be drawn upon for short-term cash loans. Thus, licensed pawnbrokers provided an essential service, and they outnumbered the savings banks in most cities.[127] Already well established in Europe, pawnbroking had begun spreading in the United States at the start of the nineteenth century. New York issued forty-four licenses for pawnbrokers and dealers of second-hand clothing in 1826 (the two were not separated), or roughly one for every 4,800 people.[128] As they did in Europe, Jewish traders entered the field in large numbers. Soon, they dominated the industry and came to represent all that was deemed repellent about it.[129]

To discourage commercial pawnbroking, reformers set up semiphilan-thropic establishments that were modeled on the European *monti di pieta* (or *monts-des-piétés*). The attempts to copy the European institutions in New York and Philadelphia during the early nineteenth century failed. By the 1850s, however, a degree of acceptance of pawnbroking allowed merchant and philanthropist Stephen Colwell to incorporate the Loan Company in Philadelphia in 1855 as a form of "banking for the poor." The venture did not last long because, unlike commercial pawnbro-kers, it would not allow borrowers to keep renewing loans or to pay them off over an extended period. More successful was the Collateral Loan Company of Boston, organized in 1857 and better known as the Pawner's Bank of Boston. A mix of philanthropy and profit seeking, it returned 8 percent annually to its shareholders. An admirer remarked that for the needy, a pawned item was like savings in the bank, and the hope of redeeming the item made the pawner work harder.[130] Like modern-day "payday lenders" and the proponents of microfinance, reformers wanted to change perceptions about short-term lending to the working poor.

In 1858, Edward Everett, the former governor of Massachusetts and U.S. secretary of state, estimated that the nation averaged about $300 ($8,200 in 2010 dollars) of debt per household, not including business debts. There was, he wrote, a "natural proclivity to anticipate income to buy on credit, to live a little beyond our means."[131] But for many households, credit was less a means to acquire assets than an expedient to survive cash-strapped times.

Bankruptcy and Imprisonment for Debt

Failure, whether in the form of unrealized business dreams or outright bankruptcies, was widespread. Failure rates are difficult to compile, but the work of a number of scholars suggests that as many as one in two business proprietors may have defaulted on their business loans.[132] Edward Balleisen's survey of court records in the southern district of New York in the early 1840s found that bankruptcy touched everyone, from multimillion-dollar banking establishments to peddlers. Popular books and magazines carried stories about how wealth could be made quickly and how it could just as swiftly be lost. Novelists warned women to be aware of the threat that bankruptcy posed and to be careful whom they married.[133]

But people also began viewing debt and failure not as stigmas but as inescapable components of a risk-taking market economy. As the ranks of debtors swelled, they became an important political constituency. The continuing shortage of labor also predisposed businesses and legislators to keep debtors productive. Although bankruptcy laws continued to protect the interests of creditors, the balance tipped toward debtors. Along with insurance and savings banks, bankruptcy laws became a defense against economic insecurity.[134] Arguments that debtors were not necessarily criminals deserving of prison sentences became common. The states began abolishing imprisonment for small debts, beginning with Massachusetts in 1811. By the 1820s, only large debtors or those suspected of fraud typically spent more than one month in jail. The Supreme Court weighed in, declaring in 1827 that the abolition of debtors' prisons by states was constitutional. In the following three decades, the states steadily abandoned the idea that defaulting debtors should be incarcerated.[135]

People's understanding of the relationship between business creditors and debtors changed. Rather than being antagonists, the two came to be seen as business partners. Credit "is a mutual risk," declared the New

THE PROVOST, OR DEBTORS' PRISON.

Built in 1756 or 1758, this three-story building was New York City's first debtors' prison. Formerly, the city had no separate accommodations for such prisoners, and they were housed in the City Hall. New York outlawed imprisonment for debt in 1831. *Source:* Picture Collection, New York Public Library, Astor, Lenox and Tilden Foundations.

Hampshire writer J. N. Bellows in 1842. Fault was difficult to assign because neither party controlled "the currency, the government, the trade of the nation. Property falls; money is scarce; the crops are cut off."[136] Trade was risky, argued another business writer, "and, in a certain sense, the seller is a co-partner with the buyer, and shares with him the profit or loss of the bargain."[137] Henry Carey, the political economist, recast the country's high failure rates by arguing that the very persistence of business failure in the United States proved that it was nothing to fear. Gustave de Beaumont, the French aristocrat who had accompanied Tocqueville in his American travels (and whom Carey liked to quote) observed that "all the Americans being engaged in business, and most of them having more or less frequently failed, it follows that to be a bankrupt is nothing. . . . The indulgence for bankrupts springs, then, from the commonness of the misfortune; but its principal cause is the facility with which men there rise from such a fall."[138] De Beaumont exaggerated, but his core intuition was correct. Recent research has established that a significant proportion of people who filed under the 1841 bankruptcy law, roughly two in five in the southern district of New York, went on to reestablish profitable businesses.[139] Tocqueville himself remarked on the "strange indulgence that is shown to bankrupts" in the United States, which, in his mind, made Americans "differ, not only from the nations of Europe, but from all the commercial nations of our time."[140]

Failure continued to have negative resonance, but the bankruptcy process was becoming more routine.[141] By the 1830s, it ceased to be a judicial matter in most states and became instead an administrative event; most defendants did not even bother to contest suits. Lenders relied on the courts to chase nonpayers.[142] The increasingly impersonal nature of business encouraged people to see failures as the result not of character flaws but of larger impersonal forces. Parallels could be seen in marine and fire insurance law, where courts began to reject the insurers' argument that disasters were the result of "negligence." Instead, judges began to consider more categories of risk as legitimately within a policy's terms of coverage.[143] The insurance industry also pioneered the idea of aggregated risks, calculated by using statistics and then set out in actuarial tables. Although there was nothing similar for predicting business failure rates, the idea that negative events were impersonal and could be aggregated to calculate risk probably influenced the way people thought about bankruptcy.

Nonetheless, the passage of a national bankruptcy law continued to be controversial. The struggle reflected many areas of disagreement among the country's numerous constituencies, and no proposal succeeded in satisfying them all. The main sticking point was whether bankruptcy should be voluntary or involuntary: should creditors alone be permitted to declare a borrower in lawful default, as was the case in England? Or should debtors be allowed to declare themselves in default?[144] The Bankruptcy Act of 1800, the nation's first bankruptcy law, permitted the former only. The law was so unpopular that Congress repealed it in 1803, even before it was scheduled to expire. Traveling to a distant federal court posed a hardship for most people and helped to sink the law. So did concerns about fraud and the perception among some conservatives that the law encouraged risk taking. Conflicts between agricultural and mercantile interests played a part in the law's repeal, as did the opposition of southern lawmakers, who objected to any federal bankruptcy law at all.[145] Traders in the South and the West feared that eastern creditors would force local businesses into bankruptcy. Merchants made up the bulk of the creditor class, and they tended to favor stricter rules; but even in this area there was a great deal of ambivalence because most creditors were themselves also debtors. After the repeal of the 1800 bankruptcy law, demands for another one quickly resumed. But not until 1818 was a bill introduced—and it was promptly defeated.

Meanwhile, the federal courts adjudicated the conflicts. In the Supreme Court decision, *Sturges v. Crowninshield* (1819), Chief Justice John Marshall held that New York's insolvency law was unconstitutional as applied to prior contracts; in other words, states could not discharge debts that were contracted before the passage of an insolvency law. In *Ogden v. Saunders* (1827), the Court declared that states could not discharge debts owed to a citizen of another state. The states nonetheless enacted laws to furnish relief to debtors. Before 1840, less than half had insolvency laws at all, but that soon changed. During the 1830s and 1840s, Pennsylvania, Virginia, Mississippi, Ohio, Illinois, and Indiana passed stay and appraisal laws that limited what creditors could claim. States also exempted debtors' property. Their legislatures and courts tended to discriminate against non-residents, forcing businesses that operated across state lines to appeal to the more accommodating federal courts.[146]

Beyond these conflicts lay other frustrations for creditors. Commercial debtors took advantage of state laws to shelter their assets, sometimes with the help of friendly preferred creditors. Besides being unfair, the arrangement was sometimes fraudulent.[147] In England, preferential assignment had been illegal for centuries.[148] But it continued in the United States, and although the national laws aimed to end the practice, many states allowed it because the arrangement worked to the benefit of creditors who lived in the same state as the debtor. As of 1853, only eleven states prohibited preferential assignment; in most states, creditors had no incentive to cooperate with one another. One business manual described how creditors had to compete to recover assets from the debtor: "If one creditor had a suspicion that a debtor was about to fail, immediately such creditor would rush to court and levy an attachment or execution. Then would begin a mad race for precedence between executions, attachments, etc.,—between the sheriff, receiver, assignee and mortgagee—to see which one would get possession of the debtor's property first."[149] Debtors also colluded with members of their families to shelter assets. According to one business writer, a bankrupt could secretly buy up his debts "at 30 or 40 per cent discount, and make a capital but dishonest speculation out of his own failure."[150]

The Whigs blamed the Panic of 1837 and the severe economic downturn that began in 1839 on the policies of the Democratic Party. A federal bankruptcy law was a critical plank of the Whig campaign platform, and they used the momentum of the Whig victory in 1840 to pass a national bankruptcy law. Daniel Webster purportedly drafted much of the bill, which passed in a very close vote, a few months after the Whigs took power.

The Bankruptcy Act of 1841 was a watershed. For the first time, debtors could fail voluntarily: they could initiate their own bankruptcy by turning over their assets to court-appointed assignees and be discharged from their debts. Creditors could contest a voluntary filing only by proving that the debtor had committed fraud. The law acknowledged that many debtors were simply unfortunate, and that bankruptcy protection should be extended to people outside of the mercantile realm. So long as filers followed the procedures and met the qualifications and requirements, they were entitled to a discharge; questions about how they had failed were irrelevant. The law differed from the bankruptcy laws of many other countries, where courts were allowed to examine in minute detail the behaviors and circumstances that lay behind commercial failures.[151]

Defenders of the law argued that voluntary bankruptcy could be a sensible business move. It allowed debtors to keep their property during economic contractions until values recovered, which enhanced the debtors' ability to repay.[152] But critics countered that voluntary bankruptcy tempted debtors to act unethically. The law's practical shortcomings alienated creditors, whose control of the proceedings was now subordinated to the courts and court-appointed assignees. Creditors recovered minimal amounts; they paid high administrative charges yet saw thousands of debtors discharged.[153] Balleisen found that in "twenty-one of the thirty-three jurisdictions that reported statistics to the House of Representatives in 1846 and 1847, creditors who proved their debts garnered 1 percent or less of their claims." In many jurisdictions, the majority of bankrupt estates paid nothing at all. (Many bankrupts who filed under the Act had failed two or more years previously, so their assets had already gone to creditors or assignees.) Although groundbreaking, the law of 1841 did not survive the controversies surrounding it, and the Democrats successfully overturned the law in 1843.[154] During its short existence, 41,000 people filed for bankruptcy, of which 33,000 received discharges—a rate of about one in every hundred white males.[155]

In the aftermath of repeal, the states continued to pass their own insolvency laws. Some, such as the lien laws, favored certain types of creditors. Most of the laws, however, exempted a steadily higher portion of debtors' property from being seized.[156] The 1841 federal law had exempted only household furniture worth up to $300 and some clothing for the debtor and his family. The states went much further. In 1846 the new state of Texas pioneered the exemption of homesteads, which included up to 200 acres and $2,000 worth of town and city lots.[157] Texas' generous exemption law became a tool for attracting immigrants, especially from neighboring states. The lesson was not lost on Californians; when California entered the Union in 1850, its legislators wrote the homestead exemption into the state constitution. Between 1848 and 1852 eighteen states, first in the lower South and then the Midwest and the Northeast, passed their own versions of a homestead exemption law, making it a typical feature of American state bankruptcy legislation. (Of course, the laws could not prevent all home losses, especially during panics.)[158] The married women's property laws, enacted in many states beginning in the 1830s, made it easier for businessmen to shelter their assets from creditors by conveying the assets to their wives.[159] Intended to protect the property of wives, the laws had the unintended consequence of enabling married couples to collude in order to keep businesses going that otherwise would have had to declare insolvency.[160]

The framers' expectations that there would be uniform bankruptcy laws across all of the states would not be realized until the very end of the nineteenth century, with the passage of the first permanent national bankruptcy law in 1898. Even though many people had begun to see business failure as a routine hazard of entrepreneurship, there were too many disagreements and obstacles to a national law that no concerted effort could overcome. There was little agreement even on the state level, which may explain why the legal evolution in every state was haphazard and piecemeal, and why state laws became simultaneously more technical and inefficient.[161]

But even so, the principle of voluntary bankruptcy became embedded in the United States' culture of credit, as did the idea that business failure did not necessarily result from moral shortcomings. And although southerners were among the fiercest opponents of a national bankruptcy law, its importance was recognized even by the Confederate government: when the eleven states that seceded to protect states' rights met in Montgomery, Alabama, in 1861 to create the Constitution of the Confederate States of America, the delegates included a provision empowering the Confederate Congress to establish uniform laws of bankruptcy. At the time, the indebtedness of southern planters and traders to northern merchants, mostly to New York, Philadelphia, Baltimore, and Boston, was an estimated $300 million. In New York, 913 mercantile houses became insolvent upon secession, each with liabilities of over $50,000.[162]

The Beginnings of Credit Reporting

While Americans debated the country's system of credit, entrepreneurs created new institutions to manage its risks. The credit-reporting agency was among the most novel and one of the few institutional innovations invented by Americans during this period: credit reporting did not exist in any other country as a profit-making venture.[163] In the large U.S. market, where there were few established mercantile relationships and the population was perpetually on the move, entrepreneurs realized that business creditors would save on the costs of gathering information and expand their potential markets if information could be collected by a third party and offered at an affordable price. Banks might have filled the role of information brokers, but the country's fragmented and unstable banking system did not facilitate the sharing of information. (This barrier had long-term consequences. According to one study, until the 1990s most U.S. banks did not make loans to small businesses located more than 51 miles away.)[164] Moreover, the information was lost when banks failed, which they did with regularity. In any case, many banks shied away from sharing information with outsiders.

The outcome of particular transactions was the most useful information. Did the borrower pay the debt, and on time? If the borrower encountered difficulties, did he or she make a good faith effort to make things right with the creditor? This information was seldom available, and never in a systematic form. Creditors therefore focused on the borrower's aptitude for business ("capacity") and on his or her character. Lenders took rumors of untrustworthy business behavior seriously; they particularly prized the testimonies of merchants and bankers. Large institutions could afford to gather this information and to keep it on file. The Massachusetts Hospital and Life Insurance Company hired its own local attorneys to investigate the creditworthiness of local farmers.[165]

Northeastern wholesalers who sought new customers came up with ad hoc ways to learn about the creditworthiness of distant traders. Nashville lawyer Robert Whyte, who collected debts for Philadelphia wholesalers, also provided them with information on Nashville storekeepers. In the late 1820s, a group of New York wholesalers hired an agent, Sheldon P. Church, to tour the country and write credit reports on existing and potential customers. The resulting volume circulated only among the wholesalers who paid for Church's services. The idea that money could be made on this type of information was therefore already spreading. In 1835 a firm called Griffen, Cleaveland and Campbell set up an agency that claimed to have a number of correspondents covering New York state. It planned to expand coverage of the surrounding areas.

The Mercantile Agency, established in 1841 by the merchant and abolitionist Lewis Tappan, bought the remains of Griffen, Cleaveland and Campbell when it went out of business. Tappan's was the first credit-reporting agency to employ an extensive network of credit reporters consisting of men who were in a position to observe or have knowledge of their fellow townspeople. Lawyers were ideal for the job because they were often involved in business deals or were positioned to hear about them. (Springfield lawyer Abraham Lincoln was one of the agency's early reporters.) Tappan's New York City–based firm opened its first branch in Boston in 1843. Competitors quickly appeared. The most enduring was the firm of John Bradstreet & Company, established in Cincinnati in the late 1840s. Bradstreet moved his head office to New York in 1855.[166]

Tappan sold his agency to Benjamin Douglass, a former cotton factor and then a clerk in the agency. Douglass tackled the problems of establishing a network; for example, he insisted that branch managers report on businesses in their district for the benefit of other branches. He also inherited the task of expanding the firm's subscriber base. By the mid-1850s, Douglass had persuaded a number of banks and insurance firms (but still no manufacturers) to subscribe to the service. He also expanded the agency's services to include debt collections and began distributing circulars on the number of failures throughout the country, gathered from court filings across the country. (The agency remained the most trusted source for this information until the 1930s, when it stopped publishing the information.)[167] In 1857 the firm opened its first international offices, in London and Montreal, to serve American exporters.

It was John Bradstreet, however, who pioneered the use of credit ratings, the numerical designations that replaced the descriptive reports on borrowers. His firm published the ratings in reference volumes that were replaced once a year. When Robert G. Dun took over the Mercantile Agency from Douglass, he copied Bradstreet's innovation, using numerical symbols from 1 to 4. The newly styled R. G. Dun and Company published its first volume of ratings in 1859, covering 20,268 firms. Numerical ratings made transmitting the information easier and allowed creditors to compare borrowers in a more systematic way.

During hard economic times the high number of failures revealed that the credit reporters often failed to detect vulnerabilities. Even so, the credit-reporting entrepreneurs argued that they provided a socially beneficial service. Later academic studies confirmed that credit-reporting firms help to prevent adverse selection, which occurs because high-risk borrowers are the most active in seeking loans. As Adam Smith had observed, these borrowers are more willing to pay high rates. When usury laws prevent lenders from charging high interest rates, they will choose not to lend at all, even though there are creditworthy borrowers that could put the funds to productive use. Credit reports allowed lenders to distinguish the good risks from the bad, giving them the confidence to lend at a reasonable rate.[168] The reports were not meant just to prevent bad debts but to enable their subscribers to make decisions about taking prudent risks.

The courts, however, struggled with the idea that information coming out of the transactions between two private parties could be sold to others who had no involvement in the transactions at all. Erroneous information that damaged the reputations of individuals and firms were another legal problem. John and Horace Beardsley, two Ohio merchants, sued Lewis Tappan for slander and libel, and Benjamin Douglass spent twenty days in jail for refusing to give the court the name of a corresponding attorney. Earlier, firms in Columbus, Mississippi, had sued Sheldon P. Church, the agent for a group of New York wholesalers, for libel. After a lengthy appeals process, the courts awarded the firms $5,000 each. But the courts could also be sympathetic to the work done by the credit-reporting firms. In *Ormsby v. Douglass* (1858), the court dismissed a suit for slander and rejected all appeals.[169]

Creditors and credit-reporting firms used an agreed-upon set of standards to evaluate creditworthiness. The standards included a person's assets (landholdings, primarily) and his or her reputation for paying debts. Rumors, whether of the failure to pay local tradespeople or of overindulging in alcohol and gambling, were taken as indicators of a lack of creditworthiness; on the flip side, the reports encouraged lenders to trust people who were hardworking and lived within their means. In the course of doing their work, the credit-reporting agencies institutionalized the informal set of rules—the norms, customs, and habits of thinking—that had served since colonial times as guides for judging who was, and was not, worthy of credit.

The founders addressed the role of credit in the new republic, but it was the next generation of Americans who grappled with the political and cultural meanings of credit and debt. They formed their ideas through daily experience, while establishing the financial institutions that made loans, invested Americans' growing savings, and issued currency. Plentiful opportunities existed in a country that was growing both more democratic and more reliant on slave labor (a contradiction that the Civil War eventually removed), but where steady economic growth was punctuated by booms and busts.

To mitigate the risks, lawmakers passed the first national bankruptcy law allowing noncommercial debtors to file for voluntary bankruptcy and discharge. Simultaneously, entrepreneurs created the for-profit credit-reporting agency. The agencies pressured business people to conform to standards of creditworthiness, standards that the agencies' networks of correspondents and reporters spread into the smallest localities. Collateral was, of course, important, but the agencies also reported on "character." Creditors wished to know about borrowers' honesty and their willingness to work hard, live thriftily, and shun drinking and gambling. Paradoxically, the fiercely democratic United States was the first country to develop an open system of credit information that relied on the surveillance of debtors by private firms.

These developments followed a period of intense ideological debates about the place of credit in a democratic republic. During the bank war, members of the new American Whig Party defended credit creation as a necessary feature of advanced democratic societies. Credit, they argued, safeguarded equality and provided opportunities for people to improve their economic circumstances. In the decades after the Civil War, those ideals would be severely tested, as access to money and credit became the central problem of American politics.

Chapter Three

"THERE IS CONSIDERABLE FRICTION"

Credit in the Reconstructed Nation

The Civil War (1861–1865) transformed the nation's financial system. When southern lawmakers left the United States at the outbreak of hostilities, they lost the power to block reforms that had been supported by northern financial interests. In February 1863, Congress passed the National Bank Act (amended in 1864).[1] Intended to help pay for the war, the act also reshaped the country's banks and currency. The new regime of national banks helped to control the nation's credit and currency for half a century, until it was subsumed into the Federal Reserve system that Congress created in 1913.

But the lawmakers also preserved much of what had gone before. Although the banks were "national," they were not allowed to branch across state lines. The government maintained the state-chartered banks, opting for a dual system of both state and federal charters. Initially, the federal charter's lower reserve requirements made it the more popular option: there were 1,612 national banks by 1870, whereas the number of state banks fell from 1,579 to 261.[2] The trend reversed in the late 1870s when state legislatures reduced the minimum capital requirements. By 1890, state-chartered banks predominated. Creating the national banks allowed Congress eventually to impose a national currency. But the national banking system did not halt the explosion of one-unit banks, nor did it improve much the problem of credit availability and the allocation of money.

The national banks did, however, galvanize the reformers, whose competing visions fueled the politics of the Reconstruction era. Greenbackers, as the opponents of the national banks were called, argued that the banks conferred benefits to an eastern moneyed elite at the expense of indebted farmers. They believed that money should be created and controlled by the federal government, not outsourced to private national banks that benefited from having federal bonds as collateral. By contrast, the financial conservatives opposed expanding the federal government's power over banks and the currency. In their view, a gold standard that was independent of government control would discipline banks in a less politicized way.[3]

Arguments about the financial system took place in a political climate in which a defeated and economically damaged South faced the rigors of Reconstruction. The states of the former Confederacy were reintegrated into a nation that was now under the sway of railroads and other large corporations—"monopolies," as many people came to regard them. Farmers in Georgia, Mississippi, Texas, and other former Confederate states continued to grow cotton, still the country's premier export. But war had destroyed the South's banking and factoring services. The pressures imposed by the imminent resumption of the gold standard and the restrictions of the new National Banking Act may have delayed the financial reintegration of the South.[4] Its citizens, both black and white, rebuilt their lives upon new structures of labor and credit.

The economy's growing complexity gave rise to unstable and shifting coalitions of interest groups, and both the Republicans and Democrats struggled to maintain party unity.[5] Intense rancor characterized the rebuilding of the nation's financial system. But beneath the heated exchanges lay a deeply pragmatic strain among the country's politicians, financiers, farmers, lawyers, and business owners. Negotiation and compromise, much of it tainted by bitterness and rooted in racism, was the overarching story of the way Americans rebuilt the financial system after the Civil War.

Gold versus Paper Money

The very large public debt to fund the Civil War forced politicians to change the financial system, in the same way the Revolutionary War debts had done eight decades earlier. Prosecuting the war cost the Union government over $3 billion (nearly $60 billion in 2011 dollars), of which taxes paid for less than one-fifth.[6] In late 1861, a few months after the start of hostilities, news of a large Treasury deficit and the prospect of continued government borrowing caused the value of government bonds to fall.[7]

Gold went into hiding, driving the banks and the Treasury to suspend specie payments. In effect, the United States went off the gold standard.

The government began issuing greenbacks the following year. Greenbacks were the United States' first fiat money—currency that was not backed by specie but which creditors were required to accept.[8] All told, the U.S. Treasury issued some $450 million worth of greenbacks and over $800 million of bonds. (With refinancings, the bond issues would double to $1.6 billion by 1869.) At its highest point in the summer of 1865, the federal debt was equivalent to one-half of GDP. Interest payments on the debt were much higher than the entire federal debt before the war.[9]

Congress established the national banks to support its war bonds. The bonds were the legal backing for the national banks' note issues (limited to a total of $300 million). Large numbers of the northern public took up the war bonds, the first mass-marketed securities in the country's history. In contrast, the greenback, the other national currency, was backed by nothing but the credit of the U.S. government. Its value rose and fell during the war, depending on the fortunes of the Union armies in the field. At the end of 1864, when the war had turned decisively in favor of the Union, it still took $185 greenbacks to buy $100 of gold.[10]

These two paper currencies—the national bank notes and the greenbacks—raised the Union's total money supply by nearly two-and-a half times during the war, causing serious inflation. The cost of living almost doubled.[11] Still, the inflation in the North never reached the level that destabilized parts of the Confederacy, where the general price index in some areas went from 100 at the beginning of the war to nearly 9,200 by war's end in April 1865.[12] The Union's note issues helped to fund the war and enlarged the North's manufacturing and agricultural bases. Northern factories and farms churned out huge volumes of war materiel, food, and supplies. The better-equipped, better-fed Union army overcame a Confederacy that eventually was unable to sustain either its armies or its home front.

When the war ended, the question of what to do with all the greenbacks became the most pressing financial problem of Andrew Johnson's administration. In the beginning, almost everyone agreed that the country had to resume the gold standard to control inflation and signal the country's creditworthiness. (The political issue became known as "resumption." Congress's limit of $300 million national bank notes, and the fact that these notes were backed by federal bonds, made them less of a problem than the greenbacks.)[13] With the strong encouragement of Secretary of the Treasury Hugh McCulloch, Congress in March 1866 passed an act for the greenbacks' gradual retirement.

For the next fifteen years, the government hesitated to contract the number of greenbacks even in good economic times. When financial panic hit in 1873, resumption once again became controversial. The railroads were among the first to cry for relief, followed by the iron and extractive industries. A coalition of Pennsylvania and western Republicans even supported an inflation bill that, after some vacillating, President Ulysses S. Grant vetoed.[14] In the long period of deflation that followed, many businesses found their profit margins narrowing. John Sherman, the Republican senator from Ohio (and elder brother of Union general William Tecumseh Sherman), assumed the difficult task of shepherding the resumption bill through Congress. In 1875, a year that saw far more business failures even than the panic year of 1873, he managed to unite enough Republicans behind the bill. Economic conditions continued to worsen, however, and the business sector remained divided about resumption. To people in the South and the West, the federal government's contention that there was too much money in the economy seemed incredible.[15] The Grant administration tried to respond by allowing the national banks to issue another $54 million of notes, primarily for the South and the West. But as of 1874, the South and the Southwest held only a little more than one-tenth of the nation's currency, despite having over a quarter of the nation's population. The high capital requirements for setting up national banks—$100,000 of U.S. bonds for country banks and $200,000 for city banks—further impeded their establishment in these regions of the country. The administration scrapped the $300 million national bank note ceiling in 1877; but even so, the volume of national notes remained unchanged and actually declined between 1882 and 1891.[16] Bank overdrafts—loans in the form of created deposits on which the borrower could write checks—became more plentiful and increased the amount of "money" in the economy.[17] But although the volume of deposits rose at first, they dropped after the Panic of 1873 and remained stagnant throughout the depression.[18]

By now, Americans had a long and mixed experience with paper money, but their memories of wartime inflation were still sharp. Even when money and credit were tight, many rural organizations still supported a specie system. At first, farmers were far more concerned about the power of the railroads and directed their political energies toward constraining these businesses. But within a few years of the Panic of 1873, farmers' groups began conflating railroads and banks—both were monopolists. From then on, the specter of a "money trust" overtook the railroads as the perceived source of agriculture's problems.[19]

A consensus began to form around enlarging the money supply, and farmers joined other groups who were agitating to add silver as the basis for paper money. A bimetallic (gold and silver) system had been in place for most of the previous eight decades, until silver was demonetized in 1873 amid great controversy.[20] Senator John Sherman tried hard not to alienate the more reasonable bimetallists, but domestic and international bond-holders took fright, believing they would be forced to redeem their federal bonds in depreciated silver. Congress passed a compromise solution, the Bland-Allison Act of 1878, which required greenbacks to be convertible to specie but also obliged the Treasury to purchase silver to sustain its price. (The act had a minimal effect on the economy; Congress repealed it in 1890.)

In the end, Sherman, who became secretary of the Treasury in 1877, managed to achieve the necessary coalition to ensure that the Resumption Act would go into force as scheduled. At the eleventh hour, he also arranged a loan from Europe with terms favorable to the United States, which guaranteed that there was enough gold for resumption. With that done, the United States resumed the gold standard on January 2, 1879. But even so, $346 million of greenbacks continued to circulate, as did millions of dollars of silver certificates.[21]

Resumption halted the momentum behind the Greenback movement, and the Greenbackers ceased to be a political force. Money remained tight for farmers, and prices dropped. The gold supporters, though, continued to blame the deflation on overproduction rather than the restrictions on money.[22] Then, in the mid-1880s, severe drought pushed the agricultural sector into depression. But the economy was far from moribund: unlike the "stagflation" (stagnant growth mixed with inflation) that would occur a century later in the 1970s, the United States in the 1870s and 1880s saw falling prices combined with GDP growth. Per capita income rose threefold between 1870 and 1910.[23]

This larger picture became clear only in hindsight. In the meantime, aggrieved farmers and small producers agitated for more money and credit, and the national banks lobbied for less federal regulation. The banks also pushed for permission to open branches, which would have enabled them to increase the scale and scope of their operations. Many Americans opposed branch banking because they feared the concentration

VOL. XIX.—No. 979.]   NEW YORK, SATURDAY, OCTOBER 2, 1875.   [WITH A SUPPLEMENT.
PRICE TEN CENTS.

Entered according to Act of Congress, in the Year 1875, by Harper & Brothers, in the Office of the Librarian of Congress, at Washington.

THE ONLY SAFE GROUND.—[FROM A SKETCH BY MARY HALL.]

of financial power. Small banks lobbied hard against allowing the branch banks, just as some local bankers had opposed the Bank of the United States' branches decades earlier.[24] The antibranch forces won out. In the 1880s, the number of national banks, state banks, and trust companies expanded dramatically, from 2,973 in 1882 to 7,147 in 1892.[25]

Other developments reduced the credit available to smaller producers. During the depression of the 1890s, bankers cut back on local loans and instead invested the funds in industrial securities. The increased demand for their securities enabled the large industrial firms to issue more, which in turn fed the great merger wave at the turn of the twentieth century. During the fifty years after the Civil War, northern firms took on larger amounts of debt in order to expand and to consolidate, prompting some commentators to observe that while railroads were more indebted than the farmers, the railroads could more easily borrow by issuing bonds.[26] But access to industrial credit was also uneven, with the large industrial firms in the North having a much easier time than struggling southern firms.[27]

The agricultural depression crystallized the opposition to industrial and financial monopolies into a national movement, Populism. The coalition contained elements of earlier political organizations such as the Texas-based National Farmers Alliance and Industrial Union (referred to as the Southern Alliance), which had unsuccessfully tried to revolutionize agricultural credit by offering farmers a program of cooperative purchasing and marketing. Like them, the Populists believed that the federal government rather than the eastern money elites should control the nation's money supply. The free coinage of silver would break the stranglehold of eastern bankers. Other proposals included a government-run postal savings bank system and a subtreasury plan to provide farmers with credit at modest rates of interest.[28] Populism reached a crescendo in 1896 when the candidate for the Democratic presidential nomination, William Jennings Bryan, denounced eastern and international creditors for creating a "cross of gold" to crucify farmers. The speech, one of the most famous in

---

This cover of *Harper's Weekly*, October 2, 1875, shows Uncle Sam on horseback, apparently having reached ground marked "Specie Basis." Uncle Sam carries the "national credit" in his bag while clouds of "Inflation" hover in the background. Congress had passed the controversial Resumption Act the previous January. The act, scheduled to take effect in January 1879, returned the United States to the gold standard. *Source:* HarpWeek (harpweek.com).

American history, won Bryan the Democratic nomination. But it was the Republican William McKinley who won the White House.

Populism had enduring legacies: the progressive income tax, agricultural price supports, and the fiat currency that the Populists supported all came to pass. And although Populists objected to a federal bankruptcy law, they influenced the first permanent one that was enacted in 1898, which formalized a number of pro-debtor provisions.

By 1910, the movement to allow free banking—a movement that had begun in the 1830s—became the norm. In most states, any group could now establish a bank so long as they met certain requirements. Pressure from the small-banking lobby continued to restrict branch banking, resulting in a further explosion in the number of one-unit banks.[29] Between 1900 and 1910, the number of nationally chartered banks alone grew from 3,732 to 7,145, while the number of state-chartered banks, including commercial banks and loan and trust companies, went from 4,659 to 13,257.[30] Most of the banks had no branches at all. A lot of small towns ended up with a high number of banks relative to population. Battle Creek, Iowa, for example, had three banks for a population of 688.[31] Unit banking had advantages, including providing incentives for bankers to know their local borrowers and to stand by them during hard economic times.[32] And the proliferation of banks may have further eroded the monopoly power of entrenched local elites and helped to narrow the differences in interest rates among regions. But the huge number of small banks became a problem during the 1920s and 1930s when they ran into trouble and contributed to the country's financial instability.

The nation's fragmented banking system aggravated other flaws: the inability to distribute money to rural areas when it was most needed, and the tendency for the money to go to Wall Street investors. Banks around the country kept their reserves in a handful of New York City banks that in turn loaned the money to investors in the stock market. During the autumn harvest season, when workers had to be paid in cash, the rural banks drew on their reserves in the city banks, who in turn drew on *their* reserves in the large New York banks. (The arrangement resembled a pyramid—six large national banks in New York held most of the nation's reserves.)[33] The New York banks then had to call in their own loans, causing stress on the stock and bond markets. Because of such arrangements, the banking system in the United States was unstable compared to some other countries at the time.[34] The problem grew even worse during financial crises, when people rushed to empty their bank accounts. Such a crisis occurred in 1907, when a falling stock market led to a bank run that spread around the country. The crisis was averted by John Pierpont (J. P.) Morgan, who injected liquidity into the banking system by pledging his own resources and strong-arming other bankers to do the same.[35]

The Panic of 1907 was a watershed. The power held by bankers such as Morgan provided the impetus for the establishment of the Federal Reserve in 1913. The Fed was a central bank, designed to inject liquidity into the financial system by making emergency loans to member banks that were temporarily under stress. The Fed's decentralized structure bore the stamp of Populism: the twelve regional ("district") banks, which increasingly held the banking reserves of the nation, issued and redeemed their own notes. But the Fed also explicitly tied the nation's monetary policy to the real-bills doctrine (discussed later in this chapter) and the gold standard. Ironically, that policy may have inhibited the Fed's ability to respond in the 1930s to the even worse crisis of the Great Depression.[36]

Alternative Sources of Credit

After the devastating shock of the Civil War, politicians and corporations embarked on the long process of building a national economy. All sectors continued to grow. Agriculture spread into Iowa, Minnesota, and the Great Plains. Industrial concerns became large, and their owners amassed wealth that dwarfed the mercantile fortunes of a generation earlier. National savings grew dramatically, from a pre–Civil War rate of around 15 percent to 28 percent in the 1880s.[37] The number of banks grew, and they now relied on deposits for their loanable funds rather than issuing paper notes as many banks had done earlier in the century.

Conservative bankers in the Northeast argued that there was no need for the government to intervene. From their viewpoint, the existing system of commercial banks was doing an adequate job. By modern standards, however, the commercial banks served only a narrow band of borrowers. Both federal and state regulations reinforced the idea that commercial banks should always have liquid assets so that they could readily meet their depositors' demands to withdraw money. This logic dictated that the only safe lending was short-term loans to creditworthy business people and farmers for the shipping of goods and produce, a practice known as "real bills."[38] Among the beneficiaries were the sellers of goods, who could borrow from banks until they collected payment from their buyers.

Recent developments reinforced the real-bills way of thinking. Transportation and communication improved, allowing trade credit terms to become shorter and accelerating the payment of the bills, which made them even safer. In New England, banks turned away from the investment-oriented model they had adopted early in the nineteenth century and toward more impersonal, short-term lending administered by "professional" bankers.[39] In his handbook on banking (1888), Albert S. Bolles, the first business professor at the University of Pennsylvania's Wharton business school, wrote that "the first and most important function of a bank . . . is to bridge over the periods of credit which necessarily intervene between production and consumption. . . . Thus defined, banking is not only one of the most useful; but it is also one of the most safe and healthy of business operations." Conservatives such as Bolles and the bank regulators reiterated the ideas of Adam Smith, who believed that credit's role was to keep assets from lying idle, not to create things that did not yet exist. Only later, during the First World War (1914–1918), did the federal government encourage more mortgage lending to farmers. It was not until the Great Depression that the government began to encourage banks to make long-term loans to businesses and home mortgage loans to ordinary Americans, and only later still would banks begin to make substantial amounts of consumer loans.[40]

Until the First World War, the national banks were prohibited from making mortgage loans, and the state-chartered banks did only a limited amount of lending in this area.[41] Commercial banks did not lend to people who wanted to buy furniture and other durables, and they certainly did not make loans for buying nondurable items like clothing and groceries. (Commercial banks did very little retail banking at all, and usually just for the wealthiest 10 percent of the population. California's Bank of Italy, founded by Amadeo Giannini in 1904, was one of the first commercial banks to seek deposits from ordinary people. It was later renamed the Bank of America.)[42] The typical bank was small and did not have the capital resources to make large loans, forcing businesses to the commercial paper markets for their large, short-term capital needs and launching the careers of "investment bankers" such as J. P. Morgan, who were able to pool together capital for long-term projects. Banks did not lend on companies' receivables because bankers did not want to manage these if companies defaulted on their loans. Mainstream banking was conservative, even in an era of growth and opportunity.

The expense and difficulty of obtaining good information on borrowers reinforced the bankers' caution. Uniform accounting methods did not exist. Small business people were unwilling to provide financial statements, and lenders did not want to offend them by asking. When banks needed to know about someone outside of their locality, they relied on other banks with whom they had a "correspondent" arrangement.[43] But there was no guarantee that a correspondent bank would be willing or able to provide the information. Credit-reporting firms such as R. G. Dun and the Bradstreet Company were sources of information. But while trade creditors may have been willing to advance goods based on the information provided by these credit-reporting firms, most commercial banks preferred to have direct knowledge of borrowers or to have a trusted merchant or correspondent bank vouch for the borrowers' creditworthiness. A handful of banks set up credit departments in the 1880s and 1890s, but even in 1899 only ten New York banks had credit departments. As late as 1914 the Federal Reserve Board reported that "the country banks which constitute the majority of our members are generally without credit files as known to the large city bank. Borrowers are personally known by the officers and directors who are usually their neighbors, and the means, business and character of such borrowers are matters of intimate personal knowledge to the bank officer."[44] The deep knowledge that local bankers had about their borrowers was advantageous, but because the knowledge was not shared with other banks, lenders could not compete for borrowers.

After the Civil War, short-term interest rates varied across regions even more widely than before the conflict. The large variations indicated that capital was not moving freely across regions; and, in the case of the West, even *within* regions.[45] The predicament of the mortgage markets provided the starkest illustration: "Under an ideal system of mortgage banking, the capital available for permanent investment would be distributed where most needed," a study in 1894 noted. "But the actual facts are different, and there is considerable friction impeding the free movement of such capital."[46]

The conservative practices of commercial banks opened up opportunities for other financial intermediaries, the new organizations that were better able to obtain information or who were just more willing to take risks. People's craving to own houses and farms gave business to building and loan societies (the forerunners of savings and loans) and mortgage companies. Personal finance companies and a few manufacturers fulfilled people's desire for durable goods by enabling customers to buy on installment. Companies in need of working capital offered their receivables as collateral to the new sales finance companies. Railroads and other large industrial companies clamored for capital, and investment bankers such as Kuhn, Loeb and Company and J. P. Morgan and Company responded by using their reputations to attract financing from investors in America and Europe. Households that could not make ends meet gave ample opportunities to pawnbrokers and loan sharks. All of these lenders constituted what a later generation would call "shadow finance," or institutions that were less regulated than the mainstream commercial banks. As the term suggests, lenders that existed in the shadows often had to fight for personal and institutional legitimacy. Some, such as the investment banks, succeeded; others, such as some loan sharks, never did.

Other institutional adaptations helped to manage credit risks. As corporations became larger, their insolvencies led to new arrangements that would maintain them as going concerns. Railroads, with their massive assets and multistate operations, came up with innovative ways to handle bankruptcy. (However, full bankruptcy procedures for corporations were not added to the national bankruptcy law until the Great Depression.) Creditor groups such as the National Association of Credit Men (NACM) set up adjustment bureaus to ensure greater fairness in dividing up the assets of failed business debtors. In 1898, Congress passed the first truly permanent national bankruptcy law, which continued the trend of leniency toward debtors. Consumer credit–reporting bureaus proliferated in hundreds of localities to help retailers assess the creditworthiness of ordinary people. These piecemeal adaptations continued the experimental mindset of the pre-Civil War era. Entrepreneurs and firms initiated new arrangements to meet the demands for credit that the commercial banks declined to fill, and they took the lead in managing the problems posed by insolvencies, especially of corporations. On the whole the federal government supported the initiatives: for example, the federal courts allowed the managers of bankrupt railroads to stay in their jobs. But the government's interventions were sporadic and uncoordinated, and would remain so until the New Deal reforms of the 1930s.

The South

The Civil War destroyed a great deal of wealth in the Confederacy, leaving its people and banks with far less to lend to one another. The end of slavery, too, fundamentally altered credit practices by shifting the basis for lending. Slaves were valuable, moveable, and tradable; as collateral, human chattel frequently was even more attractive to creditors than land.[47] The South's banks suffered severe strains during the war. They invested, willingly or under duress, in Confederate securities that lost nearly all of their value, forcing the banks to close. In the once bustling cotton hub of Louisiana, only one bank managed to survive the war.[48] Afterward the requirements imposed by the National Banking Act slowed the establishment of national banks in the South: in 1870, the twelve southern states had only sixty-nine banks of any kind, in stark contrast to the more than fifteen hundred banks serving the areas outside the South. Before the war, interest rates in the South had been roughly similar to rates in the North. But during and after the war southern interest rates rose dramatically, reflecting the insufficient capital flows into the region and the monopoly power of the few remaining banks. It took a relatively long time for interest rates in the South to reintegrate with the rest of the country.[49] The South began to catch up when its states enacted free-banking laws and the Gold Standard Act of 1900 lowered the capital requirements for national banks. But forming ties to northern commercial centers also took time.[50]

Meanwhile, the factorage system, the linked chains of middlemen and private bankers that had smoothed the flow of cotton from southern planters to buyers around the world, disappeared by the 1880s and was replaced by tenant farming and sharecropping.[51] In a sharecropping arrangement, the landowners and tenant farmers shared the risks associated with growing and marketing the crops. But in reality, the indebted farmers were in the more vulnerable position if the crop did not turn out well or if cotton prices fell. Tenant farmers and sharecroppers needed credit to tide them over until the cotton crop was harvested, but they could not obtain it from factors, who were disappearing from the scene. Nor could tenant farmers get credit from banks, which were not interested in lending to small producers. Instead, the tenant farmers and sharecroppers relied on "furnishing merchants" to advance them the supplies and equipment they needed to plant their crops. The furnishing merchants in turn depended on northern manufacturers and wholesalers.[52] Everyone in the chain of credit was paid once the cotton was harvested and sold.

The smaller credit flows into the South and the lack of competition among credit providers allowed, and perhaps even required, the furnishing merchants to charge interest rates as high as 50 to 110 percent.[53] Share-croppers who could not pay their debts in full after the harvest had no choice but to sign on for another year, perpetuating their indebtedness.[54] Cotton had a ready market—it continued to be the nation's largest export—and so most furnishing merchants agreed to lend against the crop. Sharecroppers wanting to grow other crops were out of luck; no one would advance them any supplies because only cotton was guaranteed to sell. The furnishing merchant imposed a crop lien (rights to the sharecroppers' future cotton crop) because the cotton was the sole collateral the merchant could offer to his own northern creditors. Tenant farmers and sharecroppers were also constrained by the local nature of the credit they got from furnishing merchants and local landowners. When tensions arose, the farmers were reluctant to start up somewhere new, where they were unknown and had little chance of obtaining any credit at all. Even when they had paid off their debts, most people who could pull up stakes did not move very far. The restraints were, of course, worse for black farmers, who had greater difficulty establishing relationships with local white merchants and landowners.[55]

In pre–Civil War America, mercantile credit created opportunities for people who wanted to set up their own small retail businesses, especially in the newer areas of the country. The local farmers obtained their supplies from these retailers, who helped to sell the farmers' crops and other items produced by farm households, such as eggs and butter. The relationships had allowed for some flexibility; and, most important, farmer and merchant were on a fairly equal footing. In the South after the Civil War, however, the need for credit trapped farmers in relationships that gave them little chance to progress economically and few incentives to try their luck in another locality. For farmers in the South, and for the many struggling farmers in the western sections of the country, credit and debt took on meanings that were much more negative than those held by the hopeful settlers earlier in the nineteenth century.

Credit for Business

Daniel Shaw's Lumber Company, located in Eau Claire, Wisconsin, illustrates how credit became more available to businesses in the Northeast and the Midwest. During the 1870s, Shaw obtained much of his credit from family connections in his native Maine. In his adopted home state of Wisconsin, he was forced to pay an interest rate of 10 percent; so by borrowing back east, Shaw could lower his borrowing costs by at least 2 percentage points. During the following decades, interest rates in the west fell. By the 1890s local banks discounted Shaw's paper at 7 percent, and he was able to borrow from a Chicago bank at 5 percent. (Regardless, Shaw continued to tap his eastern friends and relatives. His associates in Maine helped to place the mill's paper with businesses there.) For working capital, Shaw increasingly turned to banks in Minneapolis, St. Paul, and Milwaukee. The mill's subsidiary lumberyard companies as well as its largest customers also provided credit.[56]

More credit for small industrial concerns like Shaw's was the result of the growing surplus capital of businesses and individuals. Gross capital formation in the years 1849–1858 was 14 percent of gross national product, but this jumped to 22 percent in the period 1869–1878.[57] Older firms, especially in New England, could fund themselves through retained earnings, and they looked to other regions of the country for opportunities to invest their surplus capital. Most of the money probably still went into land and improvements, but a growing portion was now invested in the bonds of large industrial companies, railroads, and banks. Jay Cooke's hugely successful bond drives during the Civil War had taught many novice investors in the North that securities were good and (mostly) safe places to put their money. The post–Civil War generation increasingly felt comfortable investing in the stocks and bonds of industrial companies and foreign companies, as well as municipal and foreign government bonds.[58]

Commercial Paper

Commercial paper, the short-term business IOUs that firms sold directly to investors, was hardly an innovation. By the 1830s, newspapers in several of the nation's commercial cities regularly quoted discount rates on commercial paper, for the benefit of business borrowers and investors.[59] After the war, commercial paper spread into new areas and provided firms with an alternative source of business financing.[60] Dealers sprang up in most areas of the country to buy the paper and resell them to banks, which benefited by being able to diversify their portfolios outside of their immediate localities.[61] Marcus Goldman, founding partner of what became Goldman Sachs, was an early dealer of commercial paper. Starting as a peddler in Philadelphia, the German immigrant moved to New York City and set up a brokering business in 1869. Until the First World War, commercial banks were the largest buyers of commercial paper. The commercial paper markets were thus a roundabout way for banks to lend to companies: the banks trusted the commercial paper dealers to vouch for the companies whose paper the banks were buying. In time, as their own financial assets deepened, the commercial paper houses began buying the paper outright to hold for resale rather than simply acting as brokers. Some of the commercial paper houses organized credit departments to investigate the creditworthiness of issuers.[62]

A national, integrated commercial paper market took a long time to develop. In the Pacific coast states, commercial paper was not widely used until around 1900. Interest rates in most places were still determined by local conditions, including the market power of the local banks, rather than by the country's large financial centers. As a result, interest rates on commercial paper varied widely throughout the country, much more than did bond yields.[63] The market also lacked liquidity; there was no secondary market for commercial paper until the Federal Reserve was established in 1913.[64] Even so, companies who could issue commercial paper at low rates found this market convenient. Businesses could get larger loans in the commercial paper market, which saved them the trouble of having to coordinate loans from several small banks. Of course, business people with first-rate reputations could borrow from established banking connections or associates, and at lower interest.[65] But the commercial paper markets provided businesses with an alternative source of credit.

Trade (Mercantile) Credit

The credit that merchants advanced to each other in the form of goods continued to be an important source of financing, including for entrepreneurs. One department store executive recalled that his father was able to open the business in 1874 only because the Chicago wholesalers Carson, Pirie, Scott & Company were so willing to extend him long-term credits.[66] This type of credit could be extremely flexible. In 1890, credit professional Peter R. Earling observed that mercantile debts "are not looked upon like an obligation to a bank that must be paid on a certain day and by a certain hour." Few buyers held themselves to strict schedules of payment. Moreover, they felt slighted if the seller declined to extend the payment schedule.[67]

The Civil War accelerated the shortening of trade credit terms. When Congress suspended specie payments from 1862 to 1879, sellers attempted to compensate for the currency's fluctuating value by shortening credit terms to thirty days or fewer. These terms continued after resumption. As always, discounts were offered for cash payments, and merchants took advantage by obtaining the short-term loans that were now more available from banks.[68] The war also changed the calculus for manufacturers seeking working capital. Banks discounted at close to face value the federal certificates (government IOUs) that manufacturers received for war supplies. During and after the war manufacturers and railroads expanded the scale of their operations, and the huge amounts of plant and equipment they amassed changed the perception of their creditworthiness. No longer were they regarded as high-risk adventurers with few assets to back their ambitions. By the end of the nineteenth century, the large industrial concerns could fund themselves from retained earnings and borrow from banks and other lenders at competitive rates. Their securities found a national market and soon dominated the New York stock exchange.[69]

Industrialization changed the structures of markets. Businesses like meatpacking and electrical equipment became more technically complex. Oil and rubber were now dominated by a few large manufacturing companies. In these industries, manufacturers displaced merchants as the coordinators of supply chains and distribution, and they provided a greater share of the trade credit to industrial, wholesale, and retail concerns. The rise of national brands like National Biscuit, Swift, and American Tobacco and the sophisticated advertising that supported them meant that manufacturers could now sell directly to retailers. As consumers became more concentrated in urban areas, manufacturers found it economical to access them directly by establishing selling offices in the cities. Wholesalers remained important to the manufacturers of nonbranded goods, which the wholesalers bought in large batches on short credit, improving the manufacturers' cash flows.[70]

Investment Banks

The small size of most commercial banks prevented them from funding the large industrial projects of the late nineteenth century.[71] Entrepreneurs formed investment banks to fill the need. This American institution was distinct from the older British merchant banks that (as their name suggests) evolved from the merchant activities of their founders. American investment banks, in contrast, were intermediaries who pooled the capital of many investors to put into large enterprises. J. P. Morgan became one of the most powerful men in America because he could use his personal reputation to put together the financing for several mergers. His firm was behind the largest merger of the time, which united Federal Steel Company, National Steel Company, and Carnegie Steel Company to form the United States Steel Corporation, capitalized at the then-phenomenal amount of $1.4 billion.[72] Morgan also played a critical role in the governance of the corporations in which his bank invested.[73]

At the end of the nineteenth century, corporations such as U.S. Steel borrowed heavily to assemble the assets required to manufacture steel, pack meat, refine oil, and transport products throughout the country. By the First World War, corporations regularly carried long-term debt on their balance sheets and departed from the conventional wisdom that companies should only borrow short-term, to fund their working capital needs.[74] These large firms, or their investment bankers, used debt to restructure and even to save themselves from failure. In 1909, when Congress for the first time levied income taxes on corporations, it simultaneously made interest payments tax-deductible. There is little evidence that corporations immediately took advantage of this provision in the tax code to borrow large amounts. They would do so in a major way beginning in the 1970s, to fund leveraged buyouts, mergers, and acquisitions.

Bonds

The largest and most important corporations of the time, the railroads, came to rely on bond issues to achieve rapid expansion. Lines that went through sparsely populated areas or frontier regions became more dependent on debt because equity investors perceived them as too risky. Bond buyers, who have a stronger claim to companies' assets than stockholders, were more willing to invest in the new railroad lines. In addition, fixed-income securities were a good investment during a time of low inflation. Bond buyers may also have felt reassured by the lack of competition in many lines, where certain railroads held de facto monopolies.[75] The ratio of bonds to stocks rose, from 62 percent in 1875–1879 to 118 percent in 1890–1895.[76]

The popularity of bonds with investors made them a comparatively cheap source of financing for railroads. But when economic downturns hit, the railroads had reason to regret their choice of debt over equity: many could not pay the interest on the bonds and became insolvent.[77] A large number ran into serious trouble following the Panic of 1873, but the 1890s were even worse. More than 25 percent of railroads (measured by capitalization) were in receivership during the depression of the 1890s.[78] At the time, the national bankruptcy law had few provisions for corporate bankruptcies. Owners and managers worked with the courts and investment bankers to come up with a procedure that would allow the railroads to continue as going concerns. (This topic is discussed in the section on bankruptcy later in this chapter.)

Sales Finance Companies

Many businesses had significant amounts of receivables, the payments that were due to them from other businesses. Receivables were an asset, and for many businesses quite a large one, yet they could not borrow against this asset.[79] In the first decade of the twentieth century, sales finance companies began lending against receivables or buying them outright. A few specialized in funding installment sales. The first of these, Fidelity Contract Company, was organized in 1904 as a subsidiary of Foster-Armstrong Company, a piano manufacturer in Rochester, New York. Fidelity bought the installment contracts from the retail dealers of Foster-Armstrong's pianos. The first finance company to purchase open-book (as opposed to installment) accounts was also organized in 1904 and was later incorporated as the Mercantile Credit Company of Chicago.[80] These intermediaries improved their clients' cash flow and assumed the headaches of collecting payments.

Sales finance companies took on risks that conservative commercial banks declined. So it is hardly surprising that the finance companies were quick to enter the new field of automobile finance. In 1910, the first installment financing of a vehicle was done by W. P. Smith and Company of Seattle. Three years later, L. F. Weaver, a San Francisco firm that had originally financed wagons, began providing loans to dealers of passenger cars. At least twenty-five auto sales financing companies were in operation by 1917, with several having offices in a number of states.[81] In the 1920s, the companies played a critical role in enabling both dealers and consumers to purchase cars.

Mortgage Lending

Farm mortgages were a divisive political issue in the 1880s. When farmers' associations called for a federal inquiry into the subject, the federal government responded by gathering an unprecedented amount of information on the nation's mortgages during the census of 1890. Based on the information, the Department of the Census produced the Report on Home Proprietorship and Indebtedness. Its mandate was to investigate whether "the present economic condition of society tends toward the concentration of

97

wealth in the hands of a few . . . by compelling the majority of the people to become and remain debtors."[82]

The census revealed that less than one-half of the country's real property was mortgaged, and that loans typically represented 35 to 40 percent of a property's value. Individuals, not institutions, provided most of the nation's mortgage financing. The majority of these lenders (55 percent) lived in the same locality as their borrowers; individuals from outside a locality supplied an additional 18 percent of mortgages. Commercial and savings banks, life insurance companies, and building and loan societies made up the rest, which amounted to only about $2 billion out of the $7.2 billion of total mortgages outstanding.[83]

A number of restrictions limited the ability of institutions to fund mortgages. The National Bank Act prohibited the nationally chartered banks from lending on real estate, a restriction that would continue until the First World War.[84] The number of state-chartered banks grew dramatically, but they were not big players in the mortgage markets either: according to the Report of the Comptroller (1892), state and private banks collectively had assets of $1.2 billion, of which mortgages accounted for a measly $58.8 million, or less than 5 percent. Savings banks loaned out more than 41 percent of their deposits as mortgages. But these banks accounted for only 10 percent of the country's mortgage financing, and states like New York and Massachusetts prohibited their savings banks from investing in out-of-state mortgages. Building and loan societies, founded to provide mortgage funding to their depositors, accounted for an additional 7 percent of mortgages. These institutions were small: the typical building and loan society had assets of only $83,093.[85] Insurance companies were a substantial source of mortgages, but except for the largest companies, they confined most of their lending to local borrowers.[86]

The picture that emerged was of an extremely fragmented national mortgage market, in which the institutions most capable of providing loans were either prohibited from doing so or constrained by their small scale from making a meaningful number of loans. Nor was there much of a secondary market for mortgage-backed securities, instruments that were already well established in some European countries. Instead, the majority of mortgage funding came from individual lenders and investors. Like the commercial paper markets, the mortgage markets relied on agents and brokers to connect lenders with borrowers; but unlike their commercial paper counterparts, the mortgage brokers charged a high commission for their services. D. M. Frederiksen, the author of an 1894 study, estimated that for farm mortgages, agents' commissions were often above 2.5 percent on five-year loans. (The amount was deducted from the principal at the beginning of the loan period.) Over the course of the loan, commissions could total more than 10 percent of the entire amount of interest paid. Commissions on western farm mortgages were higher still—about 20 percent of the interest paid. The 1890 census, Frederiksen argued, underestimated the true cost of mortgages because it gave only the average rates of interest and did not take commissions into account. Americans, he said, paid much more for mortgages than did their counterparts in Germany, where there were well-established secondary markets for mortgage-backed bonds.[87] Subsequent research confirmed the fears of the farming sector. Beginning in 1870, the agricultural sector began a six-decades-long period of expansion that pushed up the interest rates for farm mortgages throughout the country, but especially in the southern and western markets that experienced the highest rates of agricultural growth. In contrast, long-term rates on other debt instruments such as railroad bonds fell.[88]

As with the short-term loan markets, there were large variances in regional interest rates: mortgage borrowers in the East paid about 5.5 percent; those in the South and the West about 8 percent; and in some areas like the mountain states and territories, interest rates could be above 10 percent. Significant differences in the price of mortgages indicated that capital was not moving freely to certain areas.[89] The length of mortgages varied as well, but although there were signs that they may have been lengthening overall, mortgage terms were still very short by modern standards. In the East the average length of a mortgage was almost six years, while in the South and the West they were even shorter, at three and four years, respectively.[90] Borrowers paid an annual interest rate (which was variable, not fixed), and then the entire principal was due at the end of the term.

The amount of mortgage debt in the United States rose, nonetheless, with much of the increase coming from individual rather than institutional sources. In the 1880s, mortgage debt increased three times faster than overall wealth.[91] The new borrowers, Frederiksen concluded, were not "spendthrifts"; rather, they were "persons whose circumstances are improving," such as "laborers in the cities who have bought homes, and young farmers in the West who have not yet paid for their farms." More financing could be made available, he argued, if lenders could develop a national market in mortgage-backed bonds. By aggregating mortgages into bonds ("debentures"), lenders would be able to use the capital from bond issues to make even more loans. Investors would no longer have to pay the legal fees, traveling expenses, and monitoring costs associated with holding the actual mortgages. Debentures offered investors a way to spread risk across a portfolio of mortgages. And unlike the mortgages themselves, bonds were a liquid investment. Returns would fall, of course. At the time, mortgage lending earned an average return of 6.7 percent versus 4.4 percent for railroad bonds.[92] A secondary market for mortgages, complete with an exchange, could well have equalized the returns on the two investment classes.

Variances in interest rates within the United States and between the United States and Europe provided opportunities for arbitrage, or borrowing at low rates from one place to lend at higher rates somewhere else. Some eastern lenders bought loans from western merchants and banks, while others hired agents to scour the western regions for mortgage applicants. The agents scrutinized a specific set of characteristics that signaled whether the applicants had the resources and "character" to meet their obligations, including whether they had a record of paying their debts punctually.[93] Of course, there were costs involved in hiring agents, but the eastern lenders hoped that the costs would produce higher profits later.[94]

The high returns attracted foreign investors, especially the British. There were few restrictions to the international flows of capital during this period.[95] Moreover, Britain's Companies Act of 1862 made the formation of joint-stock companies easier, and British entrepreneurs took advantage of the new law to invest in American assets. The British continued to invest in western real estate until well into the 1880s; Scottish companies even expanded their search for opportunities into the southern states.[96]

Eventually, American entrepreneurs formed mortgage companies that bought western mortgages for resale. Financiers such as J. P. Morgan and Samuel D. Babcock recognized the market's potential and organized mortgage companies during the 1870s.[97] During the next decade, some 170 mortgage companies competed for investors even in relatively new markets such as Texas.[98] Insurance companies looking to invest their funds were drawn to the mortgage companies' products. Unlike the mortgage brokers, the new mortgage companies guaranteed (or strongly implied) that they would stand behind their products. The very largest companies had over a hundred loan agents overseen by traveling supervisors.[99] The J. B. Watkins Land Company, based in Lawrence, Kansas, was one of the most substantial, operating offices in both New York and London by 1880. Watkins charged 12 percent for its mortgage loans in 1874, plus another 4 or 5 percent in charges or commissions—a total of 16 or 17 percent annually. These rates seem high by modern standards, but they were much lower than the 36 percent that borrowers had previously paid. Interest rates fell over time, but for almost two decades, Watkins provided annual dividends of 10 percent to investors.[100] Western mortgages proved to be popular; by 1890 nearly every substantial western town had a mortgage company selling paper to investors back east.[101] Unlike the commercial banks, the mortgage companies' activities were not regulated. Lawmakers in Connecticut, Massachusetts, and New York eventually passed legislation requiring them to file financial statements and apply for state licenses.[102]

In the mid-1880s the mortgage companies began bundling mortgages together and using the assets as collateral for debentures. The debentures already existed in Europe, where they were backed by farm mortgages that carried low interest rates and had maturities of up to fifty years. Conservative banks rather than mortgage companies issued the debentures, and European investors treated them like safe government debt.[103] In the United States, investor demand for the new mortgage debentures grew rapidly.[104] Investors could not inspect the underlying mortgages, so the mortgage companies gave them legally enforceable guarantees, further enhancing their attractiveness. By 1890, nearly 20 percent of the mortgage companies' loans were securitized as debentures.[105]

The debentures had a higher yield than government bonds and, in hindsight, were probably safer than railroad bonds. However, D. M. Frederiksen, the author of the 1894 study, pointed out that since the bonds were not traded on any exchanges, they were far less liquid than the equivalent European instruments. The American bonds had maturities of five to ten years, much shorter than the twenty-five years that was common in Europe; and the mortgage companies retained the option of redeeming the bonds even sooner. These characteristics compromised the bonds' safety, Frederiksen argued.[106] Frederiksen had a point. J. B. Watkins ended up securitizing the loans that would otherwise have been difficult to sell because they were too small or had short maturities. Securitization made more funds available for mortgages, but it also meant that riskier loans were being bundled into the debentures.[107]

The combination of falling interest rates, high dividends, and speculation (which drove the mortgage companies to revise the value of their land upwards) placed mortgage companies like J. B. Watkins in a fragile position. They suffered in the late 1880s when drought and low commodity prices blighted the plains states and the banks called in their loans.[108] Land prices fell. By 1890, less than 2 percent of all the mortgages of the country were in the hands of the mortgage companies.[109] (The J. B. Watkins Company went into receivership in 1894.) As historian Allan Bogue put it, "The rise of the western mortgage companies was swift, [and] their decline was catastrophically abrupt."[110] Overall, the mortgage companies failed to provide the amount of mortgage credit that the farm sector needed. Later, they were criticized for their risky practices.

The calls to help farmers coalesced around the rural credit movement. By the dawn of the First World War, a number of proposals competed for the attention of national politicians. One was a privately financed, federally chartered system of joint-stock land banks, similar to the system of national banks, that would be allowed to issue mortgage-backed debenture bonds. Proponents included the Farm Mortgage Bankers Association, who believed that oversight by the federal government would prevent the private banks from overissuing the debentures, as the mortgage companies had done in the past. By contrast, the rural credit movement favored a system of long-term, fully amortized contracts in which the mortgage and interest were paid off in regular installment, a little at a time. (This structure is familiar to all home mortgage borrowers today.) The interest rates charged would be the same throughout the country and would be no higher than 6 percent. Cooperatively owned bodies would do the lending and enforcement, and farmers would mutually ensure their mortgages. The Farm Mortgage Bankers Association vehemently opposed this proposal, arguing that conditions around the country varied too widely for standardized lending to be effective. They also claimed that farmers and lenders preferred the existing short-term, renewable mortgages because it offered them more flexibility to renegotiate and adapt to changing economic conditions. The bankers were skeptical about cooperatives, which had been unsuccessful in the past.[111]

Congress passed the Federal Farm Loan Act in 1916. It consisted of two tiers—a federally supervised cooperative lending system and private (but federally chartered) joint-stock land banks. The co-ops' mortgages would be bundled into bonds, issued by the newly created Federal Farm Loan Bank (like the Federal Reserve, made up of twelve district banks) but guaranteed by the co-ops. The private joint-stock land banks also issued bonds, which were secured by their loans. The mortgages were fully amortized, and many were long-term—up to forty years—with interest rates no higher than 6 percent. Many mortgage bankers, however, continued to resist the federal program and refused to seek federal charters.

The early twentieth century saw a period of experimentation, in which a range of different public, quasi-public, and private mortgage structures became available to farmers just when the wartime demand was pushing up crop prices and land values.[112] Some farms doubled in value within a few years, and prime agricultural land in Illinois and Iowa commanded the then-incredible price of $500 an acre. When deflation hit the agricultural sector in the early 1920s, however, indebted farmers were unable to meet their payments, forcing a significant minority into bankruptcy.[113] The problems became even worse with the climatic and economic disasters of the 1930s, prompting the federal government to pass a series of more comprehensive measures to help farmers. In 1933, the Roosevelt administration created the Farm Credit Administration, which built on the system of twelve federal land banks the government had created in 1916. The amount of farm mortgages quadrupled, with the federal government now making more than half of the loans.[114]

Residential Loans

In 1890, an estimated 37 percent of nonfarm families in the United States owned their homes. Of these homes, 29 percent were mortgaged, with an average debt of $1,139 per home. (By contrast, in 1900 home ownership in Britain was only about 10 percent.)[115] Properties in towns and cities accounted for over 60 percent of new mortgage debt in the United States, reflecting the national shift from agrarian to urban living.[116] By far the largest source of home loans was private individuals. Savings banks were a distant second. Building and loan societies were another source of mortgages, but prior to the 1880s they did not have significant membership.[117] B&Ls were confined largely to urban areas and to the Northeast, the Midwest, and the far West, particularly California.[118] Compared to other lenders, the B&Ls were innovative; they offered mortgages for as long as twelve years and amortized them so that borrowers paid off the principal and interest with regular monthly payments rather than a balloon payment at the end. Although amortization could result in higher overall payments, many people preferred it over balloon payments.[119] At the start of the twentieth century, B&Ls in Baltimore and Philadelphia provided second mortgages and lowered the amount of down payment required.[120]

Differences in regional interest rates were even more dramatic in the urban residential mortgage markets than for farm mortgages. Unlike western farm mortgages, which mortgage companies and other middlemen sold to investors in the East and abroad, there were no market makers for urban residential loans. The institutions that might have done it—life insurance companies, building and loan societies, and savings banks—confined their lending to the largest urban markets or their own localities.[121] Mortgage companies could not break into the urban markets, which continued to be served by local agents. Even *within* cities, there was evidence that capital was not flowing as freely as people would have liked.[122] Nonetheless, in the 1880s the mortgage market for urban homes grew faster than the one for farms.[123] By decade's end, the residential market accounted for more than 40 percent of all construction.[124] Real estate subdividers like William E. Harmon pioneered methods of selling urban lots for as little as 5 percent down and modest monthly payments.[125] But housing was expensive relative to most people's resources. Local builders and brokers sometimes had to offer second, third, and even fourth mortgages at effective interest rates of 18–20 percent before people could afford to buy a residence.[126]

By 1910, the funding provided by banks and other organizations (as opposed to individuals) was still only 66 percent, and rates on mortgage loans could still be 2 to 4 percentage points higher in some parts of the country than in others.[127] There was no standard home mortgage, and even individual lenders sometimes used a variety of arrangements.[128] After the First World War ended, the Calder Commission in Congress recommended that the federal government become more directly involved in residential mortgages, to address the high demand.[129] But Congress did not implement the recommendations. Only later, with the New Deal programs of the Great Depression, did the supply of residential mortgages rise and become more uniform.

Consumer Credit

For most Americans, the notion that paying with cash was more respectable than buying on credit took a firmer hold.[130] Large retailers such as Macy's and Sears tried to discourage book credit by depicting it as old fashioned. Avoiding credit sales benefited these large retailers, but they chose to position their cash-only policies as being good for *consumers*: selling for cash, they argued, lowered prices for everyone. The push to eliminate book credit had some success: after the Civil War, book credit declined as a percentage of retail sales, although it still rose in absolute terms. When the grocery chain A&P began expanding in 1913, it switched to a cash-only policy and depicted buying on credit as outmoded. In the future, A&P predicted, everyone would pay for groceries with cash. The small retailers of groceries, meat, baked goods, and other necessities, however, still allowed customers to run tabs.[131] For these neighborhood shopkeepers, credit was a way to retain customers' patronage in the face of greater competition from large chains like A&P.

Small neighborhood stores had little choice about accepting credit because their customers ran out of cash between paydays. Studies done at the time documented a widespread problem. A 1901 investigation found that 16 percent of Pennsylvania families spent more than they earned. For immigrants, the figure was nearly 19 percent. Another study revealed that in New York City, almost 24 percent of families relied on loans just to get by. Investigators in Pittsburgh cited illness, unemployment, unexpected costs such as funeral expenses, and general economic slowdowns as the main reasons people needed temporary loans. During the depression of 1907, half of the residents of Homestead, Pennsylvania, were forced to borrow.[132]

Small personal loans would have helped people when cash was tight, but such loans were hard to come by, for two reasons. One was the strong social disapproval of borrowing for nonproductive purposes, including for everyday consumption. The other obstacle was the state usury laws, which limited the profits that lenders could make on small household loans.[133] The legal maximum for interest rates had risen steadily since 1800, partly because of the high demand for mortgages in the newly settled western regions of the country.[134] In the 1880s, states reinstated their usury laws and began enforcing them more strictly. (The situation was the reverse of England and Europe, where usury laws were disappearing.)[135] By 1890, thirty-two of forty-four states, plus the New Mexico territory, had statutory ceilings on interest rates that ranged from 6 percent to 18 percent.[136] It is unclear why so many states chose to reinstate the usury laws, but the spread of loan sharks may have been a factor. These lenders came up with imaginative schemes to dodge the laws. For example, the so-called salary buyers and wage brokers "purchased" the salaries of workers at a steep discount days or weeks before the paychecks were disbursed.[137] In reality, these businesses engaged in loan-sharking, but their owners argued that they were more akin to futures traders.[138] The usury laws became associated in the public mind with consumer protection.[139] They were not relaxed again until after the First World War.[140]

Respectable providers of small loans included semiphilanthropic pawn-shops such as the Pawner's Bank of Boston, founded in 1859. Pawnbroking was a secured form of lending: the pawned item made repayment much more likely, and although interest rates were high, they were still lower than the rates for unsecured loans. Remedial loan societies, set up by entrepreneurs to make loans to the working poor, took pawnbroking as their model. The first was the Workingmen's Loan Association, established in Boston in 1888. In 1893 the Provident Loan Society opened in New York City, and it became the largest and most influential remedial loan society; soon, it was lending an average of just over $20 to 36,000 people.[141] These lenders charged a relatively modest 1 to 1.5 percent interest per month. (By contrast, New York state law allowed commercial pawnbrokers to charge 3 percent per month for the first six months on loans of $100 or less, and then 2 percent per month thereafter.) They managed to survive because their philanthropic mission gave them access to volunteer labor and their shareholders accepted lower returns. Compared to regular pawnbrokers, they made much larger loans that were backed by valuable items.[142] The remedial loan societies aimed to put commercial pawnshops out of business and instill discipline in borrowers. They attracted high-profile backers, including investment bankers J. P. Morgan, Solomon Loeb, and George Baker as well as the noted philanthropist and industrialist William E. Dodge. The societies' managers adopted more "scientific" appraisal techniques and were careful to emphasize that their organizations were businesses as well as social enterprises.[143] But these lenders targeted only the creditworthy poor who had valuables to pawn. The indigent still had to resort to loan sharks.[144]

Commercial pawnshops continued to provide more credit than their semicharitable counterparts, and to a wider variety of people. Some commercial pawnbrokers specialized in higher-value items brought in by wealthier clientele, while others dealt in clothing, shoes, and similar low-value goods—items that were likely to be pawned by the wage earners who made up their core customers. According to one estimate, in 1898 the commercial pawnbrokers of Pittsburgh made one loan for every 11.6 residents. In 1911, an estimated 2,000 pawnshops did business in 300 cities across the U.S.[145] There was a licensed pawnbroker for every 23,000 people in New York, every 27,000 in Chicago, every 15,000 in Philadelphia, and every 9,000 in Boston and San Francisco.[146]

Small-loan companies were another option. These lenders first appeared in Chicago around 1870 and soon spread to other cities. Technically, the new organizations were illegal because they charged higher rates than state usury laws allowed, but they took business away from pawn-brokers and the more criminally inclined loan sharks. Their loans were small, in the neighborhood of ten to forty dollars, made for short periods at rates that could reach 300 percent per annum. Borrowers usually were required to make weekly payments, so they had to have a steady income as well as something valuable for collateral. The loans were backed by an attachment on future wages, or chattels (movable assets) such as household furniture. The Household Finance Corporation, founded by Frank J. Mackey in 1878 in Minneapolis, was the first of many corporate chains of small-loan brokers. In 1890, Household Finance had fourteen loan offices located in cities including Omaha, Nebraska, and Newark, New Jersey. By the turn of the twentieth century, one chain had over a hundred loan offices operating around the country.[147] New York City had at least seventy small-loan offices in 1907, and Chicago had 139 offices by 1916. Borrowers consisted mostly of working people such as policemen, firemen, and workers in low-level white-collar occupations—the people who were most affected by sudden unemployment and fluctuations in the business cycle.[148]

Installment plans became more available after the Civil War. Since the mid-1800s, middle-class consumers had been able to buy durable goods such as sewing machines and pianos on installment; by century's end many more items could be bought "on time." A retail trade investigation of Boston in 1899 found that half of the city's furniture dealers sold on the installment plan. But even so, middle-income people who aspired to re-spectability declined to talk openly about their installment purchases.[149] The attitude was reinforced by the appearance of "borax" stores that sold cheaply made but overpriced items on installment to low-income cus-tomers. Astute observers noticed that installment buying led to peculiar behaviors. Women, *Scientific American* remarked, displayed a "curious reasoning" when they chose to pay a total of $50 for a sewing machine in monthly installments rather than $25 outright—even when they could afford to pay the $25.[150] Clearly, people were now making calculations about the present value of money that differed from traditional ways of thinking.

Installment buying perfectly tracked the transformation of the United States into an industrial power. The increase in the nation's production of goods and services far surpassed the increase in population during the period from the late 1860s to 1900. In the late 1860s, the United States produced $6 billion worth of goods and services; the figure expanded five-fold, in current dollars, to $30 billion by the end of the century. In contrast, population doubled between 1870 (40 million) and 1900 (nearly 80 million). The volume of goods sold at retail exploded, from $3.6 billion in 1869 to $13.2 billion in 1909.[151] Americans spent a very small percentage of their income (around 2 percent) on durable goods in 1850. Three decades later, they were spending 11 percent of their income on durable goods. As the twentieth century began, a lengthening list of mail-order companies and department stores started offering installment plans. The Philadelphia department store Wanamaker's relaxed its cash-only policy in 1903, when it began selling pianos on installment terms. Spiegel House Furnishings Company of Chicago established a mail-order business in 1904 that offered installment buying. By 1913 Sears offered installment plans on its pianos, farm implements, vehicles, encyclopedias, and other durable goods. Respectable clothing retailers in cities such as Boston began offering installment terms as a way to compete with the department stores.[152]

Chattel mortgages (short- and medium-term loans that were backed by movable assets such as livestock and farm machinery) were a common way to obtain funds from loan companies.[153] Advertisements for chattel mortgages began appearing in Chicago in 1869 and then in other cities soon after.[154] In the town of Springdale, Wisconsin, the mean amounts loaned on chattel in the years 1849–1900 could vary from under $100 to $1200, with just under $400 being typical. (For comparison, midwestern mortgages on land typically ranged from $200 to $500.) Rural households used chattel mortgages mostly for farm equipment, but also for musical instruments and other large consumer items. The commercial banks shunned chattel mortgages until the first decade of the twentieth century. Then banks, too, began dealing in the instrument.[155]

The amount of credit available to consumers expanded, yet the reality was that many people still relied on illegal lenders and paid very high interest charges for short-term loans. Annual interest rates could be very high. Virginia pawnbrokers were charging 120 percent on loans under $25.[156] Pittsburgh pawnbrokers charged administrative fees that raised the rates to 240 percent on loans under $100.[157] Loan sharks were numerous in urban areas because workers there had regular paychecks. The *New York Times* estimated in 1911 that in cities with populations of at least 30,000, one in five workers borrowed from illegal lenders. Thirty-five percent of New York City's employees relied on loan sharks.[158] Municipal workers were good targets; government paychecks may have been small, but they were regular and ensured a steady revenue stream for the lenders.

The prevalence of loan-sharking caught the attention of newspapers. Journalists began writing about the phenomenon in 1887 with the support of a few state initiatives. But their reform activities were piecemeal and ineffective. Well-organized efforts to drive out illegal lenders did not begin until 1909, when the philanthropic Russell Sage Foundation spearheaded the campaigns against loan sharks.[159] Two years later, it invested $100,000 in a new remedial loan organization, the Chattel Loan Society of New York. The society made loans of up to $200 at an interest rate of 2 percent per month. At six dollars for a ninety-day loan of $100, the society's rates compared very favorably to the $30 that loan sharks demanded.[160] The foundation sponsored educational films such as *The Usurer's Grip* (1912), about a respectable middle-class family who became hopelessly indebted to a loan shark when the child fell ill. To avoid a similar fate, the film guided its audience to credit unions, where they could save for emergencies.[161]

The reformers at Russell Sage concluded that a regulated small-loan industry was the best way to drive the worst loan sharks out of business. Ironically, the state usury laws became an obstacle to reform. Small-loan lenders had little or no access to cheap capital, so they were forced to charge high interest rates. They also took higher risks by lending to ordinary consumers and small business people rather than to the known merchants who were the bread and butter of commercial bank lending. So long as the usury laws were vigorously enforced, it was unclear who qualified as a legitimate lender, and the lack of clarity could be devastating for the small-loan companies. Daniel H. Tolman, the founder and head of one of the largest small-lending chains, was convicted of usury in New York in 1913 and sentenced to six months in prison.[162]

The Russell Sage Foundation led the development of a Uniform Small Loan law, a model piece of legislation that could be used by the states in passing their own laws. New Jersey's Egan Act (1914) was the first. A year later, six states had a version of the law, and then six more states passed legislation by 1917. The new laws raised the maximum legal interest rate to 3.5 percent a month for a yearly rate of 42 percent. In return for the higher rates, lenders were required to state their interest rates clearly. Transparency, in other words, would substitute for more restrictive regulation. The response of the small-loan lenders reflected the diversity of players in this industry. Some eagerly took the chance to become more socially acceptable by agreeing to be regulated and monitored while others preferred to remain in the shadows and continue to charge illegally high rates. The ones who chose legitimacy established the American Association of Small Loan Brokers, whose stated aim was to stamp out illegal lending. A study by academic Louis N. Robinson and industry insider Rolf Nugent concluded that although the small loan companies' profit margins shrank under the new laws, their profits still beat expectations because better quality borrowers reduced the losses from bad debts. The laws encouraged new entrants, which lowered the cost of borrowing.[163]

The U.S. census of 1890 confirmed that debt had become a significant part of Americans' personal finance strategies. Average household debt, including mortgage debt, totaled $880, a figure that the census gatherers thought was probably an underestimate. (To put this amount in perspective, the average annual wage of nonfarm workers at the time was $475.) Census Bureau statistician George K. Holmes estimated that 95 percent of private debt was used productively, to acquire capital goods or durable property. Another study found that total short-term household indebtedness was rising by over 9 percent a year. Population growth and inflation did not explain all of the increase. Rather, it was people's desire for more consumer credit that accounted for the rise.[164]

Americans demanded more consumer credit, but they also had high savings rates. In 1910 Americans had more total deposits than any other country, with New York state alone surpassing every country except Germany. But compared to Japan, Britain, and Germany, Americans had fewer institutional means to save, and some regions of the country had no savings banks at all.[165] We can only speculate about how much more Americans might have saved if convenient and reliable savings institutions had been more widely accessible. The lack of such institutions may well have driven Americans to spend more of their money on consumer items or to invest it in assets such as real estate.

Bankruptcy and Insolvency

In addition to creating the national banks and a national currency, the wartime Congress reformed the nation's bankruptcy laws. The national bankruptcy law of 1841 had embedded the notion that distressed borrowers were not necessarily criminals. But creditors who made loans in more than one state continued to wrestle with the inconsistencies among state laws.[166] After the southern states seceded, northern congressmen introduced national bankruptcy bills multiple times: in the 1862–1863 session, in 1864, and again in 1866, one year after the war ended. Congress finally passed a national bankruptcy law in 1867.

The 1867 act benefited both creditors and debtors. It allowed creditors to bring an act of bankruptcy against "any person," including farmers and laborers—the people whom Thomas Jefferson and Albert Gallatin had feared would be harmed by a national bankruptcy law. But the law also provided more help to debtors. With little debate, Congress retained the right to voluntary bankruptcy that had been so controversial in the run-up to the 1841 law; few people now questioned that the right to voluntary bankruptcy was within the constitutional power of Congress. Amendments in 1872 and 1874 further softened the 1867 law's effects on debtors. For example, debtors were allowed to propose to their creditors a repayment plan, called a composition agreement, that permitted the debtors to keep their property. Southern and western states continued to pass laws protecting debtors' property. In Louisiana, exemptions totaled $18,000 in 1871, and they applied retrospectively. In the territories, according to a credit handbook published in 1890, debtors were entitled to so many exemptions that the creditor had "no legal foothold" in those areas.[167]

At first, white southern debtors feared that the new law would further reinforce the humiliations that the Reconstruction Congress imposed on the former Confederacy. Northern creditors would press harder for collections or force insolvent southerners into bankruptcy. But federal judges in the South may instead have taken advantage of the law to allow former Confederates to protect their property. A study of three southern counties found that southerners, rather than northern merchants, held the majority of debts. The figures suggest that southern debtors took advantage of the new law. Southerners comprised one-quarter of the population in 1870, but they accounted for 36 percent of all bankruptcy filings, and the vast majority of these were voluntary. In the three counties studied, a much higher number of the filers were discharged compared to the national average. The national bankruptcy law of 1867 may well have given a fresh start to many former Confederates whose debts were magnified by the hardships of the war and its aftermath. Only after they had taken advantage of the federal law did southerners turn against it. In the late 1870s, they were among the most vocal supporters of its repeal.[168]

The nation's evolving bankruptcy regime had another drawback: it did not address the difficult issues that sprang from the insolvency of the large railroads, the country's most important industrial corporations. The companies that had overbuilt in the western territories faced default when the railroad bubble burst in 1873. Railroad failures did not affect just the companies themselves; they also laid low the networks of securities brokers and banks in the country's most important financial centers. The firm of Jay Cooke, the most prominent bond promoter during the Civil War, invested or lent heavily to the railroads, and its failure in September 1873 prompted a panic. Although not the first securities firm to go bust, Jay Cooke's personal fame ensured that his failure attracted the most attention. The shock had a knock-on effect; eventually, more than forty brokerage houses and private banks closed in New York, Philadelphia, and Washington, D.C.[169] The railroads' situation did not stabilize in the next two decades; to the contrary, their high fixed costs gave them very little leeway when competition intensified. In the late nineteenth century, up to 20 percent of all railroad mileage ended up in the hands of receivers.[170] By the time the depression of the 1890s ended, about one-third of all railroads were or had been in receivership.[171]

From an economic and social perspective, preserving the railroads as going concerns was more desirable than breaking them up and distributing their assets to creditors. State laws, however, were inadequate to deal with railroads that operated across state lines. Filing for bankruptcy under multiple state regimes was a long and arduous process, yet politicians argued that since the states granted the charters, they rather than the federal government should deal with the railroads' insolvencies. (The situation was different in England, where Parliament had sweeping powers over railroad companies.)[172] To overcome the holdup, an arrangement known as the "equity receivership" evolved, the first in response to the insolvency of the Wabash, St. Louis, and Pacific Railway in 1884.[173] Equity receiverships involved cooperation among the federal courts, investment bankers, and the managers of the railroads. The arrangements became widespread and lasted until federal reorganization laws were passed some fifty years later during the Great Depression.

Equity receiverships worked in the following way: First, the creditors petitioned to put the distressed railroad in receivership, upon which the court-appointed receiver took title to the assets. This stopped individual creditors from attempting an asset grab, which had been a long-standing problem whenever businesses went bust. The receiver could continue running the railroad while trying to find a buyer for the entire business. But what usually happened was that the courts appointed current manage-

112

ment as the receivers, and they stayed on for an average of two to three years.[174] Judges mostly denied the use of receiverships to other types of corporations. Consistent with the spirit of court decisions that stretched back to the 1840s, judges argued that railroads had an effect on the public good that other corporations did not. Railroads therefore had to be accorded special treatment.[175]

The main problem was how to force all of the debt holders, some of whom had stronger legal claims than others, to work together. Why would senior lenders voluntarily forego their rights to the subordinate lenders who were supposed to be shouldering more of the risk? Why would any of the lenders, least of all the junior holders of the debt, put more money into the distressed railroad to keep it going? The dilemma may never have been solved had the courts not directly intervened. In the name of the public good, judges redefined the claims of senior debt holders and forced them to accept receivership certificates in place of their original bonds. The courts upheld a mechanism, called the "upset value," to coerce subordinate debt holders to put more money into the distressed railroad. These actions were controversial, and bondholders sued. But, ultimately, the courts upheld the idea that preserving the distressed railroads was in the public interest. In *Union Trust Co. v. Illinois Midland Co.* (1886), the Supreme Court declared that the receivers' certificates imposed on bondholders were legal.[176]

What the courts sanctioned, the investment bankers and lawyers helped to implement. J. P. Morgan and his banking peers gained control over the railroads' reorganization committees through voting trusts that allowed them to represent the holders of the securities.[177] The bankers not only dominated the procedures; they also established precedents and shaped the legal bases of the proceedings. Soon, the reorganization of railroads became a specialty for which investment bankers charged high advisory fees. They also earned fees for the flotation of securities during the reorganization and for related banking advice afterward.[178] Of course, the bankers, attorneys, and jurists always emphasized that their actions saved the railroads for the benefit of the public. Whatever their true motivations, the procedures they invented became embedded in the way the courts dealt with corporate bankruptcies, and in the 1930s the procedures were formally incorporated into the nation's bankruptcy law.

The national bankruptcy law of 1867 lasted eleven years—longer than its predecessors, but far short of being the permanent solution that its backers had originally envisioned. Like the previous laws of 1800 and 1841, Congress passed the 1867 legislation to address the economic problems of a particular period. In common with the other two laws, it was heavily criticized for its ineffectiveness and expense.[179] It was also no better at accommodating the many tensions that persisted among interest groups. As a result of these shortcomings, large majorities in both parties repealed the law in 1878.

Almost immediately, influential creditor groups called for new legislation. Boards of trade, chambers of commerce, and other business associations petitioned Congress, urging the lawmakers to pass a lasting bankruptcy law.[180] Many of these bodies had not even existed when the 1867 law was passed, but by 1880, such creditor groups were numerous. Together they formed the National Organization of Members of Commercial Bodies to promote national bankruptcy legislation. Even more than the desire to provide relief to debtors, these groups' strong advocacy made possible the national bankruptcy act of 1898. Passage was difficult because the interests that arrayed for and against the act seemed as hopelessly divided as ever. Democrats wanted a temporary bill; they objected that the new law extended the federal courts' jurisdiction over bankruptcy proceedings (even though many railroad receiverships were already in federal courts).[181] Republicans argued that a permanent law was a necessary part of the nation's commercial law. Fortunately for the law's advocates, control of both houses of Congress swung to the Republicans in 1895 and remained there until 1911.

Among the creditor-friendly provisions of the new law was its empowerment of trustees, to prevent fraudulent transfers of property and transfers based on the preferential treatment of certain creditors. But even though creditors were behind the law's passage, the bankruptcy act of 1898 was even more protective of debtors than previous legislation. This result was perhaps not surprising. Only two years earlier, the Democratic candidate, William Jennings Bryan, had excoriated eastern bankers with his "cross of gold" speech. Debtor groups now had the power to influence bankruptcy legislation, and they pushed hard for a law allowing voluntary bankruptcy only. The new legislation reversed the 1867 law: creditors could no longer initiate involuntary procedures against farmers and wage earners. The act also removed the requirement of a minimum payment to creditors and abolished many of the remaining conditions hindering the discharge of debtors. Lawmakers now routinely accepted debtors' claims under the state exemption acts.[182]

The law of 1898 also gave corporations the right to propose a composition to their creditors. So long as the majority of creditors and the court agreed, a bankrupt corporation could make a partial payment that discharged its entire debt. (In 1910, an amendment extended to corporations the right to voluntary bankruptcy.)[183] But the 1898 law focused on individuals and small- to medium-sized businesses, not the giant corporations. Insurance, banking, and building and loan associations continued to be regulated by the states. And the law explicitly excluded distressed railroads, which were forced to continue turning to the courts for help.[184]

The law created bankruptcy referees, part-time officials who were paid a fixed percentage of the assets they distributed to creditors.[185] But the power of the referees waned because the law left the resolution of bankruptcy cases to the parties themselves. An unintended consequence was that creditors and debtors now hired bankruptcy lawyers, whose numbers grew enormously. A more adversarial process emerged, where each side aggressively pushed its own interests. In the state supreme courts, most of the cases involved small businesses or farms, where the borrower's only security consisted of the guarantees made by friends or family. Many bitter court battles arose from disputes over how these obligations should be discharged.[186]

Simultaneously, adjustment bureaus became a more common way to settle a company's debts. First set up by the San Francisco Board of Trade in 1877, the bureaus became part of the ethos of providing assistance to debtors. The bureaus eased cooperation among creditors and enhanced their ability to help borrowers who were facing temporary difficulties. The National Association of Credit Men was a driving force behind the movement. Its bureaus offered to investigate any debtor reported to be insolvent or financially embarrassed and to act as assignee, trustee, or receiver in bankruptcy.[187] The NACM recognized five local adjustment bureaus in 1904, and eighty-four by 1922.[188]

American bankruptcy laws evolved in response to repeated economic shocks. By the end of the nineteenth century, the nation's bankruptcy regime had assumed two distinguishing characteristics: it was more debtor-friendly than that of most other countries, and the proceedings were in the hands of lawyers rather than court-appointed administrators.[189] Bankruptcy lawyers became a powerful group with a vested interest in the law.[190] But adjustment bureaus, which emphasized cooperation rather than litigation, also became an important feature of business bankruptcies.

Credit Reporting

Credit-reporting agencies serving wholesalers, banks, and other business lenders were widespread by the time Reconstruction ended in 1877.[191] During the Civil War, the northern-based organizations were forced to close their southern offices but quickly reestablished them after the war ended. The largest firms, R. G. Dun and Company and the Bradstreet Company, tracked the expansion of American foreign trade by opening offices abroad. Canada was the earliest foreign market to receive attention and investment. In 1868, R. G. Dun opened an office in Halifax, Nova Scotia, and in the following decade the agency began operating in St. John (New Brunswick) and Hamilton and London (both in Ontario). In Europe, R. G. Dun established offices in Glasgow and Paris in 1872.

Rapid improvements in the credit-reporting agencies' methods occurred after the war. R. G. Dun began including information on capital worth in its published reference books. In 1874 it became one of the first companies to adopt the typewriter, along with the carbon paper technology that enabled the agency to produce multiple copies of reports to share among their branch offices. Dun's correspondents and reporters now asked for financial statements more regularly. Statements were still controversial, however, and many private businesses refused to provide them.

Problems with the accuracy of their reports continued to land the agencies in court and to attract the attention of legislators. In 1873–1874, in the wake of a severe financial panic, several state legislatures attempted to make credit-reporting agencies responsible for the losses that resulted from inaccurate reports. The lawmakers did not succeed, and the agencies vigorously resisted all attempts to constrain their practices. R. G. Dun, for example, lobbied against a bill in Ottawa, Canada, that would have required credit-reporting firms to post a bond to guarantee claims from damages incurred by their subscribers. The lawsuits continued, but as credit reporting spread, businesses found it harder to take legal action against the agencies.

By the late 1870s, R. G. Dun was one of the nation's largest businesses, with 10,000 correspondents covering 700,000 firms, plus a staff of more than 2,000. Barriers to entry were low, and the competition intensified, prompting a New York journalist to complain about the sheer number of agencies operating in that city. But creating a durable business was much more difficult than starting one; most start-ups lasted a short time, and even the larger agencies struggled. The dynamics of the credit-reporting business, where the advantages went to organizations that achieved the widest coverage, meant that the duopoly of R. G. Dun and the Bradstreet Company continued to strengthen. Their managers focused on expansion, including buying the offices of failed rivals. Dun continued to open offices in Canada and in the late 1880s and 1890s established branches in Melbourne, Australia; Mexico City; and Havana, Cuba. By the time Robert G. Dun died in 1900, his agency was covering well over one million firms, including foreign firms. U.S. trade creditors could obtain a report on businesses located almost anywhere in the world.

The trade association movement flourished in the decades after the Civil War, and several associations set up credit bureaus to share information among members.[192] The National Association of Manufacturers (NAM), founded in Cincinnati in 1895 to promote American products abroad, reportedly had files on tens of thousands of firms outside the United States by 1912. As the end of the Great War approached, the National Association of Credit Men approved the establishment of a Foreign Credit Interchange Bureau (FCIB), a mechanism for sharing information on foreign businesses. It became operational two years later. At war's end, the Foreign Credit Round Table, another forum for exchanging information, began meeting monthly in cities such as New York and Boston.[193]

Although the credit function became more professionalized, it was still stymied by the lack of reliable financial information on most businesses. Because of insufficient information and the high rate of start-ups and closures, business lenders continued to use qualitative considerations to determine creditworthiness. Of these, the notion of character, as it had been codified and standardized by the credit-reporting organizations, remained the most important. "While tangible assets are the chief basis for the extension of credits," stated one typical business manual, "yet it can be stated absolutely . . . that the rock bottom foundation upon which the whole system of credit is based is character."[194] The writer was affirming J. P. Morgan's statement during the congressional hearings on the "money trust" that character was the most important basis of commercial credit.[195]

Credit bureaus that shared information on retail customers (consumers) began operating in a number of cities after the Civil War. The ratio of consumer borrowing to consumption was growing, especially among the transient and difficult to monitor urban populations.[196] Retailers struggled to obtain information on consumers. According to the author of a storekeeping manual, "more than one-half" of most retailers' "time and thought is occupied with matters and things connected with the crediting out of the goods and the collections."[197] A credit bureau established in 1869 in Brooklyn, New York, was probably the first to report on consumers. Other bureaus soon opened in other cities, some at the instigation of the local chambers of commerce.[198]

The first consumer credit bureaus were either for-profit businesses or cooperative ventures whose running expenses were covered by membership fees. In the latter type, members pledged to share information with one another and to cooperate in debt collection. Consumer credit reporting spread just as the department stores began centralizing their credit departments.[199] Centralization gave the department stores economies of scale and the ability to develop more professional methods. By the beginning of the twentieth century the country's biggest retailers were more systematically collecting information on customers, and most large cities had some form of consumer credit reporting. (The Retail Credit Company, founded in 1899 in Atlanta, Georgia, as a for-profit organization, later became Equifax, one of America's largest consumer credit-reporting firms.)[200]

The American Mercantile Union, established in 1876, claimed to cover a number of major cities. But even the largest credit bureaus were local or (at best) regional. Not until 1906, with the founding of the National Association of Retail Credit Agencies, did the industry create mechanisms for sharing consumer credit information across cities and regions. (The group was later known as the Associated Credit Bureaus of America, and then the Consumer Data Industry Association.) To enable information sharing among independent bureaus, the Associated of Credit Bureaus (ACB) developed common procedures and methods of payment. The increase in ACB membership indicates that its services to the industry were valuable: it had 100 members in 1916, and 800 in 1927.[201] Smaller communities had credit bureaus that were housed in the chamber of commerce, board of trade, or a bank. The best-run bureaus sought information from a variety of sources that included freight depots, rental offices, and utility offices along with the more usual newspaper items and police and court records.[202] Like merchants, American consumers increasingly were brought under the surveillance of credit-reporting institutions.

Consumer lenders paid attention to the racial and ethnic origins of borrowers and were more explicit than business lenders in their refusal to lend to minorities. Boston's Workingmen's Loan Association indicated that it would "not loan to persons who frequently change their residence and are of disreputable character or to certain nationalities among immigrants, races that have not yet evolved a sense of honor, and to persons who have recently become residents of the city." A 1915 credit bureau handbook included "color" among the characteristics that determined creditworthiness, along with the length of time individuals had lived in the community and membership in churches or lodges. With no apparent sense of the incongruity the author warned that "prejudices, likes or dislikes, should not enter into your ratings at all. Facts wanted, nothing else." He emphasized that both positive and negative information should be recorded and careful distinction made between borrowers who were deadbeats and those who were merely slow (even "very slow") payers.[203] Creditors, in other words, should rank individuals along a spectrum of risk and decide for themselves which ones could potentially turn a profit.

The Civil War forced a major, and traumatic, discontinuity in the credit structures of the United States. The end of the slave-based economy was a moral victory for the Republican Party, and it brought about the end of a specific form of collateral—the human property that had backed the commercial credit of the antebellum South. The end of slavery also saw the entry into the credit economy of a group of people who until then had lived mostly outside it. (Lending to, and even borrowing from, slaves had occurred before the Civil War but on an informal basis.) With so much of the region's assets destroyed, credit dried up, and interest rates became much higher. Banking and the factorage system virtually collapsed and were replaced by tenant farming and sharecropping, whose local and inflexible contractual requirements mired both white and black farmers in debt. Reformers turned to the federal government as the only entity powerful enough to mediate among the different interest groups. Devising a system that would provide adequate credit and currency to the West and the South, while maintaining the integrity of the nation's currency (and thus the credit of the United States), became one of the political system's foremost challenges.

Funding the Civil War had required fiscal and financial experimentation. The consequences of the new institutions and instruments reverberated through the country's financial system, and its politics, for generations. But although the creation of the national banks removed the inefficiencies associated with multiple currencies, it did not solve the problems of an unstable banking system that, for political reasons, remained highly fragmented.[204] Bank runs threatened to wreck local economies whenever people lost confidence in the banks. Influenced by years of protest, politicians and academics expressed frustration with the inadequacies not just of the banks, but of the financial system as a whole. A few, such as D. M. Frederiksen, believed that the mortgage markets in particular were inefficient; capital did not easily cross regional boundaries. By the First World War, the federal government intervened directly in the farming sector. But not until the 1930s would the federal government take a radical and coherent approach to the nation's banks and mortgage markets.

The credit needs of agriculture, industry, and consumers outstripped what the commercial banks were willing or equipped to do. New institutions, including investment banks, mortgage companies, and finance companies, stepped in to fill the gaps. These financial intermediaries were the lightly regulated "shadow finance" sector of their day, providing credit to more people and businesses. Eventually, the commercial banks would enter the markets that the shadow finance industry pioneered and help to change the very meaning of consumer debt.

Chapter Four

"TO OPEN UP MASS MARKETS"

A Nation of Consumers and Home Owners

The Great Depression (1929–1939) drove the federal government once again to recast the nation's financial system. Failing banks and the threat of foreclosure on millions of properties provided the initial push for reforms. The legislation, however, went beyond these immediate emergencies; instead, the government went on to address the problems with credit that had simmered for decades. Along with the 1913 legislation establishing the Federal Reserve, the laws passed during the Great Depression constituted a systemic reform of the nation's financial regime.

Combined with the international currency controls that were set up by the Bretton Woods agreements in 1944, the reforms helped to foster financial stability in the United States after the Second World War. (In Bretton Woods, over forty countries agreed to tie their currencies to the U.S. dollar. The system diminished the ability of countries to manipulate their currencies—perceived to be one of the causes of worldwide economic depression in the 1930s—and made the U.S. dollar the world's reserve currency.)[1] Only when inflation began to spike significantly did the stability start to weaken—and even then, the United States would experience no financial crises that rivaled the Great Depression.[2] The Bretton Woods system ended in 1971, when President Richard Nixon directed the Treasury to suspend the dollar's conversion into gold. From then on, the Fed took on increasing responsibility for combating problems such as high unemployment, through its power to determine the price of money and credit.[3]

Throughout the nation's dramatic swings in fortune, Americans' demand for consumer credit and home mortgages remained strong. The 1920s saw a huge uptick in the supply of consumer credit and credit-fueled speculation, including a real estate boom in Florida in 1925 in which speculators were rumored to have bought and sold some lots up to ten times in a single day.[4] When the economy showed signs of slowing down in 1927, the Federal Reserve cut interest rates; the credit boom continued, peaking in 1928.[5] The Great Depression hit household incomes hard and demand slowed dramatically. But by 1938 consumer credit began rising once again. Regulatory controls on credit during World War II (in which the United States was a combatant from 1941 to 1945) limited the supply of consumer credit. But after the war, consumer credit rose again in tandem with exploding consumer demand. The United States was the only major combatant of the Second World War whose productive capacities were left intact. Americans' assets—their houses, savings, and pension funds—quadrupled in value between 1950 and 1970.[6] More generous unemployment and medical insurance smoothed out the disruptions in household incomes and reassured lenders that borrowers could have a means to pay their bills even in hard times.

Consumer credit acted as an engine of enterprise by powering the growth of consumer goods manufacturers, the home construction industry, and the service sector. Between 1919 and 1963, for example, General Motors' subsidiary, GMAC, financed over 43 million new cars for dealers and distributors, or an average of nearly one million cars a year. GMAC also made loans to consumers, helping them to buy 46 million new and used cars during the same period.[7] Federal programs guaranteed the mortgage loans of banks and other financial institutions and imposed standards on homebuilding. The government's participation in the housing markets made possible the long-term, fixed-rate mortgages that Americans (unlike the citizens of most other countries) enjoyed. By making both cars and houses more affordable, credit expanded the suburbs and intensified the demand for furniture, appliances, and other durable goods. Cultural critics such as William Whyte expressed ambivalence about the spread of the suburbs, and academic studies have rightly pointed to the casual racism that underpinned much of the suburban ideal.[8] But millions of Americans embraced the chance to own newer, larger homes and to raise their children in what they perceived to be a healthier environment outside of the city centers.

Table 4.1. Net public and private debt ($ billions), 1916–1976

Year	Total public and private debt ($ billions)	Public debt ($ billions)	Private debt ($ billions)
1916	82.2	5.7	76.5
1920	135.7	29.9	105.8
1930	192.3	31.2	161.1
1940	189.8	61.2	128.6
1950	486.2	239.8	246.4
1960	874.2	308.1	566.1
1970	1,881.9	484.7	1,397.2
1976	3,354.9	833.4	2,521.5
% change 1916–1976	4,081.4%	14,621.1%	3,340.0%

Source: Historical Statistics of the United States, Millennial Edition On Line, ed. Susan B. Carter et al. (Cambridge: © [copyright] Cambridge University Press, 2006), pp. 3–774.

The New Deal programs of the 1930s, and then the Great Society programs of the 1960s, accustomed people to the idea that the government should guarantee bank accounts and assist with home mortgages. College students and their families turned in greater numbers to the government for help in paying college expenses. The government indirectly subsidized borrowing through the tax deductibility of interest payments. It went even further in the case of mortgages and student loans, where the government established public and quasi-public entities (popularly known as Fannie Mae, Ginnie Mae, Freddie Mac, and Sallie Mae) to securitize the loans and create vast secondary markets to entice more private lending. (In a secondary market, investors buy securities from one another rather than from the issuing institution. The existence of a secondary market means that a security can be bought and sold more easily, which increases demand for it.) Both public and private debts grew at a rapid pace during the period 1916–1976. (See Table 4.1.)

Once again, entrepreneurs took advantage of the opportunities in the changing political economy. In addition to making use of new technologies, they exploited the regulatory loopholes to enter credit markets that were underserved by commercial banks. Public officials put up some resistance, but in general, they allowed retailers, small-loan lenders, sales finance companies, and credit card issuers to create a new world of consumer finance. The success of these lenders, in turn, diminished the reluctance of commercial banks to enter the consumer credit markets. The banks offered small personal loans and entered the domain of the sales finance companies by funding installment buying. Later they issued credit cards, dramatically expanding the supply of consumer credit for nondurables such as clothing, small appliances, and electronics goods. Eventually, Americans bought even ephemeral experiences such as vacations and restaurant meals on credit.

But people also continued to express qualms about the amount of debt they were taking on, and their political leaders voiced their ambivalence. Lenders offered reassurance: Americans, they said, were not abandoning the traditional values of thrift, hard work, and production; they were just expressing those values in a different way, by acquiring and paying for goods in a disciplined manner. Through advertisements, sponsored research, and public testimonies, lenders persuaded ordinary people and regulators that borrowing to fund consumption was aligned with American society's deepest held moral standards.

Stabilizing the Banking System

The national banking acts that were passed during the Civil War succeeded in imposing a national currency. But they failed to stabilize the banking system. In 1920 the nation had more than 30,000 state and federally chartered commercial banks, most of them small, one-unit establishments that were vulnerable to economic shocks.[9] The reserve system also contributed to the instability, with banks in New York continuing to lend the reserves of thousands of banks across the country to brokers.[10] Demand for the call loans—short-term loans that could be called in at any time—was high, and the interest paid rose accordingly, from 4.4 percent in 1922 to 7.7 percent in 1929.[11] Corporations that were flush with cash lent even more to the call money market than did the banks, further fueling the stock market boom. With the creation of the Federal Reserve the nation's banking reserves began transferring from the handful of New York City banks to the twelve Federal Reserve district banks. Progressive reformers urged the Fed to pay interest on these reserves to discourage member banks from seeking higher returns on the call money market—to no avail. Wall Street continued to enjoy easy access to call loans.[12]

Americans were accustomed to unstable banks; even in the prosperous 1920s, hundreds of banks closed their doors every year. But in the early 1930s, and despite the existence of the Federal Reserve, the bank failure rate skyrocketed. (Unlike the national banks, the state-chartered banks were not required to join the Federal Reserve, and relatively few chose to do so.) In December 1930, a run on the Bank of United States, a New York City bank, precipitated the largest bank failure in the country up to that time.[13] Home owners faced foreclosure in unprecedented numbers, which intensified the rate of bank failures. Before federal legislation stemmed the crisis, about 40 percent of all commercial banks failed, a total of over nine thousand banks.[14] Under presidents Herbert Hoover and (especially) Franklin D. Roosevelt, the federal government passed legislation and created programs to deal with the banking crises. The Hoover administration established the Reconstruction Finance Corporation (RFC) to provide liquidity to troubled banks. (The RFC went on to assist the agriculture, business, and housing sectors. It was one of the few instances when the federal government has made direct loans to individuals and businesses.) The Roosevelt administration and Congress intensified the government's intervention in the banking system beginning with the Emergency Banking Relief Act (1933).

Two pieces of Depression-era legislation that were designed to address the banking problems—Regulation Q of the Banking Act (1933) and the Federal Deposit Insurance Act (1934)—had significant unintended consequences. Regulation Q reflected the view of most policy makers that excessive competition among banks had led to the banking crisis.[15] Congress passed Regulation Q to discourage banks from competing for deposits, by limiting the interest that could be paid on savings and checking accounts. The restrictions would remain in place until the mid-1980s. Until then, Regulation Q functioned as an indirect national usury law because banks customarily charged interest rates that were only 2.5 to 3 percent above what the banks paid their depositors.[16] But competitors that were not covered by the law, such as the money markets (which includes mutual funds and commercial paper), were able to offer slightly higher interest rates. The banks lost deposits when inflation began to spike during the 1960s, and especially in the 1970s when more people transferred their savings into money market accounts. In 1949, commercial banks held one-half of all deposit assets, but by 1979 their share had fallen to just one-third. Customer deposits had been a cheap source of funds,

125

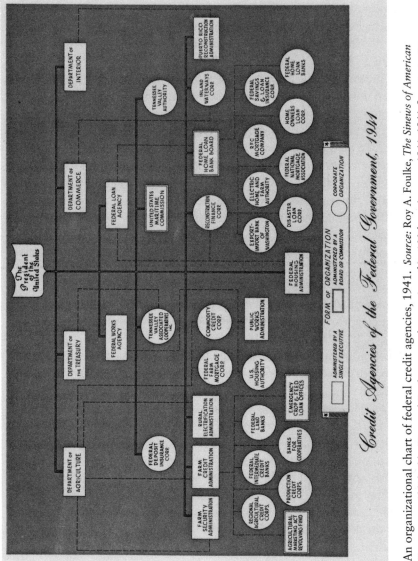

Credit Agencies of the Federal Government, 1941

An organizational chart of federal credit agencies, 1941. *Source:* Roy A. Foulke, *The Sinews of American Commerce*, published by Dun and Bradstreet on the occasion of its 100th anniversary, 1841–1941. Image courtesy of the Baker Old Class Collection, Baker Library, Harvard Business School.

and when the banks lost deposits they had less money to lend. Regulation Q started out as a way to dampen excessive competition among banks, but it ended up making them uncompetitive against new investment vehicles such as money market mutual funds.[17]

The Federal Deposit Insurance Corporation (FDIC) law worked well, but it, too, had unintended consequences for banking.[18] By guaranteeing deposit accounts, the FDIC decreased the number of bank failures, as regulators had hoped; until 1981, fewer than fifteen banks collapsed per year.[19] Deposit insurance diminished the frequency of bank runs, even on banks that were suspected of being insolvent, and more banks now held low-risk federal bonds in their portfolios.[20] Together with the capital controls imposed by legislation such as Regulation Q, these factors created a stable capital market in the United States. So long as the government kept inflation at bay, the stability could continue. But insuring people's accounts led both the banks and their depositors to pay less attention to risk. In the 1980s, the problem of moral hazard would lead banks and savings and loan associations (S&Ls) to engage in all kinds of risky lending and investing. Federal deposit insurance also may have stopped the banks from consolidating and states from relaxing their restrictions on branching. These incipient responses to the banking crises of the 1920s and early 1930s slowed when unit bankers realized that the federal government would now take on more of the risks.[21]

By 1940, the government had created many new entities whose purpose was to encourage more credit for agriculture and housing. Most of the government bodies did not lend money directly but instead encouraged private lending by (for example) guaranteeing loans. From the 1930s onward, the federal government was the senior partner and director of the U.S. credit system.

Consumer Credit

The volume of consumer debt outstanding more than doubled during the 1920s, increasing by 131 percent from $3.3 billion to $7.6 billion. Household debt, which accounted for 4 to 7 percent of disposable income (the money available to pay off the debt) between 1900 and 1920, grew to almost 10 percent of disposable income in 1929–30.[22] The Great Depression saw steep declines in the purchases of consumer durables.[23] But although high unemployment cut people's incomes, consumer borrowing remained a multibillion dollar business. A severe retrenchment occurred during the early 1930s, but by 1937 consumer debt once again reached pre-Depression levels, and it continued to rise until wartime regulations imposed limits.[24] The borrowing took two forms: small personal loans and installment buying.

Small Personal Loans

Outside of friends and family, most Americans had few places to turn to for loans. If people ran out of money before payday, their options consisted of loan sharks, pawnbrokers, "salary buyers," and other less-than-respectable lenders. A study done in the mid-1930s found that New York City's workers regularly paid 10 percent of their paychecks to salary buyers. Loans from pawnbrokers made up nearly 25 percent of all consumer credit, and even small merchants sometimes pawned a portion of their inventory.[25] The Provident Loan Society, established in 1893 as a semiphilanthropic venture, made $36 million worth of loans to over half a million borrowers during the depression year of 1931. The following year, twenty-seven such "remedial loan societies" operated across the country. Commercial pawnbroking, however, far outstripped the lending done by benevolent societies: the commercial pawnbrokers made $400 million in loans versus $53 million for the semiphilanthropic agencies.[26]

Reformers and entrepreneurs conducted a number of experiments to help wage earners get loans. One of the best known, the Morris Plan bank, was created in 1910, when attorney Arthur Joseph Morris submitted a charter to the Virginia Corporation Commission for a project that he called the Fidelity Savings and Trust Company (later changed to the Industrial Finance Corporation). Unlike the credit unions, Morris's plan was a private, profit-making enterprise funded by the sale of stock in the company. "Frankly, I don't know what it is," a perplexed commission member confessed to Morris. "It isn't a savings bank; it isn't a state or national bank; it isn't a charity." But the commissioner acknowledged that the principles of Morris's proposed company "seem sound . . . and its purposes admirable."[27] The Morris Plan institutions declined after just two decades and endured a lot of criticism, but during their heyday they provided loans to thousands of people and helped to shift public perceptions about the mass market for personal loans.

Companies organized under the Morris Plan aimed to provide working people with loans of between $50 to $5,000, based "largely on character, earning power and two indorsements [sic]." These criteria—a regular salary plus two acquaintances who vouched for the borrower's good character—were the sole collateral underpinning the scheme. Morris Plan Corporation of America, the parent company, controlled some of the banks, but most were autonomous; the Morris Plan took only a minority interest. The interest rate was high at 17 percent but far better than borrowing from loan sharks.[28] The banks engaged in a somewhat complicated maneuver to avoid running afoul of the usury laws. Borrowers received the money minus interest and fees. They then bought two certificates from the company for the whole amount, agreeing to pay $1 a week on each of the certificates. When these were paid off the borrowers could use the certificates to retire the note.[29]

Through the 1920s Morris Plan banks were the most prominent lenders of consumer credit to low-income people.[30] In 1931 the banks did about $220 million of business, which grew to $288 million in 1940. The practice became known as "industrial banking" because the banks served primarily industrial workers.[31] With loans of $3 billion spread among 15 million borrowers, the losses were less than one-half of 1 percent—lower than most banks.[32] Yet skeptics questioned whether the certificates were just a device to avoid the charge of usury.[33] The Russell Sage Foundation alleged that the Morris Plan was misleading and even fraudulent.[34] One academic critic argued instead for a new type of banking institution, authorized by federal law, "to accept deposits and to make loans on endorsed notes, salaries, chattels, and pawns at rates which would make it possible to furnish credit facilities to the masses on reasonable terms."[35] But no such institution emerged.

For many critics, schemes like the Morris Plan were not the problem. The main barriers, they argued, were the state usury laws. The laws restricted interest rates to around 6 percent, far too meager to attract nonbank lenders who had much higher costs of capital. Louis N. Robinson, a professor at Swarthmore College and author of a number of works on consumer credit, argued that the laws were "out of date or in need of serious revision to fit them to the facts of present-day economic conditions." The laws stifled the creation of lending institutions for people who had no collateral.[36] Reformers knew that usury laws presented a difficult dilemma: in order to free cash-strapped people from the grip of loan sharks and pawnbrokers, respectable institutions would have to lend to the masses. The surest incentive was to lift the usury rate ceilings and allow lenders to charge more for the risky short-term loans. In return, the lenders would agree to be licensed, monitored, and regulated—in short, they would agree to become socially acceptable members of the lending fraternity.

The Russell Sage Foundation lobbied the states to raise their legal interest rates. Along with Household Finance Corporation, a chain of small-loan lenders, Russell Sage supported the creation of a uniform small-lending law in 1916. (The campaign was part of a decades-long movement to harmonize the country's commercial laws. Reformers designed model bills that could be introduced in the state legislatures, to ensure that laws were uniform across states.)[37] Russell Sage's model law allowed licensed lenders to charge interest rates of up to 3.5 percent per month, or 42 percent annually. In return, the lenders agreed to adhere to strict standards of lending. A number of small-loan lenders embraced the opportunities that the new law made available. Members of the industry became themselves reformers, although of a self-interested sort. In 1916, cash lenders from five states met in Philadelphia to organize the American Association of Small Loan Brokers. They dedicated themselves to teaching their borrowers how to plan and to budget and used the state laws to drive out illegal lenders. In the 1920s, the association became known as the American Industrial Licensed Lenders Association, complete with a trade journal, the *Industrial Lender News*. Soon, they were depicting their offerings as "personal finance" services.[38]

By the late 1920s, forty-three out of the forty-eight states had amended their usury laws, usually by raising the ceiling to 18 percent—still lower than the 42 percent allowed by Russell Sage's model law. The movement suffered a setback during the Great Depression, when several states either repealed the law or reduced the legal maximum interest rate; by 1932 the number of states that had adopted some version of the small-lending law was down to twenty-five. The total amount outstanding of legal small loans was a relatively paltry $258 million out of a total of all cash loans outstanding of $1.7 billion. When put in the context of *total* short-term household debt outstanding ($14.4 billion, according to some estimates), it is clear that the small-loan industry represented a tiny portion of the consumer credit industry. Nevertheless, a study by M. R. Neifeld concluded that the licensed small-loan lender served 2.6 million families or one-eighth of the population, which implies that the average loan amount was tiny.[39]

The cost of capital drove the small-loan industry to consolidate, and some companies grew large. They were the first in the personal finance industry to cross state lines and open branch offices. The merger of three loan companies in 1929 formed one of the largest players, Beneficial Industrial Loan Corporation. In its first year, it operated in 228 cities and had 263 offices that together loaned out $58 million. A few loan companies even sold their stock to the public. Household Finance Corporation was the first, in 1928. By the early 1930s, state-licensed personal finance companies numbered 3,667, with the two largest—Household and Beneficial—accounting for 30 percent of total revenues. The chains came to dominate the field, and soon less than one-half of licensed lending was done by individually owned and operated companies.[40] The loan companies extended credit based on borrowers' character traits, as verified by employers and landlords. The lenders set up information exchanges to prevent overextending credit to any one borrower. In 1940 there were fifty-seven such exchanges in twenty-two states, with a total membership of 1,216 licensed lenders. Using the mail and telephone, the exchanges transacted over 174,000 clearances per month, or more than two million a year.[41] Business grew more than twenty-five-fold between 1912 and 1940, when the personal loan companies had outstanding loans of $495 million. They took business away from the remedial loan societies: from thirty-two in 1920, only nineteen remedial loan societies were left by 1940.[42]

Credit unions, financial organizations that served people in the same church, workplace, or fraternal order, were another attempt to provide affordable loans. They were modeled on the Raiffeisen (cooperative) credit societies of Germany. Canadian journalist Alphonse Desjardins organized the country's first credit union in New Hampshire in 1909. Like the building and loan societies, members bought shares in the institution on an installment basis, an arrangement designed to encourage regular saving. Members could borrow small amounts for emergencies such as doctors' bills and tax liabilities, or for minor home improvements and education. The interest on unpaid balances was around 1 percent a month. Members passed judgment on loan applications based on their personal knowledge of applicants. These unsecured loans typically were limited by state and (later) federal laws to $50. In 1920, only 142 credit unions operated in six states, but by 1930 there were over one thousand. The Federal Credit Union Act of 1934 enabled credit unions to obtain either a federal or state charter, just like the commercial banks. By 1940, 2.5 million people belonged to some 8,700 credit unions. The average loan amount was $110.[43]

The success of the personal loan industry stimulated the commercial banks to enter the field. Before the 1920s, commercial banks did not actively court retail customers. They were not interested in accommodating small-deposit accounts, nor did they want to make small consumer loans. (A rare exception was San Francisco-based Bank of America, founded by Amadeo Giannini in 1904 as the Bank of Italy.) But in 1924, a bank in

Jersey City, New Jersey, opened the first small-loan department of a commercial bank. Many others followed, probably realizing that small consumer loans were an untapped market whose riskiness was lower than conventional wisdom dictated. The nation's largest commercial bank, National City Bank of New York (later Citibank), and the Bank of United States began making small personal loans. (Bank of United States collapsed in the 1930s.) By1929, 208 banks had personal loan departments. The number increased by more than three-and-a-half times during the Depression, when banks turned to consumer lending to replace the severe decline in business borrowing. By the end of the 1930s, 766 banks had personal loan departments. Loans outstanding totaled $160 million, nearly all of it made to high- and middle-income borrowers who had regular jobs.[44]

Banks had some natural advantages over the small-loan companies. People preferred borrowing from commercial banks because they now offered convenient additional services such as savings and checking accounts.[45] And their loans were cheaper. The Russell Sage Foundation estimated that in 1928 commercial banks charged between 13 and 35 percent compared to an upper-end rate of 42 percent for small-loan companies. (In contrast, licensed pawnbrokers charged up to 60 percent, and loan sharks 480 percent.)[46] The percentage of bank loans that went to households continued to rise during the Depression, from 9 percent in 1929 to more than 20 percent a decade later. One study estimated that in 1930, 90 percent of Americans still did not have access to credit; but even so, banks were by then the largest institutional lender of cash loans to households and individuals.[47] Individuals borrowed for a variety of reasons, including debt consolidation; paying taxes, hospital bills, and insurance premiums; and to help relatives. More and more, they began taking out personal bank loans to pay for luxuries such as vacations.[48]

Installment Credit

As important as the small-loan industry became, installment buying proved in many ways to be more significant. Already in 1918–1919, almost one-quarter (22 percent) of families relied on installment buying.[49] By the end of the 1920s, installment credit amounted to more than one-half ($2.5 billion out of $4 billion) of all consumer lending, far more than the $1.4 billion provided by pawnbrokers and loan sharks.[50] Buying on installment made refrigerators, washing machines, and automobiles part of everyday life. More than the citizens of other nations, Americans were willing to go into debt to purchase these goods.[51]

The manufacturers of durable goods offered installment credit to increase sales. Installment credit was a secured form of lending: the law backed the rights of creditors to repossess the goods if the buyers failed to meet payments. The sellers could also skirt the usury laws by raising their prices to compensate for their risks.[52] These advantages made installment financing more popular than other forms of consumer credit. Household spending on nondurable items such as books, jewelry, and china remained stable, but the proportion of household money that went to durable goods such as appliances, phonographs, radios, and automobiles increased by almost one-third. Before 1916, less than 3 percent of total consumption was of durable goods, but these purchases increased to nearly 5 percent in the 1920s and reached 8 percent after World War II.[53]

Much of the growth in installment buying was in auto sales. Henry Ford's mass-assembly line revolutionized the production of cars and drove down their price, but a car still represented the most costly consumer purchase for most households. As General Motors CEO Alfred Sloan explained in his memoir, "Mass production brought with it the need for a broad approach to consumer financing, which banks did not then take kindly to . . . and so other means had to be found if the auto industry was to sell cars in large numbers."[54] Financing could not come from the auto dealers because they were themselves cash-strapped. Running a dealership required substantial amounts of working capital. The manufacturers demanded a deposit before they shipped the cars; then the dealers had to pay the balance on delivery, in cash.[55]

Sales finance companies stepped into the gap. These companies had the creditworthiness to borrow from banks, allowing funds to flow through the finance companies to less creditworthy borrowers. The finance companies, even ones that were tied to industrial concerns, could borrow more relative to their capital than manufacturing firms, which were forced to hew to more conservative ratios. In addition, the finance companies could raise working capital by selling their collateral trust notes in the capital markets. (They paid a premium because the Federal Reserve would not rediscount the finance companies' collateral notes. Banks also charged the finance companies rates that were higher than commercial paper rates.)[56] Estimates vary, but Dun and Bradstreet's Roy Foulke reported that the number of finance companies shot up to around 1,400 by 1924 before consolidating to 918 five years later.[57]

At first, the companies financed the used-car market, which was already in place by 1910 when wealthy people began replacing their cars.[58]

Then, increasingly, they funded the inventories of car dealers, improving the dealers' cash flows. Banks were reluctant to do this kind of lending because the dealers could cancel their contracts with the car manufacturers at any time, which increased the banks' risk. The finance companies offered dealers short-term loans of up to 90 percent of the cars' value, payable after two or three months. They also began extending loans to consumers through the dealers, who assumed the risk if the consumer failed to pay. Consumers who bought on credit paid a high premium: in the early 1920s, cars bought on installment were up to 22 percent more expensive, and the effective annual interest rates were more than 30 percent.[59]

In 1916 the Maxwell Motor Car Company became the first auto manufacturer to offer its products directly to consumers on the installment plan. For 50 percent down, and eight equal payments thereafter, a customer could own a Maxwell.[60] GM followed suit in 1919, after John J. Raskob, a financial executive at the company, proposed the idea for a captive sales finance subsidiary called the GM Acceptance Corporation (GMAC). Originally, GMAC helped the dealers and financed retail sales as a secondary activity only, but it soon moved heavily into retail sales. The small independent finance companies struggled to compete with GMAC, and their numbers fell.[61]

By contrast, Ford was a latecomer to auto financing. At least one independent consultant argued to Ford's management that providing credit to dealers would give Ford a number of benefits. For one, it would smooth out the company's production cycle. Sales of autos peaked between March and June, and dealers tended not to take shipments in the winter months. Providing installment financing would encourage more sales during the slow periods and enlarge the market for Ford autos. The arguments made no inroads with Henry Ford, who disapproved of installment buying. Henry's son Edsel was more open to the consultants' advice, but Henry vetoed all suggestions that Ford provide financing to its dealers, let alone to consumers. In 1919, Edsel Ford estimated that at least 65 percent of Ford cars and trucks were being sold to consumers on the installment plan, with all of the financing provided by institutions other than Ford itself. At the time, one out of every two cars in the world was a Model T, and Henry Ford was confident that he did not need to get into the financing business.

Ford was out of touch with consumers' preferences. Rival GM's financing of retail sales grew quickly, in tandem with its strategy of offering "a car for every purse and purpose." GM took business away from local sales finance companies and helped to lock people into the GM brand. In 1923, driven by narrowing margins for its Model T, Ford began offering a weekly purchasing plan. It was not a credit program; instead, the plan allowed people to open a savings account with their Ford dealer as a way to amass enough money for a Ford car. The plan was a failure, but Ford resisted establishing a sales finance company for consumers until 1928, when it formed the Universal Credit Corporation. By then it was too late. Ford had already lost market leadership to GM. Ford's share of cars was now less than 20 percent, a far cry from the 50 percent it had enjoyed in 1921.[62]

Unlike Henry Ford, Alfred Sloan publicly expressed his "complete confidence in the present situation and future development of installment selling."[63] GM sponsored Edwin Seligman, professor of economics at Columbia University, to produce the first thorough analysis of the subject, a two-volume report entitled *The Economics of Installment Selling* (1927). Seligman reported that some $38 billion worth of goods were sold in the United States in 1926, of which 12 percent was bought on deferred payment. For some goods the proportion was much higher—60 percent of all automobiles, trucks, and parts were bought on installment. GM celebrated the publication of Seligman's book with a lavish banquet in New York, where he summarized the book's conclusions for the assembled guests: "Installment selling has increased production, stabilized output, reduced production cost and increased purchasing power." Far from undermining thrift, Seligman argued that installment credit had a disciplining effect on consumers because it encouraged them to plan more carefully and motivated them to meet their payment obligations. Installment buying was progressive: consumers now had access to credit that previously had been confined to producers. Seligman asked a number of provocative questions. Can some "consumptive" activities be productive? Does installment credit distort consumers' judgment, or does it tend to make them think more rationally and to budget better? Is there really a difference between judging the creditworthiness of producers and that of consumers?[64]

As it turned out, people preferred to buy cars on installment even if it meant having to pay 15 to 22 percent more. Academic research later expressed what the auto executives already knew—that "the ability to provide credit is a more effective competitive weapon than an attractive product price," as a study in the 1950s put it.[65] Consumers did not mind the higher overall price so long as the weekly or monthly payments were low. They wanted to have the use of both the car *and* the money. Many people bought a better car than they could have afforded if they had to save for it. And they strove hard to meet payments, sometimes even going without necessities rather than lose their cars. They may even have borrowed from small-loan lenders to finance their installment buying.[66] Although two-thirds of new car purchases and one-half of used car purchases were on credit, default rates were low.[67] Even in the worst year of the Depression (1932), only 5 percent of cars sold on installment were repossessed.[68] This compared favorably to (for example) the corporate bond default rate of 6.73 percent in 1933.[69]

The GM Acceptance Company succeeded in part because customers trusted it more than the specialized finance companies. These smaller companies tacked on high finance and insurance charges as well as other fees, and they confused buyers by quoting ambiguous charges. The independent companies tried to overcome the stigma by partnering with a car manufacturer that would designate them as "preferred" providers.[70] But far from destroying the competition, GMAC stimulated the overall growth of the market by helping to make installment purchases the norm. Consumers benefited when the increased competition drove finance companies to stretch payment terms from one year to two years and longer. By 1930, installment credit financed 60–75 percent of auto sales.[71]

Finance companies had a number of advantages over banks. Technically, the finance companies did not violate the usury laws because the money they made was booked as profits on commercial transactions rather than interest charges.[72] (For many decades afterward, they would continue to be less regulated than banks.) Finance companies underwrote 40 percent of consumer installment loans by the end of the 1920s. By contrast, commercial banks provided just over 5 percent, and department stores accounted for around 13 percent of installment sales.[73] In 1926 the leading finance companies joined together to form the American Rediscount Corporation to purchase lenders' notes, enabling them to make even more loans.[74]

Even the federal government entered the consumer finance business in a limited way. During the Depression, it established the Electric Home and Farm Authority, a government entity that funded consumer purchases of electrical appliances through local utility companies. The Farm Credit Act of 1933 established a farm credit system that made loans to farmers' cooperatives, which in turn helped farmers to buy items such as appliances and cars.[75] But many bankers and most politicians continued to look

An advertisement for General Motors' installment plan. GM and other makers of durable consumer goods depicted installment finance as a smart way to buy. In this ad, the company emphasized the transparency of its finance charges and praised consumers' ability to figure out the charges for themselves. *Source: Life,* October 14, 1940. In author's possession.

askance at installment buying. Thrift and saving, they argued, lay at the core of economic recovery. The president of the American Bankers Association, Oscar Wells, was among installment credit's most severe critics. "There is no consistency," he pointed out, "in preaching this doctrine [thrift] on the one hand and on the other of encouraging an indulgence in buying on the installment plan at a cost ranging from fifteen to forty percent for the privilege." George W. Norris, governor of the Philadelphia Federal Reserve Bank, believed that the easy availability of installment credit "encourage[d] the purchase of unnecessary goods or of unnecessarily expensive goods." (But he admitted that installment buying had not discouraged saving.) No Federal Reserve officials defended installment credit during the interwar period. To the contrary, Eugene R. Black, the governor of the Federal Reserve Bank of Atlanta and later of the Federal Reserve, blamed installment credit and "the failure of the American people to live within their means" during the 1920s for the decline in business activity in the early 1930s. The Federal Reserve continued to resist expanding the supply of consumer credit by restricting its rediscount facility to commercial paper only; sales finance companies could not rely on the Fed to discount their paper. Arguably, the Fed's actions kept interest rates on installment credit high and its volume relatively lower than it might have been.[76]

Consumers, however, behaved in ways that were contrary to policy makers' hopes. Consumers retrenched when the Depression began, but from 1933 onward they once again demanded installment credit, which the finance companies provided.[77] The resilience of consumers was not lost on the commercial banks, which began financing car purchases and even experimented with buying the retail paper of installment purchases by lower-income people.[78] By 1940, the banks had become the largest providers of consumer installment credit. Many banks now bypassed the finance companies and lent directly to consumers.[79]

Researchers' interest in consumer credit intensified. In 1938 the National Bureau of Economic Research (NBER) initiated a series of reports on consumer loan lenders and the Russell Sage Foundation changed its Department of Remedial Loans to the Department of Consumer Credit Studies. Policy makers began asking questions about the impact that installment credit had on prices and the business cycle generally, and whether consumers had the information they needed to make good choices. In 1939 Rolf Nugent, who had worked in the consumer lending industry and the Russell Sage Foundation, made the case for greater government control over consumer credit in *Consumer Credit and Economic Stability.* During World War II, he helped to design Regulation W (discussed in the next section of this chapter).[80]

By contrast, M. R. Neifeld, an economist and strong supporter of consumer credit, argued that it existed "to cushion the problems of insecurity of capitalistic society and to open up mass markets in the lower income brackets by gearing production more closely to income." The problem of an industrialized society was not how to encourage thrift but how to stimulate consumption when people's incomes were inadequate.[81] Attitudes were already turning in this direction. Unlike in some European countries, the U.S. government declined to regulate consumer credit and did little to curb household overindebtedness. Many American bankers and lifestyle magazines embraced installment credit as being good for the economy; even labor unions joined in. A 1939 survey of consumer spending by the federal government's National Resources Committee stated that the country's "rich abundance of natural resources and an undreamt-of capacity to convert this natural wealth into useful goods and services," had to be matched by the ability of consumers "to buy the output of goods and services which industry can produce."[82]

But older notions of thrift continued to shape how academics and policy makers understood the role of credit in the business cycle. Over-indebtedness, many of them believed, was akin to fever; and like a fever, it had to run its course even if this temporarily weakened the patient. In his memoirs, former president Herbert Hoover wrote that his secretary of the Treasury, Andrew Mellon, had "insisted that, when the people get an inflation brainstorm, the only way to get it out of their blood is to let it collapse. He held that even a panic was not altogether a bad thing" because it led people back to "a more moral life" and removed incompetent people from the market.[83] Central bank officials were generally more tactful, but they expressed a similar outlook during the first two years of the Depression: paying down public and household debts was the best way to bring about a sustainable economic recovery.[84] Since the vast majority of policy makers held similar views, it was hardly surprising that even in the worst years of the Depression almost no one advocated that the government bring on a consumer-led recovery by making more credit available to consumers. "Every single governmental attempt to prime the business pump throughout four years of Depression has been one indirect method or another of easing credit to producers, . . ." *Time* magazine wrote in

1933, "but no serious effort has ever been made to bolster buying power by direct consumer credit."[85]

Instead, government policies encouraged people to save. The Federal Deposit Insurance Corporation guaranteed deposits and removed people's fear of unstable banks. The proportion of Americans with bank savings accounts rose from 39 percent at the end of the Second World War to 53 percent by 1960. During the war, the government ran a successful campaign to sell its war bonds as savings vehicles to a wider swath of the public. Out of a population of 132 million, 85 million people (64 percent) owned war bonds, more than had a savings account. Payroll savings plans also became more widespread during the war, which accustomed many workers to save regularly. All of these initiatives helped to embed the habit of saving into the American psyche, and for more than four decades after the Second World War ended, savings rates ranged between 7 and 11 percent. People consumed more and took on more debt, but good wages and low inflation allowed them to save. According to historian Sheldon Garon, the period from the Second World War to the 1980s was "America's Golden Age of Saving."[86]

World War II and After

Consumer credit resumed its ascent in 1937 but stalled again during World War II. The federal government caused the slowdown by policing the entire system of legal credit in the form of Regulation W. Passed by the Federal Reserve Board in 1941 and amended several times during the war, Regulation W was a sweeping piece of legislation aimed at controlling inflation. It fixed the minimum down payment and the maximum time of maturity of consumer installment credit for items like cars, aircraft, boats, motorcycles, and household appliances. (Many other articles were added to the list as the war progressed.) It also required that all persons who extended installment credit apply for a license. Federal Reserve Board chairman Marriner Eccles explained the rationale behind Regulation W: "When incomes are at high levels, that is the time when people should reduce their debts or get out of debt. Our people cannot spend their increased incomes and go into debt for more and more things today without precipitating a price inflation that would recoil ruinously upon all of us." Eccles's statement reflected the belief of many in the government that forcing people to defer purchases would conserve their buying power and prevent a slump once the conflict ended. Regulating consumer credit was the first stage of what became a coherent wartime federal policy administered by the Office of Price Administration. The OPA tried to control inflation, stabilize the economy, and redirect resources to wartime production.[87] One of the unintended consequences of Regulation W was that department stores began offering their customers revolving credit, a form of consumer borrowing that the wartime act did not regulate. Similar to modern-day credit cards, the stores' revolving-credit arrangements allowed creditworthy customers to maintain a balance on their charge accounts.[88]

Later critics of Regulation W pointed out that the war had curtailed the manufacture of consumer goods anyway. The War Production Board halted the manufacture of appliances large and small beginning in 1942. New electric washing machines, refrigerators, and stoves became unavailable, as did toasters and waffle irons. Cars, too, became a casualty of the wartime economy when General Motors, Ford, and Chrysler stopped producing civilian cars and instead began churning out tanks and aircraft engines. Even piano and organ makers Steinway, Baldwin, and Kimball reduced their output of musical instruments to make parts for military aircraft.[89] Whether because of Regulation W, the lack of durable goods available for purchase, or the increased job opportunities that gave people more cash in their pockets, the amount of consumer credit fell dramatically, and savings—including the purchase of war bonds—rose. Between September 1941 and September 1943 installment credit dropped by 80 percent, cash loans by 52 percent.[90] Significantly, consumption itself did not fall; instead, it went up, especially on food, clothing, and entertainment. The United States was the only major combatant that managed to increase its people's overall consumption during the war despite rationing and curtailed credit.[91]

When the war ended, the United States enjoyed a period of price stability combined with high economic growth. The general sense of prosperity and fulfillment of pent-up demand could be seen in the national savings rates, which fell from 26 percent towards the end of the war in 1944 to a mere 4.2 percent in 1947 before rising again to over 7 percent in the 1950s and 1960s. Credit, meanwhile, saw a dramatic rise. Installment credit grew seventeenfold between 1945 and 1960, to $45 billion, even though Regulation W was reimposed for a short time during the Korean War (1950–1953).[92] Automobiles continued to be an important part of the increase: in the mid-1950s, almost half of all installment debt was to finance cars. Appliances such as refrigerators and stoves also drove credit sales, with at least half being bought on credit. *Life* magazine observed that debt was rising faster than income. And indeed, two-thirds of American families were now indebted, with half owing installment debt.[93] Policy makers continued to wonder whether such an abundance of consumer credit would destabilize the economy. William M. Martin, chairman of the Federal Reserve from 1951 to 1970, worried that "fluctuations in installment credit accentuate cyclical swings in consumer expenditure and hence in economic activity."[94]

Still, there was little consensus that consumer credit needed controlling at all. Even during World War II, Regulation W had divided academics, with some arguing that consumer credit made people more productive— by allowing them to transfer easily to new jobs, for example.[95] In the early 1950s, marketing professor Robert Bartels proposed that the growth of consumer credit was not threatening but was instead the result of inflation, a growing population, and Americans' higher standard of living.[96] Consumer debt as a percentage of consumer expenditures was stable, indicating that more consumer credit did not stimulate overconsumption. Bartels pointed out that the savings rate had risen relative to 1929.[97] Later research confirmed that in every year during the 1950s and 1960s, Americans paid back nearly all of the installment debt they owed.[98]

In 1957, President Dwight Eisenhower and Raymond Saulnier, chairman of the President's Council of Economic Advisors, requested that the Federal Reserve undertake another research project on consumer credit.[99] The government's studies again found a significant increase in Americans' household debt. Economists pondered the larger implications of this trend, none so famously as Harvard's John Kenneth Galbraith. In his best-selling book, *The Affluent Society* (1958), Galbraith argued that classical economics was born out of an era of want, not plenty, and that its main concern was how best to achieve ever-increasing production. This argument implied that consumption had to increase proportionately, even when all natural wants had been satisfied. In very developed societies like the United States, advertisers convinced people that their wants were endless. To keep the great consumption machine going, advertisers also had to break down all traditional resistance to debt: "The process of persuading people to incur debt, and the arrangements for them to do so, are as much a part of modern production as the making of the goods and the nurturing of the wants. The Puritan ethos was not abandoned. It was merely overwhelmed by the massive power of modern merchandising." Galbraith mused, "Can the bill collector or the bankruptcy lawyer be the central figure in the good society?"[100] His observation that advertisers manipulated demand was widely shared; critics asked whether businesses were forcing consumer credit upon an unsophisticated public.[101] William Whyte, a business journalist and writer on organizations, wrote that "thrift is now un-American." It "had become quaint—as likely to invite ridicule as admiration."[102]

For corporate America, rising consumption and consumer debt levels signaled new opportunities rather than the abandonment of old values. The chairman of General Electric (GE), Philip Reed, declared that consumer credit "has made possible the acquisition of consumer goods to a greater extent than in any other country, which is a principal factor in our high standards of living." Credit created a mass market for durable goods that in turn lowered the costs of production and distribution.[103] Reed and his fellow corporate executives sometimes found themselves in the awkward position of publicly supporting the Federal Reserve's tight-credit, anti-inflation policies while they themselves were liberalizing their credit terms to customers.[104]

In the end, regulators did little to restrict consumer credit. The Federal Reserve's study concluded that the increased consumer credit, while worthy of concern, did not pose a threat to economic stability, and that monetary and fiscal measures were adequate to control the credit supply. From nearly $6 billion in 1945, consumer credit grew to $143 billion in 1970—the same year the Federal Reserve found that household debt equaled about half of Americans' disposable income—and then rocketed to more than $375 billion in 1980.[105]

Credit Cards

One reason for the steep ascent in household debt beginning in the 1970s was the spread of bank credit cards. Modern bank credit cards have two characteristics: they are all-purpose (universal) devices that can be used in multiple merchant establishments; and they have a revolving credit facility that allows their users to carry a balance from one month to the next. This facility was the first mass application of adjustable interest rates to consumer loans. Adjustable rates benefited lenders by placing the risk of fluctuating interest rates on to borrowers.[106]

In the early 1920s, some oil companies had provided "courtesy cards" that allowed customers to charge their purchases. At the end of the decade, Filene's Department Store began using the Charge-a-Plate, a metal square embossed with customers' names and account numbers. It was put through a machine at the store counter, generating a credit sales slip. A few other department stores adopted the card, and some formed cooperatives to allow customers to use the same card in a limited number of different stores. The airline industry began offering charge cards in 1936, when American Airlines formed its own credit system called the Universal Air Travel Plan.[107]

Unlike these proprietary charge cards, a universal credit card was provided by a third party, such as a bank. The third-party issuer had to attract and coordinate a large number of merchants. It had to set up mechanisms for authorizing and clearing payments to minimize fraud and ensure that merchants were paid reasonably quickly. An all-purpose credit card that also allowed customers to carry balances from month to month was even harder to set up because lenders had to keep continuous track of who owed what. They had to figure out how to make money out of a huge number of consumers. Which ones could be trusted? What interest rate could the bank charge? And what rate of default could the bank tolerate?

No single entrepreneur solved all of these problems. It wasn't even clear at first what a successful credit card business would look like. Instead, the universal bank credit card evolved out of a series of innovations and trial-and-error experiences that saw banks collectively lose millions of dollars before they figured out how to make the card profitable. But the universal bank credit card turned out to be one of the most revolutionary devices in the history of consumer credit, changing the way people thought about consumption and indebtedness. Previously, only the department stores offered revolving credit, and only to their most trusted customers. Individuals seeking personal loans had to make appointments with loan officers and fill out forms whenever they needed even small amounts of money. With credit cards, bank customers could in effect give themselves loans whenever they wished, up to their credit limit.[108]

The origins of the revolutionary product were modest. In 1947, banker John C. Biggins introduced the first bank credit card, called Charge-It.[109] It was not a "universal" card; customers could use it only within a two-square block of the issuing bank, Flatbush National Bank of Brooklyn. Two years later, Alfred Bloomingdale, Frank X. McNamara, and Ralph Snyder founded Diners Club, the first multistate third-party card. McNamara was running a finance company at the time, and over lunch one day the three acquaintances began kicking around an interesting idea: what if a third party could substitute its creditworthiness for that of individuals, much like a finance company did? And what if the requestor could get credit from establishments like restaurants and stores simply by showing a form of identification—something like the charge plates that department stores were already offering in New York? The credit product the three men came up with, the Diners Club card, was the first third-party credit card that could be used in multiple travel and entertainment establishments, in multiple cities. It was designed for convenience; Diners Club did not offer revolving credit. Merchants were charged a hefty 7 percent to participate, and the cardholders paid an annual fee.[110]

At around the same time, banks began entering the credit card market in force. For the next decade or so, there was a clear line between the travel and entertainment (T&E) cards such as Diners Club, and the cards that were issued by banks. In 1951 Franklin National Bank of Long Island introduced the first all-purpose bank credit card. By the end of 1953, there were sixty credit card plans in operation throughout the country, still a very tiny proportion of the approximately 14,000 banks in operation.[111] Four major entrants among the two types of issuers added their names to the roster in 1958: American Express and Carte Blanche in the T&E field, and Chase Manhattan and Bank of America among the banks. With significant resources behind it, American Express pulled ahead of Diners Club and Carte Blanche.[112]

The next feature of the modern charge card, the revolving credit facility, was soon added. Revolving credit already existed in some department-store credit programs such as L. Bamberger and Company in New Jersey, Filene's of Boston, and New York's Bloomingdale's and Gimbels. Gimbels' customers paid a minimum of one-sixth of their credit balance and 1 percent interest charge on the balance every month. The retailers' programs provided the model for the banks, which introduced similar credit plans in 1958 and 1959.[113]

For some banks, the competition, costs, and customer default rates proved too difficult to overcome. Chase Manhattan quit the field in 1962. Bank of America was more successful, but only after it had endured setbacks. The bank first launched its BankAmericard in Fresno, California, in 1958.[114] When rumors spread that a competitor was about to enter the California market, Bank of America expanded its card quickly to other cities in the state. Within thirteen months, it had offered the card to people throughout the whole of California. The number of frauds and delinquencies escalated. At its worst, 22 percent of all accounts were delinquent, and Bank of America lost $8.8 million on the new product. Chastened, the bank pulled back and rethought its tactics, acknowledging that it had been naïve. It set up a collections department and an antifraud unit. Bank of America's large losses, although serious, had the benefit of discouraging competitors from entering the market. This lack of competition and its much improved operations allowed Bank of America to become the dominant bank credit card issuer in California, and its profits grew. In 1966, Bank of America licensed its card across the United States. (Ten years later, it changed the name to Visa.) Of course, the bank could not keep the market to itself when its venture began turning a profit. In 1967, four banks formed the California Bankcard Association, a forerunner of what two years later would become Master Charge.

Hundreds of banks, large and small, made a stab at the credit card market, usually through mass-mailing campaigns. They discovered that consumers were less sensitive than commercial borrowers to high interest rates, and that mailing people an unsolicited card rather than an application dramatically improved the uptake. The banks also realized that too many customers paid off their entire balance, thereby depriving the banks of revenue. At first, the banks thought that only 30 percent of cardholders would do this, but in fact 70 percent of customers declined to use revolving credit. In some areas of the United States, the proportion was even higher.[115] The cards' increasing popularity attracted the attention of lawmakers, and in the late 1960s Congress conducted a series of hearings on the banks' mass-mailing campaigns. The Federal Trade Commission temporarily suspended the practice in 1970, and then President Nixon extended the ban. Except for Bank of America, banks continued to face sometimes staggering losses in their credit card operations during the 1970s. Deprived of profits and facing strong competition, most banks struggled. By the early 1970s, New York banks had lost an estimated $250 million in the credit card market.[116]

Retailers remained by far the largest issuers of credit cards, which they treated as marketing devices rather than profit centers. In 1970, only 16 percent of households had bank credit cards, whereas 35 percent used cards issued by retailers and gas companies. By 1977, the proportion of households that were bank credit card users more than doubled, to 35 percent, still far short of being the majority of households.[117] Banks also had to convince retailers to accept the cards. In 1979, when J. C. Penney began letting customers pay with Visa, less than one-half of the country's major retailers took any bank cards at all. (However, many accepted American Express, which was used by their wealthiest customers and was not seen as a major competitor to their own store cards.) With costs so high, only the largest issuers stood a chance of making any profits. The issuers of bank credit cards became more concentrated, with the top fifty issuers now accounting for over half of the total business.[118]

But even so, technological upgrades to the authorization and billing systems helped to increase the number of card-issuing banks. Edward Bontems was responsible for much of the initial work on the Interbank/MasterCharge system, and Dee Hock, who ran BankAmericard from 1970 to 1984, drove the technological upgrades there. (It was Hock who came up with the modern-sounding brand name, Visa.) Card issuers competed for customers and merchants but cooperated in establishing and maintaining the payment systems. Fortunately for the banks, antitrust regulations did not apply to this kind of cooperative venture. BankAmericard was the first to establish its national processing system as a separate company, incorporated in Delaware and jointly owned by its member banks. The system soon cut approval time from four minutes to less than one minute. In 1974 more than 200 million transactions went through the system.[119] Customers now barely noticed the name of the issuing bank. All they knew was that they had a BankAmericard (Visa) or Master Charge (changed to MasterCard in 1979). Visa and Master Charge became among the most recognized and trusted brand names ever created. By 1978 more than 11,000 banks had joined one or both national credit systems.[120] Sixty million people now held a Master Charge or Visa card, and the total spending on bank credit cards versus retailers' cards became nearly equal.[121]

Discrimination and Consumer Protection

In the 1960s, the issue of credit access broadened to include racial minorities and women.[122] Some forms of borrowing had distinctive racial patterns: for example, since the 1920s installment credit had been widely available to African-Americans, who were more likely than white families to use it. Sellers were willing to extend installment credit to a wider array of people because the goods could be repossessed if buyers failed to pay. (By contrast, book credit, which neighborhood retailers extended for nondurables such as food, was more reliant on trust.)[123] But racial and ethnic minorities faced barriers in applying for any form of credit. In 1967, 70 percent of low-income consumers either had no credit accounts at all or had them with only a few retailers in low-income areas. And even in the early 1970s, race was still a standard question on credit applications. Women, too, found it difficult to access credit, which retailers typically granted only to single women. Women who were married, divorced, or separated had no credit identities of their own but instead were regarded as extensions of their husbands' financial identities. Activists targeted the issue of credit access in part because it was easier to make political gains in this arena than in others, such as job creation.[124] Giving more Americans the opportunity to borrow became a solution to the difficult problems of stagnating wages and unequal access to education and employment.

The Equal Credit Opportunity Act, passed in 1975 and made effective in 1977, forbade discrimination on the basis of sex, marital status, race, religion, national origin, or age. Lenders who rejected applicants were required to notify them in writing and explain the basis of the rejection. The law mobilized women and minorities to bring lawsuits. In the late 1970s, for example, Amoco, Mobil, and Diners Club were sued for racial discrimination. The lawsuits charged that the companies used zip codes as a proxy for race in their credit models because areas with "undesirable" zip codes were heavily populated by ethnic and racial minorities.[125]

Protecting consumer borrowers had long been the responsibility of state governments, but starting in the 1960s the momentum shifted to the federal level. The federal government began tracking revolving credit in 1968, when Congress passed the Truth in Lending Act (Title I of the Consumer Credit Protection Act). The law for the first time required lenders to state the effective annual rate of loans, whereas previously they could disguise the rate by stating it in monthly and even weekly terms. Lenders knew that most people cared a lot about the amount they paid per week or month but gave far less attention to the total amount of interest.[126] The Truth in Lending Act was the only federal law that regulated consumer interest rates at all, and it did so by requiring disclosure of the true rates.[127] Then, in 1972, Congress passed the Fair Credit Billing Act. It targeted credit card issuers in particular and required them to disclose how they assessed finance charges. The law also mandated that card issuers handle billing complaints quickly.[128]

Overall, the laws passed to protect consumers relied on disclosure to make lenders accountable. Finance charges, debtor remedies, and other key components of consumer credit remained lightly regulated.[129] Activists derided the reforms, arguing that disclosure was not enough. Consumers needed more robust protection from manipulative lenders; they also had to be shielded from their inability to judge their own capacity to repay. The debate would flare up in the coming decades, when it became clear that simply providing information did not deter people from taking on more debt than they could handle.

Mortgage Lending

During the First World War the government began allowing national banks to make mortgage loans. After the war, when labor strikes and a housing shortage threatened social unrest, the federal government became directly involved in home ownership, although in a limited way. It took over the "Own Your Own Home" campaign that was started by the U.S. Department of Labor in conjunction with private groups—the National Association of Real Estate Boards (later the National Association of Realtors) and the National Federation of Construction Industries. Businesses supported the campaign to stimulate lending to home buyers and the housing industry.[130] No financial incentives or subsidies were offered. Instead, the Labor Department distributed posters and sponsored lectures that included advice on how to obtain a mortgage. In 1921 the campaign moved to the Commerce Department. Home ownership became a policy priority for the new secretary, Herbert Hoover, who declared it to be "the foundation of a sound economic and social system."[131] Hoover became president of the Better Homes in America movement, another campaign to persuade Americans to become home owners. Vice President Calvin Coolidge was its chairman.[132]

Between 1890 and 1930, the population of the United States doubled, but the number of housing units tripled, from 10 million to 13 million. Most of the increase occurred in the 1920s, when a residential construction boom swept states such as Florida.[133] At the peak of the boom in 1925, close to a million housing units were constructed, the highest number up to that date. Nearly 40 percent of the nation's homes were mortgaged in 1920, and that figure remained fairly stable for three decades.[134] But the sheer amount of new construction meant that from 1920 to 1930 the amount of mortgage lending tripled, much of it a mixed assortment of financing arrangements.[135] The building and loan (B&L) societies led the way, fueling the construction booms and real estate speculation. Realtors and developers sat on the boards of many B&Ls, a conflict of interest that compromised their ability to fund only creditworthy borrowers. In addition, the spread of automobile ownership expanded the suburbs, giving even more opportunities to land speculators.[136] By 1929, the B&Ls accounted for one-half of all outstanding non-farm mortgage debts. Mortgage loans further increased when, in 1923, national banks were allowed to hold real estate mortgages. Mortgage companies that had started out lending to farm families increasingly became involved in urban mortgages.

149

In 1923 the Farm Mortgage Bankers Association recognized the changes by shortening its name to the Mortgage Bankers Association.[137]

Hoover continued his support of home ownership when he became president in 1929. When the real estate bubbles burst, however, the effects were dramatic and persistent: from the peak in 1925 to the trough of 1933, new housing starts dropped by over 90 percent.[138] Hoover tried to restart the construction industry by shoring up the mortgage markets. He appealed to people's (by then) well-established desire for home ownership, declaring that "they never sing songs about a pile of rent receipts." The problem, he said, was "how we can make a home available for installment purchase on terms that dignify the name credit."[139] In 1932, Hoover signed the Federal Home Loan Bank (FHLB) Act, which set up banks that were designed to discount (buy) home mortgages so that financial institutions could make more loans. The banks were modeled after the government-sponsored land banks, created in 1916, to make more loans available to farmers.[140]

Under Franklin Roosevelt (president from 1933 to 1945), the federal government gave unprecedented help to both the housing construction industry and troubled mortgage holders. In 1933, the administration created the Federal Home Owners Loan Corporation (HOLC), which intervened more directly in the foreclosure crisis than Hoover's Federal Home Loan Bank. Rather than providing capital to lenders, HOLC purchased the mortgages of people who were in danger of default and then refinanced them on easier terms. The lenders were required to accept HOLC bonds as payment, and the government guaranteed both the interest and principal of the bonds. Between 1933 and 1935, the corporation received 1.9 million applications for loan assistance, or some 40 percent of the approximately 4.8 million one-to-four family mortgaged properties. HOLC could not help all of these home owners, but it approved about half of the applications. In its peak year of 1935, HOLC held 12 percent of the country's outstanding mortgage debt, more than either life insurance companies or commercial banks.[141] About one-fifth of home owners who received aid from HOLC defaulted. But many others were able to save their homes.[142]

Hoover's FHLB and Roosevelt's HOLC were bold moves for the time, but they did not accomplish much for the housing industry, and people continued to lose their homes: from 1931 to 1935, lenders foreclosed on a quarter of a million homes per year. The production of housing units fell dramatically, and outstanding residential mortgage debt dropped for the first time since records began. From a high of $30.2 billion in 1930, outstanding mortgages fell to $27.4 billion in 1932. By the following year, nearly half of all home mortgages were in default. Thirty-three states passed laws providing some relief for delinquent mortgages, and twenty-eight passed some form of moratoria on mortgage loans.[143]

Originally, the New Deal legislation was intended to boost the construction industry and save the financial system from the threat of so many foreclosures. But the goal of expanding home ownership, which presidents Hoover and Coolidge had also embraced, soon became important, too. Congress passed the National Housing Act (NHA; 1934) the year after HOLC. The NHA was the watershed legislation of the New Deal for housing finance, establishing the foundation for much of the nation's mortgage lending for the rest of the twentieth century. The act created the Federal Housing Administration (FHA; 1936) that provided a federally backed insurance system for mortgage lenders. Insurance decreased the lenders' costs, which allowed them to offer more attractive mortgage terms.[144] Along with the new laws that helped to stabilize the country's banking system, the FHA enabled commercial banks to increase their mortgage lending substantially.[145] Under Roosevelt, Congress intensified what Hoover began with the FHLB. In 1934, it enacted the Federal Savings and Loan Insurance Corporation (FSLIC), which insured deposits and strengthened the management of the thrifts by imposing standards. The government also granted the S&Ls tax breaks. As a result, S&Ls enhanced their status as the largest source of institutional credit for single-family housing.[146]

In another bid to enlarge the funds available for mortgages, Congress in 1938 created the Federal National Mortgage Association (FNMA, or "Fannie Mae"). FNMA issued bonds and used the proceeds to purchase Federal Housing Authority and (later) Veterans Administration (VA) mortgages at full face value from lenders. FNMA then sold the mortgages to investors nationwide. With FNMA, the federal government created what the private sector could not—a national network that connected lenders, investors, and mortgage borrowers. It was the precursor to the full-fledged secondary market for mortgages that came into being during the 1960s. By insuring mortgages, buying them at par, and establishing nationwide standards for home construction, the FHA and FNMA enhanced confidence among lenders and investors, which in turn encouraged more home building.[147] FNMA's nationwide scope helped to solve the persistent problem of unequal capital availability among the different regions of the country—inefficiencies that had frustrated writers like D. M. Frederiksen as far back as the 1890s (see Chapter 3). The FHA's national maximum interest rate for mortgages finally caused rates to converge across the country. By 1940, the regional differences had dropped to 0.6 percentage points, a huge improvement from the late nineteenth century when rates could differ by nearly 4 percentage points. FNMA also helped to moderate the nation's real estate business cycles and improved liquidity for lenders. As a result of these changes, the number of mortgages for single-family homes grew rapidly beginning in the late 1930s.[148]

In the prosperous decades that followed the Second World War, the pool of capital available for mortgages from large lending institutions continued to grow, allowing lenders to reduce down payments and spread out (amortize) mortgage payments over a longer period. Until the New Deal, residential mortgage terms had been relatively short, typically five to ten years; the entire sum then had to be paid off at once, in what was known as a balloon payment. Mortgages were for a relatively small portion of a house's purchase price because most state laws restricted mortgages to 60 percent of a property's value. Building and loan societies (which in the 1930s became known as savings and loan associations, or thrifts) offered more generous payment terms of up to fifteen years. But whatever their source, mortgages carried a variable, not fixed, rate of interest, and borrowers typically had to renegotiate their loans yearly.[149] For first mortgages, interest rates averaged between 6 and 8 percent. Most people had to resort to a second or even third mortgage that carried much higher rates. The FHA's guarantees were critical to shifting mortgage rates from variable to fixed rates, a shift that did not occur in Europe. In time, fully amortized mortgages for 80 percent of a home's selling price, paid over a much longer period, became standard even for non-FHA backed loans.[150]

After the Great Depression, the federal government would no longer hesitate to help Americans buy their homes. Unlike in Europe, governments in the United States gave little support to social housing, preferring instead to focus on home ownership.[151] On June 22, 1944, President Roosevelt signed into law another landmark piece of legislation, the Servicemen's Readjustment Act, known as the GI Bill. In addition to providing returning veterans with educational grants and unemployment compensation, the bill provided loans to buy homes and start businesses. The act was both a reward for military service and a component of the government's attempt to maintain the country's economic health. Measures such as the GI Bill were designed in part to prevent a relapse into economic depression, but it ended up advancing the cause of home ownership. Ex-servicemen became among the country's largest groups of home owners. Forty-two percent of WWII veterans owned their homes by 1956, a number that compared favorably with the 34 percent of nonveteran home owners of comparable age. By the time the original GI Bill ended in 1956, it had provided 2.4 million veterans with home mortgages.[152]

FNMA and the GI Bill helped to drive a boom in housing construction, especially in the suburbs: between 1940 and 1950, the housing stock grew by 20 percent. A total of 1.7 million single-family detached homes were built in 1950 compared to only 114,000 in 1944, one year before the war ended.[153] The rate of home ownership grew dramatically. In 1940, nearly 44 percent of Americans owned their homes; twenty years later, 62 percent had become home owners.[154] They also became more indebted: in 1949 Americans spent less than 19 percent of their disposable income on mortgages; by 1967, the figure was more than 40 percent.[155] During the high-inflation years of the 1960s and 1970s, Americans' mortgage debt burdens decreased because the market value of their homes rose while the value of their debts shrank. Combined with the wide availability of fixed-rate mortgages and relatively plentiful jobs, most home owners of this period were able to afford the payments on their mortgages without much trouble.[156]

During the 1950s another innovation, private mortgage insurance, helped to encourage more mortgage lending. Mortgage insurance companies had thrived in New York during the 1920s, but they collapsed due to bad management and fraud.[157] In 1957, the Mortgage Guarantee Insurance Corporation (MGIC) was founded in Milwaukee, Wisconsin, by Max H. Karl, a former real estate attorney who came up with the idea of insuring only the top portion (the first 20 percent) of a mortgage. This innovation limited MGIC's exposure and at the same time encouraged lenders to provide financing for mortgages with less than a 20 percent down payment. People who did not qualify for FHA or VA loans, or who could not easily save the 20 percent down payment but had good jobs with steady incomes, could now have a chance at home ownership. Karl's idea made it possible for people to qualify for a mortgage with a down payment of as little as 5 percent. *Forbes* magazine described the innovation as "one of those elegantly simple ideas that make businessmen rich."[158] The private mortgage insurance business grew even faster after 1970, when Congress passed a law allowing Fannie Mae and Freddie Mac to buy mortgages that were privately (rather than federally) insured.[159] (Freddie Mac is discussed below.)

The government's New Deal programs were not universally admired. For a long time afterwards, conservative critics argued that the programs loosened lending standards to achieve the political goal of increasing the country's home ownership rate.[160] To what extent the federal programs reinforced racial discrimination was another source of controversy. The program's underwriting standards led to racial segregation because they associated "homogeneous" (white only) neighborhoods with stability and lower risk. As part of its stricter underwriting standards, the FHA came up with uniform house appraisal guidelines that relied on a geographically based rating system. Wealthier white neighborhoods were allotted the highest ratings, while poorer areas that were populated by minorities received low grades. An FHA manual of the 1930s flagged the "infiltration of inharmonious racial or nationality groups" as a risk factor, and the Home Owners Loan Corporation produced maps coding the supposedly worst areas red, a practice that became known as "redlining." Additionally, the FHA favored single-family homes rather than the multifamily dwellings that were more common in the inner cities.[161] But in any case, home-ownership rates increased among both races between 1940 and 1960: from 23 percent to 38 percent for blacks, and from 46 percent to 64 percent for whites.[162]

Enlarging the Secondary Markets

Through FNMA, the federal government continued to enlarge the national secondary markets for mortgage loans. In 1948, FNMA began buying loans that were guaranteed by the VA. A year later Prudential Federal of Salt Lake City, Utah, sold $1.5 million of FHA/VA loans to First Federal in New York—the first private, secondary-market transaction of the government-backed loans. Private entities now bought and sold the loans just like any other type of tradable asset. Insurance companies invested in the federally insured mortgages from an early date, but the pension funds, which grew much larger beginning in the late 1950s, shied away from mortgages, preferring instead to put their money in stocks and bonds. The momentum to create mortgage-backed securities that would attract the pension funds was growing, however; for various self-interested reasons, bankers, union officials, and other groups called for the government to generate more mortgage funding.[163]

In 1968, partly in response to the credit crunch that occurred a couple of years earlier, and also with the view of creating mortgage-backed securities, the Housing and Urban Development Act split FNMA into two.

One portion became a private, government-sponsored enterprise (GSE) known as Fannie Mae, whose debts could be securitized and removed from the government's balance sheet. The government gave no explicit guarantee that it would uphold the value of the underlying mortgages, but most investors assumed that it would stand behind the securities. The other portion continued the special assistance functions that FNMA had conducted, in a new entity called the Government National Mortgage Association (GNMA, or "Ginnie Mae"). Unlike the newly privatized Fannie Mae, Ginnie Mae explicitly guaranteed the timely payment of principal and interest on securities issued by lenders of FHA-insured and VA-guaranteed loans. It was Ginnie Mae that issued the first mortgage-backed securities, in 1970.[164]

The Emergency Home Finance Act of 1970 extended Fannie Mae's remit to conventional mortgages (not just the ones backed by the FHA and VA). Although there were now twice as many conventional as federally insured mortgages, there was as yet no secondary market for them. The act created the Federal Home Loan Mortgage Corporation (FHLMC, or "Freddie Mac"), a private corporation that was meant to compete with Fannie Mae and prevent it from becoming a monopoly. Lawmakers hoped that, together, the two agencies would further enlarge the secondary market for mortgages and mortgage-backed securities.[165]

In 1970, mortgage activity in the secondary markets totaled $16 billion, of which $6 billion was attributed to Fannie Mae, Ginnie Mae, and Freddie Mac. Through them, the federal government created more and more securities to sell to investors. The three agencies together became, after the U.S. Treasury, the largest issuers of debt in the nation's capital markets. By the mid-1970s Fannie Mae sometimes supplied one-half of all new mortgages in the country.[166] The agencies also introduced uniform loan documents that standardized the guidelines on mortgage insurance, down payments, and other provisions. Soon these became the norms for the entire industry.[167] Local S&Ls were among the earliest big buyers of mortgage-backed securities, which enabled them to invest outside of their localities.[168] The agency-backed securities became popular on Wall Street, especially among fixed-income investors. (However, not until 1983, with the creation of the collateralized mortgage obligation, or CMO, would pension funds begin buying large amounts of mortgage-backed securities. The creation of the CMO is discussed in chapter 5.)[169]

Developments involving the country's savings and loan industry also increased the capital available for mortgage loans. Beginning in 1963, the federal government deregulated the S&Ls and allowed them to provide more mortgage financing.[170] Traditionally, thrifts were barred from opening branches in other states; they could make mortgage loans only to their members, within a radius of fifty miles. Congress amended the tax law to let the thrifts make loans to nonmembers and widened their geographical restriction to 100 miles.[171] Other laws passed to help the S&Ls included the Interest Rate Adjustment Act (1966), which allowed S&Ls to offer interest on deposits that was one-quarter point higher than the commercial banks. Congress believed that by attracting more deposits, the S&Ls would be able to provide even more mortgage loans. Then, beginning in 1970, Freddie Mac provided a secondary mortgage market for S&L loans, making it possible for the S&Ls to expand their lending activities even when deposit growth declined, as they did later in the decade. As a result of the legislative assistance, by 1977 S&Ls and mutual savings banks together accounted for 65 percent of all residential mortgage debt outstanding. This represented a substantial increase from 1950, when they accounted for only 36 percent.[172]

The federal government engineered the explosion in mortgage financing that began with the New Deal. Its explicit and implicit guarantees underpinned the development of a deep and liquid secondary market in mortgages, which in turn encouraged private entities, including some of the largest Wall Street institutions, to participate aggressively in these markets. S&Ls, too, were helped by tax breaks and preferential legislation. The government's direct and indirect subsidies of the mortgage markets had a predictable result: the amount of mortgages outstanding exploded, from $55 billion in 1950 to $1.2 trillion in January 1980. The mortgage markets now made up the world's largest capital market, larger than all of the U.S. stock markets combined.[173]

Inclusion in the government's programs spread to disadvantaged Americans. In 1968, President Lyndon Johnson proposed the establishment of the Department of Housing and Urban Development (HUD). "Homeownership is a cherished dream and achievement of most Americans," he stated, echoing the campaigns that Herbert Hoover had supported during the First World War. But, Johnson added, "it has always been out of reach of the nation's low-income families. Owning a home can increase responsibility and stake out a man's place in his community. The man who owns a home has something to be proud of and good reason to protect and preserve it." Until the 1960s FHA loans concentrated on newly built homes, and the profile of a typical FHA-loan recipient was not so different from one who had a conventional mortgage. The Department of Housing and Urban Development (HUD) initiated Section 235, a short-lived program that provided direct subsidies to the private sector to create mortgages for low-income people. Section 235 collapsed under allegations of fraud, but the mortgage-backed security that was created to fund it survived.[174] By 1970, the FHA was serving lower-income buyers.[175] Another legislative initiative was the Home Mortgage Disclosure Act of 1975 requiring lending institutions to make public the data on their loans. Disclosure, so the thinking went, would reveal whether financial institutions were meeting the mortgage needs of people in their communities. The data would identify which areas needed more public funding, and whether financial institutions engaged in discriminatory practices.[176] Congress intended the laws to end the practice of redlining, which discouraged ethnic minorities from buying homes in certain neighborhoods, and to pressure lenders to provide financial services to underserved communities.

Business Credit

Consumer credit receives the lion's share of attention during this stage in the country's history, and rightly so. But business credit was evolving, too. Businesses began exploiting the massive assets that they held as accounts receivable by turning to specialist sales finance companies and factors. Businesses also turned more frequently to the money markets for funding, by issuing commercial paper. Both of these trends hurt banks, whose loans to businesses fell.[177] Academics and business writers became more aware of how much trade credit there was in the economy and raised questions about the threat this posed to economic stability. Finance scholars began rethinking the nature of corporate debt. Their work helped to take some of the stigma out of borrowing to fund activities such as mergers, acquisitions, and leveraged buyouts.

Sales Finance Companies and Factors

In the 1920s, the term "factor" began to describe firms that made loans secured by receivables, or who bought the receivables of other companies outright, at a discount. (Earlier in the century, factors were almost exclusively in the textile industry.) The business-to-business installment notes they handled arose out of the sale of industrial machinery or furnishings for retail establishments.[178] When they bought receivables, the factors took on the task of managing the accounts and chasing late payers, in effect allowing companies to outsource their credit back-offices. Factors also assumed the risks of nonpaying accounts.[179] Small- and medium-sized businesses made up the bulk of the factors' clients. By providing key services at a reasonable price, factors allowed these smaller concerns to overcome their disadvantages versus big firms.[180] Factoring spread, and by the mid-1930s their total annual business was conservatively estimated at $1 billion. The types of clients they served expanded, too. From being dominated by textile firms, the customer base began to include companies that dealt in shoes, petroleum, furs, lumber, rubber, metal, paper products—and, of course, cars. In 1933, automobile retail and wholesale paper accounted for 90 percent of all receivables purchased.[181]

Sales finance companies also multiplied. They loaned money that was backed by the borrowers' accounts receivable, or they bought the accounts receivables outright.[182] Accounts receivable were a huge asset for companies, but with a few exceptions, businesses had not been able to use the asset as collateral for loans. Commercial banks shunned this potentially lucrative business because the Federal Reserve did not discount paper that was backed by accounts receivables.[183] Intermediaries such as the sales finance companies took advantage of the underexploited market; they used their own creditworthiness to obtain funds from banks or investors and then loaned the money to their clients. Most sales finance companies specialized in products such as furniture and electrical appliances and used their expertise to identify the most creditworthy borrowers.[184]

At the end of the 1950s, there were around 400 companies that specialized in commercial financing and factoring. Sales finance companies handled approximately $6.5 billion in loans, three times the volume of ten years earlier; factoring firms purchased an additional $5 billion of receivables for a combined total of $11.5 billion.[185] Major industrial companies, such as GM, GE, and Westinghouse, and retailers, such as Sears, created finance subsidiaries that helped consumers purchase the companies' products. The captive finance companies became important profit centers for their corporate parents and helped to ease the adoption of new products by customers.[186] *Fortune* magazine counted 102 "nationally significant" credit subsidiaries of major companies at the end of the 1950s, whereas only fourteen existed before 1946.[187]

Sales finance companies became known for their innovative approach to small businesses, partly because they were lightly regulated compared to commercial banks.[188] Walter E. Heller and Company was one such finance company. It was established in 1919, and by the late 1950s was involved in both financing and factoring. Heller borrowed from banks at

6 percent or less and used the funds to provide financing and factoring services to its clients.[189] Once they established a good track record, Heller's clients could borrow directly from the banks; but in the meantime, intermediaries such as Heller were an acceptable alternative. Unlike in the past, businesses that sold or assigned their accounts receivables to finance companies were no longer seen as disreputable, on the edge of bankruptcy, or both.[190]

First National Bank of Boston, Bank of America, and other commercial banks entered the factoring business, but they were rare exceptions. Most banks stayed away from buying a firm's accounts receivables because they did not see themselves as being in the business of managing and collecting trade debts. The way banks determined creditworthiness was also different: they looked at applicants' balance sheets and used asset-to-liabilities ratios to determine whether the business qualified for a loan. Heller, in contrast, scrutinized the creditworthiness of its clients' customers. The clients also benefited because Heller supplied long-term financing, which commercial banks would not. As Walter E. Heller himself explained, "Once it's resolved that the idea of the business makes sense and the people involved are good moral risks . . . the mechanics of the financing can be worked out 90 per cent of the time."[191] Companies such as Heller benefited from the healthy postwar business climate, in which government continued to buy from industry, and consumer demand was high. Businesses were willing to accept the higher rates charged by the sales finance companies, and the finance companies were happy to lend to higher-risk businesses because they were confident that borrowers could repay their loans.[192]

Trade Credit

Unlike consumer credit, trade credit received scant attention from researchers and policy makers. Then, in 1964, Martin H. Seiden published an eye-opening study for NBER that revealed the true scale of business-to-business lending.[193] Some of his findings seemed counterintuitive. A *Fortune* magazine piece on Seiden's work, published a year earlier, reported that trade credit expanded even when the economy slowed. In the recession of 1954, trade credit grew by $4.1 billion even though total sales volume fell by $15.2 billion. Bank credit, by contrast, did what one would expect—it fell by $300 million during the recession. In the boom year of 1955, when the government tightened the money supply (thereby forcing businesses to rely more on credit), trade credit increased by $10.7 billion, whereas bank credit expanded by only $6.3 billion. All of this suggested

Table 4.2. Corporate businesses, excluding farms and financial firms, trade receivables ($ billions), 1945–1990

Year	Trade receivables ($ billions)
1945	19.8
1950	38.6
1960	82.3
1970	191.4
1980	529.4
1990	967.2
% change 1945–1990	4,884.8%

Source: Historical Statistics of the United States, Millennial Edition On Line, ed. Susan B. Carter et al. (Cambridge: © [copyright] Cambridge University Press, 2006), pp. 3–806.

that trade credit was substituting for bank loans to some extent. Between 1951 and 1961, trade credit grew much faster (100 percent) than both sales (37 percent) and GNP (58 percent, all in current dollars).[194]

Seiden's study confirmed what scholars suspected and what factors and finance companies had long known: accounts receivable formed a substantial part of firms' balance sheets—fully one-third of the assets of all nonfinancial firms, according to the study. Still, even Seiden seemed surprised by the scale of it. At the end of 1962, there was about $111 billion in trade credit outstanding in the U.S. economy. "This sum," he wrote, "exceeded the volume of . . . corporate bonds and state and local securities; it was twice the volume of consumer credit outstanding, and far exceeded the business lending of the entire commercial banking system." All the more reason, then, to be worried when the quality of trade credit deteriorated. Overall, trade credit functioned smoothly after the war because businesses found it relatively easy to pay their debts. By the late 1950s, however, trade debt overall had deteriorated in quality, and the number of business failures rose. From only 14 per 10,000 firms in 1947, the business failure rate climbed to 61 per 10,000 by 1962. Seiden estimated that over 9 per cent of all failures in the postwar period resulted from the inability of firms to collect their accounts receivables. Trade credit losses totaled one billion dollars a year, more than the volume of bad-debt losses of all other forms of credit combined.[195] As with consumer credit, academic researchers worried about the effect trade credit had on the business cycle. (See Table 4.2.)

Bonds

Common stock became a more popular form of financing for businesses during the bull market of the mid-1950s, but debt was still the preferred option by far. The amount of corporate bonds issued, for example, was four times the amount of stocks.[196] And, as had been the case for most of the nation's history, loans equalled or exceeded stocks and bonds. But although corporate borrowing rose, most executives in the 1960s and 1970s continued to be conservative about debt: they believed that interest payments should be no more than one-sixth of operating profits. Businesses achieved growth primarily through reinvesting earnings rather than borrowing, even though interest on debt was tax deductible. Perhaps the Great Depression and war had instilled caution in this generation of executives. Whatever the cause, they approached debt warily rather than seeing it as an opportunity to be exploited or a financial tool that could be "engineered."[197]

Unconventional ways of thinking about business credit had surfaced, however. In the early 1920s Clarence Dillon outbid J. P. Morgan for the Dodge car company using techniques of discounted cash flow and net present value.[198] The event helped to legitimize the notion that credit extended to a business could be based on future earning capacity.[199] The idea that credit should be widely available to business to foster economic growth began making headway in academia during the 1950s. While most thinkers were preoccupied by the destabilizing effects of trade and consumer credit, economists Franco Modigliani and Merton Miller were asking very different questions about corporate debt. In a series of papers first published in 1958, they argued that how a firm was financed—whether through equity, debt, or retained earnings—made little difference to its market value.[200] Although not an endorsement of debt financing, the papers helped to take the stigma out of corporate debt.

The genesis of the leveraged buyout (LBO, in which buyers use debt to take a company private) was the "bootstrap acquisitions" of the 1960s. Banker Jerome Kohlberg invented this type of deal while at Bear Stearns in order to help the owners of family firms to pass on their companies to their heirs without paying huge estate taxes or losing family control. Kohlberg's first deal in 1965 was the acquisition of Stern Metals, a dental product maker, for $9.5 million.[201] Starting in the 1970s, Kohlberg, Kravis, and Roberts (KKR) sought to help the managers of conglomerates both to acquire businesses and sell off unprofitable divisions. Adventurous corporate executives were trying to improve their stock price-to-earnings (p/e) ratios by putting together conglomerates, using debt to acquire growing companies outside of their core businesses. By loading a company with debt, managers could shrink the equity portion of its capital structure, which they could then buy up. On the other side, corporate divestitures also increased, accounting for 53 percent of all transactions in 1977.[202] These activities were precursors of the much larger leveraged deals that would help to restructure entire industries in the 1980s and 1990s.

Bankruptcy and Debt Collection

By the second decade of the twentieth century, the idea that federal bankruptcy laws should ease the burden on business debtors had become mainstream. A 1915 Supreme Court decision, *Williams v. U.S. Fidelity*, typified the new attitude. The Court held that the bankruptcy laws were intended to give honest debtors the chance "to start afresh free from the obligations and responsibilities consequent upon business misfortunes." Subsequent decisions reinforced the idea that honest but unfortunate business debtors should be protected. *Local Loan Company v. Hunt* (1934), for example, held that debtors who had declared bankruptcy were not obliged to give over their earnings to pay off a loan against which they had pledged their future wages.[203] For business creditors, debt collection became more routinized, and fewer cases reached the courts. Private settlement mechanisms such as adjustment bureaus allowed creditors to coordinate among themselves to help distressed debtors. The National Association of Credit Men (NACM) continued to establish adjustment bureaus in major towns and cities. By 1922 the NACM recognized eighty-four bureaus around the country.[204]

Bankruptcy filings historically had been dominated by business owners, but the expansion of consumer credit during the 1920s resulted in a dramatic rise in filings by ordinary wage earners. Creditors expected to gain little by pursuing these asset-poor debtors, and unscrupulous lawyers were frequently able to obtain unlawful discharges for them. The abuses drove President Hoover to appoint a commission to investigate the issue. The commission recommended the establishment of an administrative staff, empowered to reject requests for discharges from debtors who were able to pay their debts.[205] During the Depression, however, Congress once again liberalized the bankruptcy laws. Wage earners and farmers could now seek voluntary arrangements with their creditors to repay their debts over a longer period.[206]

The Hoover report also recommended adding new procedures for corporate reorganization to the national bankruptcy law. In 1933, Congress finally passed amendments to codify equity receiverships, the arrangement that had been in use for distressed railroads since the late nineteenth century. Further amendments affected nearly the entire corporate sector. Earlier laws had required unanimous consent among creditors for a reorganization plan, causing problems if even one creditor objected. Further, any three creditors could force a company into liquidation. The amendments divided creditors into classes and allowed reorganization if just two-thirds of each class voted for it.[207] Wall Street hailed the amendments for solving the problem of corporate restructurings across state lines.

The Securities and Exchange Act of 1934 initiated an investigation of the committees that oversaw the restructuring of railroads. Since the late nineteenth century, incumbent management and investment bankers had made up the committees, leading to suspicion that they manipulated the restructurings to suit their interests. The investigations resulted in wide-ranging reforms. Chapter X of the Chandler Act, passed in 1938, required companies that were undergoing reorganization to hand the management of the business to a trustee. (The new rules initially deprived the investment bankers of a lucrative advisory business, but the setback was temporary. Congress later reversed many of the provisions and reinstated the previous practices.)[208] The Chandler Act gave distressed debtors the option of reorganizing or seeking an arrangement.[209] With the Chandler Act, American bankruptcy law attained its modern characteristics. It covered both businesses and individuals, including ordinary wage earners; it allowed both involuntary and voluntary bankruptcy; and it gave to filers the choice of a discharge or an arrangement with their creditors.[210]

After passage of the Chandler Act, the typical filer shifted from being a business to being an individual consumer. Thirty-five percent of bankruptcy filings were by wage earners when the law was enacted, but by 1958, wage earners accounted for 85 percent. This increase was partly because the business bankruptcy rate fell sharply, halving in the period from 1934 to 1988 compared to the previous sixty years.[211] Concerned about the rise in personal filings, Congress in 1968 created a commission to recommend how to update the bankruptcy laws. The commission's report came out in 1973 and formed the basis for the sweeping 1978 overhaul of the national bankruptcy law that became known as the Bankruptcy

Code. By then, the consumer protection movement had changed the terms of the debate. Lawmakers were now less concerned about the moral effects of debt and focused instead on whether creditors were behaving fairly toward debtors. The Fair Debt Collection Practices Act of 1977, for example, made harassment by collection agencies illegal and enhanced the ability of debtors to defend themselves.[212] Unlike with previous national bankruptcy laws, Congress passed the Bankruptcy Code in the absence of a severe economic downturn.[213] The code preserved the options available to corporate and individual debtors in the Chandler Act but encouraged debtors to file under Chapter 13, which allowed creditors to recoup more of their loans and debtors to preserve more of their creditworthiness.[214]

Even before the Bankruptcy Act of 1978, the bankruptcy process had undergone profound technical changes. Far fewer disputes between debtors and creditors now ended up in court. Standardized language in loan agreements covered nearly every situation that might occur so that disputes were minimized. Creditors had access to more insurance products that protected them against debtor default. Then, too, the expansion of the welfare state improved people's income security, so illness and job layoffs no longer automatically led to defaults. People's more stable income stream made creditors willing to settle for reduced payments rather than try to attach debtors' assets. Creditors were now more likely to be large, diverse institutions that were insured against losses and could consider bad debts as just a cost of doing business or even as tax write-offs.[215] Statistical calculations and administrative routines replaced the moral obligations that had traditionally tied creditors to debtors.

Credit Reporting

In 1933, R.G. Dun and its closest competitor, the Bradstreet Company, merged to form the world's largest credit-reporting firm. The amount of information on publicly listed companies increased dramatically after the creation of the Securities and Exchange Commission (1934), which required public firms to file annual and quarterly financial statements. But Dun and Bradstreet (D&B) remained one of the few national sources of information for private firms and sole proprietorships.

Consumer credit bureaus continued to proliferate in most cities, reflecting the strong growth in installment buying. By 1927, there were some 800 bureaus operating around the country.[216] Typical information in credit files included missed payments, bankruptcies, mortgages, liens on property, and marital status. As more people held salaried jobs in corporations, credit bureaus began paying more attention to the reputation of employers as an indicator of creditworthiness. The industry's trade associations helped to establish common standards of rating, so the data among the different bureaus was comparable. But information sharing among them was still limited.[217]

The small, local nature of consumer credit bureaus reflected the buying habits of ordinary people. Unlike businesses, consumers tended to do most of their shopping within a limited geographical area. The small scale of the bureaus made their managers vulnerable to criticism. In his 1938 treatise on consumer credit, M. R. Neifeld described the bureaus' methods as being "only reasonably effective." Bureau managers were not specialists and so had limited ability to distinguish between good and bad risks. They put too much emphasis on credit applicants' payment records and paid too little attention to their current condition and prospects.[218] Such criticisms did not slow the growth of the bureaus. By 1955, the membership of the Association of Credit Bureaus numbered about 1,600. (It would peak at 2,200 in 1965.) The ACB standardized reporting and helped their members obtain information from retailers such as Sears, which began computerizing its data in the 1950s. By 1960, the ACB's members collectively achieved national coverage of the nation's consumers. But even then, the largest bureaus maintained files across only a handful of cities. ACB members exchanged some information, and the industry achieved notoriety for its surveillance capabilities. But from the perspective of a truly national system of information exchange, there was scope to do much more.[219]

Scale was the key to making computerization affordable. When ACB members began consolidating in the mid-1960s, the credit bureaus in Los Angeles, New York, and San Francisco succeeded in computerizing their files. In 1969, Credit Data, a for-profit credit bureau owned by the conglomerate TRW, began shifting to computers. TRW Credit Data set up a mainframe computer with some 50 million credit files. It sold the information to lenders on condition that they shared their own data with TRW.[220] Large credit-reporting firms such as TRW Credit Data pioneered computerization because their own biggest users expected to be able to transmit and obtain information electronically. Equifax, one of the emerging Big Three firms within the industry, automated all of its files by 1970. By the 1980s Equifax, TRW Credit Data (which had changed its name to TRW Information Systems and Intelligence), and TransUnion each achieved universal coverage of consumer borrowers.[221]

The expanded coverage of the Big Three credit-reporting firms mirrored the changes in the retail sector, where the large chain stores were becoming national businesses. These retailers often had credit departments regionally or in their large branches. When they consolidated the credit function into their headquarters, they shifted from local credit bureaus to the Big Three. Banks, with their growing credit card networks, were another set of information sharing systems that were becoming national in scope. They, too, began sharing their data with the Big Three. Consumer credit reporting had begun as a fragmented, locally based activity that was an adjunct of the selling function rather than a money-making activity in its own right. By the 1970s, consumer credit reporting was dominated by a few large, for-profit firms that worked with the national retailers and banks to amass information on individuals.[222]

Modern credit scoring, the assessment of creditworthiness through statistical analysis of data, began in 1958, when Fair, Isaac and Company introduced the precursor to what would become the FICO score. Fair, Isaac's early product consisted of manually tallied scorecards. Almost no one wanted it at first; of the top fifty banks and finance companies, only one, the Louisiana-based American Investment finance company, showed any interest. Fair, Isaac developed credit scorecards for American Investment's population of customers in Louisiana. The customers answered a set of questions, and each answer was given a point value. The points were added up to produce the person's credit score. Crucially, American Investment could compare an individual's score against the outcomes of loans made to its larger population of customers to determine the probability of default. American Investment was evidently pleased by the results. It requested Fair, Isaac to develop a nationwide system, which was completed in 1960. Other types of creditors soon adopted the scoring system. Retailers (Montgomery Ward was an early client), oil companies, then the issuers of travel and entertainment cards used credit scoring to manage their accounts.[223]

By the late 1960s, the use of consumer credit reports by lenders was so ubiquitous that people who lacked credit histories found it nearly impossible to borrow: banks would not lend to them, and retailers declined their credit applications. Access to credit became a political issue that the civil rights and women's movements helped to inflame. But even as women and minority groups clamored to be included in the credit-reporting firms' files, consumer advocates demanded regulations to restrict the ways credit information could be used. As early as the 1920s utility companies, law enforcement entities, and landlords applied to the credit bureaus for information; employers and marketers would later do so, too. Fears about surveillance increased when magazines such as *Time* ran stories about how the credit bureaus could now easily discover people's private lives and past mistakes.[224] Yet it was many decades before privacy concerns led Congress to act. In 1970 it passed the Fair Credit Reporting Act, the first law to explicitly target the information industry in the United States. The law limited the types of information that could be reported on individuals, as well as the purposes for which the information could be used. But the issue of privacy remained contentious, and consumer activists such as Ralph Nader attacked the industry for its lack of safeguards.[225]

Bonds and Credit Rating

Bond rating had a slower start in the United States than did credit reporting. U.S. railroad bonds had been traded on exchanges since the 1850s, but bond-rating services did not appear until much later.[226] At the beginning of the twentieth century, entrepreneurs founded businesses to serve stock and bond investors. These included John Moody and Company (1901), Roger Babson's Stock and Bond Card System (1903), and Luther Lee Black's Standard Statistics Bureau (1906). The first stock- and bond-rating service, however, appeared only in 1909, when John Moody created the *Analyses of Railroad Investments,* using rating symbols that were copied from the older credit-reporting firms. The symbols, AAA to DD, became standard for the bond credit-rating business. Poor's Publishing issued its first ratings of stocks and bonds in 1916 using essentially the same rating system as Moody's.[227]

The First World War changed the American capital markets and created more business for the new credit-rating agencies. The federal government issued a huge amount of public debt, war bonds that were sold in massive numbers to both seasoned American investors and ordinary citizens.[228] Moody's began rating U.S. government and municipal securities in 1918. It also compiled a separate rating book on securities that were issued outside of North America. By 1924, Moody's was rating nearly all U.S. corporate bonds, and two years later it created a formal rating department. Competition appeared when Standard Statistics entered the rating field in 1922, and Fitch (established in 1913) published its *Bond Rating Book* a year later.[229]

A combination of factors contributed to the growing authority of the rating agencies, despite the uneven quality of their services. Between 1929 and 1937, a wave of state and municipal bond defaults hit investors. More than 90 percent of the municipal bonds (by dollar volume) had been rated Aaa or Aa in 1929.[230] The corporate bond default rate rose, too: from less than 1 percent in 1930, it increased to between 6 and 7 percent in 1933.[231] There were, as well, a number of very high-profile corporate bond frauds, such as the scandals around the Swedish "Match King," Ivan Kreuger, and utilities and railroads magnate Samuel Insull.[232] Even so, when Congress passed laws to reform the way information was reported to the capital markets, the regulators incorporated ratings into the new regulations. For example, the comptroller of the currency specified that bonds rated Baa/BBB and above could be carried on the issuer's books at cost, but lower-rated bonds had to be recorded at their current market value. State regulators then adopted similar rules. Credit rating thus became enshrined in law and in the bond markets. The authority of the credit-rating agencies also grew simply because they served the bond markets in the United States, which collectively were the world's largest.[233]

Poor's merged with Standard Statistics Company in 1941 to form Standard and Poor (S&P). S&P became a public company in 1962 and was acquired by McGraw-Hill in 1966 through a share swap. Dun & Bradstreet bought Moody's in 1962.[234] S&P, Moody's, and Fitch progressively rated more types of investments, nearly all of them American in origin.

Over the years, a number of studies assessed the effectiveness of credit-rating agencies. In 1958 W. Braddock Hickman, director of the Corporate Bond Research Project at NBER, oversaw the first major study to assess the performance of corporate bond rating. Hickman praised the agencies' "remarkably good" record in gauging the risk of default. They made some mistakes, but on the whole the corporate bonds rated as high-grade defaulted at lower rates than low-grade bonds. (However, Hickman was less impressed by the agencies' success in rating municipal bonds before and during the Great Depression.)[235] Congress initiated hearings on the agencies whenever bonds experienced unusual downgrades, as happened with New York City's bonds in the mid-1960s. The hearings focused on the agencies' methods and their impact. But none of the hearings resulted in legislation. The twenty-five-year period that followed the end of the Second World War was economically stable, and there were very few bond defaults: between 1945 and 1965, the default rate of corporate

The pioneers of credit reporting, credit rating, and credit scoring. Lewis Tappan (a) founded the Mercantile Agency, a precursor of Dun and Bradstreet, in 1841; John Moody (b) began analyzing the stocks and bonds of America's railroads in 1909; Bill Fair and Earl Isaac (c) established Fair, Isaac and Company, the inventor of the FICO score, in 1956. *Sources:* Lewis Tappan, photograph 81.635 from Portraits of American Abolitionists, Collection of the Massachusetts Historical Society; John Moody, photograph, NYT/Redux/ eyevine © New York Times; Bill Fair and Earl Isaac, photograph courtesy of Fair Isaac Corporation.

bonds was less than 0.1 percent of outstanding debt. Higher corporate earnings and the introduction of term loans by commercial banks meant that bonds came to account for a smaller portion of corporate financing during this period.[236] There was therefore little cause to castigate the agencies.

*　　*　　*

From the 1920s to the Second World War, private and public reforms transformed the basis for consumer and mortgage lending. Reformers in the private sector lobbied to raise the state usury laws, arguing that higher rates would entice more lenders to make loans to low-income consumers. The New Deal programs that helped to stabilize the economy during the Great Depression ended up radically changing people's mortgage terms and the mortgage markets themselves. Begun as emergency measures, the government's policies shifted. Increasing home ownership—and by implication, mortgage financing—became the goal of American public policy.

During the three decades of affluence and economic stability that followed the war, the suppliers and users of mortgage and consumer credit resisted attempts to constrain growth. The federal government deliberately enlarged the secondary markets for mortgage-backed securities through the government-sponsored enterprises, Fannie Mae, Ginnie Mae, and Freddie Mac. Stoking demand for these investment products became the key to financing the American dream of home ownership. Once the subsidies began, everyone was incentivized both to create and take on more mortgage debt.[237] In later federal laws such as the Community Reinvestment Act (1977), the government compelled banks and savings associations to provide more services, including mortgage financing, to residents in disadvantaged communities. The federal government further shaped Americans' borrowing habits with the establishment of student loan programs. Beginning in 1957, government-backed loans transformed how young people and their parents thought about debt. (Student loans are discussed in Chapter 5.) Perhaps inevitably, the number of personal bankruptcies rose dramatically.

Innovations also occurred in trade credit. Businesses unlocked the value of their accounts receivables by turning to the sales finance companies and factors. Smaller concerns were now able to borrow against their accounts receivable or sell them outright, which enhanced their cash flows.

After the war, academics and policy makers worried that the huge and growing supply of consumer and trade credit could potentially destabilize the economy. But at the same time, academics began rethinking the nature of corporate finance, and a few even questioned whether relying on debt was any better or worse than using retained earnings to accomplish corporate objectives. Proponents of consumer credit subverted traditional thinking by suggesting that installment credit had a disciplining effect on borrowers. (These two ideas—that debt was just like any other form of funding, and that the pressure of debt regulates and focuses borrowers—would be taken up by the corporate raiders of the 1980s.) The new ways of thinking set the stage for the explosion of credit that occurred during the last two decades of the twentieth century.

Chapter Five

"CHILDREN, DOGS, CATS, AND MOOSE ARE GETTING CREDIT CARDS"

The Erosion of Credit Standards

In the 1980s, the amount of credit available to American governments, businesses, and households became vast—so immense that it had no counterpart to the experiences of previous generations. Historically, the growing savings of American businesses and individuals and investment from abroad had provided the basis for ever more credit. But nothing matched the massive increase, in absolute terms, that began around the late 1970s. (See Table 5.1.) Looking just at bank lending gives some idea of the scale of the increase: in the century from the 1870s to the 1970s, the ratio of bank loans to gross domestic product was 40 percent to 50 percent. But afterwards, bank loans grew until they were as large as the nation's GDP.[1]

A linked cluster of events explains why the United States saw such a huge amount of credit creation. The low inflation of the postwar period came to an end in 1970, when the inflation rate hit 6 percent and rapidly began climbing. With the oil crisis in 1974, Americans experienced the first double-digit inflation since 1947. Inflation again went above the 10 percent mark in 1979–1981.[2] The cost of credit rose, too: in December 1980, the prime rate hit 21.5 percent, a staggeringly high price by the standards of any peacetime period in the nation's history.

High inflation, along with continuing improvements in information technology, destabilized the financial regime that had been in place since the end of the Second World War. An ideology that pushed for freer markets gained ground, accelerating the changes. At the same time, and somewhat at odds with the support for free markets, the popular conviction

Table 5.1. Credit market debt securities, selected sectors ($ billions), 1945–1990

Year	U.S. government securities	Commercial paper/bankers' acceptances	Corporate/ foreign bonds	Bank loans (not elsewhere classified)	Mortgages	Consumer credit
1945	252.4	0.3	26.9	11.4	35.7	6.8
1950	218.4	1.3	40.9	26.0	72.8	23.9
1960	242.8	6.5	91.8	58.3	207.9	61.2
1970	341.6	40.2	204.3	154.8	471.4	133.7
1980	1,008.3	163.8	508.4	458.5	1,462.2	355.4
1990	3,911.7	609.9	1,705.7	820.0	3,800.8	805.1
% change 1945–1990*	1,550.0%	203,300.0%	6,340.9%	7,193.0%	10,646.5%	11,840.0%

* For comparison, the population of the United States increased by around 90 percent during the period 1940–1990.
Source: Historical Statistics of the United States, Millennial Edition On Line, ed. Susan B. Carter et al. (Cambridge: © [copyright] Cambridge University Press, 2006), pp. 3–789.

that the federal government should support home ownership intensified. The twin ideals of less regulated markets and expanded home ownership resulted in the government liberalizing some financial markets while increasing its subsidies of mortgage lending. It also enlarged dramatically the secondary markets for mortgage-backed securities.

Higher inflation, volatile interest rates, better information technology, liberalized markets, and federal support for mortgage lending gave financial institutions the incentives to invent new credit and debt instruments. Some of the instruments were risky, but regulators declined to put obstacles in the way of innovation. At any rate, creative bankers and their lawyers found ways around most regulations. One result was a marked deterioration in the assets that backed lending. In the case of credit cards, the credit was not even secured at all.

For ordinary people, federal deposit insurance and other protections took away the urgent need to monitor what their banks were doing. So did the strong possibility that the Federal Reserve and Treasury would step in to prevent large financial institutions, including Fannie Mae, Ginnie Mae, and Freddie Mac, from going under. Commercial banks and S&Ls, facing new competition and threatened with crippling losses, successfully lobbied for permission to make riskier loans and invest in new financial products. From having 60 to 70 percent of their assets in safe government securities in 1950, banks ended up holding almost no such securities in the 2000s.[3] Instead, their balance sheets became laden with assets that promised greater returns, but whose riskiness was often exponentially higher.

The dramatic rise of Japan, South Korea, China, and other export-led economies was another contributing factor. These countries depended on the U.S. and western European markets to absorb the goods that they were churning out in greater and greater quantities. Americans proved to be the world's most willing consumers, and the federal government mostly declined to impose high tariffs on the imports. The nation as a whole consumed beyond its means, and its trade deficit with countries such as China widened. Determined to keep their own currencies low relative to the dollar, and also driven by the wish to build up their dollar reserves, the export powerhouses bought U.S. debt instruments in huge quantities. They enabled Americans to obtain mortgages, home equity loans, car loans, and other consumer credit at relatively low interest rates.

The story of credit was, of course, also one of demand—of the willingness to borrow by American businesses, consumers, and governments.

Indebtedness came to be regarded as normal and even prudent. Fears that large corporate bankruptcies might destabilize the financial system made the government willing to step in to prevent defaults. Academic theorists, many of them believers in free markets, began changing their calculations of business risk, and corporations and financial institutions were only too happy to adopt the new views. Pressures on the federal government to provide mortgage loans to lower-income households led Congress and successive presidential administrations to encourage more credit creation for mortgage lending. The massive quantities of credit pushed lenders to work harder to find borrowers, including ones who did not meet traditional standards of creditworthiness. When demand for credit weakened, lenders stimulated it through marketing campaigns and government lobbying.

It is worth looking more closely at each of these developments while bearing in mind that they were intertwined in complex ways. The federal government's support of mortgage markets is a particularly important development that is treated in a separate section later in this chapter.

Volatile Inflation and Interest Rates

After the Second World War, interest rates remained mostly stable for two decades. In the 1950s, the interest rates on three-month Treasury bills were between 1 percent and 3.5 percent. Beginning in the 1960s, and especially during the 1970s and 1980s, interest rates fluctuated much more—between 4 percent and 15 percent.[4] Inflation spiked higher, too, when President Richard Nixon took the United States off the gold standard, effectively ending the Bretton Woods agreement that had been in place since 1944. Bretton Woods had helped to stabilize the world's monetary and currency regimes, and its demise resulted in the devaluation of the U.S. dollar. (One effect was that the oil-exporting countries, deprived of purchasing power because oil is valued in dollars, raised their prices significantly.)[5]

High inflation along with higher and more volatile interest rates profoundly affected the credit markets. Bank and S&L depositors were no longer content with earning the legal maximum of 6 percent that Regulation Q had set during the Depression. Many depositors instead placed their funds in the money markets, which were exempt from the interest-rate ceilings. Money markets had existed since the nineteenth century and were used by businesses and governments to lend and to borrow large amounts of money for short-term needs. (Businesses did this by issuing

175

commercial paper.) Now, mutual funds—professionally managed investment funds with diversified holdings—were available to ordinary savers, allowing them to participate in the money markets where the lure of higher yields proved irresistible. The proportion of deposits held in commercial banks shrank dramatically, from one-half in 1949 to just one-third by 1979.[6] In losing their depositors, banks lost their cheap source of loanable funds. The model of paying a low interest rate to their depositors and then lending the money at a slightly higher interest rate had for decades ensured steady profits for the banks. Now the model was changing, just at the time that banks faced greater competition from other financial service institutions.

The more volatile interest rates also made it very difficult for both lenders and borrowers to plan ahead. Financial institutions, ever alert to opportunities, came up with new products to manage the uncertainty. Adjustable-rate mortgages, for example, caught on in the early 1980s because they enabled lenders to escape the rigidities of long-term fixed-rate mortgages. Other innovations included the negotiable order of withdrawal (NOW) account, which was invented to skirt the ban imposed by Regulation Q.[7] To hedge risks, institutions used financial derivatives. The instruments became more and more complicated, and financial institutions competed to create derivatives that promised to eliminate risks for investors.[8] Big financial firms began making deals to take on each other's credit risks. In 1982 they came up with interest-rate swaps, where (for example) one party traded a floating rate of interest for another party's fixed rate of interest. The existence of a large interest-rate swap market meant that debts had become a tradable commodity, much like any other asset.[9]

Perhaps most significantly, the volatile interest rates transformed the bond markets. Bond prices are closely tied to interest rates, and once the rates began to fluctuate, so did bond prices. Suddenly, a market that was known for being safe and boring became interesting to speculators.[10] As the asset-backed and mortgage-backed bonds issued by American governments and businesses gained popularity with investors all over the world, a familiar pattern emerged: the makers of the securities (Wall Street, in this case) were driven to produce more of them. That meant that the raw materials—home mortgages, auto loans, and credit card charges—that underlay these securities had to increase, too.

Improved Information Technology

New information technology made the gathering and dissemination of information faster and cheaper. Financial institutions harnessed the technology to enlarge the market for products like credit cards. Improved technology also gave investors access to better information about corporations: they became more willing to take risks on firms that until that point had not been as visible as the Fortune 100 or the Dow Jones industrials. Markets, such as the one for commercial paper, grew larger as information became easier to obtain and the speed of trading accelerated. From $33 billion outstanding in 1970, the commercial paper market grew to more than $2.2 trillion outstanding by 2006.[11] Technology transformed credit reporting because firms like Dun and Bradstreet and Experian could now devise algorithms to calculate quickly the creditworthiness of businesses and individuals. (An algorithm is a process or set of rules that a computer follows to make calculations or solve problems.) Automated decision making enabled lenders to make more loans, faster.

More Liberal Markets

Accelerating these changes was a general trend toward the liberalization of markets. The development crossed political party lines. Democrat Jimmy Carter, president of the United States from 1977 to 1981, presided over the deregulation of airlines, railroads, trucking, and financial services. (By contrast, workplace and environmental regulations grew much more numerous.) His successor, the Republican Ronald Reagan, president from 1981 to 1989, championed the idea that firms and markets functioned best without government interference. Democrat Bill Clinton subscribed to this view while he was president from 1993 to 2001, especially when it came to the financial sector. Many of the Reagan and Clinton initiatives concerned banks and S&Ls. The new regulations allowed banks and S&Ls to enter riskier markets and provided more opportunities for them to exploit regulatory loopholes.[12]

Emergencies like the near-collapse of Continental Illinois National Bank in 1984 and the S&L crisis of the 1980s led to new attitudes and legislation. Continental Illinois, one of the country's biggest banks, made loans mostly at the wholesale level. The frightening prospect that it might close its doors led regulators, including Fed chairman Paul Volcker, to accept the idea that a financial institution could be "too big to fail." To prevent the bank's closure, the FDIC guaranteed its deposits and even paid in full the depositors whose accounts exceeded the insurance limit of $100,000. Some bondholders were saved as well. In congressional testimony, the comptroller of the currency stated that other large banks would receive similar treatment.[13] The changes that the Continental Illinois episode set in motion became permanent: by the 1990s, the ratings agencies began factoring the "too big to fail" assumptions into their ratings.[14] In response, the Bank for International Settlements (BIS) imposed new capital requirements in September 1987. (The BIS, based in Basel, Switzerland, acts as a bank to the world's central banks.) Banks' capital reserves now had to be equal to 8 percent of their loans outstanding. If a bank could not meet the requirements, the excess loans had to be taken off its balance sheet. Banks responded not by making fewer loans but by securitizing a greater proportion of them. Securitization, in turn, led to an explosion of credit for mortgages and other consumer debts.

Traditional commercial banks found it harder to compete in this new environment. To stay viable, a number of the surviving banks merged. States had already experimented with allowing their banks to be owned by out-of-state banks. (Maine was the first, in 1975.) In the 1980s the states went further, allowing the formation of superregionals such as Northern Trust, a Chicago-based bank that expanded into California, Florida, Texas, and Arizona. The giants were so large that they rivaled some of the financial institutions in New York and other money centers. The willingness of state and federal regulators to let superregionals exist went against nearly two hundred years of American practice. Until the 1970s, state laws kept most banks small by prohibiting branches, even within a state. Just twelve states permitted unrestricted banking within their borders; New York allowed statewide branch banking only in 1976.[15] A series of new laws and technological changes rapidly struck down the prohibitions against bank branching. In 1982 Congress allowed bank holding companies to acquire failed banks in any state. Then, automatic teller machines (ATMs) gave banks a means to circumvent the anti-branching laws, especially after a Supreme Court decision in 1985 held that ATMs were not branch banks. Banks with national branch networks soon predominated—comprising more than 70 percent of all banks—by the 1990s. In 1994 a new federal law permitted branch banking within and across states.[16]

The growth of international trade and the establishment by American companies of branches outside the United States drove the expansion of

American banks overseas.[17] Another way that banks tried to replace lost profits was by lending to governments in the developing world. (State laws often restricted them from conducting business in other U.S. states, but nothing prevented them from operating in other countries.)[18] Banks also engaged in riskier lending. They made more commercial real estate loans and funded leveraged buyouts and corporate takeovers. Banks began to use and invest in financial instruments such as junk bonds, swaps, and futures. Regulators, committed to liberalizing the financial markets and concerned about the health of the S&Ls and mutual savings banks, over-turned conventional practices by allowing these depositary institutions to invest in risky instruments, too.[19] Eventually, financial institutions were allowed back into businesses from which they had been barred by Depression-era laws. Insurance, which state laws had kept separate from banking, could now be combined with banking services.[20]

The mania for deregulation culminated in the Financial Services Modernization Act (1999), which repealed portions of the Banking Act of 1933, known as Glass-Steagall. Firms could now engage simultaneously in commercial and investment banking, securities trading, and insurance. (Even before the act was passed, the Federal Reserve had quietly allowed banks to use loopholes in Glass-Steagall to underwrite securities. In 1998 the nation's second-largest bank, Citicorp, merged with Travelers Group, a large insurance company and securities firm. The merger hastened the repeal of Glass-Steagall.)[21] Supporters of the repeal argued that letting financial institutions merge into large, one-stop financial supermarkets would smooth out the effects of the business cycle: the banks could provide services that Americans used in good times, when they increased their investment activities, and in bad times, when people pulled back from investing and saved their money instead. The repeal of Glass-Steagall would also allow American firms to compete globally with the large institutions, many based in Germany and Japan, that were allowed by their home countries to engage in all aspects of the financial services industry. The Financial Services Modernization Act received broad bipartisan support. Its main sponsor, Republican senator Phil Gramm of Texas, was an unapologetic champion of financial deregulation, and the bill was endorsed by the Clinton administration.

Despite the opportunities presented by entering new businesses and markets—or perhaps because of them—more than 2,500 banks and thrifts failed in the period 1985–1995. Liberalization allowed banks and thrifts to benefit from upswings in volatile markets such as junk bonds, real estate, and other risky assets and instruments. But they were now more vulnerable to the downturns in those markets.[22]

Securitization

Perhaps the single biggest factor increasing the amount of credit was securitization. In 1960, at least 73 percent of bank loans, including mortgages, car loans, and personal loans, were "secured," meaning that banks could take tangible assets like houses, cars, appliances, and jewelry if debtors failed to pay. "Securitization," however, changed the model by making collateral meaningless. The value of securitized loans did not lie primarily in the underlying assets but in the income stream the assets produced: what mattered was not the real estate but the mortgages; not the airplanes but the leases on them; not the cars but the payments made by their owners.[23] Crucially, investors in securitized loans often had no means of checking either the quality of the underlying assets or the income stream. Instead, investors relied on a third party, the credit-rating agencies, to judge the quality of these investments. When investment banks began creating much more complex securities, the credit-rating agencies struggled to keep up with the technical challenges presented by the new instruments.[24]

The investment banks Salomon Brothers and First Boston invented one of the most technically sophisticated instruments, the collateralized mortgage obligation (CMO), for Freddie Mac in 1983. CMOs were debt instruments that pooled together residential mortgages and then sliced the pool into "tranches" that had varying degrees of riskiness that could be bought by different kinds of investors. (Many pension funds, for example, could legally invest only in the least risky tranches.) The first mortgages to make up the CMOs were ones backed by Fannie Mae and Freddie Mac, but eventually, even subprime mortgages were included. Within a few years, pension funds and international investors became the biggest buyers of the securities: American pension funds alone held about $30 billions worth in 1986. High investor demand for securitized debt products channeled $60 billion of new money into American home finance during the 1980s.[25]

Mortgages were a huge source of raw material, but any loan that generated a regular cash flow could be securitized. The first securities backed by auto loans came on the market in 1985. (General Motors Acceptance Corporation was the first of the auto manufacturers' credit subsidiaries to issue them.) Then, in 1986, Bank One in Ohio issued securities backed by credit card loans. They were popular because, unlike mortgages, credit card loans have a short maturity and don't have the uncertainty of pre-payment. Within a year of their introduction, investors bought more than $2 billion worth of credit card securities.[26]

In the late 1980s, banks began dealing in collateralized debt obligations (CDOs). Unlike a collateralized mortgage obligation, CDOs were backed by riskier loans or by other bonds.[27] Instead of lending out their depositors' money, banks created huge amounts of debt instruments, increasingly backed by low-grade assets. Then they quickly cleared the products off their books. It was an exercise in credit creation that made even the worst banks of the Jacksonian era seem very tame in comparison.

Securities houses developed debt and derivatives instruments that were so innovative that their creators took out patents. They also began speculating on instruments such as the interest-rate swaps that had been developed in the early 1980s to hedge risk.[28] As had happened with western land during the 1880s and 1890s, growing investor demand prompted the investment products' makers to create larger amounts. Creative Wall Street financiers who invented successful new types of securities were richly rewarded. Stories of Wall Street bankers' extravagant lifestyles filled the popular press. With the creation of so much new credit, lenders had strong incentives to push governments, companies, and consumers to borrow more.

Imbalances in World Trade

Meanwhile, developments in global finance led to a phenomenon that was unique in modern history: capital now migrated from emerging economies to mature ones. South Korea and China became export powerhouses, whereas countries like the United States began importing far more goods relative to their GDP. To encourage the consumption of their products in the United States, the central banks of China and South Korea devalued their currencies relative to the dollar. They bought the U.S. dollars that private American companies invested in their countries and reinvested them in short-term U.S. government bonds.[29] Simultaneously, the financial crises that many developing countries endured during the 1980s and 1990s made them far less willing to borrow from abroad to fund their internal investments. The East Asian economies, in particular, began building up their dollar reserves. They bought U.S. Treasuries and lots of bonds issued by the GSEs—Fannie Mae, Ginnie Mae, and Freddie Mac—because of the implicit protection that the GSEs received from the U.S. government. By the beginning of the twenty-first century, the amount of reserves in the emerging markets may have totaled about $14 trillion, a far greater amount than any previous time in history.[30]

The Chinese and other Asian countries were not the only buyers of GSE bonds. Other foreign investors, including the traditionally conservative European banks, purchased them too. As discussed in the section on mortgage lending (later in this chapter), the GSEs created more and more of the bonds, including ones that were backed by subprime mortgages.[31]

The great demand for U.S. debt securities gave the U.S. government unprecedented access to cheap funds. The Federal Reserve could keep interest rates low, which encouraged even more borrowing by Americans. Beginning in the mid-1980s, the United States went from being the world's largest creditor nation to being its biggest debtor.[32] Its trade deficits also widened. In 1990, the trade deficit with China alone totaled $10.4 billion. Ten years later, it had risen to $83.8 billion.[33]

Drivers of Credit Demand

Stagnant wages drove Americans to borrow just to maintain their standard of living. Even at interest rates of 12–18 percent, credit card spending more than tripled between 1975 and 1978. Total consumer borrowing reached nearly $315 billion, a rise of 90 percent in just three years.[34]

By the 1980s, traditional ideas about indebtedness had changed significantly. Beginning with the New Deal programs and continuing through the post–World War II period, government protection of depositors, debtors, large financial institutions, and the GSEs decreased the incentives to be cautious. In the past, lending or borrowing beyond what was prudent could result in great loss and pain for individuals and their communities. People avoided defaulting on loans because the prospect of being shamed and of losing access to credit was so great. Understandably, voters supported legislation that promised to mitigate such pain. Once enacted, however, the laws were difficult to overturn. Bankruptcy laws extended protections to individuals and businesses that were brought down by debt. The FDIC insurance limit for bank and S&L deposits rose steadily, reaching $100,000 per account in 1980. Banks and other lenders pressured people to borrow more while assuring them that debt was a smart way to save and to invest for the long run. All of these developments accelerated the cultural acceptance of borrowing by consumers and firms.

Taken together, these disparate but interlocked events vastly increased the supply of credit available for all sorts of purchases and activities. In 1977, governments, corporations, and consumers owed a combined total of $323 billion, most of it in the form of commercial bank loans. Less than ten years later, total borrowing had reached $7 *trillion,* and a much higher proportion was in the form of securitized debt (bonds).[35] The Federal Reserve, led by individuals who believed that markets should be less constrained, did little to control the expansion of consumer credit and business loans.[36]

Consumer Credit

By the 1980s, the American economy was more dependent on consumption, and more of the consumption was maintained through borrowing. Whereas in 1953 the interest payments on debt accounted for 2.5 percent of household income, in 1985 the figure had risen to 8 percent.[37] Total household debt as a percentage of disposable income was just under 72 percent in 1979. By 1999, it had jumped to 103 percent. Borrowing now exceeded people's discretionary income.[38]

The critical role of credit in fueling consumption was made clear to federal officials in the spring of 1980, when President Carter's administration tried to fight inflation by imposing credit controls, including on credit cards and other short-term instruments. Creditors who had more than $2 million of outstanding consumer credit were required to establish deposit accounts with the Federal Reserve. After March 14, 1980, they had to deposit the equivalent of 15 percent of any new consumer lending. They would get no interest on the deposits, whose purpose was to discourage new consumer loans.[39] The ploy worked too well: banks ceased making new loans, consumers stopped borrowing, and the economy began to collapse immediately—"within a matter of days," according to the then-chairman of the Federal Reserve, Paul Volcker. The administration quickly reversed the policy, and Volcker undid the credit controls within four months.[40] Under Carter's successor, Ronald Reagan, the Keynesian belief that government should spend to stimulate demand fell out of fashion. Consumers, however, were urged to keep on spending.[41]

Americans' growing indebtedness did not necessarily constitute a negative trend, so long as the savings rate remained unaffected. For most of the postwar period, consumer debt soared, yet savings as a percent of disposable income remained high. Consumer repayments began to fall in the 1970s—that is, consumers were maintaining higher balances on their accounts rather than paying them off. Yet despite high inflation, people tried to protect themselves against difficult economic times by saving. Recently revised statistics show that the savings rate was even higher than previously thought: it was 9 to 11 percent during the first half of the 1980s and remained above 7 percent even during the early 1990s.[42]

Then the savings rate began to decline. Within a few years, a gap appeared between the growth of consumer debt (including mortgage debt) and the savings rate. The rate at which people saved fell to 3.7 percent in the 1990s and to less than 1.4 percent in 2005. If we were to point to the most important discontinuity in consumer finance trends during the latter half of the twentieth century, this decrease in the savings rate may well be it. People stopped saving. Instead, encouraged by the finance industry and by regulations such as the tax code, many Americans began seeing themselves less as savers and more as investors—in money market funds, mutual funds, certificates of deposit (CDs), and their homes.[43] New consumer credit instruments spread to the masses, even to people whose incomes traditionally would have disqualified them from getting so many loans.

Credit Cards

Beginning in the 1960s, credit cards began to replace installment sales. Adoption of this credit instrument accelerated in the 1970s, and the amount that people charged on their cards increased. By 1986, 55 percent of families had a bank credit card, more than triple the number for 1970.[44] By 1998, two-thirds of American households had bank credit cards.[45] The amount they charged kept rising. In the space of the 1980s, the average household's charges jumped from $885 to $3,753 per year, more than twice as fast as the rise in disposable income. By 1994, the typical cardholder had almost $4,000 of credit-card debt, with an average annual interest rate of 17 percent. Nearly sixteen percent of households had credit card debt equal to income, and 8 percent had debts that were more than twice their income.[46] The cards spread to poorer households, whose use of bank credit cards more than doubled between the early 1980s and the mid-1990s. In the space of thirty-two years, from 1968 to 2000, the amount of revolving credit in the economy grew from just $2 billion to $626 billion, most of it generated by credit cards.[47]

The credit card fundamentally changed the power of consumers by allowing them to decide when and where to grant themselves credit, up to the limits imposed by the card issuer. Previously, credit applicants had to fill out forms or go to their bank managers whenever they wanted to borrow money, and then they had to wait for approval and for the funds to be transferred to them. Small-loan agencies such as D. H. Tolman's asked not just for marital status but also parents' names and the names of at least six people, including in the applicant's workplace, to vouch for his or her creditworthiness. If the bank approved the loan, the applicant then had to sign, in front of a witness, a promissory note, a chattel mortgage or an assignment of wages, a statement of current indebtedness, and legal forms giving the lender power of attorney. The applicant then had to return a day or two later to pick up the funds.[48] The credit card freed consumers from such inconvenience and embarrassment, including the shame of having a "repo man" show up at the door if they were unable to pay.

But credit cards were not an immediate moneymaker for banks, largely because of the high cost of capital and operating costs (as a percentage of total costs) that were nearly three times that of commercial credit operations. Citibank, one of the largest issuers, struggled to make a profit in credit cards during the 1960s and 1970s. Between 1979 and 1981 alone, Citibank lost over $500 million on its credit card products, in part because high inflation made their cost of obtaining funds very expensive. Citibank persevered despite the gigantic losses, largely because the stubborn head of its credit card operations, John Reed, refused to cut spending. Eventually, the credit card operations began turning a profit, and by the mid-1980s, it had become one of Citibank's most important businesses. (Reed went on to become Citibank's chairman and chief executive officer [CEO] in 1984.) Large institutions such as Citibank discovered that their economies of scale gave them advantages over smaller banks. The credit card business became concentrated, with the top fifty banks holding 70 percent of outstanding balances by the early 1980s.[49]

To fund their growing credit card receivables, banks obtained capital from the money markets rather than from their depositors. Most banks set up finance subsidiaries to issue commercial paper which, unlike deposits, was not subject to reserve requirements and was a cheaper source of funds when interest rates were low. Throughout the 1980s and into the early 1990s, the amount of commercial paper issued by banks increased by almost 20 percent per year.[50] Finance companies, too, accessed the commercial paper market, which enabled them to compete with the banks while escaping the banking sector's tighter regulations.[51] In 1990, the finance subsidiaries of corporations such as Sears, GE, and Ford provided one-third of all consumer credit and one-quarter of all commercial loans.[52] Consumers benefited by having more sources to turn to for financing cars, appliances, and home improvement projects.

The next great innovation, securitization, was introduced by Bank One, and it revolutionized the bank credit card market. After two years of working on the problem of how to structure and price credit card payments, Bank One securitized $50 million of credit card receivables in 1986. Its success drew other card issuers into the securitized bonds market.[53]

Competition drove credit card issuers to attract new customers more aggressively. They started mass-marketing credit cards on college campuses and signing up students without parental consent. Colleges collaborated with the card issuers by providing mailing lists in return for a commission.[54] By 1996, two-thirds of students in four-year institutions had a bank credit card.[55] Credit card issuers also marketed corporate cards to small businesses and the self-employed. By the mid-1990s, personal credit cards were the most important source of financing for small businesses. Within a few years, and despite the rising availability of small business loans, 46 percent of small-business owners were using their personal credit cards to fund their enterprises. American Express began offering tax and business services to small-business owners as part of its Corporate Card benefits. In 1999 the services made up a quarter of American Express's revenues.[56]

Card issuers discovered other ways to increase their revenues. By the early 1970s, they were charging interest of around 18 percent a year.[57] In the mid-1970s, they switched from assessing interest from the time the payment was due to the day the charge was made, a simple change that increased revenues by an estimated 15 to 25 percent.[58] Banks adapted their credit card businesses to the changing economic climate and to new regulations. High inflation in the late 1970s and early 1980s, and the Federal Reserve's requirement in the spring of 1980 that banks hold reserves against outstanding credit card debts, drove the card issuers to impose annual fees. They were forced to do it, the issuers argued, because the regulations had prevented them from soliciting new customers. When the consumer market collapsed, the Fed withdrew its requirement, but the banks' annual fees remained in place. Initially, about 8 percent of the cardholder base dropped out as a result of the new charges. But once the banks discovered that most cardholders tolerated the fees, the charges became a permanent feature of most credit cards.[59]

Even after the inflation rate fell, the annual fees, mandatory minimum payments, and high interest rates continued. Between 1983 and 1988, major credit card issuers earned from three to five times the ordinary rate of return in banking, through keeping interest rates high even when the cost of borrowing dropped. When the proportion of convenience users rose in the late 1990s, card issuers responded by raising penalty fees. (Convenience users were the unprofitable cardholders who paid their balances in full every month. Perversely, they were known in the business as "freeloaders.")[60] Banks also figured out better ways to deal with their bad debts. In 1989, Bank of America made the first sale of charged-off credit card debt to an intermediary, for 2 cents on the dollar.[61]

Credit card loans were significantly more profitable than most other loans—during most of the 1980s, returns on credit card loans were 8.2 times greater than the average return on all loans.[62] Predictably, the banks began issuing more cards. In 1982, they held about one-half of all outstanding credit card balances; four years later, the banks held almost two-thirds.[63] They had changed their thinking about the credit card business: so long as losses were under 3 percent, the banks were happy to continue issuing credit cards to more and more people. In Citibank's case, if fewer than a quarter of a million households defaulted on their card payments, Citibank could shrug it off as just a cost of doing business. Citibank simply regarded the riskier loans as part of its diversified portfolio.[64]

Until the late 1970s, state usury laws presented something of a barrier to the credit card issuers. The maximum rates varied. California, Hawaii, and New Hampshire had no ceilings at all, but most states imposed ceilings of between 12 and 18 percent.[65] Like other creditors throughout history, the banks found ways around the usury laws. They were helped by the Supreme Court, which in 1978 affirmed the right of banks to impose their home state's higher interest rates on credit card accounts in other states *(Marquette National Bank v. First National Bank)*. South Dakota took advantage of the ruling by agreeing to waive its usury laws for Citibank; essentially, the state allowed Citibank to charge as high a rate as it thought fit. In return Citibank agreed to locate its headquarters in the state. Freedom from the usury laws allowed Citibank to survive the high inflationary environment of the late 1970s and early 1980s; it could now charge consumers a higher interest rate than its own cost of funds.

South Dakota attracted other companies' card-processing operations, enabling several more credit card companies to operate nationally with no interest-rate limit. (Banks also continued to consolidate, and the lack of competition may have resulted in higher costs for consumers.)[66] Soon, two-thirds of states either had no interest-rate ceilings or had raised them substantially. The rate of bad loans in these states was much higher than in the states that controlled interest rates—1.38 percent compared to 0.85 percent in 1984.[67] In 1996 another Supreme Court ruling, *Smiley v. Citibank*, removed the remaining regulations controlling interest rates and fees.[68]

American households, suffering from flat wages and bombarded by credit card offers, succumbed to the lure of easy credit, especially revolving credit. Seventy million households had credit cards in 1993, and each household had an average of three active accounts.[69] In 2002 an American Bankers Association survey found that nearly half of all credit cardholders paid only the minimum on their balances outstanding.[70] In the meantime, more retailers began accepting the cards. Supermarkets, which traditionally shunned credit cards, now readily accepted the popular form of payment. At the beginning of the 1990s, just 5 percent of supermarkets allowed shoppers to pay with credit cards, but by 2003 almost all supermarkets permitted it. Not every household had credit cards; more than 25 percent did not have any at all. But the cards were penetrating even the poorest households. Thirty-eight percent of households whose incomes were in the bottom 20 percent now had credit cards and were acquiring them at a faster rate than wealthier households.[71]

The Chairman of the Federal Reserve, Alan Greenspan, a supporter of bank deregulation, acknowledged that "abnormalities" in the credit card industry sometimes enabled "children, dogs, cats, and moose" to obtain them. But he continued to view the spread of credit cards as generally positive for the economy. In testimony before a congressional committee in 2000, he said, "It's something which is a major good, if I may put it that way, in the United States in that it brings a significant portion of the population into the financial mainstream." Greenspan pointed out that the amount of interest paid, as a percentage of household income, "has not gone up all that much" because interest rates were lower and the repayment periods for many loans had grown longer. People were using home equity loans (discussed later in this chapter) to pay off their higher-rate credit card debts. Greenspan concluded, "We have very high debt, but it is not yet something which creates concerns as far as the economy overall is concerned."[72] The Fed chairman's benign assessment of the rise in consumer lending signaled to the financial markets that federal officials were not likely to curtail their very profitable consumer lending businesses.

Fringe Lending

Not everyone qualified for mainstream products such as credit cards or loans from banks and finance companies. In the 1980s and 1990s, a significant proportion of low-income Americans—between 35 to 45 percent—did not even have bank accounts.[73] Fringe lenders served people who could not or would not access credit through mainstream sources. Despite public disapproval of these businesses, some fringe lenders grew large, and a number of them even traded on the national stock exchanges. Ace Cash Express, established in 1968, became the premier company in the check-cashing industry, and its shares were publicly traded on NASDAQ. Cash America, which became the nation's largest chain of pawn shops, was founded in Texas in 1984. It listed on the New York Stock Exchange in 1987, becoming the first publicly traded pawnshop company. Rent-A-Center, started in 1986, grew to be the nation's largest rent-to-own company; it, too, listed on NASDAQ. (In a rent-to-own arrangement, consumers rent a product that they can later choose to own. The final price is invariably much higher than if they had just bought the product outright.) In 1993, another form of fringe banking appeared when Title Loans of America (later Community Loans of America), which offered loans backed by car titles, opened in Georgia. It soon became the industry leader.[74]

The 1978 Supreme Court decision, *Marquette National Bank v. First National Bank,* made it possible for fringe banking services that were chartered in a deregulated state to "export" the privileges to every state in which it operated.[75] In the 1990s, some states enacted safe-harbor laws, further enlarging the fringe credit industry. ("Safe harbor" is a legal provision that reduces liability, especially in cases where the law is vague.) The prospect of large profits enticed the first-tier banks into the fringe lending markets. Citigroup bought the subprime lender Associates First Capital Corporation. Wells Fargo formed a joint venture with Cash America to develop automated payday loan kiosks.[76] Payday loans had existed since at least the early twentieth century, but payday lenders proliferated in earnest during the 1990s.[77] To obtain a payday loan, a customer left a predated personal check that the lender cashed on the customer's next payday. Customers had to prove they had regular jobs or income (including Social Security), but even those with poor credit could obtain loans because lenders did not run credit checks.[78]

Rent-to-own stores, despite their name, were a form of consumer lending. They first emerged in the late 1960s, but their explosive growth occurred during the 1980s. According to its national trade association, the number of establishments rose from 3,000 in 1983 to 8,000 nine years later. Rent-A-Center, at one time owned by Thorn EMI Rental Americas, was one of the largest, operating 2,400 stores in mostly poor neighborhoods in 2001. *Fortune* magazine named it among the country's fastest-growing companies.[79] Rent-to-own stores were lightly regulated by the states and could charge very high rates of interest. Only Pennsylvania imposed a cap (18 percent), and some states circumvented the issue by treating the contracts as rentals rather than sales, even though a 1999 survey by the Federal Trade Commission (FTC) established that 70 percent of households eventually bought the products they had been renting.[80] Reformers argued that fringe banking services took advantage of low-income consumers, but the FTC survey found that 75 percent of rent-to-own patrons were generally satisfied with their experience. Sixty-seven percent intended at the outset to buy the items they rented.[81] Although they probably were aware that they paid far more than people who just bought the products outright, the customers knew that they would not have been able to obtain the items any other way. Similarly, pawnbrokers provided benefits to borrowers, including a degree of certainty and privacy. Pawning was by then a well-regulated industry where the terms of the loans were clearly spelled out. Because the loans were secured by the pawned item, collection agents never harassed borrowers, and credit reporting agencies were not informed if pawners failed to redeem their items. According to the National Pawnbrokers Association, as of the early twenty-first century more than 92 percent of pawners were employed, and more than 25 million Americans used pawn services annually.[82]

Consumer activists berated the federal government for failing to protect consumers from predatory lending and payday loan abuses. But although journalists and academics referred to consumer "movements," the collective sense of grievance among consumers was different from the Populist and labor movements of the past. Consumers barely constituted an interest group; they were fragmented and difficult to organize. And activists' calls for protecting consumers from "toxic" financial products were less radical than the Populist agenda a century earlier.[83] Despite wide-

190

spread anger at the perceived abuses by banks and other lenders, radical reforms did not occur.

The U.S. government's response was markedly different from that of France, which in the late 1980s reimposed stricter controls on consumer credit. Households in continental Europe had sharply lower consumer debt levels (as a percentage of disposable income) than the 25 percent or so that was common in the United States and Great Britain in 2004. In Germany, the debt level was 16 percent, and in France it was 12 percent. The Germans and Dutch used "credit cards," but the cards did not allow them to carry balances from month to month. The divergence between the Anglo-American and continental European approaches to household debt represented fundamentally different ideological beliefs. Sheldon Garon has observed that "continental European states tend to respond to life's emergencies by providing social benefits, while the American system offers families more credit."[84]

An area of contention was whether credit card issuers encouraged borrowers to remain in debt. For banks, the key attraction of consumer loans was the cash flow they generated. When the banks securitized credit card debts in the 1980s, cash flow became more important; even if customers made only the minimum payments on their balances, banks could still achieve enough cash flow to support securitization. Consumer advocates argued that banks' securitization of credit card debt was a clear instance of interests becoming nonaligned: although securitized debt was good for banks and investors, it was not necessarily good for credit card users.[85] Only the intervention of a federal consumer protection agency could right the balance, according to critics. But the banking lobby succeeded in heading off any stringent regulations. Instead, the Fair Credit and Charge Card Disclosure Act of 1988 emphasized "transparency" rather than controlling interest rates or prohibiting high fees.[86] Whether average consumers could make good decisions based on more information, however, remained debatable.

Mortgage Lending

In 1980, the rate of home ownership in the United States reached nearly 70 percent. From the perspective of the federal government, this figure indicated a stunning success that vindicated the federal support of mortgage markets. Congress passed an important amendment to the tax code in 1986 that ended the ability of taxpayers to deduct interest payments on consumer loans. But the interest on mortgages and home equity loans continued to be tax deductible, a clear sign that borrowing to achieve home ownership and home improvements had become a sacrosanct right in the minds of Americans and their representatives in Congress. Mortgages accounted for a growing share of household debt. Of the $1.5 trillion of outstanding household debt in 2000, more than 80 percent consisted of home mortgages. From being equal to 46 percent of total household income in 1979, mortgage debt grew to 73 percent of household income by 2001.[87]

Savings and Loans

Government support of the mortgage markets transformed the savings and loan industry, and Wall Street along with it. S&Ls were established as building and loan societies (B&Ls) in the early 1800s, and increasingly became an important source of mortgage loans. But in the 1980s, S&Ls faced a number of dilemmas. They had made thirty-year home loans at a low fixed-interest rate, but when the inflation rate spiked, their cost of capital rose. The 1981–1982 recession that hit areas such as Texas hard exacerbated the problem. People defaulted on their mortgages, imposing losses on the S&L industry of around $10 billion. (Commercial banks, too, suffered large losses.) By the end of 1982, about one-half of all S&Ls were insolvent. The number of S&Ls that closed their doors dwarfed the number in previous decades. From the time of the New Deal to 1980 only 143 S&Ls failed, with a total of $4.5 billion in assets. By comparison, the first three years of the 1980s alone saw 118 S&Ls fail, with total assets of $43 billion. Their failures cost the federal government $3.5 billion to resolve.[88]

Congress passed a series of laws to help the banks and S&Ls. Most significantly, and with the strong support of the Carter administration, Congress removed the deposit rate ceiling that was imposed during the Depression.[89] These limits had been intended to prevent banks from competing for customers. Lifting them allowed the banks and S&Ls to vie with mutual funds for depositors. Congress also permitted the S&Ls to engage in riskier lending, including on commercial real estate development and consumer loans. Depositors, meanwhile, were protected for up to $100,000 per account.[90] The greater freedom to invest in riskier loans and investments plus the government's protection of their depositors' money created dangerous incentives for S&Ls, turning the boring institutions portrayed in the Hollywood film *It's a Wonderful Life* into fearless gamblers on risky assets and instruments.

In September 1981, Congress passed a tax break that was triggered if S&Ls sold their mortgage loans. The thrifts promptly did so and ignited a boom on Wall Street. Investment banks bought the mortgage loans and turned them into bonds. Institutional investors, convinced that the bonds carried an implicit guarantee by the U.S. government through Fannie Mae, Ginnie Mae, and Freddie Mac, eagerly bought the securities. There was little incentive to check the quality of the underlying mortgages, and few investors bothered. When short-term interest rates fell in late 1982, the surviving S&Ls were able to borrow at 12 percent and make mortgage loans at 14 percent, prompting them to add a large number of new loans to their previous loss-making ones. Once the S&Ls got rid of the loans on their own books, investment banks such as Salomon Brothers persuaded them to buy mortgage bonds made up of other thrifts' loans. (The S&Ls also were allowed to buy junk bonds, but most stuck to mortgage bonds.) Their bond holdings increased from $12.6 billion in 1977 to $150 billion in 1986.[91]

Regulators did not stop the S&Ls from buying the mortgage bonds or the investment banks from selling it to them. The regulators were underfunded, understaffed, and ill-trained to understand the new instruments. The ideology of deregulation and the successful lobbying by the S&L industry further prevented an aggressive federal response. In fact, the regulators made the problem worse: they lowered the capital requirements and liberalized the accounting rules, in the belief that distressed S&Ls just needed to be kept alive until the markets recovered. Once the federal regulators showed their laxity, many states did the same. The result was the opposite of prudent consolidation and the closure of problematic thrifts. Instead, enterprising people took advantage of the relaxed regulations to found new thrifts. In just three years, 1982 to 1985, total S&L assets went from $686 billion to $1,068 billion, a growth of 56 percent. All sorts of people entered the industry, investing in everything from ski resorts to derivatives. (A derivative is a contract between one or more parties, whose value is determined by fluctuations in some underlying entity, such as an asset or an index. Derivatives are used to hedge risk but are also popular with speculators.) Above all, the S&Ls invested in commercial property development. Commercial banks and S&Ls poured funds into commercial real estate projects, causing bubbles in these markets. When the bubbles burst, as they inevitably did in the highly cyclical real estate markets, the S&Ls paid the price. In some cases, S&L entrepreneurs also committed outright fraud.

The government protected the S&Ls' depositors. As a result, people put their money into the S&Ls without worrying about the integrity or competence of their managers. The risk taking of the worst-run S&Ls affected even the well-run institutions, who felt pressured to engage in similar practices or face losing funds and customers. Lots of money pouring in, plus bad regulations and risky practices, resulted in the failure of even more S&Ls. In 1988, as a number of real estate markets around the country collapsed, the thrift industry's losses amounted to more than $10 billion. They nearly doubled the following year, to almost $20 billion.[92]

Congress finally responded by passing the Financial Institutions Reform, Recovery, and Enforcement Act (FIRREA) in 1989. Essentially, it was a bailout of the industry. Thrifts that were in receivership were placed under the supervision of a new agency, the Resolution Trust Corporation (RTC). The RTC took over the assets of some fifty troubled S&Ls and sold most of them, recovering more than 85 percent. Taxpayers eventually paid $150 billion to bail out the thrifts. So, after a decade of removing the constraints from the S&L industry, lawmakers reimposed them. S&Ls were once again restricted as to the types of assets they could hold.[93] But the industry had already shrunk dramatically: of the 3,175 thrifts that had been in existence in 1987, only 1,670 remained six years later. Taxpayers were left with a huge bill of some $124 billion. Other official estimates placed the final tab even higher.[94]

Secondary Markets Become Huge

In 1969, Ginnie Mae guaranteed the first mortgage "pass-through," an arrangement in which home owners' mortgage payments pass from the originating bank through a government agency or investment bank to investors, usually in the form of a mortgage-backed certificate. Freddie Mac, created in 1968 to compete with Fannie Mae, issued its first pass-through a few years later, in 1971. Investors liked the pass-through instruments because they had higher yields than traditional bonds and provided monthly cash flows. From the government's perspective, helping banks to sell their mortgage loans to investors ensured that the banks would make even more loans.[95]

Freddie Mac's invention, with the help of the Wall Street banks, of the collateralized mortgage obligation in 1983 was a significant event that further enlarged the market for mortgage loans. The CMO fixed the critical flaws of the earlier mortgage-backed instruments: the varying amounts of the underlying mortgages, their different maturities, and the risk that they would be prepaid in full at any time. All of these features had made mortgage bonds problematic for the secondary markets. The prepayment option was the most serious because it gave mortgage bonds an unknown maturity, and the uncertainty spooked investors. By aggregating and then slicing mortgage bonds into tranches, CMOs eliminated the uncertainty and allowed conservative investors like pension funds to invest in the supposedly safest tranches. The bonds flourished. By the early 1980s, the securities that Fannie Mae, Ginnie Mae, and Freddie Mac first introduced in the late 1960s had become very popular with investors, including the pension funds that had once avoided the securities as too risky. Underlying the growth in the mortgage-backed instruments was the assumption that the federal government would never allow the agencies to default.[96] By 1985, about half of all new mortgages were being sold in the secondary market.[97] For a while in the mid-1980s, mortgage bonds constituted the world's biggest capital market.[98]

The tax code continued to drive home buying. By keeping mortgage interest tax-deductible, Congress stacked the incentives in favor of buying rather than renting. And there was even more to come: in 1996, the Taxpayer Relief Act increased the amount of capital gain (the profits made when a house was sold) that was exempt from tax. The amounts rose to $250,000 for a single taxpayer and $500,000 for a married couple. Like other provisions in the tax code, the act encouraged people to view their homes not just as places to live but as investments. In the low-interest-rate environment, borrowing today to reap large and mostly tax-free rewards in the future made eminent sense.

In addition, the federal government explicitly set goals regarding disadvantaged Americans. In 1989 new regulations dictated that 10 percent of the Federal Home Loan Banks' earnings should support housing initiatives for low- and moderate-income people. (Chartered during the Depression, the FHLB was the system of twelve banks designed to help keep financial institutions liquid so that they could provide more loans.) The Cranston-Gonzales National Affordable Housing Act, passed in 1990, stated the objective that "every American family be able to afford a decent home in a suitable living environment." The rise of the megabanks contributed to the relaxation of mortgage-lending standards. In order to obtain approval for their mergers and demonstrate their good citizenship, the large banks agreed to accede to the demands of housing activists.[99]

Pushed by community activists, a number of banks in the Boston area, for example, began extending mortgage loans to households making less than $25,000.[100] In 1995 the Clinton administration announced a National Homeownership Strategy to increase home ownership and aid to minority groups. "One of the great successes of the United States in this century," President Bill Clinton stated, "has been the partnership forged by the national government and the private sector to steadily expand the dream of home ownership to all Americans."[101] The administration pushed the Federal Housing Administration to reduce minimum down-payment requirements to only 3 percent of a property's value. (Formerly, most banks had insisted on 20 percent.) The FHA also had to enlarge the maximum size of the mortgages it guaranteed without charging borrowers an equivalent premium reflecting the increased risks.[102]

The government-sponsored enterprises, especially Fannie Mae and Freddie Mac, were key to expanding the number of loans. The troubles of the S&L industry had already enhanced the importance of the Federal Home Loan Banks and the GSEs in subsidizing mortgage credit. Then, in 1992, the GSE Act imposed targets for affordable housing, requiring Fannie Mae and Freddie Mac to make mortgages more available to low-income households. At first the GSEs required a higher down payment from the risky borrowers and made them obtain private mortgage insurance. But then political pressures and perverse incentives, including rich rewards for the GSEs' shareholders and managers for making more loans, chipped away at the GSEs' standards. Beginning in 1994, they bought mortgages with down payments of just 3 percent. Crucially, the 1992 GSE Act set low capital standards: the GSEs were now required to hold just $2.50 of reserves for every $100 in mortgages in their portfolios. (By contrast, banks were required to hold $4.00 for every $100 of mortgages.) Securitizing the mortgages took them off the GSEs' balance sheets, which further lowered the capital reserves they were required to keep.[103] Encouraged by the government's endorsement of the riskier loans, Wall Street banks intensified their involvement in the secondary markets. The investment banks Bear Stearns and First Union Capital began to securitize the risky loans in 1997.[104]

Thus, the GSEs were the vehicles through which the federal government, in partnership with private financial institution, created money for all the new loans. Between 1990 and 2003, the share of single-family home mortgages accounted for by Fannie and Freddie doubled, from roughly one-quarter to about one-half. More significant was the growing number of risky mortgages in the GSEs' portfolios. In 2001, two-thirds of these mortgages were in categories that were mandated by the government: low- and moderate-income, "underserved areas," and "special affordable" (that is, very low-income) mortgages. By 2004 the GSEs were even buying "no-docs loans"—mortgages that banks had extended without checking the information provided by applicants. Not everyone believed that the GSEs' role in mortgage lending was sustainable. The diverse array of critics included Federal Reserve chairman Alan Greenspan and consumer activist Ralph Nader. Greenspan warned in 2000 and again in 2005 about the dangers to the economy posed by the GSEs. He recommended that the government limit their growth.[105] But exactly the opposite occurred: the GSEs bought even more mortgages whose underlying quality was worse than ever.

The banks were themselves engaging in more creative types of mortgage financing. They encouraged people to see the equity in their residences as "savings" that they could tap to pay for purchases. In the 1970s and early 1980s, banks transformed second mortgages into "home equity loans." These were essentially consumer loans that were secured by people's equity in their homes. The federal laws now allowed mainstream banks to offer them, along with adjustable-rate mortgages (ARMs), interest-only loans, and piggyback loans that creatively combined first and second mortgages. Originally, finance companies and some S&Ls had used these alternative products to target lower-income customers. Now, repackaged by the banks as a smart way to borrow, home equity loans spread among middle-income householders. From $1 billion of home equity loans outstanding in 1982, the amount rose a hundredfold, to $100 billion just six years later. Federal laws continued to encourage home buying. The 1986 tax overhaul, for example, eliminated the tax deductibility of credit card interest but left home equity loans untouched.[106] Americans could still deduct the interest payments on them, even if they used the loans to finance vacations, recreational vehicles, sporting equipment, or anything at all, since no one was monitoring how they used the borrowed money. By 1986, 4 percent of home owners had taken out home equity loans. Banks liked these loans because the interest on them was variable, not fixed, which reduced the banks' risks.[107]

Similarly, adjustable-rate mortgages transferred the riskiness attached to fluctuating interest rates from lenders to borrowers. ARMs were exempt from usury laws, which applied only to fixed-rate mortgages. When the 1980s began, adjustable-rate mortgages barely existed, but by 1984

197

they represented nearly half of all new residential home loans. Other mortgage products proliferated until, in the mid-1990s, banks were offering up to twenty ways to finance a home.[108] Congress provided some consumer protection in the form of the Home Ownership and Equity Protection Act (1994). An amendment of the Truth in Lending Act, it provided safeguards against certain deceptive and unfair practices in home equity lending. But it set no limits on what could be charged for loans. And, as would become clear a decade later, the laws failed to protect mortgage borrowers from taking on loans that they could not repay.

Student Loans

As in the mortgage markets, federal aid to students in higher education increased, and government participation in the market encouraged private lenders to enter it. The federal government had begun giving aid to individuals for higher education just after the Second World War, with the GI Bill. The bill was innovative, but it also represented the cultural limits of what the American public would accept. Americans welcomed federal aid that they saw as a reward for military service, but aid that was based on need remained controversial. The Soviet launch of Sputnik in 1957 changed people's attitudes by sparking worries that the United States was falling behind the Soviet Union in the sciences. There was also widespread concern about the shortage of mathematicians, who were being hired in large numbers by industry. In response, Congress quickly passed the National Defense Education Act to provide college students with low-interest loans.[109]

The Johnson administration's Great Society programs widened the government's commitment to make higher education accessible to needy students. Title IV of the Higher Education Act (HEA) of 1965 provided financial aid in the form of loans and grants and encouraged the states to create additional programs. The Guaranteed Student Loan program, a part of the HEA, was designed to help middle-income college students and their families. It relied on private lenders, who were given incentives and subsidies to make more loans. As it had done for home mortgages, the federal government in 1972 established a GSE, the Student Loan Marketing Association ("Sallie Mae"), to enable more private sector lending to students and their families.

Congress passed other amendments to the Higher Education Act to give the states incentives to establish their own loan guarantee agencies. In 1979, Congress tied the federal subsidies to the Treasury bill rates. This little-noticed change guaranteed the banks that were receiving subsidies a favorable rate of return on their student loans. Many more banks signed up to participate in the Guaranteed Student Loan program, just as the government policy makers had hoped. In the early 1980s, the ratio of grants to loans shifted. Whereas federal, state, and private grants had previously accounted for the lion's share of aid, loans now became more important.

The original intent of the HEA and the 1972 amendments was to provide taxpayer support to students based on need. But demand from middle-income families drove Congress to raise the income eligibility limits. The change had little effect on grants, but it significantly affected the Guaranteed Student Loans. The volume of loans exploded, more than doubling to $9 billion in the short period from 1977 to 1980. Congress reimposed the caps on eligibility based on family income, but the caps proved unpopular and Congress removed them again in 1992. The number of loans increased even more.

The demand for student loans seemed unlimited. Seeing the opportunities, more private lenders entered the market. Unlike the federally backed loans, private ones charged higher rates of interest and were not suspended if the borrower decided to pursue more education. Private loans accounted for an ever-larger proportion of all student loans. Concerned observers wrote about a "student loan culture" that had gone awry and of unscrupulous colleges that took advantage of naïve students and their families. Critics went further, accusing the colleges of taking advantage of the loan culture to raise tuition and fees at a rate that was far above the level of inflation.

The federal government's programs helped to change fundamentally how students and their families approached paying for higher education. In the decades-long evolution of federal student aid, loans became a much more important component even for the needy students who were the programs' original target. The dynamics in higher education, where rising costs made even publicly funded colleges and universities more reliant on tuition, reinforced the switch to loans. Demand for college degrees rose in response to the higher-education premium, the pay gap between those with college degrees and those without. The loss of good-paying blue-collar jobs made the premium even larger. Such jobs had once been available to people with only a high school diploma.

In the late 1980s, a large percentage of students found themselves unable to cope with the high levels of debt. Default rates on government-guaranteed student loans ran as high as 30 percent, the highest of any type of loans.[110] In late 1977, the median student debt was a manageable

$2,000, but by the early 1990s, the median had risen to $7,000. In 1996, it was $15,000. The average public university student graduated with nearly $12,000 in loans, while students who attended private universities were in debt for more than $14,000. Adding to the already heavy debt burden was credit card debt. Two-thirds of students now had at least one bank credit card, often with very high interest rates. In 2002, these student borrowers had an average credit card debt of $3,176.[111]

Corporate Debt

Changes in the capital markets also affected the nature and extent of corporate indebtedness. Throughout the nation's history, most corporate expansion was financed by companies' retained profits rather than loans, and this reliance on internally generated funds continued into the beginning of the twenty-first century.[112] Nonetheless, corporations became more sophisticated at accessing the domestic and international capital markets. Beginning in the 1970s, they issued more bonds and deepened their reliance on commercial paper.[113] The corporations' shrewdness added to the woes of commercial banks, whose corporate borrowers and depositors were being lured away by new financial vehicles.

The work of academics Harry Markowitz, William Sharpe, Franco Modigliani, Merton Miller, Edward Altman, Michael Jensen, and William Meckling changed the negative connotations of corporate debt. In 1964, the capital asset pricing model (CAPM) that was developed by Markowitz, Sharpe, and others differentiated between market risks and specific risks. Market risk could not be avoided, but specific risks could be tackled by diversifying the investments in a portfolio. Further, a specific security's relationship to the market could be measured by a beta coefficient: securities that tracked the market perfectly had a beta of 1.00. Higher or lower betas indicated higher or lower volatility, which helped investors to calculate the expected return of an asset. Sharpe also showed that debt was a better source of funding when the stock market was volatile because—thanks to the tax deductibility of interest—debt usually cost less than equity. Franco Modigliani and Merton Miller theorized that the value of the firm is not dependent on whether it is financed through equity (stocks) or debt (bonds and bank borrowing). Edward Altman developed quantitative techniques for assessing the likelihood of corporate bankruptcy. The works of these academic theorists led managers, investors, and investment bankers to believe that the risks associated with indebtedness could be managed. Investors saw that as long as the returns on debt were greater than the cost of capital (usually the cost of issuing commercial paper), corporate debt instruments could be regarded as simply part of a prudent portfolio of investments.[114] Later, Michael Jensen and William Meckling argued that debt was superior to equity in disciplining managers because indebtedness incentivized them to work harder to meet debt payments.[115] They echoed the earlier arguments of Edwin Seligman and others that installment credit disciplined households to stick to their budgets.

LBOs and Junk Bonds

In 1979 Kohlberg, Kravis and Roberts, a firm specializing in private equity, arranged the first-ever leveraged buyout, or LBO, of a large public company. Bryan Burrough and John Helyar, the authors of the best-selling *Barbarians at the Gate* (1990, an account of the LBO of the food and tobacco conglomerate RJR Nabisco), give a succinct explanation of the device: "In an LBO, a small group of senior executives, usually working with a Wall Street partner, proposes to buy its company from public shareholders, using massive amounts of money . . . raised from banks and the public sale of securities; the debt is paid down with cash from the company's operations and, often, by selling pieces of the business."[116] Previously, KKR had confined its buyouts to private, family-owned firms, usually to help the families retain control when the founder retired. The publicly listed company that KKR bought in 1979, Houdaille Industries, was an industrial manufacturer based in Florida. KKR financed the deal with a complex structure that gave both Wall Street and regulators a glimpse of what could be accomplished by creative financing.[117] It soon became clear that LBO firms like KKR could acquire very large companies, so long as the companies had steady cash flows. In the process, the partners of the buyout firms could become spectacularly rich. In 1982 William Simon, a partner of Wesray Capital, engineered the buyout of Gibson Greeting Cards, earning himself a phenomenal $66 million. The vast profits that could be made along with the anemic state of the stock market in the early 1980s made people on Wall Street very interested in LBOs. Eighteen LBOs were completed in 1985, each valued at $1 billion or more.[118]

The intellectual rationale for doing LBOs had to do with "agency costs," the downsides associated with professionally managed firms. According to this theory, managers have very different incentives from owners. Managers try to reduce the firm's market risks by retaining earnings rather than paying out the money to shareholders. The problem was made worse by regulations, such as the 1968 act to limit tender offers, that removed the market's power to discipline managers. Antitrust laws, moreover, constrained firms from merging with their competitors. Managers thus targeted companies that were in unrelated industries, and over time these conglomerates became unwieldy and inefficient. In the case of RJR Nabisco, the tobacco business dragged down the food operations: "We are sitting on food assets that are worth twenty-two, twenty-five times earnings," CEO Ross Johnson reportedly complained, "and we trade at nine times earnings, because we're still seen as a tobacco company!"[119] The obvious solution was to break up RJR Nabisco to "release" the financial value of the food businesses. KKR and other LBO firms defended their activities, arguing that they helped to realign the incentives of managers with that of shareholders: by substituting debt for retained earnings, LBOs gave managers a stake in the company. Although debt increased a company's financial risks, it also imposed the discipline that overregulated financial markets could no longer provide. Managers had to make their bloated companies more efficient to generate enough cash to meet their debt payments. They often accomplished this end by breaking up the companies and laying off employees.

KKR had another advantage: being a small limited partnership, it could coordinate its activities more quickly and effectively than could a dispersed shareholder base, which would have spent ages trying to agree about anything. Although KKR itself consisted of only twenty partners and associates, at its peak it owned a stable of companies that collectively employed nearly 400,000 people. They included household names like Duracell, RJR Nabisco, and Safeway.[120] If it had been an industrial company, KKR would have ranked among the top ten corporations in the United States.[121]

The sources of KKR's funding shifted during the 1970s and 1980s. At first, they tapped wealthy individual investors, but soon KKR went to the commercial banks, which were facing greater competition and searching for additional revenue streams. Investment banks, too, were looking for new sources of revenue. Inflation played a role by driving investors out of the stock market to look for higher returns.[122] The tax code, which taxed dividends but not the interest on debt, inadvertently subsidized the LBOs. KKR turned to pension funds. Oregon and Washington states were the first to sign up. They did very well, which attracted other state pension funds to invest in corporate debt. Tapping all of these sources, KKR was able to raise $1 billion of funding in 1983. Its average annual return to investors was a very impressive 63 percent.[123]

What turned LBOs into investment bubbles was a debt instrument, the high-yield ("junk") bond. Junk bonds were issued by firms who were considered less than absolutely creditworthy—that is, rated lower than Baa3 by Moody's, or BBB- by Standard and Poor's. Michael Milken, a partner in Wall Street investment bank Drexel Burnham Lambert (referred to hereafter as Drexel), had spotted the potential of junk bonds, and his tireless promotion during the 1970s and 1980s dramatically enlarged the market for this previously little-used instrument. Junk bonds had been around for decades: ever since the 1920s, the term had referred to noninvestment-grade paper—around 15 to 20 percent of all corporate bond issues—and "fallen angels," or investment-grade bonds that had been downgraded. Such bonds appealed to a small, specialized group of investors like Milken who sniffed opportunities in these supposedly undesirable securities. Now, thanks to Milken and Drexel, the junk bonds were being used to fund hostile takeover bids, in which Drexel and its clients first announced that they were targeting a company before putting together the financing from investors. Usually, the point was not to obtain the company but just to sell their stakes in it at a higher price.[124] KKR's inclusion of Milken and Drexel in its funding network enabled KKR to go after some of America's largest corporations. KKR conducted only a few of the 2,385 leveraged buyouts that occurred in the 1980s, but its deals were by far the biggest, totaling about one-fourth the value of all LBOs from 1985 to 1989.[125] Eventually, KKR began to accumulate stock in its targets, in the manner of high-profile takeover mavens such as T. Boone Pickens. When KKR acquired a company's stock it intensified its monitoring of managers, sometimes arm-twisting them to get the desired result.[126]

Junk bonds typically financed only a fraction of an LBO deal: commercial banks provided 60 percent (the secured debt), and the buyer put in an additional 10 percent. An important advantage of junk bonds, however, was speed. In contrast to the months it took to secure funds from insurance companies (which previously provided the junior, or subordinated debt), Milken and Drexel could come up with 20 or 30 percent of the overall financing very quickly.[127] As the buyouts became larger, the absolute amounts financed by junk bonds grew, too. Ronald Perelman bought the cosmetics firm Revlon in 1985, after a bidding war that raised the price from $45 to $58 a share. In 1986, KKR did a $6.2 billion LBO of food conglomerate Beatrice. Many of the target firms were in stable, humdrum industries such as consumer products.[128]

Investors trusted Michael Milken because he did his due diligence and closely monitored the firms whose bonds he issued. Milken did whatever it took to support the market for junk bonds, even if that meant buying back fallen bonds at the price at which they had originally been issued, if investors complained. At times Milken renegotiated the firms' debts and even advanced funds when they ran into trouble. Under him, Drexel virtually guaranteed the liquidity of the secondary market for junk bonds because investors knew that Drexel was prepared to be the buyer of last resort.[129] From almost nothing in the 1970s, new junk-bond issuance reached $32 billion in 1986.[130] Milken attracted media attention for the size of his compensation as much as his market-making skills. In 1987, fees of 2 to 3 percent per junk-bond issue made Drexel the most profitable firm on Wall Street. Milken made a staggering $1 billion-plus of personal income between 1983 and 1987.[131]

But, as so often happens with hot investment instruments, the quality of the underlying assets eventually degraded. Milken ran out of the kinds of undervalued companies that most benefited from junk bonds—small, new, or fallen companies that were good bets but had trouble accessing the capital markets. By 1985, investors were still piling into junk bonds, but Milken struggled to find worthy companies to take all the cash. Milken and Drexel had done such a good job transforming the image of junk bonds that mainstream investors like pension funds and university endowments now wanted them. Investment banks like Morgan Stanley and Merrill Lynch had begun competing in this market, too. They used their own money to make bridge loans to cover the interim financings; later, they refinanced the loans by issuing junk bonds. By 1987 the LBO field was so crowded that bidding wars became common. The stock market crash in October 1987 made the stock of many companies seem very cheap, encouraging a large number of takeovers in the first half of 1988. From having the field to itself, KKR was now forced to pay ever-higher prices for companies.[132]

In a strange twist, the targeted companies asked KKR and other buyout firms to become their "white knights," or rescuers. A cynical appraisal offered by the authors of *Barbarians at the Gate* was that the whole thing "was a symbiotic relationship: raider seeks target; target seeks LBO; and raider, target, and LBO firm all profit from the outcome. The only ones hurt were the company's bondholders, whose holdings were devalued in the face of new debt, and employees, who often lost their jobs."[133] The managers of public companies also used junk bonds to raid their own companies and take them private, especially if the companies had under-valued assets that could be sold off. By turning companies into takeover targets and loading them up with debt, raiders turned the bonds of even the most stable firms into junk bonds.[134]

Corporate raiders caught the public imagination. They appeared as Hollywood anti-heroes, epitomized by the character of Gordon Gekko in the 1987 movie *Wall Street*. His famous speech, elevating greed as a pro-ductive force that focused peoples' energies, was the cinematic version of a real-life commencement speech given by arbitrageur Ivan Boesky to the graduating class of the University of California, Berkeley, in 1986. But the case for the corporate raider was made most eloquently by a character in another movie, *Other People's Money* (1991). In a meeting of shareholders, Larry "the Liquidator" Garfield, the corporate raider of an inefficient wire and cable firm, declares,

> You know, at one time there must have been dozens of companies making buggy whips. And I'll bet the last company around was the one that made the best . . . buggy whip you ever saw. Now, would you have liked to have been a stockholder in that company? You invested in a business, and this business is dead. Let's have the intelligence—let's have the decency—to sign the death certificate, collect the insurance, and invest in something with a future. . . . Take the money. Invest it somewhere else. Maybe . . . maybe you'll get lucky, and it'll be used productively. And if it is, you'll create new jobs and provide a service for the economy and, God forbid, even make a few bucks for yourself.[135]

But when *Other People's Money* opened in movie theaters in 1991, the junk-bond bubble had already burst. It was partly deflated by the Tax Re-form Act of 1986, which circumscribed the ways that cash flow could be accounted for after a company was purchased, severely limiting the com-panies' ability to service the debts. Congress closed the loopholes in the tax code after members became concerned about the consequences of LBOs on employment and productivity. Both unions and business groups such as the Business Roundtable lobbied to place restrictions on deal making, arguing that it resulted in mass layoffs and diverted managers' attention from long-term objectives.[136] Then the credit crunch of 1989–1990 forced banks to curtail the loans they made to buyout companies by 86 percent.[137] Some $4 billion worth of junk-bond defaults occurred in the period from January to August 1989.[138] The collapse of the junk-bond market occurred in conjunction with the severe problems of the S&Ls, which had bought a large portion of junk-bond issues. Fraud also played a part when Michael Milken and Drexel were convicted of insider trading. Drexel's $650 million in fines helped to drive it into bankruptcy in 1990; Milken went to jail. With the main support of the junk-bond market gone, 250 companies defaulted between 1989 and 1991.[139]

Junk bonds continued to be a part of many investors' diversified port-folios, and in fact the junk-bond market became several times larger during the 1990s.[140] But the deals they made possible were no longer the cultural and financial spectacles that they had been in the 1980s.

Bankruptcy

For more than a century, the nation's bankruptcy laws became increasingly favorable to debtors. The 1978 overhaul (known as the Bankruptcy Code) continued the trajectory. The overhaul was a response to debtors' complaints that their confiscated assets went to pay the costs of bankruptcy administration rather than creditors. The new code streamlined the process and established bankruptcy courts in each judicial district, with each court presided over by a bankruptcy judge.[141] Filers were now called debtors rather than bankrupts. In many ways, the bankruptcy laws substituted for the kind of social welfare programs that in other countries helped to cushion people from the effects of long-term unemployment and medical hardships, two common reasons for bankruptcy. The laws also functioned as a form of consumer protection.[142]

Personal filings went up dramatically—by 60 percent in the year after the Bankruptcy Code was passed in 1978. Between 1979 and 1997, the filings increased by over 400 percent, to more than one million.[143] More lawyers entered the consumer bankruptcy field. (They formed a national association in 1992.) The dramatic rise in filings drew a backlash from the consumer credit industry, which successfully lobbied for amendments to the code, in 1984 and 1994. The 1984 amendments failed to deter most debtors from getting immediate discharges. In 1994, Congress tasked a new commission to recommend changes to the laws. To the dismay of creditors, the commission took a strong pro-debtor stance and stoutly defended the right of consumer debtors to an immediate discharge.[144] Creditors fought back by introducing amendments that made discharges

Table 5.2. Bankruptcy petitions filed by businesses and nonbusinesses, 1948–1998

Year	Business	Business as % of total	Nonbusiness (consumers and family farms)	Nonbusiness as % of total
1948	4,973	26.9%	13,537	73.1%
1960	12,284	11.2%	97,750	88.8%
1970	16,197	8.3%	178,202	91.7%
1980	46,071	12.8%	314,886	87.2%
1990	64,689	8.9%	660,796	91.1%
1998	50,202	3.5%	1,379,249	96.5%
% change 1948–1998	1,009.5%		10,188.7%	

Source: Historical Statistics of the United States, Millennial Edition On Line, ed. Susan B. Carter et al. (Cambridge: © [copyright] Cambridge University Press, 2006), pp. 3–552.

harder to obtain. They also sought to push more filers into the Bankruptcy Code's Chapter 13, which allowed debtors with regular incomes to pay their creditors, in part or in full, in installments. Debtors could spread these payments over three years, and creditors were prohibited from attempting to collect during that period. Chapter 7, the other option, required the immediate liquidation of a debtor's assets, apart from some exempt property. The proceeds were then distributed among the creditors. Unlike Chapter 13, the process took months rather than years. Filers preferred Chapter 7 because it gave them a fresh start quickly; in 1991, 71 percent of cases were Chapter 7.[145] Legislation in 1996 aimed to curb access to Chapter 7 if debtors were capable of making payments under Chapter 13. Creditors pointed to a controversial study by the Credit Research Center, which argued that many Chapter 7 filers could have paid at least half of their debts.[146]

Consumer bankruptcies continued to rise, even during periods when the unemployment rate was below 4 percent.[147] According to the *Historical Statistics of the United States,* the number of bankruptcy petitions filed by consumers and family farms increased by over 100 times between 1948 and 1998. (See Table 5.2.) Some of the increase may have been due to the Bankruptcy Code's more generous provisions for debtors and aggressive advertising by bankruptcy lawyers, which made people more aware of bankruptcy as a means to a fresh start.[148] But the most important reason was that consumers were taking on more debt, and they had little savings to rely upon. Unexpected medical payments, divorce, or unemployment rendered them unable to meet their loan payments. Some consumer filers were actually small entrepreneurs whose businesses got into trouble.[149]

The 1978 Bankruptcy Code also fundamentally transformed corporate bankruptcy by combining Chapters X and XI into Chapter 11, a term that became synonymous with the American form of corporate bankruptcy. Professional service firms benefited from the 1978 code. Previous laws had attempted to preserve the value of a distressed business by strongly recommending limits on the fees paid to professionals. There was therefore little incentive for first-tier lawyers, bankers, and consultants to enter the business. The 1978 code reversed the incentives by allowing the bankruptcy trustee to hire a "professional person on any reasonable terms" to help with the reorganization. Soon, advisory services sprang up in firms like Lehman Brothers and First Boston, and corporate reorganizations became a lucrative specialist business.[150] The code also diminished the SEC's role in corporate bankruptcy by establishing an entity called the U.S. Trustee that was in charge of bankruptcy administration.

Reorganization (rather than liquidation) of distressed corporations was the overriding goal of the new bankruptcy regime. Even more than in the past, the U.S. system favored rescuing companies rather than salvaging whatever value they still contained for their creditors. The code made it harder even for secured creditors to obstruct a company's reorganization efforts. For the legal profession, the new rules meant that lawyers rather than government administrators called the shots; as a result, the nation's most prestigious law firms entered the field for the first time. The rise in large corporate bankruptcies during the LBO craze of the 1980s further enhanced the lure. Most importantly, the new bankruptcy regime changed the incentives for managers, who could now continue to run their troubled firms while being protected from their creditors, often for years. No longer did corporate executives make heroic efforts to avoid bankruptcy. Ironically, the protection they enjoyed often disadvantaged their healthy competitors. (The airline industry, where every major U.S. player spent time in bankruptcy reorganization, is perhaps the leading example.) Critics accused the new bankruptcy rules of encouraging more risk taking.

The U.S. bankruptcy regime was unique. In other countries, court- or government-appointed administrators replaced the managers of troubled firms, and the administrators sold the firms' assets quickly at fire-sale prices. In the United States, troubled corporations were given more leeway, and they began using the bankruptcy laws creatively. For example, companies facing large tort liabilities (such as asbestos) have resorted to bankruptcy as a way to preempt large class action suits. And prepackaged bankruptcies have become routine. In a "prepack," a company can shorten the process by agreeing to a reorganization with its creditors before filing for bankruptcy.[151]

Credit Reporting and Credit Rating

Consumer credit reporting grew alongside the explosion in consumer credit. The industry diverged into two types of organizations. There were the Big Three (Experian, TransUnion, and Equifax), and the much smaller credit bureaus, most of which had just one office and an average of ten employees. Some of the smaller bureaus were part of exchanges that served a particular industry such as the medical profession or personal finance companies.[152] For decades, the small bureaus had proliferated, but after hitting a peak in 1965, the industry began to consolidate. Between 1972 and 1997, the number of credit bureaus fell by 20 percent, to around 1,000 bureaus. They employed some 22,000 people and generated $2.8 billion in sales. Only fourteen companies had more than five offices, but they accounted for over one-fifth of all offices, two-thirds of revenues, and one-half of employees. The four largest firms alone generated more than one-half of the industry's revenues.[153] The dominance of the Big Three firms paralleled the industry's developments in most other mature economies, where activity tended to be concentrated in the hands of a small number of credit-reporting firms or bureaus.[154]

At the end of the twentieth century, the credit bureaus of the United States collectively covered every individual in the country who accessed credit from a mainstream creditor, whether a bank, a major credit card, a large retailer, or a car dealer. Increasingly, they also collected information from fringe lenders such as payday loan providers.

Credit Scoring

The use of credit scores was an established practice with nearly all consumer credit grantors at the end of the twentieth century. (By contrast, credit scoring for business borrowers was still in its infancy. Business borrowers were fewer and more diverse than consumer borrowers, making it harder to develop scoring models for business loans.)[155] Banks found credit scoring especially useful in their credit card businesses. Scoring eliminated the labor-intensive work of assessing applicants, allowing the banks to save on costs and make more loans.[156] Banks and other lenders used the algorithms developed by firms like Fair, Isaac to prescreen their existing client base for promotional mailings.

In the late 1970s, Fair, Isaac began eyeing the data banks of the Big Three as the basis for an improved scoring system.[157] The largest credit-reporting firms had digitized their data much sooner than the smaller bureaus; as late as 1989, more than one-third of small bureaus had not automated their files.[158] Fair, Isaac worked closely with the Big Three, and it was for a time the only credit-scoring firm that had access to all of their databases. Fair, Isaac had to be careful about maintaining clear boundaries so that it did not violate the abilities of the Big Three firms to compete with one another or inadvertently give one firm an advantage over the others.[159]

Equifax debuted the first general-purpose FICO score, called BEACON, in 1989. By 1991, Fair, Isaac had negotiated joint ventures with the Big Three to develop unique scoring systems for each. The scoring systems had different brand names because they were based on calculations of risk that were specific to each Big Three firm. All, however, came to be known as a FICO score, and the meaning of the score was consistent; a score of 650 (or 700 or 800) indicated the same level of risk whether it came from Experian, TransUnion, or Equifax.[160] The existence of one authoritative scoring system made it easier for credit grantors to assess applicants. And the more credit grantors relied on the FICO score, the more authoritative the score became.

FICO received an even greater boost in 1995, when both Fannie Mae and Freddie Mac began recommending the use of FICO for evaluating mortgage loans. Freddie's officials used FICO in its new automated systems, believing that a standardized score would prevent local brokers from manipulating borrowers' credit scores. A score of 660 became the benchmark for prime-investment loans issued by both Freddie and Fannie. The GSEs wrote it into their proprietary software, literally embedding the score into the industry standards. Soon, lawmakers were explicitly using the FICO scores as an indication of creditworthiness, partly because it was something that the public could easily understand.[161]

From the GSEs, FICO spread throughout the mortgage industry. When Standard and Poor began using FICO in its analyses of mortgage-backed bonds, it provided incentives for lenders to incorporate FICO into *their* models. The change happened swiftly. In 1998, only 50 percent of prime and 30 percent of "nonprime" (loans that did not meet the standards set by Fannie Mae and Freddie Mac) mortgages incorporated credit scores. Five years later, nearly all mortgages did so. The incorporation of FICO allowed the riskiness of mortgages to be quantified along a spectrum and borrowers to be charged accordingly. Risk that was quantified could be managed rather than simply avoided, giving lenders and investors the confidence to venture into previously untouched areas such as subprime lending. First Franklin Financial, a home mortgage lender that specialized in subprime loans, made their reliance on risk quantification explicit in their slogan: "Score it, price it, close it." Yet the credit scores often left out important information, such as borrowers' income and occupation, that was too expensive to access and difficult to keep current.[162] (See Table 5.3.)

The dominance of the three large credit-reporting firms worried the regulators. But the oligopoly may have enabled the industry to police itself better. Unlike the smaller bureaus, the Big Three's customers tended to be stable users of the firms' services, the sort of customers that could be relied upon to provide data on a regular basis. And as the large credit-reporting firms became well-known national brands, they had a further incentive to guard their reputations for reliability and fairness.[163]

But even so, the unprecedented authority of consumer credit-reporting firms posed a dilemma for regulators and consumer advocates. Ensuring the accuracy of credit reports had always been a challenge. Now that credit reports and credit scores had become a prerequisite for obtaining almost any kind of loan, the inaccuracies had even larger consequences. Congress passed laws to ensure that consumers who discovered mistakes in their credit files had adequate recourse. The Fair Credit Reporting Act (FCRA; passed in 1970) required all providers of credit reports to take reasonable actions to ensure that data in their files were accurate. The FCRA gave consumers the right to see the information in their files, be informed if lenders used the information to take adverse actions against them, and correct any misinformation. However, the responsibility for monitoring the reports lay with consumers themselves. To encourage vigilance, the act gave consumers the right to request free copies of their credit reports if lenders had used them to take negative actions. Congressional hearings led to amendments, enacted in 1996, that further strengthened the protections accorded to consumers, and the FTC prosecuted a number of credit information providers for devoting inadequate resources to resolve consumer disputes.[164]

211

Table 5.3. Criteria for creditworthiness, 1850s versus 2014

The Bradstreet Co., early 1850s	FICO score, 2014*
1 Making money	Payment history—35%
2 Making money rapidly	Amounts owed—30%
3 Losing money	Length of credit history—15%
4 Losing money rapidly	New credit—10%
5 Expenses large	Types of credit used—10%
6 Economical	
7 Business too much extended	
8 Business not too much extended	
9 Temperate	
10 Not temperate	
11 Attends closely to business	
12 Does not attend closely to business	
13 Pays large interest	
14 Does not pay large interest	
15 Often hard run for money	
16 Often pays before maturity	
17 Good moral character	
18 Not very good private character	
19 Sometimes suffers notes to be protested	
20 Does not always pay accounts at maturity	
21 Credits prudently	
22 Takes large risks in crediting	
23 Does not value prompt payments sufficiently	
24 Sued	
25 Not sued	
26 Purchases east	
27 Purchases in Cincinnati	
28 Purchases in East and West	
29 Pays promptly	
30 Rather slow pay	
31 Honest	
32 Honesty not fully endorsed	
33 Good business qualifications	
34 Medium business qualifications	
35 Endorses too much	
36 Does not endorse	

* The emphasis on the five categories may vary for particular individuals, such as those who do not yet have a long credit history.

Sources: The Bradstreet ratings were reconstructed from *Bradstreet's Commercial Reports . . .*, 2nd ed., vol. 7, July 31, 1860, p. 8, and earlier looseleaf versions. (The mention of Cincinnati reflects the company's origins in that city.) The FICO standards are from myFICO.com.

The accumulation of personal data by bureaus and large financial institutions aggravated the concerns of consumer activists about privacy and discrimination. FCRA confined access to credit files to parties such as lenders, landlords, insurers, and employers, who intended to engage in legitimate business transactions. To reduce the potential for discrimination, credit information became highly standardized, eliminating the rich details that had gone into traditional credit reports. Although credit reports and credit scores were promoted as tools to help creditors assess risks, organizations now also used them as a defense against charges of discrimination. Taking subjective human judgments out of credit decisions, in other words, was driven as much by political considerations as by the belief that "scientific" algorithms were inherently superior.[165]

Credit Rating

The credit rating agencies continued to garner good reviews into the 1970s, including from the Twentieth Century Fund, a progressive think tank. The Fund's Task Force on Municipal Bond Credit Ratings published its findings in 1974. According to the study, called *The Rating Game,* the agencies were doing a credible job. To put them under public ownership and regulate them more strictly, as some in Congress were advocating, was an extreme solution to an ill-defined problem.[166] Criticisms of the agencies intensified, however, in the wake of New York City's moratorium on payment of its short-term notes in 1975. Senator Thomas Eagleton accused the credit-rating firms of having done an inadequate job of flagging the risks. (Fitch, however, had downgraded New York City's credit prior to the crisis.) Congress again conducted hearings—and again, they resulted in no legislation.

Also controversial were the changes in the way the agencies charged for their services. S&P announced in 1968 that it would charge municipalities for rating their bonds. Previously, S&P had offered municipal ratings free of charge to the municipalities, but the amount of tax-exempt bonds had increased dramatically. Moody's began charging municipal and corporate bond issuers in 1970, and in 1974 S&P also started charging corporate issuers. The agencies' revenue streams shifted from investors and subscribers to the issuers of the securities, prompting complaints about conflict of interest.[167] The situation became even more complicated when the Securities and Exchange Commission designated certain ratings agencies as nationally recognized statistical ratings organizations (NRSROs) in 1975 and began integrating their ratings into the SEC's own regulations.

By the 1970s, the ratings industry had become an oligopoly of three large players—Standard and Poor (S&P), Moody's, and Fitch—that were granted quasi-regulatory powers by federal regulators.[168]

In the late 1970s and early 1980s, high inflation drove most major bond buyers to manage their fixed-income portfolios on a day-by-day basis. The demand for timely research by the credit-rating agencies increased. In 1980 a new agency, Duff and Phelps, began issuing public bond ratings.

Until the 1970s, the United States was the world's largest bond market, by far. When the capital markets began to globalize in the late 1970s, the credit-rating agencies adapted by expanding the scope of their ratings. Ratings now included securities that were issued in the international capital markets, or denominated in foreign currencies. Following S&P, Moody's began to assign unsolicited ratings to the Eurobonds of companies based in the United States. (A "Eurobond" is a bond issued in a currency other than that of the country in which the bond was issued.) In 1985, Moody's began issuing sovereign credit reports, evaluations of the economic and political risks associated with particular countries. The credit-rating agencies also opened more international offices. After having closed its London office in 1975, Moody's reopened it in 1986. S&P opened a London office in 1983 and moved its international operations there five years later.[169] The agencies continued expanding internationally, and the rivalry among them intensified. In the late 1980s, additional competition came in the form of new rating agencies in eastern Europe and Asia that were established with the support of their governments and local institutions. By the mid-1990s, one-third of Moody's analytic staff consisted of non-U.S. nationals, and it began affiliating with the rating agencies in emerging markets. The Asian financial crisis of 1997 spurred even more credit rating activity in the developing world.

The agencies also responded to the spread of new investment instruments. Moody's began a speculative grade (junk bond) research service. S&P first rated mortgage-backed securities in 1975; Moody's entered this market in the early 1980s. In 1987, S&P rated the first bonds backed by credit card receivables, and in 1991, Moody's issued its first-ever rating of a derivatives products company (Merrill Lynch). Moody's launched a program to rate banks throughout the emerging markets in 1994 and began rating bank loans the following year.[170] At century's end, the agencies were rating trillions of dollars worth of global debt, including a number of non-traditional instruments. The industry had come a long way from its beginnings early in the twentieth century, when Moody's, Poor's Publishing, and a handful of other small enterprises rated only a few types of securities, primarily industrial and government bonds.

As with credit reporting, the credit-rating industry became an oligopoly. But credit rating differed from credit reporting in its relationship with the federal regulators. For credit-reporting firms like Dun and Bradstreet, Experian, Equifax, and TransUnion, there was no equivalent to the NRSRO status that the SEC bestowed on S&P, Moody's, and Fitch. In effect, federal regulators had given to the credit-rating agencies a quasi-regulatory function, even though they were publicly listed, for-profit enterprises. The Department of Justice conducted antitrust investigations of the credit-rating agencies in 1996, but it ended the following year with no action taken. S&P, Moody's, and Fitch would continue as the primary guardians of investors in the bond markets.

At the end of the twentieth century, a confluence of historical forces brought about an explosion in the supply of credit. Rising levels of consumer debt were of course nothing new. The difference now lay in people's savings rates.[171] Depending on how it is defined, the rate had hovered at around 7 to 10 percent from the early 1950s until the late 1980s. Then it fell precipitously: in 2005, Americans had a historically low savings rate of just 1.5 percent.[172] One explanation for the fall in savings was simply that corporations and public policies had changed the norms. As one scholar put it, "In an affluent economy [that is] churning out an abundance of goods, thrift becomes a hindrance."[173] Although wage growth stagnated, the rate of unemployment was stable from the mid-1980s to 2008, which may have diminished the urgency to save for bad times. (The unemployment rate fluctuated between 3.5 and 9.7 percent in the years between 1961 and 1983 but moderated to between 4 percent to 7.5 percent until 2008.)[174] The growth in housing prices might also have been a factor, leading home owners to regard their fast-appreciating dwellings as a form of saving. Rather than rely on rainy-day funds, people now tapped their home equity lines to meet living expenses or just to buy more consumer goods. Rising debt and falling savings had the predictable result—bankruptcy rates continued to rise. Creditors lobbied hard to stem the filings, with limited success.

The way lenders and intermediaries measured creditworthiness changed. The standards for "whom to trust" (the title of a well-regarded credit handbook of the 1890s) had originated in the world of trade, where lenders needed informal rules for judging whether potential borrowers were willing and able to pay their debts.[175] John Bradstreet's innovative rating system of the 1850s tried to codify the elements of trustworthiness in business (Table 5.3). Although the order was somewhat idiosyncratic, contemporaries recognized and approved Bradstreet's list of thirty-six traits. Within a few decades, business people shortened the list of traits to the "three Cs": capital, capacity (ability), and character. Credit professionals sometimes argued about the relative weighting of the "Cs," but they did not doubt that capital, capacity, and character were the basis of responsible lending and borrowing.

When the economy became more reliant on consumer credit, the spirit of the three Cs lived on, although it was modified by increased attention to individuals' salaried employment. Until well into the 1970s, local bankers exercised power over people's access to credit, and personal reputations still mattered hugely, especially in mortgage lending. But once technology, industry consolidation, government bailouts, the politicization of the mortgage markets, and other factors severed that link, having a reputation for clean living, hard work, and integrity mattered much less. Creditors now had more sophisticated means at their disposal for assessing applicants; the large credit bureaus achieved universal coverage, and the FICO score became ubiquitous. FICO did not take into account a person's capital or capacity, and it measured "character" only indirectly, through the individual's recent payment history. These developments did not prevent loans from going to households that could not properly afford them. Meanwhile, in the corporate sector, attitudes about debt and creditworthiness were upended by new academic thinking and the increasingly bold practices of Wall Street banks and financiers such as Michael Milken. The federal tax laws, which exempted the interest paid on debts, also encouraged companies and households to increase their leverage.[176]

Then, too, the booms and busts that had dogged the American economy now seemed a thing of the past. Encouraged by federal policies and with no major panics and crashes to stop it, the credit binge continued. Wall Street, Main Street, lawmakers, political leaders, and the Federal Reserve—all seemed content for the excesses to continue.

POSTSCRIPT

Creative and Destructive Credit

The U.S. credit markets of the early twenty-first century exhibited paradoxical features. On the one hand, they were highly efficient because lenders could now automate their decisions by running immense amounts of data through algorithms. But on the other hand, credit markets were more complex than ever, and instruments such as derivatives defied the ability of credit-rating agencies to assess risk correctly.

New regulations continued to lift the barriers to financial "innovation." The Commodity Futures Modernization Act of 2000 removed derivatives securities such as CMOs and CDOs from regulatory oversight. In 2004 the Securities and Exchange Commission further relaxed the regulatory standards; it loosened the capital requirements of the five largest securities firms and allowed investment banks greater self-regulation.[1] The newly liberated banks and securities firms plowed their capital into yet more asset-backed and mortgage-backed securities and derivatives. The result was a boom in the number and type of securitized debts, which by 2006 reached a volume of $28 trillion. Three-fifths of all American mortgages and a full one-quarter of consumer debt provided the raw materials for the popular investments.[2] The massive expansion of household debt can best be grasped by expressing it as a share of the nation's GDP: it went from 100 percent in 1980 to 173 percent in 2009, or the equivalent of around $6 trillion of additional borrowing.[3]

A number of academics, journalists, policy makers, and even some lenders warned that the boom was unsustainable. No one, however, could predict when the credit markets would turn negative, and until then, there was no incentive for lenders to stop lending or financial institutions to stop creating the debt-based securities. True to historical patterns, the assets that underpinned the securities deteriorated: at the height of the credit bubble in 2006, one-quarter of all new mortgages were subprime. Thanks mostly to the rise in mortgages and home equity loans, household debt went from 86 percent of household disposable income in 1989 to 141 percent by 2007. One-third of households were using home equity loans to pay their credit card debts; they were trading unsecured debt for secured debt and placing themselves at greater risk. In the process, they eroded the equity they had in their homes, which constituted the greatest portion of many Americans' total wealth. And their savings rates fell to the lowest level since World War II.[4]

In 2006 the housing mortgage markets began declining. By 2007, the default rates reached alarming proportions. Defaults mounted in the subprime lending markets in particular, causing trouble for lenders such as Countrywide Financial (a conservative mortgage lender until it entered the subprime market in a big way) and many of the mortgage-backed securities funds. The credit-rating agencies downgraded a number of the securities and firms, but not until the spring of 2007—too late, according to critics. By August 2007, interbank liquidity—the ease with which banks lend to one another—had diminished, signaling that the credit markets were tightening. The next institutions to encounter serious difficulties were the government-sponsored enterprises (GSEs). In July 2008 the Federal Reserve and the U.S. Treasury authorized increased borrowing facilities for Fannie Mae and Freddie Mac. Shortly afterward, President George W. Bush authorized the Treasury Department to buy the GSEs' obligations. His actions vindicated those who had believed that the federal government would never allow the GSEs to fail.

The crisis came to a head in September 2008. First, the Treasury placed Fannie Mae and Freddie Mac in government conservatorship, the equivalent of receivership for public institutions. The government continued to ensure that the GSEs would continue operating; it bought the GSEs' stock and mortgage-backed securities and extended a secured lending facility. But then Lehman Brothers, the nation's fourth-largest investment bank, filed for Chapter 11 bankruptcy protection on September 15, 2008. Lehman had borrowed substantially to fund its investments in mortgage-related assets, and its bankruptcy filing was the largest in U.S. history. The next day, the Federal Reserve authorized up to $85 billion of lending to the international insurance company, AIG. AIG's credit rating had been downgraded, causing a liquidity crisis and imminent bankruptcy. According to federal officials, AIG held so many credit default swaps (described later in this postscript) that the claims against it threatened the entire financial system.

In the end, the U.S. government bailed out the financial sector.[5] Congress stabilized the U.S. debt markets through the Troubled Asset Relief Program (TARP, enacted in 2008), which invested in, loaned to, or subsidized 945 financial institutions, turning much of their toxic debt into taxpayer-owned securities. The Federal Reserve encouraged more credit availability to individuals and businesses through "quantitative easing": it purchased huge amounts of troubled mortgage-backed securities and GSE debts as well as long-term Treasury securities. (Buying Treasuries kept interest rates low.) The amount of debt the Fed held ballooned by some $3 trillion from 2007 to 2013, or nearly four times the average debt that it held before the crisis. (The amount was unprecedented in absolute terms, but as a fraction of GDP it was a bit lower than during the Great Depression and World War II.)[6] Lawmakers and regulators hoped that the government's actions would restore confidence in the markets. Taxpayers might even make money through the securities' dividend and interest payments and the sale of bank equities that the government had acquired. The decision to save so many private companies at public expense ignited political controversy, and it led to organized citizen protests in the United States, of which the Occupy Wall Street movement was the most newsworthy. On the other end of the political spectrum, the members of the conservative Tea Party movement also voiced objections.

The historic bailouts led to yet another attempt, the Third Basel Accord, to bolster the liquidity and capital strength of financial institutions. These goals had supposedly been accomplished in 2004 when the Second Basel Accord was agreed. (The accords were agreements about bank laws and regulations, including capital requirements, issued by the Committee on Banking Supervision. The committee is part of the Bank for International Settlements, based in Basel, Switzerland.) But financial institutions had quickly figured out that they could take a large portion of loans off their balance sheets by securitizing them. And, of course, they benefited from the higher returns the securities provided.[7] Technically, the institutions were in compliance with the Second Basel Accord requirements. But their actions violated the intent of the regulations, which was to enhance the robustness of financial institutions, and by extension the entire global financial system.[8] The Third Basel accord was designed to fix the loopholes.

The shocking events of September 2008 forced a great deal of soul-searching in the U.S. and other countries that had participated in the frenzy of borrowing. Nearly two years after the crisis, the *Economist* ruefully observed how completely debt had seeped into American and British life: "The answer to all problems seemed to be more debt. Depressed? Use your credit card for a shopping spree 'because you're worth it.' Want to get rich quick? Work for a private-equity or hedge-fund firm, using borrowed money to enhance returns. Looking for faster growth for your company? Borrow money and make an acquisition. And if the economy is in recession, let the government go into deficit to bolster spending."[9] The United States had not been unique in the scale of its indebtedness. Rising debt was a feature in the world's ten mature economies, where the average total debt (public and private combined) rose from 200 percent of GDP in 1995 to 300 percent in 2008.[10]

Ironically, before the crisis, academics had pointed to credit as an important reason for why the economy had been so stable. New financing techniques and better methods for assessing creditworthiness, they argued, resulted in more credit, which allowed people to bridge temporary gaps in spending power—for example, when households ran out of money before the next paycheck. On the face of it, the dream of the early twentieth-century reformers had been fulfilled: middle- and low-income households could now access credit much more easily. Their spending and investment were no longer strictly tied to today's income and cash flow but could be linked to income over the long term. For firms, this meant that temporary slowdowns in consumer earnings no longer led, necessarily, to a slowdown in consumption. And given that consumer spending now accounted for about 70 percent of the American economy, the ability to smooth out the peaks and troughs of consumer demand meant that the business cycle was less likely to wreak the kind of havoc that characterized the era prior to the Second World War.[11]

But instead of moderating the pattern of consumer demand, the credit boom resulted in a consumption binge. Credit, moreover, was no longer backed by real assets or by people's "character." Instead, assets whose price rises were driven by irrational beliefs and unfounded hope became the basis for lending.

The Securitized Debt Markets

Securitized debts played a central role in the crisis. Few bankers worked in structured finance, the name given to the area concerned with the securitization of debt. But in 2006, structured finance instruments accounted for 20–30 percent of the big investment banks' earnings. Merrill Lynch's fees from collateralized debt obligations alone peaked that year at $700 million.[12] In the early 2000s, structured finance instruments were used on credit card debt, student loans, auto loans, aircraft leases—anything that generated a cash flow. But they made the biggest difference in home mortgages.

The guarantees provided by the GSEs kept the secondary markets for mortgage debt vibrant. But between 2003 and 2006 the quality of the underlying mortgages deteriorated substantially. In 2003 nearly two-thirds of mortgage originations were conventional loans that conformed to GSE guidelines; by 2006 only about one-third were conventional, conforming loans. When the crisis hit in 2008, the GSEs held some $170 billion in subprime securities—products that they themselves would not have deemed creditworthy, but which they bought because of government-mandated targets for increasing the number of loans and because the credit-rating agencies had rated the products triple-A.[13]

The riskier loans were included in the CDOs. Properly done, a CDO allows investors to choose among different tranches of securities, according to their appetite for risk. But Wall Street firms (and their subsidiaries in London) abused the instrument by improperly selling even the highest-risk tranches as low-risk. They were helped by the credit-rating agencies, which gave the low-quality tranches the highest ratings of AAA, a near-guarantee that the bonds would not default. Reassured, investors such as pension funds and municipalities bought the bonds. CDO issues went from $100 to $150 billion a year in the early 2000s to over $500 billion in 2006. The healthy market for CDOs continued even when housing markets declined. In February 2007, Freddie Mac announced that it would no longer buy the riskiest subprime mortgages and mortgage-backed securities. But between February and June 2007, as mortgage defaults rose, Wall Street firms created and sold $50 billion of new CDOs.[14]

The now-familiar pattern repeated itself. As happened with western mortgages in the 1880s and junk bonds during the 1980s, strong demand for the securities drove banks and securities firms to create more even though the underlying assets were becoming steadily worse. This time, however, there was an additional factor—the GSEs, which were required by the federal government to buy increasing amounts of securities that were backed by risky mortgage loans. Just before the crisis hit, Fannie Mae and Freddie Mac between them had $2 trillion worth of very risky mortgages on their books, and they were acquiring nearly all new high-risk lending. Because the GSEs were guaranteed buyers, the mortgage lenders dispensed with traditional credit standards. As recently as 1990, Americans found it difficult to obtain mortgage loans without first proving that they had a hefty 20 percent down payment, a good credit history, and stable employment. Fifteen years later, a 3 percent down payment, a less-than-stellar credit score, and an oral statement about one's employment and salary sufficed to get a subprime loan. In 2006, nearly half of first-time buyers had no down payments at all.[15]

Eventually, the supply of even the riskiest subprime mortgages began to dry up. And yet the sellers of the investment instruments had no incentive to stop; while there was money to be made from buyers who were clamoring for the bonds, the investment banks and securities firms had strong inducements to keep going. Financial institutions accelerated the frenzied dance by dealing in a derivative, the credit default swap (CDS).[16] CDSs were a form of insurance against default by a credit instrument such as a CDO, or a downgrade of the instrument by a credit-rating agency. The CDS was originally invented to allow banks and insurers, which have different regulatory requirements, to swap their loans and insurance policies with one another, in what economists call regulatory arbitrage.[17] But with CDSs, the banks did not even need to accumulate the underlying mortgages. Instead, the CDS was an agreement between two parties that was based on the principles of insurance: if the bond defaulted, the buyer of the CDS would get a payment. Originally used as a hedge, the CDS became a speculative instrument. Investors began buying the insurance on securities they did not even own, a situation that was akin to a person buying life insurance on someone he did not even know. Even more strange, many investors could buy insurance on the same security, meaning that if the security defaulted, they would all be paid. Unlike regular insurance, with CDSs there was little understanding of the risks involved.[18] At the peak of the CDS market in 2008, outstanding CDSs totaled more than $62 trillion, a figure that was significantly higher than the gross national product of the entire planet! The Wall Street firms bet that CDOs, CDSs, and other such securities would never collapse because U.S. house prices would never collapse. AIG alone insured $400 billion of these securities, of which a significant portion ($57 billion) was backed by sub-prime mortgages.[19]

The credit default swaps market posed great risks to the economy. Because there was no central clearing mechanism for the CDSs (an equivalent to the New York Stock Exchange), no one was sure what the potential liabilities were. This huge unknown intensified the alarm that spread through the financial markets in September 2008, when Lehman Brothers and then AIG were threatened with bankruptcy. Both held large amounts of structured finance instruments, but AIG's bets on CDSs were so large that a wave of bond defaults would have seriously threatened not just AIG but, the regulators argued, the financial system itself. Henry Paulson, the secretary of the Treasury when Lehman Brothers and AIG were facing collapse, later wrote about his support for bailing out AIG: "I understood that we had to hold our noses and save the company in order to protect the frail financial system."[20]

Why the supposedly smart Wall Street bankers participated in the structured finance markets up to the point when they collapsed can be explained by a combination of factors: regulations that created perverse incentives, the lack of competence of regulators and credit-rating agencies, actions that bordered on fraud, and cognitive mistakes that critics labeled as arrogance ("it can't happen," or "it won't happen to me"). Short-term profit taking and competition among financial institutions to be at the top of the league tables overrode concerns about risk. Banks feared they would lose their luster in the competitive investment banking sphere unless they participated aggressively in the structured finance markets. There was, as well, a tacit expectation that the Federal Reserve and Treasury would continue to rescue institutions that were deemed too big to fail.[21] The government's implicit guarantee diminished the urgency for banks to strengthen their capital reserves by, for example, issuing new shares. Instead, they counted on the price of their existing shares to rise.[22]

Academics and policy makers struggled to explain the events that had nearly destroyed the financial system of the United States. In 2013, former chairman of the Federal Reserve Alan Greenspan admitted, "When I was sitting there at the Fed, I would say, 'Does anyone know what is going on?' And the answer was 'Only in part.' I would ask someone about synthetic derivatives [such as credit default swaps], say, and I would get detailed analysis. But I couldn't tell what was really happening."[23] The complexities of the credit markets baffled even those who were supposed to monitor and to control them.

Credit and the American Dream

Throughout the four phases of credit, American businesses, households, and governments willingly took on the risks associated with credit to accomplish their goals. Why they did so may be debated, but surely one explanation was people's optimism about the economy and their own prospects within it. According to this thinking, the prices of houses, equities, land, and other assets tend to go up. So do wages and salaries, especially of the people who are wise enough to invest in education. "The essence of a capitalist system," writes historian Thomas McCraw, "is a strong psychological orientation toward the future. And that orientation is best expressed in the system's pervasive reliance on credit."[24]

Americans historically have been not just future-oriented but optimistic. Extending credit and, on the flip side, going into debt appeared sensible in light of the very real possibility that the future would be better than the past. The expansion (albeit uneven) of democracy combined with a large endowment of valuable natural resources, especially undeveloped land, was a perpetual source of hopefulness. More Americans have become wealthy by betting on real estate than in any other enterprise. Whether it was the New York frontier of the 1790s, Chicago in the 1830s, Los Angeles in the 1880s, midwestern farmland in 1910, or San Francisco in the 1990s, many people—not just speculators—have shown great willingness to go into debt for the prospect of future gains.[25] Through every phase of the history of credit, Americans have believed in the power of the future to render today's indebtedness irrelevant, and even prudent.

The busts that followed credit bubbles (or, more rarely, equities bubbles) periodically shook this faith but never completely destroyed it. From the viewpoint of individuals, panics and depressions were the exception, not the norm. For most Americans, "normal" meant economic growth, and they behaved accordingly. Confidence—the collective belief that risks were worth taking because economic and political conditions would continue to be good, that other people would honor their contracts, and that methods existed that allowed creditors and investors to calculate risks reasonably accurately—remained strong despite the volatility of the business cycle. The numbers suggest that the faith was not misplaced: real GDP per capita grew in 162 out of the 223 years from 1790 to 2012.[26] Or put another way, for 73 percent of the nation's history, when the population grew to *75 times* its initial number, Americans as a whole became steadily better off. Crashes and panics resulted in high default rates. But in normal times the vast majority of borrowers paid their debts, the economy grew, and creditors were right to be confident of making a return. For nearly all of the nation's history, therefore, the use of credit to achieve future prosperity was well supported by both hope and experience.

Through the first three phases, credit increasingly became more available to ordinary people. Even so, lenders, borrowers, investors, and insurers faced constraints, including the prospect of losing their capital or collateral. Debtors also bore the risk of losing their good reputations, and with it the ability to borrow at reasonable rates. The late twentieth century, however, was an inflection point. A number of global developments in the political and financial spheres fundamentally shifted the assumptions about credit that had existed since the eighteenth century: that credit should be backed by assets, or (especially in the business realm) by a person's character. In the 1980s, lending institutions, credit-reporting and credit-rating agencies, and the political establishment began removing the constraints. The steady erosion of lending standards along with government guarantees of bailouts severed the link between risk and reward. Nothing illustrated this break so starkly as the incidents of bank employees reaping outsized bonuses by taking risks with other people's money while having no responsibility for losses. This unsustainable state of affairs culminated in the crisis of 2008, when the world's largest and supposedly most advanced financial system nearly collapsed. Credit was still an engine of enterprise, but it had also become, more than at any time in the past, an agent of destruction whose reach was global. Today we have credit creation on a gargantuan scale, accomplished with instruments so complicated that they stumped even a highly intelligent chairman of the Federal Reserve.[27] Credit drives new forms of speculation (on derivatives and virtual money, for example) and unaffordable levels of consumption for some people. Credit now comes from institutions that are larger and more efficient, but whose imminent failures pose consequences so catastrophic that governments feel pressured to choose bailouts over bankruptcy.

The moral and political ambiguities of a credit economy drove the founders and their successors to rethink credit's power to build and to destroy. Alexander Hamilton staked his federal bonds on his conviction that a large class of entrepreneurs would benefit from the private credit that a stable United States could unleash. He believed that there existed among his countrymen not just pent-up demand, but ambitions that the imperial system—with its prohibitions against money creation, banks, and the settlement of western lands—too often suppressed. The subsequent growth of the American economy proved Hamilton right. Despite problems with credit that were at times severe, and which Americans have never fully solved, credit has been the invigorating principle that turned potential wealth into national prosperity.

APPENDIX: AN EXPLANATION OF TERMS

NOTES

ACKNOWLEDGMENTS

INDEX

APPENDIX

An Explanation of Terms

Lending and borrowing are simple concepts, but the arrangements and instruments for doing these activities can be somewhat complex. (In the late twentieth century, they became very complex indeed.) Although we often speak of "credit" as if it were monolithic, there are many kinds; they evolved over millennia in different areas of the world, as responses to the specific problems of trade, public policy, and warfare. For most countries, we can divide credit into a few broad categories: business, consumer, and public (or government) credit. Within these categories, things get more complicated. Business credit, for example, involves both short- and long-term credit. Short-term credit is working capital, for funding inventories and payroll; long-term credit funds the building of factories, offices, and other physical plant. Consumer credit can be anything from an informal tab at a local establishment (such as a grocery store or bar) to a thirty-year home mortgage. We can speak of public credit to mean a government's ability to borrow on the strength of its credibility and reputation. In the United States, the federal government has rarely made direct loans to individuals and businesses. More often, it has expanded the credit markets for certain targeted groups such as farmers, home buyers, small businesses, and students by insuring the loans made by private entities. Important exceptions include the Reconstruction Finance Corporation (RFC), established by the Hoover administration at the start of the Great Depression. The RFC made direct loans to banking, agriculture, and other troubled sectors of the economy. Today the departments of agriculture and education make loans directly to farmers and students, respectively. The Export-Import Bank, an independent government agency, lends to the foreign buyer of U.S. goods.

Financial tools such as bonds and commercial paper (bills of exchange and promissory notes belong in the latter category) evolved to meet the specific needs of lenders and borrowers. Many are very old and were first introduced to facilitate trade. This book refers only to a small number of the most important credit and debt instruments that Americans have used over the course of their history. The instruments' basic workings are explained below, but there can be variations, and many of these instruments became more complex over time.

Bill of credit. The colonial governments issued bills of credit, primarily during wartime, to pay for supplies. The bills were accepted for tax payments at a future date. Bills of credit were a roundabout way of borrowing from the populace. They allowed governments to avoid levying taxes, which were politically unpopular. Issuing government IOUs had the added benefit of supplying colonists with a form of paper money for conducting their everyday business. In this way, a society that lacked specie substituted a paper currency that was backed by debt. Bills of credit were fiat money—that is, backed by nothing other than the colonial governments' credibility. Even so, the bills of credit worked well, especially in the middle colonies.

Bill of exchange (also known as a draft). An instrument used primarily in international trade. The bill of exchange binds one party to pay another a specific amount of money, at a specific date. If the maker of the bill had a good reputation, the bill could be endorsed (transferred) to another party at a discount. (See Discounting in this appendix.) The new owner then received the payment from the original maker of the bill. A bill of exchange could be endorsed many times in the course of its life, passing hand to hand as a kind of currency. Merchants with very high reputations charged a fee for guaranteeing the bills of their lesser-known brethren so that the bills could be used even in overseas markets. Bills of exchange were for large denominations. They were used less in inland (domestic) trade, which generally involved smaller sums.

Bond. A debt instrument representing a loan from an investor. Along with equities, bonds are a form of security. They are issued by the borrower, who can be either a business or a government body, to finance a variety of short- or long-term projects and activities. Bond terms vary, but usually the bond's "maturity" is the date when it is paid off; the "coupon" is the interest that the borrower pays the investor at fixed intervals. From the early nineteenth century, bonds could be bought and sold in exchanges located in U.S. commercial centers, and this negotiability made bonds very attractive to a wide range of investors. Investors see bonds as conservative investments; in the event of bankruptcy, bondholders are repaid before stockholders. However, there are many different grades of bonds, ranging from U.S. Treasuries (the safest) to high-yield or "junk" bonds, which carry greater risks.

Call loans. Short-term loans to stockbrokers, which can be called in at any time. Call loans were in place in New York by the 1840s. After the Civil War, the large New York commercial banks began making call loans. This exacerbated the problems with the nation's payments system: when banks in the agricultural portions of the country withdrew their reserves from the New York banks during the harvest season, the New York banks had to call in *their* loans, which destabilized the stock market. In the early twentieth century, corporations sought higher returns on their money; eventually, they surpassed the banks to become the biggest lenders of call loans. The large amount of call loans helped to fuel the stock market boom of the late 1920s.

Commercial bank. Today, commercial banks offer a diverse range of services, including taking deposits from ordinary people and issuing credit cards. For most of U.S. history, however, the primary function of commercial banks was making short-term business loans to fund the transportation and marketing of goods. Retail banking was done by institutions such as savings banks.

Commercial paper. A short-term debt instrument issued by businesses, usually maturing between 30 and 270 days. Commercial paper allows businesses to go to the money markets and borrow directly from investors. Along with commercial banks, the commercial paper market is the largest source of short-term credit for businesses. Commercial paper markets have existed in the United States since the 1830s. The markets spread to other areas after the Civil War, but a national market did not emerge until the turn of the twentieth century. The lack of a secondary market for commercial paper constrained its liquidity; the problem continued until the Federal Reserve (established in 1913) began to discount commercial paper. The market grew much larger in the 1960s and 1970s, when banks set up finance subsidiaries to fund their credit card businesses. These subsidiaries issued commercial paper rather than depending on bank deposits for funding. Other financial intermediaries such as consumer finance companies also depend on the commercial paper markets for their funds.

Debentures. A bond that is backed by a portfolio of financial assets, such as real estate mortgages. Western mortgage companies in the United States began experimenting with debentures in the 1880s, following a well-established practice in Europe. Unlike the mortgages themselves, the bonds were a liquid investment. The drawback was that investors could not evaluate the underlying assets. This weakness prompted the mortgage companies to write explicit guarantees into their contracts with investors. The other drawback was the debentures' relative lack of liquidity; unlike in Europe, there was no exchange that would have allowed investors to trade the bonds easily. Today, U.S. debentures are unsecured loan certificates issued by a company. In Britain, the term has retained its older meaning—a security that is backed by assets. (See also Securitization in this appendix.)

Discounting (of bills). A person who receives a bill of exchange can sell it to another party before the maturity date for an amount that is slightly less than the bill's face value. This amount is called the discount. The original maker of the bill then pays the new owner of the discounted bill its original face value. Confidence that bills of exchange could be readily discounted allowed these instruments to circulate as currency among commercial people. In the United States in the early nineteenth century, the endorsements and guarantees of key merchants made it possible for bills to travel across the continent. Bills of exchange that contained two names—that of the maker and that of the endorser who guaranteed the bill—were called "trade acceptances" and were readily discounted by banks.

Factor. One of the many middlemen linking buyers, sellers, creditors, and debtors across the Atlantic world. The term "factor" originated in the English cloth trade, but the function itself probably has existed since the very earliest days of trade. In the United States, a good example was the cotton factor of the pre–Civil War era—the New York merchants and their partners in the southern ports who paid advances to cotton planters, transmitted information about creditworthiness, acted as guarantors for planters and buyers, provided supplies on credit, and endorsed planters' notes. The term was resurrected in the 1920s to refer to entities that bought accounts receivable at a discount, thus allowing companies to outsource their credit back-offices. Today factoring continues to be an important service in domestic and international trade.

Finance company. Specialized financial institutions that provide funding to businesses or consumers. In the United States, finance companies became important financial intermediaries at the beginning of the twentieth century, especially for automobile purchases. Finance companies borrowed from the banks and made loans to small or new borrowers who otherwise could not obtain financing. Some manufacturers such as General Electric and General Motors set up captive finance companies as subsidiaries to their core businesses. Sales finance companies had the advantage of being less regulated than commercial banks and so could tailor their services to meet their customers' needs.

Investment bank. Unlike commercial banks, investment banks do not take deposits or make short-term credit available to businesses. Instead, they underwrite debt and equity securities and provide guidance to corporations on issuing and placing their shares. Modern investment banking began in the United States after the Civil War to exploit the commercial banks' inability to fund large industrial projects. Investment bankers such as J. P. Morgan and Jacob Schiff pooled the capital of investors in the United States and Europe to put into large enterprises. This American institution was distinct from the older British merchant banks that evolved from the merchant activities of their founders.

Mercantile (trade) credit.   A form of business-to-business lending in which payment for goods is deferred until the goods are sold, with the goods themselves serving as collateral. This type of credit appears on the borrower's records as accounts payable (a liability), and on the creditor's records as accounts receivable (an asset). Historically, the transactions were formalized by bills of exchange and promissory notes, but sometimes the arrangements were less formal. Trade credit terms vary by industry and the types of goods involved. Sellers use generous trade credit to compete for buyers or to encourage buyer loyalty. Discounts are offered for immediate payment. Mercantile credit can serve as a form of start-up financing for businesses that may otherwise struggle to attract funding from banks.

Real-bills doctrine.   The belief that commercial banks should lend only to commercial entities, on short term. The doctrine evolved from bankers' long experience with bills of exchange and other mercantile paper—and, even further back in time, to the overseas merchants of the seventeenth and eighteenth centuries, who restricted their lending to fellow merchants. The bills that merchants produced during the course of trade represented actual goods in transit. In contrast to manufacturing and real estate, mercantile activities required only short-term borrowings—the very opposite of speculative lending on undeveloped land and industrial enterprises. In the late nineteenth century, the doctrine was reinforced by the need for banks always to have adequate reserves on hand to meet their depositors' demands.

Securitization.   The process of creating a financial instrument (such as a bond) by combining financial assets such as mortgages, car loans, or other securities. The securitized assets are then divided into tiers (tranches) and marketed to investors based on their tolerance for risk. Securitization helps to make financial assets such as mortgages more tradable. Slicing the large asset pools into smaller tranches also allows a wider range of investors to participate. Securitization only works when investors trust that someone (the bond issuer, or a credit-rating agency) is monitoring the quality of the underlying assets. For companies, banks, and other financial institutions, securitization is a convenient way to take loans off their balance sheets, which improves their reserves-to-loans ratios. (See also Debentures in this appendix.)

NOTES

Introduction

1. "Credit Market Debt Outstanding by Sector," table D.3, in Board of Governors of the Federal Reserve System, *Flow of Funds, Balance Sheets, and Integrated Macroeconomic Accounts,* Third Quarter 2014, p. 5.

2. Alexander Hamilton, "Report on a Plan for the Further Support of Public Credit," January 16, 1795, communicated to U.S. House of Representatives on January 19, 1795; to U.S. Senate on January 21, 1795, http://founders.archives .gov/documents/Hamilton/01-18-02-0052-0002.

3. Alexander Hamilton, "Second Report on the Further Provision Necessary for Establishing Public Credit" (Report on a National Bank), December 13, 1790, communicated to U.S. House of Representatives on December 14, 1790, http://founders .archives.gov/?q=alexander%20hamilton%20december%2014%201790%20 national%20bank&s=1111311111&sa=&r=7&sr=.

4. Benjamin Franklin, *Poor Richard's Almanack,* widely available, including online, https://archive.org/details/poorrichardsalm01frangoog; and "Advice to a Young Tradesman" [July 21, 1748], originally printed in George Fisher, *The American Instructor: or Young Man's Best Companion . . .* , 9th ed., rev. (Philadelphia: B. Franklin and D. Hall, 1748), pp. 375–377; National Archives, Founders Online, http://founders.archives.gov/documents/Franklin/01-03-02-0130. In his will, Franklin left funds to be loaned out to deserving young craftsmen. Wilbur C. Plummer, "Consumer Credit in Colonial Philadelphia," *Pennsylvania Magazine of History and Biography* 66, no. 4 (October 1942): 385–409, p. 404.

5. Alexander Hamilton, "Report Relative to a Provision for the Support of Public Credit," January 9, 1790, communicated to U.S. House of Representatives on January 14, 1790, http://founders.archives.gov/?q=alexander%20hamilton%201790%20 public%20credit&s=1111311111&sa=&r=20&sr=.

6. Hamilton estimated that the U.S. government owed about $29 million to domestic (U.S.) bondholders, and $12 million to Dutch and French creditors. His

235

very rough estimate of the states' debts was about $25 million. All told, Hamilton reckoned that the public debt from the war totalled about $79 million. Thomas K. McCraw, *The Founders and Finance: How Hamilton, Gallatin, and Other Immigrants Forged a New Economy* (Cambridge, MA: Harvard University Press, 2012), pp. 47, 93–95.

7. Hamilton, "Report on a Plan for the Further Support of Public Credit." For a very different view of debt, see David Graeber, *Debt: The First 5,000 Years* (Brooklyn, NY: Melville House, 2011). Graeber argues that the basis of all modern debt is governments' creation of money to fund wars.

8. Benjamin Franklin, *The American Weekly Mercury,* March 27, 1729; "A Modest Enquiry into the Nature and Necessity of a Paper-Currency," pamphlet, April 3, 1729.

9. Daniel Defoe, *The Complete English Tradesman,* 2nd ed., vol. 1 (London 1727 [1726]), letters 18 and 23.

10. Anthony Di Renzo, "The Complete English Tradesman: Daniel Defoe and the Emergence of Business Writing," *Journal of Technical Writing and Communication* 28, no. 4 (October 1998): 325–334.

11. Charles Calomiris and Stephen Haber, *Fragile by Design: The Political Origins of Banking Crises and Scarce Credit* (Princeton, NJ: Princeton University Press, 2014), pp. 75, 103.

12. Adam Smith, *An Inquiry into the Nature and Causes of the Wealth of Nations,* vol. 1, bk. 2, ch. 2, para. 86, widely available, including online, http://www.econlib.org/library/Smith/smWN.html. Smith was aware that the Scottish banks regularly created credit by offering overdrafts—cash advances that were not underpinned by merchants' IOUs. Neil T. Skaggs, "Adam Smith on Growth and Credit: Too Weak a Connection?" *Journal of Economic Studies* 26, no. 6 (1999): 481–496.

13. Smith, *Wealth of Nations,* vol. 1, bk. 2, ch. 3, para. 16.

14. Joseph Schumpeter, *Business Cycles: A Theoretical, Historical and Statistical Analysis of the Capitalist Process* (New York: McGraw-Hill Book Company, Inc., 1939), p. 216.

15. Joseph Schumpeter, *The Theory of Economic Development: An Inquiry into Profits, Capital, Credit, Interest, and the Business Cycle* (1934 [1911]), pp. 70–74, 116, 126; Thomas K. McCraw, *Prophet of Innovation: Joseph Schumpeter and Creative Destruction* (Cambridge, MA: Belknap Press of Harvard University Press, 2007), pp. 74–75.

16. Henry C. Carey, *The Credit System in France, Great Britain, and the United States* (Carey, Lea & Blanchard, 1838), p. 40. The original paragraph was in italics.

17. John Stuart Mill, "Of Credit, as a Substitute for Money," in *Principles of Political Economy with Some of Their Applications to Social Philosophy,* bk. 3, ch. 11, widely available, including online, http://www.econlib.org/library/Mill/mlP.html.

18. Mill, *Principles of Political Economy,* bk. 3, ch. 11, para. 2–4.

19. On the views of the philosopher and economist David Hume, see Richard H. Popkin, "Hume and Isaac de Pinto," *Texas Studies in Literature and Language* 12,

no. 3 (1970); and John Christian Laursen and Greg Coolidge, "David Hume and Public Debt: Crying Wolf?" *Hume Studies* 20, no. 1 (April 1994): 143–150. French economist Jean-Baptiste Say echoed Smith's notions about credit. Credit, according to Say, "does not cause to be born one *sou* of capital value; but it causes often to pass an idle capital value, into the hands where it bears fruit." Gilles Jacoud, *Money and Banking in Jean-Baptiste Say's Economic Thought*, Routledge Studies in the History of Economics (Abingdon, UK: Routledge, 2013), p. 211.

20. Alexander Hamilton to James Duane, September 3, 1780, National Archives, Founders Online, http://founders.archives.gov/?q=%22public%20authority%20 and%20faith%20with%20private%20credit%22&s=1111311111&sa=&r=1 &sr=. Parliament granted shareholders of the Bank of England valuable advantages in return for loans enabling the government to continue financing its wars. Among the bank's advantages was the right to be structured as a joint-stock company, whereas other banks were limited to the partnership form, with a maximum of six partners. See Calomiris and Haber, *Fragile by Design,* chap. 4.

21. Alexander Hamilton to Robert Morris, April 30, 1781, National Archives, Founders Online, http://founders.archives.gov/?q=%22the%20happiest%20en gines%20that%20ever%22&s=1111311111&sa=&r=1&sr=; McCraw, *Founders and Finance,* pp. 52–53, 63–64.

1. "The Sound of Your Hammer"

1. Advice books for merchants, tradesmen, and artisans began appearing in the seventeenth century. The market for these "manuals" attracted many entrepreneurial writers, including Franklin. Sheldon Garon, *Beyond Our Means: Why America Spends while the World Saves* (Princeton, NJ: Princeton University Press, 2011), p. 25.

2. The *Autobiography* was published after Franklin's death. The first English version appeared in London in 1793 as *The Private Life of the Late Benjamin Franklin, LL.D.* Benjamin Franklin, "Advice to a Young Tradesman" [21 July 1748], originally printed in George Fisher, *The American Instructor: or Young Man's Best Companion* . . . , 9th ed., rev. (Philadelphia: B. Franklin and D. Hall, 1748), pp. 375–377; National Archives, Founders Online, http://founders.archives.gov/documents /Franklin/01–03–02–0130.

3. A number of historians have made this point. See, e.g., Thomas Doerflinger, *A Vigorous Spirit of Enterprise: Merchants and Economic Development in Revolutionary Philadelphia* (New York: W. W. Norton, 1987 [1986]), pp. 60–61.

4. Keith Wrightson, *Earthly Necessities: Economic Lives in Early Modern Britain* (New Haven, CT: Yale University Press, 2000), pp. 302–303.

5. B. L. Anderson, "Money and the Structure of Credit in the Eighteenth Century," *Business History* 12 (1970): 95–96; Jacob M. Price, *Capital and Credit in British Overseas Trade: The View from the Chesapeake, 1700–1776* (Cambridge, MA: Harvard University Press, 1980), p. 142; Jacob M. Price, "What Did Merchants Do? Reflections on British Overseas Trade, 1660–1790," *Journal of Economic History* 49, no. 2 (June 1989): 267–284, pp. 278–279; Neil McKendrick, John

Brewer, and J.H. Plumb, *The Birth of a Consumer Society: The Commercialization of Eighteenth-Century England* (Bloomington: Indiana University Press, 1982).

6. Reliance on credit differed among merchant types. Importers, e.g., relied more heavily on long-term credits from Britain than did the exporters of American commodities. Doerflinger, *Vigorous Spirit of Enterprise,* pp. 77–97. For the early republic, see N. S. Buck, *The Development of the Organisation of Anglo-American Trade, 1800–1850* (New Haven, CT: Yale University Press, 1925; repr., Newton Abbott, UK: David and Charles, 1969).

7. See, e.g., David Hancock, *Citizens of the World: London Merchants and the Integration of the British Atlantic Community, 1735–1785* (New York: Cambridge University Press, 1997). For a general discussion of commercial risk during the early decades of American history, see "Special Forum: Reputation and Uncertainty in Early America," *Business History Review* 78 (Winter 2004): 595–702.

8. Kenneth O. Morgan, "Remittance Procedures in the Eighteenth-Century British Slave Trade," special issue, *Business History Review* 79, no. 4 (Winter 2005): 715–749, p. 718. See also Christine Daniels and Michael V. Kennedy, eds., *Negotiated Empires: Centers and Peripheries in the Americas, 1500–1820* (New York: Routledge, 2002).

9. Price, "What Did Merchants Do?" p. 278.

10. Daniel Defoe, *The Complete English Tradesman,* 2nd ed., vol. 1 (London, 1727 [1726]), letters 18 and 23. See also Peter Earle, *The World of Defoe* (New York: Atheneum, 1977 [1976]).

11. Price, "What Did Merchants Do?" pp. 273–274. See also Kenneth O. Morgan, *Slavery, Atlantic Trade and the British Economy, 1660–1800* (Cambridge University Press, 2000); Edward Edelman, "Thomas Hancock, Colonial Merchant," *Journal of Economic and Business History* 1, no. 1 (November 1928): pp. 85–86.

12. Price, "What Did Merchants Do?" p. 273.

13. Morgan, *Slavery, Atlantic Trade and the British Economy,* pp. 78–79. Robert Morris stated in 1786 that English merchants extended goods free of interest for a year but raised the price of the goods. After one year, and depending on how long it took to pay the debts, Morris estimated the interest rate charged to be "equal to fifteen, twenty, or perhaps thirty percent." *Debates and Proceedings of the General Assembly of Pennsylvania, on the Memorials Praying a Repeal or Suspension of the Law Annulling the Charter of the Bank,* ed. Matthew Carey (Philadelphia: Seddon and Pritchard, 1786).

14. Cotton Mather, *Fair Dealing between Debtor and Creditor . . .* (Boston, 1716); Bruce H. Mann, *Republic of Debtors: Bankruptcy in the Age of American Independence* (Cambridge, MA: Harvard University Press, 2003), p. 41.

15. Morgan, *Slavery, Atlantic Trade and the British Economy,* pp. 77–78. Nine million pounds in 1770 equal $1.8 billion in 2013 dollars, using a purchasing power parity calculator. Lawrence H. Officer and Samuel H. Williamson, "Five Ways to Compute the Relative Value of a UK Pound Amount, 1270 to Present," MeasuringWorth, http://www.measuringworth.com/ukcompare/.

16. Edwin J. Perkins, *The Economy of Colonial America* (New York: Columbia University Press, 1988), pp. 36–37.

17. Morgan, *Slavery, Atlantic Trade and the British Economy,* pp. 86–87.

18. T. H. Breen, *The Marketplace of Revolution: How Consumer Politics Shaped American Independence* (New York: Oxford University Press, 2004), pp. 122–123.

19. Gordon S. Wood, *Radicalism of the American Revolution* (New York: Random House, 1993 [1991]), p. 142.

20. Quoted in Price, *Capital and Credit in British Overseas Trade,* pp. 125–126.

21. Quoted in Breen, *Marketplace of Revolution,* p. 124.

22. Mann, *Republic of Debtors,* pp. 132–133, 136–137; Perkins, *Economy of Colonial America,* p. 38. See also T. H. Breen, *Tobacco Culture: The Mentality of the Great Tidewater Planters on the Eve of Revolution* (Princeton, NJ: Princeton University Press, 1985).

23. Morgan, "Remittance Procedures," p. 720.

24. Price, "What Did Merchants Do?" pp. 278–281.

25. Kenneth Morgan, ed., *An American Quaker in the British Isles: The Travel Journals of Jabez Maud Fisher, 1775–1779* (Oxford: Oxford University Press, 1992).

26. For the opportunities available in the expanding British empire to ambitious young men with little capital and few connections, see Hancock, *Citizens of the World.*

27. Morgan, *Slavery, Atlantic Trade and the British Economy,* pp. 78–79.

28. Doerflinger, *Vigorous Spirit of Enterprise,* pp. 53, 160.

29. Gordon S. Wood, *Radicalism of the American Revolution,* p. 137.

30. Importing so many goods drained the colonies of specie, causing the price of credit to rise while the price of the goods fell. Mann, *Republic of Debtors,* pp. 171, 177. For the competitiveness of the Philadelphia market, see Doerflinger, *Vigorous Spirit of Enterprise,* pp. 45–47, 62–67, 88–90.

31. Doerflinger, *Vigorous Spirit of Enterprise,* p. 333.

32. Richard S. Chew, "Certain Victims of an International Contagion: The Panic of 1797 and the Hard Times of the Late 1790s in Baltimore," *Journal of the Early Republic* 25, no. 4 (Winter 2005): 565–613, pp. 575, 577.

33. S. R. Cope, "The Goldsmids and the Development of the London Money Market During the Napoleonic Wars," *Economica* 9, no. 34 (May 1942): 180–206, p. 181; Charles Calomiris and Stephen Haber, *Fragile by Design: The Political Origins of Banking Crises and Scarce Credit* (Princeton, NJ: Princeton University Press, 2014), pp. 95–98, 113.

34. Morgan, "Remittance Procedures," p. 723.

35. Morgan, *Slavery, Atlantic Trade and the British Economy,* pp. 75–76.

36. Morgan, "Remittance Procedures," pp. 726, 729–730.

37. For an argument that all money was originally "virtual," see David Graeber, *Debt: The First 5,000 Years* (Brooklyn, NY: Melville House, 2011), p. 17.

38. John J. McCusker and Russell R. Menard, eds., *The Economy of British America, 1607–1789* (Chapel Hill, NC: University of North Carolina Press, 1991 [1985]), pp. 340–341.

39. Roy A. Foulke, *The Sinews of American Commerce* (New York: Dun and Bradstreet, 1941), pp. 59–60.

40. Calomiris and Haber, *Fragile by Design*, p. 159.

41. Wood, *Radicalism of the American Revolution*, p. 66.

42. Perkins, *Economy of Colonial America*, pp. 172–173, 181.

43. Wood, *Radicalism of the American Revolution*, pp. 140–141.

44. John Adams, "To the Inhabitants of the Colony of Massachusetts-Bay," February 13, 1775, Massachusetts Historical Society, www.masshist.org/publications /apde2/view?id=ADMS-06-02-02-0072-0005.

45. Sidney Homer and Richard Sylla, *A History of Interest Rates*, 4th ed. (New Brunswick, NJ: Rutgers University Press, 2005 [1963]), p. 276.

46. Precedents include the Chinese empire during the Song dynasty (tenth to thirteenth centuries) and the Venetian government (twelfth century). Graeber, *Debt*, pp. 258, 269–270, 338.

47. Perkins, *Economy of Colonial America*, pp. 175–176.

48. Mann, *Republic of Debtors*, p. 135.

49. See McCusker and Menard, *Economy of British America*, pp. 336–337, 340.

50. Benjamin Franklin, *American Weekly Mercury,* March 27, 1729; "A Modest Enquiry into the Nature and Necessity of a Paper-Currency," pamphlet, April 3, 1729; Farley Grubb, "Benjamin Franklin and the Birth of a Paper Money Economy," lecture, repr., Federal Reserve Bank of Philadelphia and the Library Company of Philadelphia, 2006.

51. Letter from Thomas Jefferson to Edward Carrington, May 27, 1788, National Archives, Founders Online, http://founders.archives.gov/?q=%22only%20the%20 ghost%20of%20money%22&s=1511311111&r=1. See Donald F. Swanson, "Bank Notes Will Be But as Oak Leaves: Thomas Jefferson on Paper Money," *Virginia Magazine of History and Biography* 101, no. 1 (January 1993): 37–52, p. 43.

52. Wood, *Radicalism of the American Revolution*, p. 66.

53. The Continental Congress authorized forty emissions of paper notes, totaling $240 million. The states emitted $209 million, for a total of $150 per capita. By contrast, the whole circulating specie was estimated at $12 million. Homer and Sylla, *History of Interest Rates*, p. 277.

54. Henry Laurens in Wood, *Radicalism of the American Revolution*, p. 248.

55. E. James Ferguson, *The Power of the Purse: A History of American Public Finance, 1776–1790* (Chapel Hill: University of North Carolina Press, 1961).

56. Mann, *Republic of Debtors*, p. 170.

57. Wood, *Radicalism of the American Revolution*, pp. 140–141, 248.

58. Stanley L. Engerman and Kenneth L. Sokoloff, *Economic Development in the Americas Since 1500: Endowments and Institutions* (Cambridge: Cambridge University Press, 2012), p. 255.

59. House of Commons [Great Britain], "Report from the Secret Committee on the Expediency of the Bank Resuming Cash Payments," London, 1819.

60. Doerflinger's examination of three Philadelphia merchants in the 1780s found that book debts receivable far outweighed notes and bills receivable. *Vigorous Spirit of Enterprise*, p. 307. See also Wilbur C. Plummer, "Consumer Credit in Co-

lonial Philadelphia," *Pennsylvania Magazine of History and Biography* 66, no. 4 (October 1942): 385–409.

61. Perkins, *Economy of Colonial America,* p. 167; Foulke, *Sinews of American Commerce,* p. 65.

62. Barter may occur in economies where money is (or has become) scarce but people remain familiar with using it. Graeber, *Debt,* pp. 36–37.

63. Only around one-third of debts was paid in cash; the remainder was settled by barter. W. T. Baxter, "Accounting in Colonial America," in *Studies in the History of Accounting,* ed. Ananias C. Littleton and Basil S. Yamey (New York: Arno Press, 1978), pp. 272–274.

64. Breen, *Marketplace of Revolution,* p. 120.

65. Wood, *Radicalism of the American Revolution,* pp. 67–68.

66. Studies of early modern England and France that situate credit within social relations include Craig Muldrew, *The Economy of Obligation: The Culture of Credit and Social Relations in Early Modern England* (New York: St. Martin's Press, 1998); Margot Finn, *The Character of Credit: Personal Debt in English Culture, 1740–1914* (Cambridge: Cambridge University Press, 2003); Laurence Fontaine, "Antonio and Shylock: Credit and Trust in France, c. 1680–c. 1780," trans. Vicki Whittaker, *Economic History Review* 54, no. 1 (February 2001): 39–57.

67. The large planters of Virginia considered their business relationships in highly personalized terms. Mann, *Republic of Debtors,* pp. 134–135; Breen, *Tobacco Culture.* Even in the nineteenth century, business people based their credit relations on local ties and defended fellow residents from outside creditors. Tony A. Freyer, *Producers versus Capitalists: Constitutional Conflict in Antebellum America* (Charlottesville: University Press of Viriginia, 1994).

68. Letter from John Adams to James Warren, February 12, 1777, National Archives, Founders Online, http://founders.archives.gov/?q=%22who%20live%20 upon%20their%20income%22&s=1511311111&r=1.

69. McCusker and Menard, *Economy of British America,* pp. 335–336.

70. Wood, *Radicalism of the American Revolution,* p. 69.

71. Ibid., pp. 68–71.

72. Ibid., pp. 139–140. A similar phenomenon occurred in England in the seventeenth century. Muldrew, *Economy of Obligation.*

73. Robert A. Kagan, "The Routinization of Debt Collection: An Essay on Social Change and Conflict in the Courts," *Law and Society Review* 18, no. 3 (1984): 323–372, p. 341; Robert A. Silverman, *Law and Urban Growth: Civil Litigation in the Boston Trial Courts, 1880–1900* (Princeton: Princeton University Press, 1981), p. 135.

74. Breen, *Marketplace of Revolution,* p. 136.

75. Ibid., pp. 136–137.

76. McCusker and Menard, *Economy of British America,* pp. 279–281 and table 13.1.

77. Breen, *Marketplace of Revolution,* pp. 49, 55. See also Ann Smart Martin, *Buying into the World of Goods: Early Consumers in Backcountry Virginia* (Baltimore, MD: Johns Hopkins University Press, 2008).

78. Quoted in Breen, *Marketplace of Revolution,* pp. 136–137.

79. *New London Gazette,* 1769, in Breen, *Marketplace of Revolution,* p. 139.

80. Breen, *Marketplace of Revolution,* p. 137. "Father Abraham's Speech" was as widely reprinted in America and Europe as *The Way to Wealth.*

81. Wood, *Radicalism of the American Revolution,* p. 136.

82. Quoted in Charles R. Geisst, *Beggar Thy Neighbor: A History of Usury and Debt* (Philadelphia: University of Pennsylvania Press, 2013), p. 77.

83. Breen, *Marketplace of Revolution,* p. 14.

84. Wood, *Radicalism of the American Revolution,* p. 135.

85. Usury was a civil rather than a criminal offense in most of the colonies. Geisst, *Beggar Thy Neighbor,* p. 116.

86. For a survey of early colonial and state usury and bankruptcy laws, see Peter J. Coleman, *Debtors and Creditors in America: Insolvency, Imprisonment for Debt, and Bankruptcy, 1607–1900* (Madison: State Historical Society of Wisconsin, 1974).

87. Medieval Hindu law codes and Buddhism permitted interest-bearing loans but did not tolerate abusive lenders. Islamic law permitted service fees and adding the price of credit on to the sales price. Graeber, *Debt,* pp. 11, 275.

88. Homer and Sylla, *History of Interest Rates,* p. 68.

89. Gregory Clark, "A Review of Avner Greif's *Institutions and the Path to the Modern Economy: Lessons from the Medieval Trade,*" *Journal of Economic Literature* 45, no. 3 (September 2007): 725–741, p. 734; Graeber, *Debt,* p. 290.

90. Graeber, *Debt,* pp. 288–289.

91. These state-run institutions charged 5 percent or less, and they were exempt from the Church's usury laws. Geisst, *Beggar Thy Neighbor,* p. 28. See also Rosa-Maria Gelpi and Francois Julien-Labruyere, *The History of Consumer Credit: Doctrines and Practices,* trans. Mn Liam Gavin (New York: St. Martin's Press, 2000).

92. Mauro Carboni and Massimo Fornasari in Thomas M. Safley, ed., *The History of Bankruptcy: Economic, Social and Cultural Implications in Early Modern Europe* (London: Routledge, 2013), p. 120; Geisst, *Beggar Thy Neighbor,* p. 9.

93. Wendy Woloson, *In Hock: Pawning in America from Independence through the Great Depression* (Chicago: University of Chicago Press, 2009), p. 155.

94. Geisst, *Beggar Thy Neighbor,* pp. 92, 102.

95. Martin Lewison, "Conflict of Interest? The Ethics of Usury," *Journal of Business Ethics* 22, no. 4 (December 1999): 327–339, p. 333; Graeber, *Debt,* pp. 321–322.

96. Hugh Rockoff, "Prodigals and Projectors: An Economic History of Usury Laws in the United States from Colonial Times to 1900," National Bureau of Economic Research (hereafter NBER), Working Paper Series, no. 9742 (May 2003), p. 3.

97. Cotton Mather, *Thirty Important Cases Resolved with Evidence of Scripture and Reason* (Boston, 1699); Mark Valeri, "The Rise of Usury in Early New England," *Common-Place* 6, no. 3 (April 2006), www.common-place.org/vol-06/no-03/valeri/. Earlier generations of Puritans did not interpret Calvin as condoning

usury. Calvin himself rejected all forms of usury later in his career. See Mark Valeri, "Religious Discipline and the Market: Puritans and the Issue of Usury," *William and Mary Quarterly*, 3rd ser., vol. 54, no. 4 (October 1997): 747–768.

98. On Adam Smith and Jeremy Bentham, see Rockoff, "Prodigals and Projectors." David Ricardo argued that the laws' repeal would not raise interest rates because competition between lenders would bring them to a sustainable level. David Ricardo, *The Works and Correspondence of David Ricardo,* ed. Piero Sraff and M. H. Dobb, vol. 5, *Speeches and Evidence 1815–1823* (Indianapolis: Liberty Fund, 2005), April 12, 1821, and June 17, 1823.

99. For an example of a colonial trader who was prosecuted for charging too much for goods, see John Cotton, Boston, 1639, in John Winthrop, *The History of New England from 1630 to 1649,* 2 vols. (Boston, 1853), 1:377–382.

100. Rockoff, "Prodigals and Projectors," p. 12.

101. Mann, *Republic of Debtors,* p. 47.

102. Ibid.; Morton Horowitz, *The Transformation of American Law,* 1780–1860 (Cambridge, MA: Harvard University Press, 1979). See also Thomas Max Safley, ed., *The History of Bankruptcy: Economic, Social and Cultural Implications in Early Modern Europe* (New York: Routledge, 2013).

103. Charles Jordan Tabb, "The History of the Bankruptcy Laws in the United States," *American Bankruptcy Institute Law Review* 3, no. 5 (1995): 5–51, p. 8.

104. Ibid., p. 9.

105. Thomas Max Safley, "Business Failure and Civil Scandal in Early Modern Europe," *Business History Review* 83, no. 1 (Spring 2009): 35–60, p. 37; Safley, *History of Bankruptcy.*

106. Safley, "Business Failure and Civil Scandal," pp. 48–49. The first English bankruptcy law (1542) distinguished between bankrupts and insolvents, the latter of whom were nontraders. Geisst, *Beggar Thy Neighbor,* pp. 104–105.

107. Safley, introduction to *History of Bankruptcy,* p. 12.

108. Tabb, "History of the Bankruptcy Laws," p. 11.

109. Defoe, *The Complete English Tradesman,* vol. 1, letter 13.

110. Coleman, *Debtors and Creditors in America*; Mann, *Republic of Debtors,* p. 76.

111. Kurt H. Nadelmann, "On the Origin of the Bankruptcy Clause," *American Journal of Legal History* 1 (July 1957): 215–228, pp. 222–223.

112. William Blackstone, "Of Title by Bankruptcy," in *Commentaries on the Laws of England,* bk. 2, chap. 31.

113. Thomas K. McCraw, *The Founders and Finance: How Hamilton, Gallatin, and Other Immigrants Forged a New Economy* (Cambridge, MA: Harvard University Press, 2012), pp. 46–47.

114. Mann, *Republic of Debtors,* pp. 177–182.

115. Roger Sherman of Connecticut gave the only dissenting vote. He was concerned that bankruptcies could be punished by death, as specified (but very rarely imposed) in English law. Tabb, "History of the Bankruptcy Laws," p. 13.

116. Nadelmann, "Origin of the Bankruptcy Clause," p. 216; James Madison (Publius), *Federalist,* no. 42 (January 22, 1788).

117. Mann, *Republic of Debtors,* p. 112ff.

118. Doerflinger, *Vigorous Spirit of Enterprise,* p. 311.

119. Mann, *Republic of Debtors,* p. 193.

120. Doerflinger, *Vigorous Spirit of Enterprise,* p. 311.

121. McCraw, *Founders and Finance,* pp. 353–354.

122. Richard Sylla, Robert E. Wright, and David J. Cowen, "Alexander Hamilton, Central Banker: Crisis Management during the U.S. Financial Panic of 1792," *Business History Review* 83 (Spring 2009): 61–86; McCraw, *Founders and Finance,* pp. 353–354.

123. Mann, *Republic of Debtors,* pp. 198–199.

124. Doerflinger, *Vigorous Spirit of Enterprise,* pp. 319, 325.

125. Mann, *Republic of Debtors,* pp. 200–203.

126. Chew, "Victims of an International Contagion," pp. 567–568, 578–581.

127. Mann, *Republic of Debtors,* pp. 199–201.

128. Wood, *Radicalism of the American Revolution,* p. 266.

129. Mann, *Republic of Debtors,* p. 203.

130. Ibid., p. 222.

131. Tabb, "The History of the Bankruptcy Laws in the United States," pp. 14–15.

132. Mann, *Republic of Debtors,* pp. 32, 218.

133. Letter from Thomas Jefferson to James Madison, September 6, 1789, National Archives, Founders Online, http://founders.archives.gov/?q=%22earth%20belongs%20in%20usufruct%22&s=1511311111&r=5. This argument is in Herbert T. Sloan, *Principle and Interest: Thomas Jefferson and the Problem of Debt* (New York: Oxford University Press, 1995).

134. Joseph J. Ellis, "Money and That Man From Monticello," *Reviews in American History* 23, no. 4 (December 1995): 590.

135. Sloan, *Principle and Interest,* pp. 14–21, 24.

136. Thomas Jefferson to Jean-Nicolas Démeunier, January–February 1786, National Archives, Founders Online, http://founders.archives.gov/?q=%22these%20debts%20had%20become%20hereditary%22&s=1511311111&r=1. Démeunier had written with questions about bills of credit.

137. Letter from Thomas Jefferson to Lucy Ludwell Paradise, August 27, 1786, National Archives, Founders Online, http://founders.archives.gov/?q=%22there%20never%20was%20an%20instance%20of%20a%20man%27s%20getting%20out%22&s=1511311111&r=1.

138. Sloan, *Principle and Interest,* p. 32. Many state courts were reluctant to help British creditors to collect prewar debts. McCraw, *Founders and Finance,* p. 150.

139. Alexander Hamilton, "Report Relative to a Provision for the Support of Public Credit," January 9, 1790, communicated to U.S. House of Representatives on January 14, 1790, http://founders.archives.gov/?q=alexander%20hamilton%201790%20public%20credit&s=1111311111&sa=&r=20&sr=. Hamilton's task was complicated by the diversity of debt sources, interest rates and maturities, and debt holders. McCraw, *Founders and Finance,* pp. 93–94.

140. Graeber, *Debt: The First 5,000 Years,* p. 49.

141. Calomiris and Haber, *Fragile by Design,* pp. 93–94.

142. Ultimately, the states' debts were equalized on a per capita basis across all the states.

143. See Joseph J. Ellis, *Founding Brothers: The Revolutionary Generation* (New York: Vintage, 2002 [2000]), pp. 48–80; McCraw, *Founders and Finance,* p. 107.

144. Letter from Thomas Jefferson to George Washington, September 9, 1792, American History: From Revolution to Reconstruction and Beyond, www.let.rug .nl/usa/presidents/thomas-jefferson/letters-of-thomas-jefferson/jefl100.php.

145. Foulke, *Sinews of American Commerce,* p. 133.

146. Letter from Thomas Jefferson to Thomas Cooper, September 10, 1814, National Archives, Founders Online, http://founders.archives.gov/?q=%22dupery%20 of%20our%20citizens%22&s=1111311111&r=1. See Swanson, "Bank Notes Will Be But as Oak Leaves," p. 48.

147. Mann, *Republic of Debtors,* pp. 196–197.

148. 9 Annals of Cong., 5th Cong., 3rd Sess., 2666–2667 (1799); Mann, *Republic of Debtors,* p. 209 and chap. 7. Mann reports that some of the filings were probably initiated by debtors with the help of friendly creditors.

149. See, e.g., Drew McCoy, *The Elusive Republic: Political Economy in Jeffersonian America* (Chapel Hill: University of North Carolina Press, 1980); Joseph Ellis, *American Sphinx: The Character of Thomas Jefferson* (New York: Knopf, 1997).

2. "To Be a Bankrupt Is Nothing"

1. Joseph Angell, *A Practical Summary of the Law of Assignments in Trust for the Benefit of Creditors* (Boston: Hilliard, Gray & Co., 1835), p. iii.

2. John Joseph Wallis, "What Caused the Crisis of 1839?" NBER, Historical Paper Series, no. 133 (2001), p. 1.

3. Roy A. Foulke, *The Sinews of American Commerce* (New York: Dun and Bradstreet, 1941), pp. 122, 129.

4. Foulke, *Sinews of American Commerce,* pp. 146–148. By the 1850s, building and loan societies operated in Boston, Brooklyn, and Chicago. Robert A. Lynn, "Installment Credit before 1870," *Business History Review* 31, no. 4 (Winter 1957): 414–424, p. 415.

5. Foulke, *Sinews of American Commerce,* pp. 139–140.

6. Alan L. Olmstead, "Investment Constraints and New York City Mutual Savings Bank Financing of Antebellum Development," *Journal of Economic History* 32, no. 4 (December 1972): 811–840, pp. 811–813.

7. Tamara Plakins Thornton, "'A Great Machine' or a 'Beast of Prey': A Boston Corporation and Its Rural Debtors in an Age of Capitalist Transformation," *Journal of the Early Republic* 27, no. 4 (Winter 2007): 567–597, p. 589. Safe investments included government bonds, mortgages secured by good local real estate, and (in Boston) the shares of local commercial banks. Foulke, *Sinews of American Commerce,* pp. 142–144.

8. Foulke, *Sinews of American Commerce,* pp. 134–136, 138–139.

9. For the number of U.S.-chartered banks in this period, see Joseph Van Fenstermaker, *The Development of American Commercial Banking, 1782–1837* (Kent, OH: Kent State University, 1965), tables 4, 12, 13, 14, 16, 17, and A-1.

10. See esp. Howard Bodenhorn, *A History of Banking in Antebellum America: Financial Markets and Economic Development in an Era of Nation Building* (Cambridge: Cambridge University Press, 2000).

11. Naomi R. Lamoreaux, *Insider Lending: Banks, Personal Connections, and Economic Development in Industrial New England* (Cambridge: Cambridge University Press, 1994); Howard Bodenhorn, "Antebellum Banking in the United States," EH.net Encyclopedia, ed. Robert Whaples, March 26, 2008, http://eh.net /encyclopedia/article/bodenhorn.banking.antebellum.

12. Howard Bodenhorn and Hugh Rockoff, "Regional Interest Rates in Antebellum America," in *Strategic Factors in Nineteenth Century American Economic History: A Volume to Honor Robert W. Fogel,* ed. Claudia Goldin and Hugh Rockoff (Chicago: University of Chicago Press, 1992), p. 173.

13. John Joseph Wallis, Richard Sylla, and Arthur Grinath III, "Land, Debt, and Taxes: Origins of the U.S. State Default Crisis, 1839 to 1842," unpublished paper presented at a conference on Sovereign Debt and Default after the Financial Crisis of 2007–2008, Federal Reserve Bank of Atlanta, November 28–29, 2011, pp. 15–16.

14. Bodenhorn, "Antebellum Banking."

15. Carole E. Scott, "Banking Lessons from the Antebellum South," B>Quest, 2000, www.westga.edu/~bquest/2000/antebellum.html.

16. Wallis, Sylla, and Grinath, "Land, Debt, and Taxes," pp. 15–16; Philip S. Bagwell and G. E. Mingay, *Britain and America: A Study of Economic Change, 1850–1939* (London: Routledge & Kegan Paul, 1970), pp. 18–22.

17. Richard Sylla, "U.S. Securities Markets and the Banking System, 1790–1840," *Federal Reserve of St. Louis Review* (May–June 1998): 83–98, p. 95.

18. Thomas K. McCraw, *The Founders and Finance: How Hamilton, Gallatin, and Other Immigrants Forged a New Economy* (Cambridge, MA: Harvard University Press, 2012), p. 293.

19. Richard Sylla, John B. Legler, and John J. Wallis, "Banks and State Public Finance in the New Republic: The United States, 1790–1860," *Journal of Economic History* 47, no. 2 (June 1987): 391–403, p. 402; Sylla, "U.S. Securities Markets," p. 96.

20. Charles Calomiris and Stephen Haber, *Fragile by Design: The Political Origins of Banking Crises and Scarce Credit* (Princeton, NJ: Princeton University Press, 2014), p. 163.

21. Banking was a lucrative enterprise in New York, tempting many entrepreneurs to try to establish banks without a charter. In a few instances, entrepreneurs founded insurance companies, not to insure anything, but in order to lend money. Eric Hilt, "Rogue Finance: The Life and Fire Insurance Company and the Panic of 1826," *Business History Review* 83, no. 1 (Spring 2009): 87–112, pp. 91–92.

22. Sylla, "U.S. Securities Markets," p. 95.

23. Scott, "Banking Lessons."

24. Jane Knodell, "Rethinking the Jacksonian Economy: The Impact of the 1832 Bank Veto on Commercial Banking," *Journal of Economic History* 66, no. 3 (2006): 541–574, pp. 569–570. See also Howard Bodenhorn, "Private Banking in Antebellum Virginia: Thomas Branch & Sons of Petersburg," *Business History Review* 71, no. 4 (Winter 1997): 513–542.

25. Sylla, "U.S. Securities Markets," pp. 93–94.

26. Bodenhorn, "Antebellum Banking."

27. Bodenhorn presents evidence that antebellum banks were an important factor in economic growth. Similarly, Lamoreaux argues that New England banks were critical in funding the enterprise of that region. Lamoreaux, *Insider Lending*.

28. However, Calomiris and Haber argue that the restrictions on banks prevented competition and gave rise to "segmented monopolies." *Fragile by Design*, pp. 163–171.

29. Lamoreaux, *Insider Lending*, pp. 19–20.

30. Sylla, "U.S. Securities Markets," pp. 89–90, 94.

31. For a discussion of eighteenth-century "projectors," see Anthony Di Renzo, "The Complete English Tradesman: Daniel Defoe and the Emergence of Business Writing," *Journal of Technical Writing and Communication* 28 (Winter 1998): 325–334.

32. Inflation, as measured by the Consumer Price Index (CPI), was generally not much of an issue in the antebellum period. We do not have comparable data on asset prices. For the inflation rate (using the CPI), see Lawrence H. Officer and Samuel H. Williamson, "Annual Inflation Rates in the United States, 1775–2013, and the United Kingdom, 1265–2013," MeasuringWorth, 2013, www.measuringworth.com/inflation.

33. Cathy Matson and Wendy Woloson, *Risky Business: Winning and Losing in the Early American Economy, 1780–1859: An Exhibition Drawn from the Collections of the Library Company of Philadelphia* (Library Company of Philadelphia, 2003), p. 11.

34. Lynn, "Installment Credit before 1870," p. 415.

35. Harry L. Watson, *Liberty and Power: The Politics of Jacksonian America* (New York: Hill and Wang, 1990), pp. 161–164. The historiography of the Bank War is extensive. The classic work is Bray Hammond, *Banks and Politics in America from the Revolution to the Civil War* (Princeton, NJ: Princeton University Press, 1957). Many of the most important speeches and writing on the subject are contained in Herman E. Krooss, *Documentary History of Banking and Currency in the United States*, vol. 2 (New York: McGraw-Hill, 1969).

36. Watson, *Liberty and Power*, pp. 161–164.

37. Matson and Woloson, *Risky Business*, p. 14.

38. Sidney Homer and Richard Sylla, *A History of Interest Rates*, 4th ed. (New Brunswick, NJ: Rutgers University Press, 2005 [1963]), p. 281.

39. Matson and Woloson, *Risky Business*, p. 14.

40. Cathy D. Matson, "Capitalizing Hope: Economic Thought and the Early Modern Economy," *Journal of the Early Republic* 16, no. 2 (Summer 1996): 273–291, p. 276.

41. The idea that a bank could act as lender of last resort appeared in England beginning in 1833, when Parliament gave the Bank of England's notes legal-tender status that it could use to assist other banks during times of crisis. Calomiris and Haber, *Fragile by Design*, pp. 79–80, 116–117.

42. Estimates of the number of bank failures may have been exaggerated by contemporaries for political reasons. Richard Sylla, "Early American Banking: The Significance of the Corporate Form," *Business and Economic History*, 2nd ser., vol. 14 (1985): 105–123, p. 119.

43. Paul B. Trescott, *Financing American Enterprise: The Story of Commercial Banking* (New York: Harper and Row, 1963), pp. 29–33.

44. New York state's bank commissioners' report to the General Assembly (1833) stated that the true function of banks was not to make loans but to supply a sound currency. Bodenhorn, *History of Banking*, pp. 90, 92–96.

45. The precursor to the free banking idea was the Scottish banking system. See Fritz Redlich, *The Molding of American Banking: Men and Ideas* (New York: Hafner, 1947). The New York model was unique not because of free entry but because of the free incorporation of banks. It is unclear why Americans decided to incorporate banks rather than rely more heavily on the partnership form, as was more usual in Britain. Sylla, "Early American Banking," pp. 109, 113.

46. Bodenhorn, "Antebellum Banking." The banks were required to deposit the securities with the state comptroller of the currency, essentially granting the government a loan. Calomiris and Haber, *Fragile by Design*, p. 169.

47. William Gouge, *A Short History of Paper Money and Banking in the United States* (Philadelphia: T. W. Ustick, 1833).

48. Lamoreaux, *Insider Lending*, pp. 38–39.

49. Homer and Sylla, *History of Interest Rates*, p. 283.

50. Ibid., p. 284.

51. Stephen Mihm, *A Nation of Counterfeiters: Capitalists, Con Men, and the Making of the United States* (Cambridge, MA: Harvard University Press, 2007). From 1790 to 1860, the money supply increased about fortyfold, from $15 million to $600 million. In contrast, population multiplied eightfold, so the amount of money per head increased dramatically. The discovery of gold in California alone added an estimated $320 million into the economy from 1848 to 1854. Together, deposits and bank notes comprised about three-fourths of the country's money by 1860. Benjamin Klebaner, *American Commercial Banking: A History* (Boston: Twayne Publishers, 1990), p. 54; Trescott, *Financing American Enterprise*, p. 18.

52. Martin van Buren, "Special Session Message," September 4, 1837. Online by Gerhard Peters and John T. Woolley, The American Presidency Project, http://www.presidency.ucsb.edu/ws/?pid=67234.

53. Sylla, "U.S. Securities Markets," pp. 88–89.

54. Homer and Sylla, *History of Interest Rates;* William B. English, "Understanding the Costs of Sovereign Default: American State Debts in the 1840s," *American Economic Review* 86, no. 1 (March 1996): 259–275, p. 261.

55. Homer and Sylla, *History of Interest Rates*, p. 326.

56. Edwin J. Perkins, *Financing Anglo-American Trade: The House of Brown, 1800–1880* (Cambridge, MA: Harvard University Press, 1975); Niall Ferguson, *The*

House of Rothschild, vol. 1, *Money's Prophets, 1798–1848* (New York: Viking, 1998); Niall Ferguson, *The World's Banker: The History of the House of Rothschild* (London: Weidenfeld and Nicolson, 1998).

57. English, "Understanding the Costs of Sovereign Default," p. 261. Foreigners probably did not own shares in state-chartered banks, although they were willing to hold state debt that was issued to establish banks. Sylla, "U.S. Securities Markets," p. 93 n6.

58. Mira Wilkins, *The History of Foreign Investment in the United States to 1914* (Cambridge, MA: Harvard University Press, 1989), pp. 50–51.

59. Wallis, Sylla, and Grinath, "Land, Debt, and Taxes," pp. 7, 9–10. The quotation is on pp. 9–10.

60. John Joseph Wallis, Richard E. Sylla, and Arthur Grinath III, "Sovereign Debt and Repudiation: The Emerging-Market Debt Crisis in the United States, 1839–1843," NBER, Working Paper Series, no. 10753 (September 2004).

61. Wallis, "What Caused the Crisis of 1839?" p. 1.

62. Wallis, Sylla, and Grinath, "Land, Debt, and Taxes," pp. 15–16.

63. Alan D. Morrison and William J. Wilhelm Jr., *Investment Banking: Institutions, Politics, and Law* (Oxford: Oxford University Press, 2007), p. 147.

64. Ron Chernow, *The Death of the Banker: The Decline and Fall of the Great Financial Dynasties and the Triumph of the Small Investor* (New York: Vintage, 1997), p. 21.

65. Richard Sylla, "An Historical Primer on the Business of Credit Ratings," in *Ratings, Rating Agencies and the Global Financial System,* ed. Richard M. Levich, Giovanni Mainoni, and Carmen M. Reinhart (Boston: Kluwer Academic Publishers, 2002).

66. McCraw, *Founders and Finance,* pp. 210–211, 262, 356.

67. Albert Gallatin, *Considerations on the Currency and Banking System of the United States* (Philadelphia: Carey & Lea, 1831), p. 68.

68. Daniel Webster, Speech on the Sub-Treasury Bill, U.S. Senate, January 31, 1838, p. 6. See also Melvin Dubofsky, "Daniel Webster and the Whig Theory of Economic Growth," *New England Quarterly* 42 (December 1969): 551–572, pp. 566–568. Webster speculated heavily in midwestern land. He lost heavily during the financial Panic of 1837 and never repaid the debts. See Robert Remini, *Daniel Webster: The Man and His Time* (New York: W. W. Norton, 1998).

69. Cong. Globe, 25th Cong., 2nd Sess., appendix, 606 (1938).

70. Henry S. Geyer, *Speech . . . in reply to the Hon. Thomas H. Benton* (St. Louis, 1831), p. 17.

71. George Chambers, *Speech . . . on the Currency and Banks, December 22 and 26, 1837* (Philadelphia: James Kay, Jun. & Brother, 1838), pp. 11–12.

72. Abel P. Upshur, *A Brief Enquiry into the True Basis of the Credit System; and into the True Basis of Bank Credit as Part Thereof* (Petersburg, VA: Edmund & Julian C. Ruffin, 1840), p. 24.

73. Calvin Colton, "The Currency," May 1843, in *The Junius Tracts* (New York: Greeley & McElrath, 1844), pp. 4–5.

74. Paul C. Conkin, *Prophets of Prosperity: America's First Political Economists* (Bloomington: Indiana University Press, 1980), p. 309. See also Daniel Walker

Howe, *The Political Culture of the American Whigs* (Chicago: University of Chicago Press, 1980), pp. 108–122.

75. Henry C. Carey, *The Credit System in France, Great Britain, and the United States* (Philadelphia: Carey, Lea & Blanchard, 1838), pp. 15–16, 37–38.

76. Trescott, *Financing American Enterprise,* p. 23; Klebaner, *American Commercial Banking,* p. 51.

77. Glenn Porter and Harold Livesay, *Merchants and Manufacturers: Studies in the Changing Structure of Nineteenth-Century Marketing* (Baltimore: Johns Hopkins Press, 1971). See also Bill R. Moeckel, *The Development of the Wholesaler in the United States, 1860–1900* (New York: Garland, 1986); Fred M. Jones, *Middlemen in the Domestic Trade of the United States, 1800–1860* (Urbana: University of Illinois, 1937); Shelby D. Hunt and Jerry Goolsby, "The Rise and Fall of the Functional Approach to Marketing: A Paradigm Displacement Perspective," in *Historical Perspectives in Marketing: Essays in Honor of Stanley C. Hollander,* ed. Terence Nevett and Ronald A. Fullerton (Lexington, MA: D. C. Heath, 1988), pp. 35–51, and appendix. The term "merchant" became democratized in the United States and was used to describe even small shopkeepers.

78. Chernow, *Death of the Banker,* p. 8. The term "merchant banker" survived in the City of London until the very end of the twentieth century.

79. Elva C. Tooker, "A Merchant Turns to Money Lending in Philadelphia," *Bulletin of the Business Historical Society* 20, no. 3 (June 1946): 71–85, pp. 71–74, 81–82, 84; Porter and Livesay, *Merchants and Manufacturers.* Henry Clay described the United States as "a country where every description of paper imparting an obligation to pay money or deliver property is assignable," i.e., can be used as currency. Clay, *Speech . . . on a Deliberate Design,* p. 20.

80. Richard Sylla, "Forgotten Men of Money: Private Bankers in Early U.S. History," *Journal of Economic History* 36, no. 1 (March 1976): 173–188, pp. 175–177; Alice E. Smith, "Banking without Banks: George Smith and the Wisconsin Marine and Fire Insurance Company," *Wisconsin Magazine of History* 48, no. 4 (Summer 1965): 268–281. We know very little about private banking and the precise role it played in the economy.

81. Bodenhorn, "Private Banking," p. 514. Quantifying the total amount of private notes in circulation is impossible, but incorporated banks had a total note circulation of between $150 and $200 million, so we can surmise that private bankers such as Smith were significant contributors to the country's money supply. Richard Sylla estimates that in the 1850s private banks may have accounted for one-third of all commercial banks, and over one-quarter of all bank capital. Sylla, "Forgotten Men of Money," pp. 175–177, 185.

82. Morton J. Horwitz, *The Transformation of American Law, 1780–1860* (Cambridge, MA: Harvard University Press, 1977), pp. 212–226.

83. Howard Bodenhorn, "Capital Mobility and Financial Integration in Antebellum America," *Journal of Economic History* 52, no. 3 (September 1992): 585–610, pp. 597–600; Bodenhorn, *History of Banking,* chap. 5.

84. Historians disagree about the extent to which regional capital markets were integrated before the Civil War. For evidence that the short-term capital markets

were integrated, see Bodenhorn and Rockoff, "Regional Interest Rates in Antebellum America." The seminal paper arguing that short-term interest rates varied widely across regions after the Civil War is Lance Davis, "The Investment Market, 1870–1914: Evolution of a National Market," *Journal of Economic History* 25 (September 1965): 355–399.

85. Tony Freyer, "Business Law and American Economic History," in *The Cambridge Economic History of the United States,* vol. 2, *The Long Nineteenth Century,* ed. Stanley Engerman and Robert E. Gallman (Cambridge: Cambridge University Press, 2000), pp. 440–441, 455–456.

86. Lamoreaux, *Insider Lending,* p. 2; Bodenhorn, "Private Banking," p. 528.

87. Donald R. Adams, Jr., "The Role of Banks in the Economic Development of the Old Northwest," in *Essays in Nineteenth Century Economic History: The Old Northwest,* ed. David C. Klingaman and Richard K. Vedder (Athens: Ohio University Press, 1975), pp. 238–239.

88. Julian Hoppit and Thomas Doerflinger make the same point about businesses in eighteenth-century England and Philadelphia, respectively. Julian Hoppit, "The Use and Abuse of Credit," *Historical Journal* 33 (June 1990); Thomas Doerflinger, *A Vigorous Spirit of Enterprise: Merchants and Economic Development in Revolutionary Philadelphia* (New York: W. W. Norton, 1987).

89. Lewis E. Atherton, *The Frontier Merchant in Mid-America* (Columbia: University of Missouri Press, 1971), pp. 18, 147.

90. William Endicott, *Reminiscences of Seventy-Five Years,* quoted in Foulke, *Sinews of American Commerce,* p. 154; Herman E. Krooss and Martin R. Blyn, *A History of Financial Intermediaries* (New York: Random House, 1971), p. 17.

91. Norman S. Buck, *The Development of the Organisation of Anglo-American Trade, 1800–1850* (Hamden, CT: Archon Books, 1969 [1925]), p. 160; Atherton, *Frontier Merchant,* p. 150.

92. Mercantile Agency circular, January 1858, repr., *Business History Review* 37, no. 4 (Winter 1963): 438–439. The nominal GDP figure is from Samuel H. Williamson, "What Was the U.S. GDP Then?" MeasuringWorth, http://www.measuringworth.org/usgdp/.

93. Harold D. Woodman, *King Cotton and His Retainers: Financing and Marketing the Cotton Crop of the South, 1800–1925* (Lexington: University of Kentucky Press, 1968), p. 159.

94. Moeckel, *Development of the Wholesaler,* pp. 13–14.

95. Morrison and Wilhelm, *Investment Banking,* pp. 142–143.

96. Robert G. Albion, *The Rise of New York Port, 1815–1860* (New York: C. Scribner's Sons, 1939); Alfred D. Chandler Jr., *The Visible Hand: The Managerial Revolution in American Business* (Cambridge, MA: Belknap Press, 1977), chap. 1.

97. Woodman, *King Cotton,* pp. 35–40.

98. Scott P. Marler, "Merchants in the Transition to a New South: Central Louisiana, 1840–1880," *Louisiana History* 42, no. 2 (Spring 2001): 165–192.

99. Bodenhorn, *History of Banking,* p. 233.

100. Woodman, *King Cotton,* pp. 16, 41.

101. Tooker, "Merchant Turns to Money Lending," pp. 82–83. The firm of Nathan Trotter continues to operate as a manufacturer of metals.

102. Lamoreaux, *Insider Lending,* p. 82; Barbara Vatter, "Industrial Borrowing by the New England Textile Mills, 1840–1860: A Comment," *Journal of Economic History* 21, no. 2 (June 1961): 216–221.

103. Lance E. Davis, "The New England Textile Mills and the Capital Markets: A Study of Industrial Borrowing, 1840–1860," *Journal of Economic History* 20, no. 1 (March 1960): 1–30, pp. 3, 6–8.

104. "Between 1850 and 1860, capital per [manufacturing] establishment increased at an average annual rate of 5.2 percent. Even the manufacturing-impaired South Atlantic states experienced real growth." Bodenhorn, *History of Banking,* pp. 86, 88, 90.

105. Tooker, "Merchant Turns to Money Lending," p. 84.

106. William Sheldon, *Cursory Remarks on the Laws Concerning Usury, and on Late Proceedings in Cases of Usury* (Norwich, CT: John Trumbull, 1798). See also George Hay, *Speech Delivered in the Legislature of Virginia in the Session of 1816–1817: In Support of a Bill to Repeal All the Laws Concerning Usury* (Richmond, VA: Shepherd and Pollard, 1817).

107. Bodenhorn and Rockoff, "Regional Interest Rates," pp. 176–179. They reproduce a chart from *Hunt's Merchants' Magazine and Commercial Review,* 1841, indicating the legal rate and usury penalty in each state.

108. Horwitz, *Transformation of American Law,* pp. 237–240, 243–244.

109. Tooker, "Merchant Turns to Money Lending," p. 74; Bodenhorn and Rockoff, "Regional Interest Rates," p. 178.

110. Atherton, *Frontier Merchant,* pp. 143–144.

111. Charles R. Geisst, *Beggar Thy Neighbor: A History of Usury and Debt* (Philadelphia: University of Pennsylvania Press, 2013), pp. 151–152.

112. Davis, "New England Textile Mills," pp. 8–9, 18.

113. Hugh Rockoff, "Prodigals and Projectors: An Economic History of Usury Laws in the United States from Colonial Times to 1900," NBER, Working Paper Series, no. 9742 (May 2003), p. 25.

114. For developments in Britain, see Geisst, *Beggar Thy Neighbor,* p. 146.

115. Lynn, "Installment Credit before 1970," p. 415; Foulke, *Sinews of American Commerce,* p. 182.

116. Olmstead, "Investment Constraints," pp. 811–813.

117. MHLIC later shifted its investments to textile mills. Thornton, "Great Machine," pp. 567, 572.

118. Research in the bankruptcy records shows that in New York City in the late 1830s, merchant tailors, furniture makers, stonemasons, and other artisans extended book credit in order to survive that very competitive market. Edward J. Balleisen, *Navigating Failure: Bankruptcy and Commercial Society in Antebellum America* (Chapel Hill: University of North Carolina Press, 2001), pp. 44–45.

119. Lynn, "Installment Credit before 1870." He could find almost no credit terms in advertisements for furniture during the 1850s.

120. Lendol Calder, *Financing the American Dream: A Cultural History of Consumer Credit* (Princeton, NJ: Princeton University Press, 1999), p. 160.

121. Lynn, "Installment Credit before 1870," pp. 417–419.

122. John P. Watkins, "Corporate Power and the Evolution of Consumer Credit," *Journal of Economic Issues* 34, no. 4 (December 2000): 909–932, p. 916.

123. Robert A. Kagan, "The Routinization of Debt Collection: An Essay on Social Change and Conflict in the Courts," *Law and Society Review* 18, no. 3 (1984): 323–372, p. 342.

124. Allan G. Bogue, Brian Q. Cannon, and Kenneth J. Winkle, "Oxen to Organs: Chattel Credit in Springdale Town, 1849–1900," *Agricultural History* 77, no. 3 (Summer 2003): 420–452. This type of mortgage existed during colonial times. Wilbur C. Plummer, "Consumer Credit in Colonial Philadelphia," *Pennsylvania Magazine of History and Biography* 66, no. 4 (October 1942): 385–409, p. 396.

125. The advertisement is dated November 7, 1848, and appeared in the *Illinois Daily Journal*.

126. Daniel Wadhwani, "Institutional Foundations of Personal Finance: Innovation in the U.S. Savings Banks," *Business History Review* 85, no. 3 (Autumn 2011): 499–528, p. 503; Sheldon Garon, *Beyond Our Means: Why America Spends while the World Saves* (Princeton, NJ: Princeton University Press, 2011), pp. 24–25, 86–88.

127. Wendy A. Woloson, *In Hock: Pawning in America from Independence through the Great Depression* (Chicago: University of Chicago Press, 2010), pp. 156–157.

128. Calder, *Financing the American Dream*, p. 45; Foulke, *Sinews of American Commerce*, p. 118; Woloson, *In Hock*, p. 60. According to Foulke, in 1828 when the licenses were separated, there were only nine licensed pawnbrokers.

129. Woloson, *In Hock*, chap. 2 and p. 71. In Chicago, the Irish predominated in pawnbroking. Later, they entered the field in significant numbers in other big cities.

130. Woloson, *In Hock*, pp. 119, 159–163.

131. Calder, *Financing the American Dream*, pp. 39, 120.

132. Balleisen, *Navigating Failure*, p. 3 and introduction, n. 5.

133. Ibid., pp. 3, 7, 216–217.

134. For insurance, see Sharon Murphy, *Investing in Life: Insurance in Antebellum America* (Baltimore: Johns Hopkins University Press, 2010).

135. Peter J. Coleman, *Debtors and Creditors in America: Insolvency, Imprisonment for Debt, and Bankruptcy, 1607–1900* (Madison: State Historical Society of Wisconsin, 1974), chap. 18.

136. *Hunt's Merchants' Magazine* 6 (March 1842), pp. 253–254.

137. *Hunt's Merchants' Magazine* 7 (September 1842), pp. 274–275.

138. Quoted in Carey, *Credit System*, pp. 17–18.

139. Balleisen, *Navigating Failure*, pp. 117–118, 184.

140. Alexis de Tocqueville, "Of Honor in the United States and in Democratic Communities," in *Democracy in America, vol. 2* (New York: Vintage Books, 1990 [1840]), sec. 3, chap. 18.

141. For the cultural meanings of business failure in the United States, see Scott Sandage, *Born Losers: A History of Failure in America* (Cambridge, MA: Harvard University Press, 2006).

142. Thomas D. Russell, "The Antebellum Courthouse as Creditors' Domain: Trial-Court Activity in South Carolina and the Concomitance of Lending and Litigation," *American Journal of Legal History* 40, no. 3 (July 1996): 331–364, pp. 343, 349.

143. Horwitz, *Transformation of American Law,* pp. 228–230.

144. David Skeel, *Debt's Dominion: A History of Bankruptcy Law in America* (Princeton, NJ: Princeton University Press, 2001), pp. 27–28.

145. Charles Jordan Tabb, "The History of the Bankruptcy Laws in the United States," *American Bankruptcy Institute Law Review* 3 (1995): 5–51, pp. 15–16.

146. Tony A. Freyer, "Negotiable Instruments and the Federal Courts in Antebellum American Business," *Business History Review* 50, no. 4 (Winter 1976): 435–455, p. 436.

147. Balleisen, *Navigating Failure,* chap. 3.

148. Joseph K. Angell, *A Practical Summary of the Law of Assignments* (Boston: Hilliard, Gray, 1835), p. 27.

149. R. P. Ettinger and D. E. Golieb, *Credits and Collections* (New York: Prentice-Hall, 1917), pp. 331–332.

150. *Hunt's Merchants' Magazine* 26 (January 1852), pp. 91–92.

151. Balleisen, *Navigating Failure,* pp. 106–107, and chap. 4 generally.

152. *Hunt's Merchants' Magazine* 7 (August 1842), p. 182.

153. Tabb, "History of the Bankruptcy Laws," p. 18.

154. Balleisen, *Navigating Failure,* p. 120, and chap. 4 generally. David Skeel argues that the quick repeal occurred because the original coalition that passed the law was highly unstable. Skeel, *Debt's Dominion,* pp. 31–32.

155. Balleisen, *Navigating Failure,* pp. 120, 124.

156. Paul Goodman, "The Emergence of Homestead Exemption in the United States: Accommodation and Resistance to the Market Revolution," *Journal of American History* 80 (September 1993): 470–498. See also Tony A. Freyer, *Producers versus Capitalists: Constitutional Conflict in Antebellum America* (Charlottesville: University Press of Virginia, 1994), which finds that the Mid-Atlantic states continued to pass laws to protect debtors, which contradicted the pro-creditor stance of the Supreme Court rulings.

157. Charles Warren, *Bankruptcy in United States History* (Cambridge, MA: Harvard University Press, 1935), pp. 87–88, 91, 181n7; Freyer, "Business Law and American Economic History," p. 452.

158. Goodman, "Emergence of Homestead Exemption," pp. 470–471, 477, 481.

159. Linda E. Speth, "The Married Women's Property Acts, 1839–1865: Reform, Reaction, or Revolution?" in *Women and the Law: The Social Historical Perspective,* ed. D. Kelly Weisberg, vol. 2 (Cambridge, MA: Schenkman, 1982), pp. 69–91.

160. Clyde Griffen and Sally Griffen, "Family and Business in a Small City: Poughkeepsie, New York, 1850–1880," *Journal of Urban History* 2 (May 1975): 316–338, pp. 329–330.

161. Lawrence M. Friedman, review of Peter J. Coleman, *Debtors and Creditors in America: Insolvency, Imprisonment for Debt, and Bankruptcy, 1607–1900,*

in *Reviews in American History* 3, no. 1 (March 1975): 42–46. The same phenomenon occurred in Europe during the early modern era. See Thomas M. Safley, ed., *The History of Bankruptcy: Economic, Social and Cultural Implications in Early Modern Europe* (London: Routledge, 2013).

162. Warren, *Bankruptcy in United States History*, p. 97.

163. This section relies on Rowena Olegario, *A Culture of Credit: Embedding Trust and Transparency in American Business* (Cambridge, MA: Harvard University Press, 2006); and James D. Norris, *R. G. Dun and Co., 1841–1900: The Development of Credit-Reporting in the Nineteenth Century* (Westport, CT: Greenwood Press, 1978).

164. Calomiris and Haber, *Fragile by Design*, pp. 166–167.

165. Thornton, "'A Great Machine,'" pp. 571–572.

166. In England, a different institutional form, the mutual protection society, spread and formed networks. C. McNeil Greig, *The Growth of Credit Information: A History of UAPT-Infolink* (Wiley-Blackwell, 1992).

167. Gary Richardson and Michael Gou, "Business Failures by Industry in the United States, 1895 to 1939: A Statistical History," NBER, Working Paper Series, no. 16872 (March 2011).

168. For contemporary evidence, see Margaret J. Miller, ed., *Credit Reporting Systems and the International Economy* (Cambridge, MA: MIT Press, 2003).

169. Sandage, *Born Losers.*

3. "There Is Considerable Friction"

1. State bankers in the North delayed the law but could not destroy it. The act passed in the Senate by a margin of 23 to 21. Irwin Unger, *The Greenback Era: A Social and Political History of American Finance, 1865–1879* (Princeton, NJ: Princeton University Press, 1964), p. 19.

2. Some banks switched charters whenever the state or the federal regime became more advantageous. Michael D. Bordo, Angela Redish, and Hugh Rockoff, "Why Didn't Canada Have a Banking Crisis in 1908 (or in 1930, or 1907, or . . .)?" NBER, Working Paper Series, no. 17312 (August 2011), pp. 7–8.

3. Gretchen Ritter, *Goldbugs and Greenbacks: The Antimonopoly Tradition and the Politics of Finance in America* (Cambridge: Cambridge University Press, 1997), pp. 92, 107.

4. Howard Bodenhorn and Hugh Rockoff, "Regional Interest Rates in Antebellum America," in *Strategic Factors in Nineteenth Century American Economic History: A Volume to Honor Robert W. Fogel,* ed. Claudia Goldin and Hugh Rockoff (Chicago: University of Chicago Press, 1992), p. 186.

5. For an explanation of the shifting alliances among creditor and debtor groups, and the arguments of the "Bullionists" versus the "Greenbackers," see Unger, *Greenback Era;* Bruce G. Carruthers and Sarah Babb, "The Color of Money and the Nature of Value: Greenbacks and Gold in Postbellum America," *American Journal of Sociology* 101, no. 6 (May 1996): 1556–1591.

6. The estimate of the cost is from Stephen Daggett, "Costs of Major U.S. Wars," U.S. Congressional Research Service, June 29, 2010, table 1, p. 1, http://cironline.org/sites/default/files/legacy/files/June2010CRScostofuswars.pdf.

7. Charles Calomiris and Stephen Haber, *Fragile by Design: The Political Origins of Banking Crises and Scarce Credit* (Princeton, NJ: Princeton University Press, 2014), p. 176.

8. Fiat currencies are legal tender—by government decree, they must be accepted if offered as payment for debts. By this definition, the colonial bills of credit and state currencies were something less than fiat money. Colonial bills of credit, for example, were often refused by British merchants. According to Calomiris, "The primary purpose of creating this depreciated currency [the greenback], and making it legal tender, was to bail out the nation's banks . . . The net worth of the banks was restored, while depositors and note holders were effectively expropriated." Calomiris and Haber, *Fragile by Design*, p. 177.

9. Unger, *Greenback Era*, pp. 14–17.

10. Ibid., p. 15.

11. The constitutionality of making the greenbacks legal tender remained uncertain. Unger, *Greenback Era*, pp. 15–16, 20, 172.

12. Eugene Lerner, "Money, Prices and Wages in the Confederacy, 1861–1865," *Journal of Political Economy* 63, no. 1 (February 1955): 20–40, p. 24.

13. Ritter, *Goldbugs and Greenbacks*, p. 74. A gold standard need not restrict the supply of money. In the eight years after 1848, when gold was first discovered in California, the supply of money in the United States increased by 82 percent and prices went up by an average of 28 percent. Gary M. Walton and Hugh Rockoff, *History of the American Economy*, 9th ed. (Stamford, CT: Thomson Learning, 2002), p. 264.

14. Unger, *Greenback Era*, pp. 43, 165, 247–248.

15. Similar complaints arose during the Bank War of the 1830s. See the speeches of Missouri senator Thomas Hart Benton, 8 Reg. Deb. 974 (1833); and *Speech . . . on the Motion of Mr. Webster for . . . the Charter of the Bank of the United States, Delivered in the Senate, March 21, 1834* (Washington, DC: Francis Preston Blair, 1834), p. 16.

16. Ritter, *Goldbugs and Greenbacks*, pp. 68–69, 94.

17. Walton and Rockoff, *History of the American Economy*, p. 411. The Bank of New York offered this form of credit during the Jacksonian period, but it was the rare exception. Roy A. Foulke, *The Sinews of American Commerce* (New York: Dun and Bradstreet, 1941), pp. 138–139.

18. Historians do not agree about the exact supply of money during this period. Ritter writes that "the overall money stock rose only 17 percent in the twelve years between 1867 and 1879. The per capita money stock shrank over the greenback period." However, according to Unger, "the actual per capita money stock, defined to include bank deposits, grew from $5 to $72 between 1869 and 1879." Ritter, *Goldbugs and Greenbacks*, p. 75; Unger, *Greenback Era*, p. 36.

19. Unger, *Greenback Era*, chap. 6.

20. The Coinage Act of 1792 established both gold and silver as standards. In the following decades, and especially with the discovery of gold in California, gold

was undervalued relative to silver, and so tended to circulate in greater amounts (a phenomenon known as Gresham's Law).

21. Unger, *Greenback Era*, pp. 360, 370, 406.

22. Ritter, *Goldbugs and Greenbacks*, pp. 90, 154–158, 167.

23. Bernard Bailyn, et al., *The Great Republic: A History of the American People*, vol. 2, 4th ed. (Lexington, MA: D. C. Heath, 1992), pp. 92, 114–115.

24. Calomiris and Haber, *Fragile by Design*, p. 164.

25. There was healthy competition among New York banks, whereas country bankers were local monopolists. Ritter, *Goldbugs and Greenbacks*, pp. 155, 172–176, 202–203.

26. Gene Smiley, "The Expansion of the New York Securities Market at the Turn of the Century," *Business History Review* 55 (1981): 75–85; Charles R. Geisst, *Beggar Thy Neighbor: A History of Usury and Debt* (Philadelphia: University of Pennsylvania Press, 2013), p. 199.

27. Ritter, *Goldbugs and Greenbacks*, pp. 200–203 and the works cited therein.

28. Ibid., p. 187.

29. George A. Selgin and Lawrence H. White, "Monetary Reform and the Redemption of National Bank Notes, 1863–1913," *Business History Review* 68, no. 2 (Summer 1994): 205–243, pp. 238–239; James, "National Money Market, 1893–1911," p. 895.

30. U.S. Department of the Treasury, Annual Report of the Comptroller of the Currency, 1931, pp. 3, 5, https://fraser.stlouisfed.org/docs/publications/comp/1930s/compcurr_1931.pdf.

31. James, "National Money Market," pp. 888–889, 891, 896–897.

32. Economists would argue that these bankers had no choice, as they had a smaller pool of potential borrowers. Calomiris and Haber, *Fragile by Design*, p. 171.

33. Bordo, Redish, and Rockoff, "Why Didn't Canada," p. 14.

34. Selgin and White, "Monetary Reform," pp. 206–212; Calomiris and Haber, *Fragile by Design*, p. 183.

35. Ron Chernow, *The House of Morgan* (London: Simon & Schuster, 1990), chap. 7.

36. Allan H. Meltzer, *A History of the Federal Reserve*, vol. 1, *1913–1951* (Chicago: University of Chicago Press, 2002).

37. Bailyn, *Great Republic*, 2:92.

38. For antebellum proponents of the real-bills doctrine, see Condy Raguet, *A Treatise on Currency and Banking* (London: Ridgway, 1839), p. 97; Charles Francis Adams, "The Principles of Credit," *Hunt's Merchants' Magazine* 2 (March 1840): 197–198. At the time, short-term lending was the law only in New Orleans. Benjamin Klebaner, *American Commercial Banking: A History* (Boston: Twayne Publishers, 1990), p. 38.

39. Naomi R. Lamoreaux, *Insider Lending: Banks, Personal Connections, and Economic Development in Industrial New England* (Cambridge: Cambridge University Press, 1994).

40. Eugene N. White, "Were Banks Special Intermediaries in Late Nineteenth Century America?" *Federal Reserve Bank of St. Louis Review* 80, no. 3 (May–June

1998): 13–32, pp. 16–18, 23. Albert S. Bolles, Practical Banking (New York: Homans Publishing Co., 1884), p. 52.

41. However, see Richard H. Keehn and Gene Smiley, "Mortgage Lending by National Banks," *Business History Review* 51, no. 4 (Winter 1977): 474–491. They argue that the national banks may have made more mortgage loans than previously thought.

42. Geisst, *Beggar Thy Neighbor,* p. 183.

43. Gene Smiley, "Postbellum Banking and Financial Markets in the Old Northwest," in *Essays on the Economy of the Old Northwest,* ed. David C. Klingaman and Richard K. Vedder (Ohio University Press, 1987), p. 213.

44. White, "Were Banks Special Intermediaries," p. 21.

45. Historians offer a diverse set of reasons why regional short-term interest rates after the Civil War varied so widely and converged slowly. These range from increased bank competition to the development of the stock market. See Bodenhorn and Rockoff, "Regional Interest Rates," p. 159; Ritter, *Goldbugs and Greenbacks,* p. 71.

46. D. M. Frederiksen, "Mortgage Banking in America," *Journal of Political Economy* 2, no. 2 (March 1894): 203–234, p. 209.

47. Gavin Wright, *Old South, New South: Revolutions in the Southern Economy since the Civil War* (New York: Basic Books, 1986), pp. 87–89.

48. Howard Bodenhorn, *A History of Banking in Antebellum America: Financial Markets and Economic Development in an Era of Nation Building* (Cambridge: Cambridge University Press, 2000), p. 230; Howard Bodenhorn, "Capital Mobility and Financial Integration in Antebellum America," *Journal of Economic History* 52, no. 3 (September 1992): 585–610, p. 601.

49. Bodenhorn and Rockoff, "Regional Interest Rates," p. 183.

50. Bodenhorn, "Capital Mobility and Financial Integration," p. 602.

51. The factors' disappearance was also the result of improved transportation and communication facilities, which helped to replace the factors' networks. Harold D. Woodman, *King Cotton and His Retainers: Financing and Marketing the Cotton Crop of the South, 1800–1925* (Lexington: University of Kentucky Press, 1968).

52. Bodenhorn, "Capital Mobility and Financial Integration," pp. 601–602.

53. Ritter, *Goldbugs and Greenbacks,* p. 203; Roger L. Ransom and Richard Sutch, "Debt Peonage in the Cotton South after the Civil War," *Journal of Economic History* 32 (1972): 641–667.

54. Stanley L. Engerman, "Slavery and Its Consequences for the South," in *The Cambridge Economic History of the United States,* ed. Engerman and Robert E. Gallman, vol. 2, *The Long Nineteenth Century* (Cambridge: Cambridge University Press, 2008), pp. 360–361.

55. Wright, *Old South, New South,* pp. 97–98.

56. A. R. Reynolds, "Rafting Down the Chippewa and the Mississippi: Daniel Shaw Lumber Company, a Type Study," *Wisconsin Magazine of History* 32, no. 2 (December 1948): 143–152.

57. Ritter, *Goldbugs and Greenbacks,* p. 71.

58. Bailyn, *Great Republic,* 2:92; Geisst, *Beggar Thy Neighbor,* p. 185.

59. Bodenhorn, *History of Banking,* p. 153.

60. White, "Were Banks Special Intermediaries," p. 19.

61. James, "National Money Market," pp. 885–886.

62. White, "Were Banks Special Intermediaries," pp. 25–26.

63. James, "National Money Market," pp. 888, 896–897.

64. White, "Were Banks Special Intermediaries," pp. 25–26.

65. Sidney Homer and Richard Sylla, *A History of Interest Rates,* 4th ed. (New Brunswick, NJ: Rutgers University Press, 2005 [1963]), p. 317.

66. Wayland A. Tonning, "Department Stores in Down State Illinois, 1889–1943," *Business History Review* 29 (December 1955), pp. 341–342.

67. Peter R. Earling, *Whom to Trust: A Practical Treatise on Mercantile Credit* (Chicago: Rand, McNally, 1890), p. 209; Samuel Terry, *Retailer's Manual: Embodying the Conclusions of Thirty Years' Experience in Merchandizing* (Newark, NJ: Jennings Brothers, 1869), p. 189.

68. Herman E. Krooss and Martin R. Blyn, *A History of Financial Intermediaries* (New York: Random House, 1971), p. 72; J. H. Tregoe, *Credit and Its Management* (New York: Harper & Brothers, 1930), p. 32.

69. Glenn Porter and Harold Livesay, *Merchants and Manufacturers: Studies in the Changing Structure of Nineteenth-Century Marketing* (Baltimore: Johns Hopkins Press, 1971), chap. 7; Gene Smiley, "Postbellum Banking and Financial Markets in the Old Northwest," in *Essays on the Economy of the Old Northwest,* ed. David C. Klingaman and Richard K. Vedder (Athens: Ohio University Press, 1987), p. 213.

70. Porter and Livesay, *Merchants and Manufacturers,* pp. 12, 165, 216–218, 228.

71. Calomiris and Haber, *Fragile by Design,* p. 185.

72. Edward Sherwood Meade, "Capitalization of the United States Steel Corporation," *Quarterly Journal of Economics* 16, no. 2 (February 1902): 214–232.

73. See J. Bradford Delong, "Did J. P. Morgan's Men Add Value? An Economist's Perspective on Financial Capitalism," in *Inside the Business Enterprise: Historical Perspectives on the Use of Information,* ed. Peter Temin (Chicago: University of Chicago Press for NBER, 1991), pp. 205–236; Susie J. Pak, *Gentlemen Bankers: The World of J. P. Morgan* (Cambridge, MA: Harvard University Press, 2013); Alan D. Morrison and William J. Wilhelm Jr., *Investment Banking: Institutions, Politics, and Law* (Oxford: Oxford University Press, 2007).

74. George P. Baker and George David Smith, *The New Financial Capitalists: Kohlberg Kravis Roberts and the Creation of Corporate Value* (Cambridge: Cambridge University Press, 1999), p. 47.

75. Jonathan Barron Baskin and Paul J. Miranti Jr., *A History of Corporate Finance* (Cambridge: Cambridge University Press, 1999), pp. 160–161.

76. Peter Tufano, "Business Failure, Judicial Intervention, and Financial Innovation: Restructuring U.S. Railroads in the Nineteenth Century," *Business History Review* 71, no. 1 (Spring 1997): 1–40, p. 7.

77. Ibid., p. 6.

78. Baskin and Miranti, *History of Corporate Finance,* pp. 150–151.

79. Some financing of accounts receivables existed in the nineteenth century. See Lendol Calder, *Financing the American Dream: A Cultural History of Consumer Credit* (Princeton, NJ: Princeton University Press, 1999), p. 187.

80. Wilbur C. Plummer and Ralph A. Young, *Sales Finance Companies and Their Credit Practices* (Cambridge, MA: NBER, 1940), pp. 33–34; Foulke, *Sinews of American Commerce,* pp. 196–197.

81. Foulke, *Sinews of American Commerce,* p. 197.

82. Kenneth A. Snowden, "Mortgage Rates and American Capital Market Development in the Late Nineteenth Century," *Journal of Economic History* 47, no. 3 (September 1987): 671–691, pp. 671, 674.

83. Frederiksen, "Mortgage Banking in America," pp. 206–209.

84. However, see Keehn and Smiley, "Mortgage Lending by National Banks."

85. The average capital of stock savings banks was only $115,000, and the average surplus of the American mutual savings banks was $190,000. Frederiksen, "Mortgage Banking in America," pp. 225–226.

86. A few large eastern insurance companies invested in western mortgages. In 1890, four insurance companies—Aetna, Connecticut Mutual, Phoenix, Travelers (all in Connecticut), and Northwestern Mutual of Wisconsin—"held 30 percent of the life insurance industry's mortgage loan portfolio and an even larger share of inter-regional lending in both the commercial and farm mortgage markets." Kenneth A. Snowden, *Mortgage Banking in the United States, 1870–1940,* Research Institute for Housing America, Special Report, 2013, p. 22.

87. Frederiksen, "Mortgage Banking in America," pp. 217, 222, 230.

88. Snowden, "Mortgage Rates and American Capital Market Development," p. 681.

89. Loans to westerners by life insurance companies and mutual savings banks would have been greater had New York, where many of the institutions were based, not forbidden them from lending outside of the state. H. Peers Brewer, "Eastern Money and Western Mortgages in the 1870s," *Business History Review* 50, no. 3 (Autumn 1976): 356–380, pp. 358–359.

90. Frederiksen, "Mortgage Banking in America," pp. 206, 209.

91. Kenneth A. Snowden, "Mortgage Lending and American Urbanization, 1880–1890," *Journal of Economic History* 48, no. 2 (June 1988): 273–285, p. 275.

92. Frederiksen, "Mortgage Banking in America," pp. 206–210, 223.

93. Barry Eichengreen, "Mortgage Interest Rates in the Populist Era," *American Economic Review* 74, no. 5 (December 1984): 995–1015, pp. 997–999.

94. Snowden, "Mortgage Rates and American Capital Market Development," p. 678.

95. According to one estimate, the international flow of capital increased by nearly fifty times from 1825 to 1913. Hartmut Berghoff, "Civilizing Capitalism? The Beginnings of Credit Rating in the United States and Germany," *Bulletin of the GHI [German Historical Institute]* (Fall 2009): 9–28.

96. Lance E. Davis and Robert Gallman, *Evolving Financial Markets and International Capital Flows: Britain, the Americas, and Australia, 1865–1914* (Cambridge: Cambridge University Press, 2001), pp. 257–258 and the works cited therein.

97. Brewer, "Eastern Money and Western Mortgages," pp. 360–362. The evidence strongly suggests that lenders were able to skirt usury laws. In Kansas, the legal

maximum was 12 percent, but lenders charged 15 percent and called the extra percentage points a commission. Eichengreen, "Mortgage Interest Rates in the Populist Era," p. 999.

98. Eichengreen, "Mortgage Interest Rates in the Populist Era," p. 997.

99. Borrowers paid the loan agents a commission, which was taken out of the loan's principal. Allan G. Bogue, *Money at Interest: The Farm Mortgage on the Middle Border* (Ithaca, NY: Cornell University Press, 1955), pp. 86–90.

100. Over the course of its existence, the Watkins company provided over 22,000 loans worth a total of $19 million. Allan G. Bogue, "The Land Mortgage Company in the Early Plains States," *Agricultural History* 25, no. 1 (January 1951): 20–33, pp. 23–26. See also Bogue, *Money at Interest*.

101. Brewer, "Eastern Money and Western Mortgages," p. 361.

102. Snowden, *Mortgage Banking in the United States*, pp. 14, 18.

103. Eichengreen, "Mortgage Interest Rates in the Populist Era," p. 997; Snowden, *Mortgage Banking in the United States*, p. 29. The first to issue mortgage-backed bonds was the Iowa Loan and Trust Company of Des Moines, Iowa, in 1881. Frederiksen, "Mortgage Banking in America," p. 210.

104. Bogue, *Money at Interest*, pp. 129–130.

105. Snowden, *Mortgage Banking in the United States*, pp. 19–20.

106. Frederiksen, "Mortgage Banking in America," pp. 217–222.

107. Snowden, *Mortgage Banking in the United States*, pp. 21–22.

108. Bogue, "Land Mortgage Company," pp. 23–26. See also Bogue, *Money at Interest*. Bogue found that the rates charged by resident and nonresident investors were nearly identical. He argues that local agents, working with little supervision, were responsible for the high costs of loans. Moreover, mortgage company officials were often too optimistic and knew little about farming.

109. Frederiksen, "Mortgage Banking in America," p. 209.

110. Bogue, "Land Mortgage Company," p. 33.

111. Snowden, *Mortgage Banking in the United States*, pp. 30–36.

112. Ibid., pp. 27–41.

113. Walton and Rockoff, *History of the American Economy*, p. 482.

114. Calomiris and Haber, *Fragile by Design*, p. 193.

115. Sheldon Garon, *Beyond Our Means: Why America Spends while the World Saves* (Princeton, NJ: Princeton University Press, 2011), p. 89; Calder, *Financing the American Dream*, p. 68. The depression of the 1890s, however, caused residential housing starts to fall dramatically. They did not recover until the First World War. Snowden, *Mortgage Banking in the United States*, p. 56. The British statistic is from *A Century of Change: Trends in UK Statistics Since 1900*, House of Commons Library, December 1999, p. 12, http://www.parliament.uk/documents/commons/lib/research/rp99/rp99-111.pdf.

116. Snowden, "Mortgage Lending and American Urbanization," p. 275. Homeownership rates, urban versus non-urban mortgage figures, and other information on mortgage indebtedness in 1890 are available in George K. Holmes and John S. Lord, *Report on Real Estate Mortgages in the United States at the Eleventh Census: 1890* (Washington, DC, 1892).

117. Daniel Wadhwani, "Institutional Foundations of Personal Finance: Innovation in the U.S. Savings Banks," *Business History Review* 85, no. 3 (Autumn 2011): 499–528, p. 505.

118. Garon, *Beyond our Means,* p. 94. See also David L. Mason, *From Buildings and Loans to Bail-Outs: A History of the American Savings and Loan Industry, 1831–1955* (Cambridge: Cambridge University Press, 2004).

119. Marc A. Weiss, "Marketing and Financing Home Ownership: Mortgage Lending and Public Policy in the United States, 1918–1989," *Business and Economic History,* 2nd ser., vol. 18 (1989): 109–118, p. 111.

120. The antibranching laws prevented the expansion of savings banks. In the first quarter of the twentieth century, their numbers declined, whereas the numbers of building and loan societies and commercial banks increased. Wadhwani, "Institutional Foundations of Personal Finance," pp. 518, 523–524.

121. Snowden, "Mortgage Rates and American Capital Market Development," p. 689.

122. Frederiksen, "Mortgage Banking in America," p. 221.

123. Snowden, "Mortgage Rates and American Capital Market Development," p. 673.

124. Snowden, "Mortgage Lending and Urbanization," pp. 274–275; Calder, *Financing the American Dream,* p. 68.

125. William E. Harmon, "The Sale of City Real Estate on Instalments," *Proceedings of the Academy of Political Science in the City of New York* 2, no. 1, *Capital and Labor Unified* (October 1911): 15–22. Harmon noted that when he first began, in the 1880s, selling land on installment carried a "social stigma."

126. Weiss, "Marketing and Financing," p. 110.

127. Ibid., p. 111.

128. Calder, *Financing the American Dream,* pp. 64–66.

129. Snowden, *Mortgage Banking in the United States,* p. 63.

130. David Graeber, *Debt: The First 5,000 Years* (Brooklyn, NY: Melville House, 2011), p. 354.

131. Calder, *Financing the American Dream,* pp. 58–59, 70–71, 167–170.

132. Pittsburgh's neighborhood retailers charged about 10 percent more than the large, cash-only chains and department stores. Peter R. Shergold, "The Loan Shark: The Small Loan Business in Early Twentieth-Century Pittsburgh," *Pennsylvania History* 45, no. 3 (July 1978): 195–223, pp. 196–199.

133. Calder, *Financing the American Dream,* p. 112.

134. Hugh Rockoff, "Prodigals and Projectors: An Economic History of Usury Laws in the United States from Colonial Times to 1900," NBER, Working Paper Series, no. 9742 (May 2003), p. 19. Although the national banking act imposed a usury ceiling on federally chartered banks, state banks did not fall under the law. Geisst, *Beggar Thy Neighbor,* p. 193.

135. Calder, *Financing the American Dream,* pp. 114–115.

136. Eichengreen, "Mortgage Interest Rates in the Populist Era," p. 998.

137. Paul R. Moo, "Legislative Control of Consumer Credit Transactions," *Law and Contemporary Problems* 33 (Fall 1968): 656–670, p. 657.

138. Calder, *Financing the American Dream,* pp. 50, 52.

139. Geisst, *Beggar Thy Neighbor*, p. 169.

140. The U.S. Uniform Small Loan Law' (USLL') defined a small loan as $300 or less. Bruce Carruthers, Timothy Guinnane, and Yoonseok Lee, "Bringing 'Honest Capital' to Poor Borrowers: The Passage of the U.S. Uniform Small Loan Law, 1907–30," *Journal of Interdisciplinary History* 42, no. 3 (Winter 2012): 393–418, p. 400.

141. Wendy A. Woloson, *In Hock: Pawning in America from Independence through the Great Depression* (Chicago: University of Chicago Press, 2010), p. 76.

142. Calder, *Financing the American Dream,* pp. 49, 120; Foulke, *Sinews of American Commerce,* p. 117.

143. Woloson, *In Hock,* p. 163.

144. Shergold, "The Loan Shark," p. 220.

145. Calder, *Financing the American Dream,* pp. 44, 46, 49; Woloson, *In Hock,* table 3.1, p. 63; Shergold, "The Loan Shark," p. 200.

146. Woloson, *In Hock,* table 3.1, p. 63.

147. Calder, *Financing the American Dream,* pp. 50–54, 117–118. There is little evidence that the chains made loans across state lines.

148. Calder, *Financing the American Dream*, pp. 51–52.

149. Martha L. Olney, *Buy Now, Pay Later: Advertising, Credit, and Consumer Durables in the 1920s* (Chapel Hill: University of North Carolina Press, 1991), pp. 130–131.

150. Calder, *Financing the American Dream,* pp. 56, 181. Consumers may have made a rational choice because installment financing gave them the use of both the product and the money. Behavioral economists offer another perspective: the tendency of individuals to undervalue the future relative to the present. Thus, individuals prefer having the cash in the present, even if they know they will (eventually) pay a higher overall price. See Dan Ariely, *Predictably Irrational: The Hidden Forces That Shape Our Decisions* (New York: HarperCollins, 2008).

151. Paul B. Trescott, *Financing American Enterprise: The Story of Commercial Banking* (New York: Harper and Row, 1963), p. 64; Gilbert C. Fite and Jim E. Reese, *An Economic History of the United States,* 3d ed. (Boston: Houghton Mifflin, 1973 [1965, 1959]), p. 321.

152. Calder, *Financing the American Dream,* pp. 72, 167–173.

153. Allan G. Bogue, Brian Q. Cannon, and Kenneth J. Winkle, "Oxen to Organs: Chattel Credit in Springdale Town, 1849–1900," *Agricultural History* 77, no. 3 (2003): 420–452, pp. 421–422. See also Robert A. Lynn, "Installment Credit before 1870," *Business History Review* 31, no. 4 (Winter 1957): 414–424, p. 422.

154. Calder, *Financing the American Dream,* p. 117.

155. Bogue, Cannon, and Winkle, "Oxen to Organs," pp. 431–433, 435–436.

156. Woloson, *In Hock,* p. 58.

157. Shergold, "The Loan Shark," pp. 215–217.

158. Calder, *Financing the American Dream,* p. 118.

159. Ibid., pp. 124–135.

160. "Aims to Fight Loan Sharks," *New York Times,* February 16, 1912; "Compete with Loan Sharks," *New York Times,* February 19, 1912. It was sold to a

commercial lender in 1925. See Carruthers, Guinnane, and Lee, "Bringing 'Honest Capital' to Poor Borrowers."

161. *The Usurer's Grip,* film, dir. Charles Brabin, 1912, http://www.library.hbs .edu/hc/credit/credit4f.html.

162. "Loan Shark Fined $1,000," *New York Times,* August 2, 1913; "Has Pardon Plea Backed by $500,000," *New York Times,* December 24, 1913; "Tolman Has Rivals Who Buy Salaries," *New York Times,* December 27, 1913; "Daniel H. Tolman, 'Loan Shark,' Dies," *New York Times,* February 14, 1918.

163. Louis N. Robinson and Rolf Nugent, *Regulation of the Small Loan Business* (New York: Russell Sage Foundation, 1935); Carruthers, Guinnane, and Lee, "Bringing 'Honest Capital' to Poor Borrowers."

164. Calder, *Financing the American Dream,* pp. 40, 73, 100.

165. In 1910, only 10 percent of Americans had savings accounts compared to 30–39 percent of the populations of Germany, Japan, France, Britain, Belgium, Sweden, and the Netherlands. Garon, *Beyond Our Means,* pp. 91, 93, 186.

166. Charles Jordan Tabb, "The History of the Bankruptcy Laws in the United States," *American Bankruptcy Institute Law Review* 3 (1995): 5–51, p. 19.

167. Tabb, "History of the Bankruptcy Laws," pp. 19, 21; Peter J. Coleman, *Debtors and Creditors in America: Insolvency, Imprisonment for Debt, and Bankruptcy, 1607–1900* (Madison: State Historical Society of Wisconsin, 1974), pp. 25–26. The quote is from Earling, *Whom to Trust,* p. 51.

168. Elizabeth Thompson, *The Reconstruction of Southern Debtors: Bankruptcy after the Civil War* (Athens: University of Georgia Press, 2004), pp. 49, 51, 84.

169. In New York only one national bank and two trust companies failed (as opposed to brokerage houses and private banks, many more of which shut their doors). Yet depositors in Chicago, Memphis, and the southern Atlantic coast lost confidence in their banks and began trying to withdraw their money. Elmus Wicker and Ellis W. Tallman, "Banking and Financial Crises in United States History: What Guidance Can History Offer Policymakers?" Social Science Research Network (hereafter SSRN), Working Paper (July 31, 2009), pp. 11–12, http://ssrn.com /abstract=1544015.

170. Tufano, "Business Failure," pp. 2–3.

171. Morrison and Wilhelm, *Investment Banking,* p. 176. See also Richard White, *Railroaded: The Transcontinentals and the Making of Modern America* (New York: W. W. Norton, 2011).

172. David Skeel, *Debt's Dominion: A History of Bankruptcy Law in America* (Princeton, NJ: Princeton University Press, 2001), pp. 52–54.

173. Bradley Hansen, "The People's Welfare and the Origins of Corporate Reorganization: The Wabash Receivership Reconsidered," *Business History Review* 74, no. 3 (Autumn 2000): 377–405, pp. 379–382. One party who retained control of the reorganized railroad was Jay Gould.

174. Tabb, "History of the Bankruptcy Laws," p. 22; Tufano, "Business Failure," p. 20.

175. Bradley Hansen, "Bankruptcy Law in the United States," EH.net Encyclopedia, ed. Robert Whaples, August 14, 2001, http://eh.net/encyclopedia/article

/hansen.bankruptcy.law.us. Hansen makes the argument of continuity in "People's Welfare."

176. Tufano, "Business Failure," pp. 8, 11, 32.

177. Ibid., p. 29; David A. Skeel Jr., "Competing Narratives in Corporate Bankruptcy: Debtor in Control vs. No Time to Spare," University of Pennsylvania Law School, Faculty Scholarship Paper, no. 328, pp. 1191–1192, http://scholarship.law.upenn.edu/faculty_scholarship/328.

178. Morrison and Wilhelm, *Investment Banking,* pp. 181–182.

179. Charles Warren, *Bankruptcy in United States History* (Cambridge, MA: Harvard University Press, 1935), pp. 112–114; Bradley Hansen, "Commercial Associations and the Creation of a National Economy: The Demand for Federal Bankruptcy Law," *Business History Review* 72, no. 1 (Spring 1998): 86–113, p. 108.

180. Skeel, *Debt's Dominion,* p. 37.

181. Hansen, "Commercial Associations and the Creation of a National Economy," pp. 98–99, 104, 107–108.

182. Skeel, *Debt's Dominion,* pp. 41–42.

183. Thomas Bak, John Golmant, and James Woods, "A Comparison of the Effects of the 1978 and 2005 Bankruptcy Filing Rates," *Emory Bankruptcy Developments Journal* 25, no. 1 (2008): 11–38, p. 12, note 10.

184. The constitutionality of state exemptions under the federal law was not clarified until 1902. Skeel, *Debt's Dominion,* pp. 48, 54; Gary Richardson and Michael Gou, "Business Failures by Industry in the United States, 1895 to 1939: A Statistical History," NBER, Working Paper Series, no. 16872 (March 2011).

185. Skeel, *Debt's Dominion,* p. 41.

186. Robert A. Kagan, "The Routinization of Debt Collection: An Essay on Social Change and Conflict in the Courts," *Law and Society Review* 18, no. 3 (1984): 323–372, pp. 354–355.

187. Peter P. Wahlstad, *Credit and the Credit Man* (New York: Alexander Hamilton Institute, 1917), p. 225.

188. Hansen, "Commercial Associations and the Creation of a National Economy," p. 96.

189. Skeel, *Debt's Dominion,* p. 43.

190. Hansen, "Bankruptcy Law in the United States."

191. For this section, see Rowena Olegario, *A Culture of Credit: Embedding Trust and Transparency in American Business* (Cambridge, MA: Harvard University Press, 2006).

192. Hansen, "Commercial Associations and the Creation of a National Economy," p. 112; Jesse R. Sprague, *The Romance of Credit* (New York: D. Appleton-Century Co., Inc., 1943), p. 187.

193. Rowena Olegario, "Credit Information, Institutions, and International Trade," in *The Foundations of Worldwide Economic Integration: Powers, Institutions, and Global Markets, 1850–1930,* ed. Niels P. Petersson and Christof DeJung (Cambridge: Cambridge University Press, 2013), pp. 60–88.

194. Edward M. Skinner, "Essentials in Credit Management," in *Credits, Collections and Finance: Organizing the Work, Correct Policies and Methods: Five Credit and Collection Systems* (Chicago: A. W. Shaw, 1914), pp. 14–15.

195. *Report of the Committee Appointed Pursuant to House Resolutions 429 and 504 to Investigate the Concentration of Control of Money and Credit,* submitted by Mr. Pujo, February 28, 1913 (Washington, DC: Government Printing Office, 1913), p. 136.

196. Later research has confirmed that these circumstances tend to be important in explaining the establishment of credit bureaus worldwide. See Marco Pagano and Tullio Japelli, "Information Sharing in Credit Markets," *Journal of Finance* 48, no. 5 (December 1993): 1693–1718.

197. Terry, *Retailer's Manual,* p. 151.

198. J. R. Truesdale, *Credit Bureau Management* (New York: Prentice Hall, Inc., 1972), p. 13.

199. Calder, *Financing the American Dream,* p. 72.

200. William A. Flinn, "History of Retail Credit Company: A Study in the Marketing of Information about Individuals," Ph.D. thesis, Ohio State University, 1959, pp. 47–64; Louis Hyman, *Debtor Nation: The History of America in Red Ink* (Princeton: Princeton University Press, 2011), pp. 207–208.

201. Robert M. Hunt, "The Development and Regulation of Consumer Credit Reporting in America," Federal Reserve of Philadelphia, Working Paper Series, no. 02–21 (November 2002); Nicola Jentzsch, *Financial Privacy: An International Comparison of Credit Reporting Systems,* 2nd ed. (Berlin: Springer Verlag, 2006), pp. 63–64.

202. C.O. Hanes, *The Retail Credit and Adjustment Bureaus: Their Organization and Their Conduct* (Columbia, MO: n.p., 1915), pp. 5, 7, 27.

203. Woloson, *In Hock,* pp. 175–178; Hanes, *Retail Credit and Adjustment Bureaus,* pp. 4–5, 11, 15, 19, 21–22, 29, 33. The mercantile agencies and handbooks were less explicitly exclusive, and they did not emphasize membership in churches, lodges, or political parties. Olegario, *A Culture of Credit,* chap. 3.

204. Fragmentation may have hurt both banking and economic growth in the United States. Calomiris and Haber, *Fragile by Design.* See also Charles W. Calomiris, *U.S. Bank Deregulation in Historical Perspective* (Cambridge: Cambridge University Press, 2006).

4. "To Open Up Mass Markets"

1. See Michael D. Bordo, "The Bretton Woods International Monetary System: A Historical Overview," in *A Retrospective on the Bretton Woods System: Lessons for International Monetary Reform,* ed. Michael D. Bordo and Barry Eichengreen (Chicago: University of Chicago Press, 1993). The American government promised to keep the dollar convertible to gold, and the other signatories pledged to buy and to sell dollars to keep their own currencies within 1 percent of the fixed exchange rate. The dollar's reserve currency status reduced the United States' exposure to exchange risk and its transaction costs, among other benefits.

2. Alan M. Taylor, "The Great Leveraging," NBER, Working Paper Series, no. 18290 (August 2012), p. 2. From the end of the Second World War to the financial crisis of 2007–2008, none of the world's advanced economies experi-

enced financial crises that were of the same intensity as those of the 1920s and 1930s.

3. Charles Calomiris and Stephen Haber, *Fragile by Design: The Political Origins of Banking Crises and Scarce Credit* (Princeton, NJ: Princeton University Press, 2014), p. 81.

4. Baker Library Historical Collections exhibit, "The Forgotten Real Estate Boom of the 1920s," Harvard Business School, www.library.hbs.edu/hc/crises/forgotten.html.

5. Barry Eichengreen and Kris Mitchener, "The Great Depression as a Credit Boom Gone Wrong," Bank for International Settlements (hereafter BIS), Working Papers Series, no. 137 (September 2003), pp. 21, 25.

6. Louis Hyman, *Debtor Nation: The History of America in Red Ink* (Princeton: Princeton University Press, 2011), p. 118; Joseph Nocera, *A Piece of the Action: How the Middle Class Joined the Money Class* (New York: Simon and Schuster, 1994), p. 128.

7. Alfred Sloan, *My Years with General Motors* (New York: Doubleday, 1964), p. 305.

8. William Whyte, *The Organization Man* (Garden City, NY: Doubleday, 1956); Kenneth T. Jackson, *Crabgrass Frontier: The Suburbanization of the United States* (New York: Oxford University Press, 1985).

9. *Historical Statistics of the United States,* Millennial Edition On Line, ed. Susan B. Carter, et al. (Cambridge: Cambridge University Press, 2006), pp. 3–651.

10. Richard Sylla, "U.S. Securities Markets and the Banking System, 1790–1840," *Federal Reserve of St. Louis Review* (May–June 1998): 83–98, p. 97.

11. Gary M. Walton and Hugh Rockoff, *History of the American Economy,* 9th ed. (Stamford, CT: Thomson Learning, 2002), p. 491.

12. Charles R. Geisst, *Collateral Damaged: The Marketing of Consumer Debt to America* (New York: Bloomberg Press, 2009), p. 56; Charles R. Geisst, *Beggar Thy Neighbor: A History of Usury and Debt* (Philadelphia: University of Pennsylvania Press, 2013), p. 197. The Fed acquired the authority to pay interest on the reserves of member banks in 2008.

13. James Butkiewicz, "Reconstruction Finance Corporation," EH.Net Encyclopedia, ed. Robert Whaples, July 19, 2002, http://eh.net/encyclopedia/reconstruction-finance-corporation/. The national banks opposed bailouts of their less-regulated competitors, which may have affected the decisions of the Federal Reserve not to intervene. During the Depression, the Federal Reserve was freed from the gold standard so that it could more easily inject liquidity into the banking system. Michael D. Bordo, Angela Redish, and Hugh Rockoff, "Why Didn't Canada Have a Banking Crisis in 1908 (or in 1930, or 1907, or . . .)?" NBER, Working Paper Series, no. 17312 (August 2011), p. 18.

14. Calomiris and Haber, *Fragile by Design,* p. 189.

15. Regulation Q "was apparently motivated by a desire that commercial banks not put money on deposit in reserve city banks, but rather lend it out." Bordo, Redish, and Rockoff, "Why Didn't Canada . . . ," p. 21. See R. A. Gilbert, "Requiem of Regulation Q: What It Did and Why It Passed Away," *Federal Reserve Bank of St. Louis Review* 68, no. 2 (February 1986): 22–37. The Federal Deposit Insurance

Corporation (FDIC) was strongly supported by small, one-unit bankers, whereas larger banks opposed it. See Calomiris and Haber, *Fragile by Design;* Charles Calomiris, *U.S. Bank Deregulation in Historical Perspective* (Cambridge: Cambridge University Press, 2000).

16. Geisst, *Collateral Damaged,* p. 72.

17. Hyman, *Debtor Nation,* p. 253.

18. Calomiris and Haber argue that deposit insurance was not passed to save the banking system, but was instead "the product of lobbying by unit bankers who wanted to stifle the growth of branch banking." The American Bankers Association lobbied President Franklin D. Roosevelt to veto it, but populist congressman Henry B. Steagall of Alabama was able to get it through. Calomiris and Haber, *Fragile by Design,* pp. 189–190.

19. Frederic S. Mishkin and Stanley Eakins, *Financial Markets and Institutions* (Essex, UK: Pearson Education, 2012), p. 466.

20. Bordo, Redish, and Rockoff, "Why Didn't Canada . . . ," p. 20.

21. Calomiris and Haber, *Fragile by Design,* pp. 188–189, 194.

22. Lendol Calder, *Financing the American Dream: A Cultural History of Consumer Credit* (Princeton, NJ: Princeton University Press, 1999), pp. 18–19; Martha L. Olney, *Buy Now, Pay Later: Advertising, Credit, and Consumer Durables in the 1920s* (Chapel Hill: University of North Carolina, 1991), pp. 86–92. Estimates of total consumer and installment debt prior to World War II differ among researchers.

23. Christina D. Romer, "The Great Crash and the Onset of the Great Depression," *Quarterly Journal of Economics* 105, no. 3 (August 1990): 597–624. The buildup of credit in the 1920s probably contributed to the length and depth of the subsequent economic slowdown, but there is no scholarly agreement about this. See Eichengreen and Mitchener, "Depression as a Credit Boom Gone Wrong."

24. Calder, *Financing the American Dream,* p. 18.

25. Geisst, *Collateral Damaged,* p. 52; Wendy A. Woloson, *In Hock: Pawning in America from Independence through the Great Depression* (Chicago: University of Chicago Press, 2010), pp. 76, 90.

26. Woloson, *In Hock,* pp. 174, 178.

27. "New Morris Plan," *Time,* November 13, 1933.

28. Ibid.

29. Louis N. Robinson, "The Morris Plan," *American Economic Review* 21, no. 2 (June 1931): 222–235, pp. 222–223.

30. Ronnie J. Phillips and David Mushinski, "Morris Plan Banks," Economic History Association, EH.Net Encyclopedia, ed. Robert Whaples, August 14, 2001, http://eh.net/encyclopedia/morris-plan-banks.

31. Robinson, "The Morris Plan"; Roy A. Foulke, *The Sinews of American Commerce* (New York: Dun & Bradstreet, 1941), pp. 205–207.

32. *Time,* November 13, 1933.

33. See Robinson, "Morris Plan," for other criticisms.

34. Phillips and Mushinski, "Morris Plan Banks."

35. Robinson, "Morris Plan," p. 233. Morris did not succeed in using the Plan to finance installment buying and second mortgages.

36. Robinson, "Morris Plan," p. 235.

37. Bruce Carruthers, Timothy Guinnane, and Yoonseok Lee, "Bringing 'Honest Capital' to Poor Borrowers: The Passage of the U.S. Uniform Small Loan Law, 1907–30," *Journal of Interdisciplinary History* 42, no. 3 (Winter 2012): 393–418.

38. Calder, *Financing the American Dream,* pp. 135–137, 153.

39. M. R. Neifeld, *The Personal Finance Business* (New York: Harper and Bros., 1933), p. 138; Calder, *Financing the American Dream,* pp. 134, 147; Carruthers, Guinnane, and Lee, "Bringing 'Honest Capital' to Poor Borrowers," p. 405.

40. Foulke, *Sinews of American Commerce,* p. 202; Calder, *Financing the American Dream,* pp. 147–148.

41. M. R. Neifeld and A. E. Robichaud, "Lenders Exchanges in the Personal Finance Business," *Journal of Marketing* 4, no. 3 (January 1940): 268–273, pp. 269–270.

42. Foulke, *Sinews of American Commerce,* p. 201.

43. Ibid., pp. 202–205.

44. M. R. Neifeld, "What Consumer Credit Is," *Annals of the American Academy of Political and Social Science* 196 (March 1938): 63–73, p. 72; Geisst, *Collateral Damaged,* p. 48; Calder, *Financing the American Dream,* p. 284. The Federal Housing Administration's Title I program, which ensured small bank loans for home improvements, further accustomed the banks to consumer lending. Hyman, *Debtor Nation,* pp. 78–79.

45. Phillips and Mushinski, "Morris Plan Banks."

46. Geisst, *Collateral Damaged,* p. 50.

47. Calder, *Financing the American Dream,* p. 285; Geisst, *Beggar Thy Neighbor,* p. 188.

48. Jesse R. Sprague, *The Romance of Credit* (New York: D. Appleton-Century Company, Inc., 1943), pp. 168–169.

49. Martha L. Olney, "When Your Word Is Not Enough: Race, Collateral, and Household Credit," *Journal of Economic History* 58, no. 2 (June 1998): 408–431, p. 410.

50. Martha Olney, "Avoiding Default: The Role of Credit in the Consumption Collapse of 1930," *The Quarterly Journal of Economics* 114, no. 1 (February 1999): 99, 319–335; Sheldon Garon, *Beyond Our Means: Why America Spends while the World Saves* (Princeton, NJ: Princeton University Press, 2011), p. 333; Geisst, *Collateral Damaged,* pp. 40, 44.

51. Eichengreen and Mitchener, "Depression as a Credit Boom Gone Wrong," p. 40.

52. Edwin R. A. Seligman, "Economic Problems Involved in Installment Selling," *Proceedings of the Academy of Political Science in the City of New York* 12, no. 2 (January 1927): 83–94, p. 84.

53. Olney, *Buy Now, Pay Later,* chap. 2.

54. Sloan, *My Years with General Motors,* p. 302.

55. Martha L. Olney, "Credit as a Production-Smoothing Device: The Case of Automobiles, 1913–1938," *Journal of Economic History* 49, no. 2, *The Tasks of Economic History* (June 1989): 377–391.

56. The financial markets tolerated higher debt-to-capital ratios for finance companies that were capitalized above $500,000. Ibid., pp. 386–388.

57. Foulke, *Sinews of American Commerce,* pp. 198–199.

58. Calder, *Financing the American Dream,* p. 185.

59. Olney, "Credit as a Production-Smoothing Device," pp. 380–381.

60. Geisst, *Beggar Thy Neighbor,* p. 188.

61. Olney, "Credit as a Production-Smoothing Device," p. 383; Hyman, *Debtor Nation,* pp. 23, 26. Other industrial corporations began establishing their own sales finance subsidiaries, including General Electric in 1921. It sold the subsidiary to Industrial Acceptance Corporation in 1928.

62. Ibid., pp. 195–199; Louis Hyman, *Borrow: The American Way of Debt* (New York: Vintage Books, 2012), p. 55.

63. Alfred P. Sloan, "I Believe in Time Payments—Why?" *Nation's Business* 52 (April 1926): 18; Paul J. Kubik, "Federal Reserve Policy during the Great Depression: The Impact of Interwar Attitudes regarding Consumption and Consumer Credit," *Journal of Economic Issues* 30, no. 3 (September 1996): 829–842, p. 837.

64. Seligman, "Economic Problems Involved in Installment Selling"; "Installment Selling," *Time,* November 28, 1927.

65. Paul H. Banner, "Competition, Credit Policies, and the Captive Finance Company," *Quarterly Journal of Economics* 72, no. 2 (May 1958): 241–258, p. 243.

66. Calder, *Financing the American Dream,* p. 151.

67. Ibid., p. 267; Olney, "Credit as a Production Smoothing Device," pp. 377–378.

68. Calder, *Financing the American Dream,* pp. 189–191.

69. Kay Giesecke, Francis A. Longstaff, Stephen Schaefer, and Ilya Strebulaev, "Macroeconomic Effects of Corporate Default Crises: A Long-Term Perspective," unpublished paper, February 2012, p. 1, n. 1.

70. In 1938, the Department of Justice brought an antitrust suit against the three largest car manufacturers for forcing car dealers to use certain preferred sales finance companies. Banner, "Captive Finance Company," pp. 252–253. The case was in the courts until 1952.

71. Calder, *Financing the American Dream,* pp. 192–201. Martha Olney, relying on another source, reports that there were nearly 1,500 auto sales finance companies in 1925. Olney, "Credit as a Production-Smoothing Device," p. 377. For durable goods other than cars, the sales finance companies did not deal directly with consumers but instead bought the sellers' notes (the evidence of the unpaid balances). Neifeld, "What Consumer Credit Is," p. 65.

72. Paul R. Moo, "Legislative Control of Consumer Credit Transactions," *Law and Contemporary Problems* 33 (Fall 1968): 656–670, p. 658.

73. The 40 percent included installment contracts bought by sales finance companies and personal installment loans. Olney, *Buy Now, Pay Later,* p. 108; Robert M. Hunt, "The Development and Regulation of Consumer Credit Reporting in America," Federal Reserve of Philadelphia, Working Paper no. 02-21 (November 2002), p. 10.

74. Geisst, *Collateral Damaged,* pp. 43–44.

75. Calder, *Financing the American Dream,* pp. 279–280.

76. Kubik, "Federal Reserve Policy during the Great Depression," pp. 831–836.

77. Calder, *Financing the American Dream,* p. 274; Moo, "Legislative Control of Consumer Credit Transactions," p. 658.

78. Neifeld, "What Consumer Credit Is," p. 72.

79. Calder, *Financing the American Dream,* p. 285.

80. Rolf Nugent, *Consumer Credit and Economic Stability* (New York: Russell Sage Foundation, 1939). The study covers the period from 1860 to the early 1920s.

81. Neifeld, "What Consumer Credit Is," pp. 64–65.

82. Garon, *Beyond Our Means,* pp. 326, 334.

83. Herbert Hoover, *Memoirs,* vol. 3: *The Great Depression* (New York: Macmillan, 1951–52), p. 30.

84. Kubik, "Federal Reserve Policy during the Great Depression," p. 830.

85. "New Morris Plan," *Time,* November 13, 1933.

86. Garon, *Beyond Our Means,* pp. 191, 204, 206, 208, 321–322.

87. "Regulation of Consumer Credit," *Federal Reserve Bulletin* 28, no. 5 (May 1942): 399–409, p. 401; Walter J. Matherly, "The Regulation of Consumer Credit," *Southern Economic Journal* 11, no. 1 (July 1944): 34–44.

88. Hyman, *Debtor Nation,* chap. 4.

89. Thomas K. McCraw, *American Business, 1920–2000: How It Worked* (Wheeling, IL: Harlan Davidson, 2000), p. 91.

90. Matherly, "Regulation of Consumer Credit," p. 39.

91. Garon, *Beyond Our Means,* p. 201; McCraw, *American Business,* pp. 92–93.

92. Geisst, *Collateral Damaged,* pp. 61, 318; Robert D. Manning, *Credit Card Nation: The Consequences of America's Addiction to Credit* (New York: Basic Books, 2000), pp. 31, 38.

93. Joseph Nocera, *A Piece of the Action: How the Middle Class Joined the Money Class* (Simon and Schuster, 1994), pp. 21–22.

94. *Consumer Credit Controls, Extracts Reprinted from the Report of the Subcommittee on General Credit Control and Debt Management of the Joint Committee on the Economic Report* (reprinted by the Federal Reserve of Cleveland, 1952), pp. 4, 5, 7, cited in Robert Bartels, "Justification for Direct Regulation of Consumer Credit Reappraised," *Journal of Finance* 8, no. 2 (May 1953): 261–271, p. 262, n. 1.

95. Matherly, "Regulation of Consumer Credit," p. 41.

96. Eric H. Shaw and Robert D. Tamilia, "Robert Bartels and the History of Marketing Thought," *Journal of Macromarketing* 21 (2001): 156–163.

97. Bartels, "Consumer Credit Reappraised," pp. 267–268.

98. Garon, *Beyond Our Means,* p. 338.

99. Dwight D. Eisenhower, "White House Statement on Regulation of Consumer Installment Credit," May 25, 1957, *Public Papers of the Presidents of the United States: Dwight D. Eisenhower* (Washington, DC: Government Printing Office, 1957), pp. 413–415. The Eisenhower administration tasked the Federal Reserve Board with investigating whether credit controls ought to be reimposed to avoid economic destabilization. John P. Watkins, "Corporate Power and the Evolution of

Consumer Credit," *Journal of Economic Issues* 34, no. 4 (December 2000): 909–932, p. 918.

100. John Kenneth Galbraith, *The Affluent Society* (London: Penguin Books, 1999 [1958]), pp. 145–147.

101. See, e.g., Arch W. Troelstrup, "The Influence of Moral and Social Responsibility on Selling Consumer Credit," *American Economic Review* 51, no. 2 (May 1961): 549–557, pp. 550–551.

102. William H. Whyte Jr., "Budgetism: Opiate of the Middle Class," *Fortune* (May 1956): 133; Garon, *Beyond Our Means*, p. 320.

103. Board of Governors of the Federal Reserve System, *Consumer Installment Credit: Growth and Import*, pt. 1, vol. 2 (Washington, DC: Government Printing Office, 1957), p. 127.

104. Banner, "Captive Finance Company," p. 250.

105. Lewis Mandell, *The Credit Card Industry: A History* (Boston: Twayne Publishers, 1990), p. 22. The figures do not include mortgage debt.

106. Geisst, *Beggar Thy Neighbor*, p. 216.

107. Mandell, *Credit Card Industry*, p. xii.

108. Nocera, *Piece of the Action*, p. 22.

109. Mandell, *Credit Card Industry*, p. 26.

110. Ibid., pp. 1–10.

111. Timothy Wolters, "'Carry Your Credit in Your Pocket': The Early History of the Credit Card at Bank of America and Chase Manhattan," *Enterprise and Society* 1 (June 2000): 315–354, pp. 323, 327.

112. The T&Es were used primarily by business people and were not seen as competing with the bank cards. Despite their problems, Diners Club and Carte Blanche were profitable for much of the 1970s. Mandell, *Credit Card Industry*, pp. 107, 116.

113. Ibid., pp. 23–25, 29–30.

114. The best accounts of this episode are Nocera, *Piece of the Action*, pp. 23–33; and Wolters, "'Carry Your Credit in Your Pocket.'" If Bank of America had used Chase's more conservative accounting standard, BoA's credit card business would have shown a longer period of losses.

115. Hyman, *Borrow*, pp. 156–157; Mandell, *Credit Card Industry*, pp. 29, 71.

116. Mandell, *Credit Card Industry*, pp. 34, 53; Nocera, *Piece of the Action*, p. 61.

117. Hyman, *Debtor Nation*, p. 240.

118. Mandell, *Credit Card Industry*, pp. xviii, 37.

119. Ibid., p. 61; Nocera, *Piece of the Action*, pp. 101, 103.

120. Mandell, *Credit Card Industry*, p. 38.

121. Nocera, *Piece of the Action*, p. 190. In the mid-1970s, thrifts and credit unions began issuing credit cards, too. Mandell, *Credit Card Industry*, pp. 48–51.

122. Lizabeth Cohen, *A Consumer's Republic: The Politics of Mass Consumption in Postwar America* (New York: Knopf, 2003), chap. 8.

123. Olney, "When Your Word Is Not Enough," pp. 408–409.

124. Hyman, *Debtor Nation*, pp. 174–206, 224.

125. Ibid., p. 215.

126. The regulation did not apply to corporate credit or mortgage loans. Geisst, *Collateral Damaged*, p. 73.

127. Ibid., p. 217. Title IV of the Consumer Credit Protection Act established a National Commission on Consumer Finance. See Thomas A. Durkin and Michael E. Staten, "The Origins of the Credit Research Center," in *The Impact of Public Policy on Consumer Credit*, ed. Thomas A. Durkin and Michael E. Staten (Boston: Kluwer Academic, 2002), pp. 1–22.

128. Both the Truth in Lending and the Fair Credit Billing acts are administered by the Federal Reserve System under Regulation Z.

129. Durkin and Staten, "Origins of the Credit Research Center"; Moo, "Legislative Control of Consumer Credit Transactions," p. 662.

130. Marc A. Weiss, "Marketing and Financing Home Ownership: Mortgage Lending and Public Policy in the United States, 1918–1989," *Business and Economic History*, ser. 2, vol. 18 (1989): 109–118, pp. 109–110.

131. Lawrence J. Vale, "Ideological Origins of Affordable Homeownerhip Efforts," in *Chasing the American Dream: New Perspectives on Affordable Homeownerhip*, ed. William M. Rohe and Harry L. Watson (Ithaca, NY: Cornell University Press, 2007).

132. Vincent J. Cannato, "A Home of One's Own," *National Affairs* 3 (Spring 2010): 69–86, p. 72.

133. Jackson, *Crabgrass Frontier*, p. 205. The housing bubble may have been nationwide; more research is needed. See "The Forgotten Real Estate Boom of the 1920s," Baker Library Historical Collections, Harvard Business School, www.library .hbs.edu/hc/crises/forgotten.html.

134. F. John Devaney, *Tracking the American Dream: 50 Years of Housing History from the Census Bureau: 1940 to 1990* (Washington, DC: U.S. Department of Commerce, Economics and Statistics Administration, Bureau of the Census, 1994), p. 49.

135. Weiss, "Marketing and Financing Home Ownership," pp. 111–112.

136. Eichengreen and Mitchener, "Depression as a Credit Boom Gone Wrong," p. 35.

137. Hyman, *Borrow*, p. 70.

138. Weiss, "Marketing and Financing Home Ownership," p. 112.

139. Herbert Hoover, "Address to the White House Conference on Home Building and Home Ownership," December 21, 1931, http://www.presidency.ucsb .edu/ws/?pid=22927; Weiss, "Marketing and Financing Home Ownership," pp. 109, 117.

140. A bill for such a system was introduced in Congress in 1919 but did not pass. Weiss, "Marketing and Financing Home Ownership," p. 112.

141. Kent W. Colton, "Housing Finance in the United States: The Transformation of the U.S. Housing Finance System," working paper, Joint Center for Housing Studies, Harvard University, July 2002, p. 4. HOLC stopped making loans in 1936 and was liquidated in 1951.

142. Cannato, "Home of One's Own," p. 73.

143. Colton, "Housing Finance in the United States," p. 2; Richard K. Green and Susan M. Wachter, "The American Mortgage in Historical and International Context," *Journal of Economic Perspectives* 19, no. 4 (Fall 2005): 93–114, pp. 94–95.

144. Cannato, "Home of One's Own," p. 73. On the FHA, see Jackson, *Crabgrass Frontier,* pp. 204–218.

145. Weiss, "Marketing and Financing Home Ownership," p. 113.

146. Ibid., p. 113. Other institutional lenders—mortgage bankers and life insurance companies—did not benefit from the FHLB and continued to oppose it. Kenneth A. Snowden, *Mortgage Banking in the United States, 1870–1940,* Research Institute for Housing America, Special Report (2013), pp. 83–84.

147. "Buying at par meant banks had no exposure to interest rate risk when lending long term and funding these loans by FNMA-issued bonds." Green and Wachter, "American Mortgage," p. 96.

148. Snowden, *Mortgage Banking in the United States,* pp. 75, 82, 89, 92; Hyman, *Debtor Nation,* p. 69.

149. Green and Wachter, "American Mortgage," p. 93.

150. Cannato, "Home of One's Own," p. 73.

151. Garon, *Beyond Our Means,* p. 340.

152. Cohen, *Consumer's Republic,* p. 141. See also Glenn C. Altschuler and Stuart M. Blumin, *The GI Bill: A New Deal for Veterans* (Oxford: Oxford University Press, 2009).

153. Devaney, *Tracking the American Dream,* p. 8; Carolyn Merchant, *American Environmental History: An Introduction* (New York: Columbia University Press, 2007), p. 128.

154. Cannato, "Home of One's Own," p. 74.

155. Robert D. Manning, "Credit and Debt in the Age of Influence: Can U.S Bankruptcy Reform Avoid the Recessionary Abyss?" University of Houston Law Center, Institute for Higher Education Law and Governance Monograph 02–08 (2002), p. 4.

156. Garon, *Beyond Our Means,* p. 341.

157. Snowden, *Mortgage Banking in the United States,* pp. 64–68.

158. MGIC History, www.mgic.com/aboutus/mgichistory.html; Paul Goldberger, "The Lives They Lived: Martin Bucksbaum and Max H. Karl; Settling the Suburban Frontier," *New York Times,* December 31, 1995.

159. Michael Quint, "Max H. Karl, 85, Pioneer in Mortgage Insurance," *New York Times,* April 20, 1995.

160. See, e.g., Jack Cashill, *Popes and Bankers: A Cultural History of Credit and Debt, From Aristotle to AIG* (Nashville, TN: Thomas Nelson, 2010).

161. Carliner, "Development of Federal Homeownership 'Policy,' " pp. 306–307; Cannato, "Home of One's Own," p. 75; Jackson, *Crabgrass Frontier,* pp. 206–218.

162. William J. Collins and Robert Margo, "Race and Home Ownership from Civil War to the Present," NBER, Working Paper Series, no. 16665 (January 2011), p. 18.

163. U.S. Department of Housing and Urban Development, *The Secondary Market in Residential Mortgages* (1982), p. 12 (the HUD website lists the publication date as 1982, but the document contains information for 1983); Hyman, *Debtor Nation,* pp. 224–225.

164. Hyman, *Debtor Nation,* pp. 223–224.

165. Carliner, "Development of Federal Homeownership 'Policy,' " pp. 309, 312; Hyman, *Debtor Nation,* pp. 230–231. "Initially, the shares of Freddie Mac were owned by the FHLBs and their member banks, but in 1989, Freddie Mac was converted into a publicly owned GSE like Fannie Mae and with the same special privileges." Calomiris and Haber, *Fragile by Design,* p. 230.

166. Hyman, *Debtor Nation,* pp. 232–234.

167. Geisst, *Collateral Damaged,* p. 125.

168. Hyman, *Debtor Nation,* p. 229.

169. Ibid., pp. 237–239. In 1976, for the first time, Fannie Mae's purchases of conventional mortgages ($2.5 billion) exceeded the purchases made by the FHA and the VA combined ($820 million). U.S. Department of Housing and Urban Development, *Secondary Market in Residential Mortgages,* p. 14.

170. The Federal Home Loan Bank Board and Federal Savings and Loan Insurance Corporation issued nationwide regulations permitting S&Ls to purchase conventional residential loans up to 5 percent of their assets.

171. Mishkin and Eakins, *Financial Markets and Institutions,* p. 373.

172. Green and Wachter, "American Mortgage"; Weiss, "Marketing and Financing Home Ownership," p. 113.

173. Michael Lewis, *Liar's Poker: Rising through the Wreckage of Wall Street* (New York: W. W. Norton, 1989), p. 105.

174. Kevin Fox Gotham, "Separate and Unequal: The Housing Act of 1968 and the Section 235 Program," *Sociological Forum* 15, no. 1 (2000): 13–37, p. 14; Hyman, *Debtor Nation,* p. 227.

175. Carliner, "Development of Federal Homeownership 'Policy,' " pp. 307, 312; Jackson, *Crabgrass Frontier,* p. 205.

176. "Home Mortgage Disclosure Act," Federal Financial Institutions Examination Council, www.ffiec.gov/hmda/default.htm, accessed August 2010.

177. Calomiris and Haber, *Fragile by Design,* p. 196.

178. Foulke, *Sinews of American Commerce,* pp. 198–199.

179. William H. Hillyer, "Four Centuries of Factoring," *Quarterly Journal of Economics* 53, no. 2 (1939): 302–311, p. 309; Foulke, *Sinews of American Commerce,* pp. 188–191.

180. Hillyer, "Four Centuries of Factoring," pp. 310–311.

181. Wilbur C. Plummer and Ralph A. Young, "Sales Finance Companies as Credit Agencies," in *Sales Finance Companies and their Credit Practices,* National Bureau of Economic Research, 1940, p. 38.

182. For modern-day finance companies, see Frederic S. Mishkin and Stanley Eakins, "Finance Companies," in Mishkin and Eakins, *Financial Markets and Institutions,* chap. 26, p. W-5, http://wps.aw.com/aw_mishkin_finmkts_5/0,10613,2146070-,00.html.

183. Ibid., p. W-4.

184. Plummer and Young, "Sales Finance Companies as Credit Agencies," pp. 35, 37, 40.

185. "The Autocrat of 12 Per Cent Money," *Fortune,* March 1958.

186. In the 1950s both GM and GE used their finance arms to maintain sales and market share. Banner, "Captive Finance Company," pp. 244, 246.

187. Many were set up during 1953–1957 to counter the government's tight money policies and the need to find other ways to finance customers. "The Autocrat of 12 Per Cent Money."

188. Mishkin and Eakins, "Finance Companies," p. W-4.

189. Finance companies borrowed large amounts from the money markets and loaned small amounts to clients. Banks did the opposite: they collected small deposits from their customers and often made large loans. Ibid., p. W-2.

190. "The Autocrat of 12 Per Cent Money."

191. Ibid.

192. Ibid. See also Mishkin and Eakins, "Finance Companies," p. W-2.

193. Martin H. Seiden, *The Quality of Trade Credit* (Cambridge, MA: NBER, 1964).

194. Carl Rieser, "The Great Credit Pump," *Fortune,* February 1963, pp. 122–124, 148, 150, 152, 157.

195. Seiden, *Quality of Trade Credit,* pp. 1–5, 15, 26.

196. Geisst, *Collateral Damaged,* pp. 64, 66.

197. George P. Baker and George David Smith, *The New Financial Capitalists: Kohlberg Kravis Roberts and the Creation of Corporate Value* (Cambridge: Cambridge University Press, 1999), p. 48.

198. Discounted cash flow is a method of valuation that uses the projected free cash flow of a company at a future date and then discounts this amount to arrive at a net present value.

199. Geisst, *Collateral Damaged,* pp. 53–54.

200. Franco Modigliani and Merton H. Miller, "The Cost of Capital, Corporate Finance and the Theory of Investment," *American Economic Review* 48, no. 3 (June 1958): 261–297.

201. Bryan Burrough and John Helyar, *Barbarians at the Gate: The Fall of RJR Nabisco* (New York: HarperCollins, 1990), pp. 133–134.

202. Baker and Smith, *New Financial Capitalists,* pp. 48, 50; Allen Kaufman and Ernest J. Englander, "Kohlberg Kravis Roberts & Co and the Restructuring of American Capitalism," *Business History Review* 67, no. 1 (Spring 1993): 52–97, pp. 66–67.

203. "Debt's Honor: Bankruptcy, the American Morality Tale," *New York Times,* March 13, 2005.

204. Bradley Hansen, "Commercial Associations and the Creation of a National Economy: The Demand for Federal Bankruptcy Law," *Business History Review* 72, no. 1 (Spring 1998): 86–113, p. 96.

205. Bradley Hansen, "Bankruptcy Law in the United States," EH.net Encyclopedia, ed. Robert Whaples, August 14, 2001, http://eh.net/encyclopedia/article/hansen.bankruptcy.law.us.

206. Charles J. Tabb, "The History of the Bankruptcy Laws in the United States," *American Bankruptcy Institute Law Review* 3 (1995): 5–51, p. 28; Hansen, "Bankruptcy Law in the United States."

207. Gary Richardson and Michael Gou, "Business Failures by Industry in the United States, 1895 to 1939: A Statistical History," NBER, Working Paper Series, no. 16872 (March 2011).

208. Thomas Bak, John Golmant, and James Woods, "A Comparison of the Effects of the 1978 and 2005 Bankruptcy Filing Rates," *Emory Bankruptcy Developments Journal* 25, no. 1 (2008): 11–38.

209. For the reasons why Congress's original intentions for Chapter X and XI were sidelined, see David Skeel, *Debt's Dominion: A History of Bankruptcy Law in America* (Princeton, NJ: Princeton University Press, 2001), pp. 161–170.

210. Hansen, "Bankruptcy Law in the United States."

211. Failure rates climbed again in the 1980s. Hansen, "Bankruptcy Law in the United States." The business failure rates are from D&B.

212. Robert A. Kagan, "The Routinization of Debt Collection: An Essay on Social Change and Conflict in the Courts," *Law and Society Review* 18, no. 3 (1984): 323–372, p. 347.

213. Tabb, "History of the Bankruptcy Laws in the United States," p. 32.

214. "The 1978 code combines chapters X and XI into chapter 11, a single corporate reorganization chapter." Bak, Golmant, and Woods, "1978 and 2005 Bankruptcy Filing Rates," p. 15.

215. Kagan, "Routinization of Debt Collection," pp. 342, 355, 365–366. Among the "systemic developments" that also led to fewer court cases were the stabilization of banking, spread of insurance, and diversification of credit markets.

216. Hunt, "Consumer Credit Reporting in America," p. 9.

217. Sprague, *Romance of Credit,* p. 170. For credit bureaus worldwide at the end of the twentieth century, see Marco Pagano and Tullio Japelli, "Information Sharing in Credit Markets," *Journal of Finance* 48, no. 5 (December 1993): 1693–1718.

218. Neifeld, "What Consumer Credit Is," pp. 72–73.

219. Kenneth Lipartito, "The Narrative and the Algorithm: Genres of Credit Reporting from the Nineteenth Century to Today," January 6, 2011, pp. 29–31, http//ssrn.com/abstracts+1736283. Even in the 1970s, two-thirds of ACB's member bureaus were located in towns with populations of 20,000 or fewer. Hunt, "Consumer Credit Reporting in America," pp. 9, 11.

220. Experian came about in 1996 when the TRW sold off its information division to an investor group that then sold it to the British company, GUS plc. Nigel Watson, "A Brief History of Experian: Our Story," 2013, on the company's website. There is not much written on the history of TransUnion. According to its company website, TransUnion entered the credit reporting business when it acquired the Credit Bureau of Cook County in 1969.

221. Hunt, "Consumer Credit Reporting in America," p. 11.

222. Lipartito, "The Narrative and the Algorithm," pp. 30–31.

223. Martha Poon, "Scorecards as Devices for Consumer Credit: The Case of Fair, Isaac & Company Incorporated," *Sociological Review* (2007): 284–306, p. 289.

224. Josh Lauer, "The Good Consumer: Credit Reporting and the Invention of Financial Identity in the United States, 1840–1940," *Enterprise and Society* 11, no. 4 (December 2010): 686–694, pp. 691–693.

225. Mandell, *Credit Card Industry,* p. 59.

226. Henry Varnum Poor and his son Henry William Poor published the first series of manuals on the railroad industry, called *Poor's Manual of Railroads,* in 1868. In 1900, the first *Moody's Manual of Industrial and Miscellaneous Securities* was published. See Alfred D. Chandler, *Henry Varnum Poor: Business Editor, Analyst, and Reformer* (Cambridge, MA: Harvard University Press, 1956).

227. Institutions such as credit-reporting firms, the business/financial press, and investment banks were important antecedents. Richard Sylla, "An Historical Primer on the Business of Credit Ratings," in *Ratings, Rating Agencies and the Global Financial System,* ed. Richard M. Levich, Giovanni Mainoni, and Carmen M. Rienhart (Boston: Kluwer Academic Publishers, 2002), pp. 23–25. See also Timothy J. Sinclair, *The New Masters of Capital: American Bond Rating Agencies and the Politics of Creditworthiness* (Ithaca, NY: Cornell University Press, 2005), pp. 24–25; David Stimpson (with Christopher Mahoney), "Moody's: The First Hundred Years," Moody's Investors Service, Inc., 2008, unpublished manuscript, pp. 66–68.

228. Sylla, "Business of Credit Ratings," p. 34. See also Julia Ott, *When Wall Street Met Main Street: The Quest for an Investors' Democracy* (Cambridge: Harvard University Press, 2011), chap. 3.

229. Frank Partnoy, "The Siskel and Ebert of Financial Markets: Two Thumbs Down for the Credit Rating Agencies," *Washington University Law Review* 77, no. 3 (1999): 619–714, pp. 638–639.

230. The Federal Municipal Bankruptcy Act was passed in 1937 to deal with the defaults. Henry W. Lehrmann, "The Federal Municipal Bankruptcy Act," *Journal of Finance* 5, no. 3 (September 1950): 241–256; Stimpson and Mahoney, "Moody's," p. 103; Paul Heffernan, "When Moody's Comment is Baa, That is Merely a Passing Grade," *New York Times,* September 2, 1958.

231. Giesecke, Longstaff, Schaefer, and Strebulaev give a corporate default rate figure of 6.73 percent in 1933 in "Macroeconomic Effects," p. 1, n. 1. Stimpson and Mahoney give a corporate bond default rate of 6.1 percent in 1933 in "Moody's," p. 90.

232. Geisst, *Beggar Thy Neighbor,* p. 206.

233. Sinclair, *The New Masters of Capital,* pp. 26, 42; Stimpson and Mahoney, "Moody's," p. 92.

234. "A History of Standard and Poor's," http://www.standardandpoors.com /about-sp/timeline/en/us/

235. W. Braddock Hickman, *Corporate Bond Quality and Investor Experience* (Princeton, NJ: Princeton University Press, 1958), p. 141.

236. Sylla, "Business of Credit Ratings," p. 30.

237. Calomiris and Haber, *Fragile by Design,* p. 229. However, some scholars argue that explicit federal support for home ownership was limited because most policies had other intentions, such as economic stimulus. See, e.g., Carliner, "Development of Federal Homeownership 'Policy,'" p. 317.

5. "Children, Dogs, Cats, and Moose Are Getting Credit Cards"

1. The total assets of banks grew even larger, to twice GDP. Alan M. Taylor, "The Great Leveraging," NBER, Working Paper Series, no 18290 (August 2012), p. 10.

2. "FRBSF Economic Letter," December 3, 2004 [October 6, 1979], Federal Reserve Bank of San Francisco, no. 2004–35. For historical inflation rates, see InflationData.com.

3. Taylor, "Great Leveraging," p. 10.

4. Frederic S. Mishkin and Stanley Eakins, *Financial Markets and Institutions* (Essex, UK: Pearson Education, 2012), p. 498. The rates violated existing state usury laws. For example, rates on commercial paper reached 15 percent—much higher than New York's legal limit of 4 percent. Charles R. Geisst, *Beggar Thy Neighbor: A History of Usury and Debt* (Philadelphia: University of Pennsylvania Press, 2013), p. 218.

5. Geisst, *Beggar Thy Neighbor,* p. 231.

6. Louis Hyman, *Debtor Nation: The History of America in Red Ink* (Princeton, NJ: Princeton University Press, 2011), p. 253. On Regulation Q, see Mishkin and Eakins, *Financial Markets and Institutions*, pp. 73, 307, 505–506, 510–511, 539.

7. NOW accounts technically were not demand deposit accounts, and so did not fall under Regulation Q. Sidney Homer and Richard Sylla, *A History of Interest Rates,* 4th ed. (New Brunswick, NJ: Rutgers University Press, 2005 [1963]), p. 328. On the creation of the NOW account, see Joseph Nocera, *A Piece of the Action: How the Middle Class Joined the Money Class* (New York: Simon and Schuster, 1994).

8. The origins of financial derivatives is somewhat cloudy. The Chicago Board of Trade may have started the widespread trading of financial derivatives during the 1970s. Mishkin and Eakins, *Financial Markets and Institutions*, p. 499.

9. Charles R. Geisst, *Collateral Damaged: The Marketing of Consumer Debt to America* (New York: Bloomberg Press, 2009), p. 8.

10. For a first-hand account of how Wall Street took advantage of the change in bond markets, see Michael Lewis, *Liar's Poker: Rising through the Wreckage of Wall Street* (New York: W. W. Norton, 1989).

11. Both banks and mutual funds now go to the money markets when they need funds at short notice; for example, when their customers withdraw funds. Mishkin and Eakins, *Financial Markets and Institutions,* p. 504.

12. For the argument that legal rules provide market opportunities, see Richard H. K. Vietor, "Regulation-Defined Financial Markets: Fragmentation and Integration in Financial Services," in *Wall Street and Regulation,* ed. Samuel Hayes (Boston: Harvard Business School Press, 1987).

13. Mishkin and Eakins, *Financial Markets and Institutions,* p. 468. Continental Illinois was renamed Continental Bank. It was sold to BankAmerica in 1994.

14. Charles Calomiris and Stephen Haber, *Fragile by Design: The Political Origins of Banking Crises and Scarce Credit* (Princeton, NJ: Princeton University Press, 2014), p. 215.

15. Branching was regulated by the states and the McFadden Act of 1927 (amended in 1956). Mishkin and Eakins, *Financial Markets and Institutions,* pp. 514–517; Calomiris and Haber, *Fragile by Design,* p. 191; Nocera, *Piece of the Action,* p. 145.

16. Calomiris and Haber, *Fragile by Design,* pp. 154, 195, 201.

17. In 1960, eight U.S. banks operated foreign branches, with total assets of less than $4 billion. In 2012 the number of banks with foreign branches had risen to around one hundred, with more than $1.5 trillion of assets. American banks have engaged in the international markets by underwriting foreign securities, selling insurance, and tapping into Eurodollars, sometimes known as "offshore" deposits. Mishkin and Eakins, *Financial Markets and Institutions,* pp. 523–525.

18. Geisst, *Beggar Thy Neighbor,* p. 232.

19. Mishkin and Eakins, *Financial Markets and Institutions,* pp. 511–512. Conventional practices were overturned, specifically by the Depository Institutions Deregulation and Monetary Control Act (DIDMCA) of 1980 and the Depository Institutions (Garn–St. Germain) Act of 1982.

20. However, a number of commercial banks were already performing investment banking activities through the syndicated loan and Eurobond markets. Geisst, *Beggar Thy Neighbor,* pp. 234, 303.

21. "The loophole allowed affiliates of approved commercial banks to engage in underwriting activities as long as the revenue didn't exceed a specified amount. . . . After the US Supreme Court validated the Fed's action in July 1988, the Federal Reserve allowed JP Morgan, a commercial bank holding company, to underwrite corporate debt securities (in January 1989) and then stocks (in September 1990), with the privilege later extended to other bank holding companies. The regulatory agencies also allowed banks to engage in some real estate and insurance activities." Mishkin and Eakins, *Financial Markets and Institutions,* p. 520.

22. Geisst, *Collateral Damaged,* pp. 80–81.

23. Ibid., p. 100.

24. "Technically, the bank or finance company wanting to securitize would create a special purpose vehicle, or trust in this case, which would issue the bonds and pledge the receivables as collateral. Since the assets were now off the balance sheet of the original lender, the trust was considered 'bankruptcy remote,' meaning that even if the bank or finance company went bankrupt the bonds would survive standing alone and be paid by the trust." Geisst, *Beggar Thy Neighbor,* p. 227.

25. Lewis, *Liar's Poker,* pp. 136–137.

26. Lewis Mandell, *Credit Card Industry: A History* (Boston: Twayne Publishers, 1990), p. 88.

27. Geisst, *Collateral Damaged,* pp. 132–133.

28. Ibid., pp. 8–9.

29. Raghuram G. Rajan, *Fault Lines: How Hidden Fractures Still Threaten the World Economy* (Princeton, NJ: Princeton University Press, 2010), pp. 69, 109, 132.

30. Taylor, "Great Leveraging," pp. 14–15.

31. Rajan, *Fault Lines,* pp. 69, 109, 132.

32. Stephen A. Meyer, "The U.S. as a Debtor Country: Causes, Prospects, and Policy Implications," *Business Review,* Federal Reserve Bank of Philadelphia

(November/December 1989): 19–31; Homer and Sylla, *History of Interest Rates,* p. 329.

33. U.S. Census, Foreign Trade, Trade in Goods with China, 1990 and 2000, www.census.gov/foreign-trade/balance/c5700.html#2000.

34. Nocera, *Piece of the Action,* pp. 128, 191.

35. Lewis, *Liar's Poker,* pp. 35–36.

36. Geisst, *Collateral Damaged,* p. 103.

37. Nocera, *Piece of the Action,* p. 298.

38. The measure does not include car leases, payday loans, pawns, and rent-to-own contracts. Robert D. Manning, "Credit and Debt in the Age of Influence: Can U.S Bankruptcy Reform Avoid the Recessionary Abyss?" University of Houston Law Center, Institute for Higher Education Law and Governance Monograph 02–08 (2002), p. 4.

39. Mandell, *Credit Card Industry,* p. 77.

40. Nocera, *Piece of the Action,* pp. 185–186.

41. Sheldon Garon, *Beyond Our Means: Why America Spends while the World Saves* (Princeton, NJ: Princeton University Press, 2011), p. 331.

42. Ibid., p. 344.

43. Before the revisions, the savings rate was thought to have been around 8 percent until the early 1980s. Ibid., pp. 344, 353.

44. However, the greatest *number* of credit cards (as opposed to billings) was held by retailers. Mandell, *Credit Card Industry,* pp. xxi, 92.

45. Hyman, *Debtor Nation,* p. 220.

46. Robert D. Manning, *Credit Card Nation: The Consequences of America's Addiction to Credit* (New York: Basic Books, 2000), pp. 11–13; John P. Watkins, "Corporate Power and the Evolution of Consumer Credit," *Journal of Economic Issues* 34, no. 4 (December 2000): 909–932, p. 924.

47. Thomas A. Durkin, "Credit Cards: Use and Consumer Attitudes, 1970–2000," *Federal Reserve Bulletin* (September 2000): pp. 623–634; Edward J. Bird, Paul A. Hagstrom, and Robert Wild, "Credit Card Debts of the Poor: High and Rising," *Journal of Policy Analysis and Management* 18, no. 1 (Winter 1999): 125–133, pp. 129, 132. The authors found that default rates among poor households actually fell between 1989 and 1995, a fact that was "difficult to reconcile" with higher bankruptcy rates. In 2000, the combination of credit card debt and consumer loans for autos and appliances totaled $1.5 trillion. Twenty years earlier, total credit card debt had been very much smaller—just $50 billion. Manning, "Credit and Debt in the Age of Influence," p. 3. In 1978, commercial banks held as much revolving credit as retailers, but by 1993, the banks held five times as much. J. C. Penney became the first major department store to accept Visa in 1979; Sears, one of the holdouts, did not do so until 1993. Robert M. Hunt, "The Development and Regulation of Consumer Credit Reporting in America," Federal Reserve of Philadelphia, Working Paper Series, no. 02–21 (November 2002), p. 11; Nocera, *Piece of the Action,* p. 306.

48. Peter R. Shergold, "The Loan Shark: The Small Loan Business in Early Twentieth-Century Pittsburgh," *Pennsylvania History* 45, no. 3 (July 1978): 195–223.

49. Hyman, *Debtor Nation*, p. 245; Lawrence Ausubel, "The Failure of Competition in the Credit Card Market," *American Economic Review* 81, no. 1 (March 1991): 50–81; Manning, *Credit Card Nation*, p. 21.

50. Geisst, *Collateral Damaged*, p. 89; Hyman, *Debtor Nation*, p. 253.

51. Geisst, *Collateral Damaged*, p. 102.

52. Congressional Budget Office, *The Changing Business of Banking: A Study of Failed Banks from 1987 to 1992* (June 1994), p. 8. Sears in 1993 spun off its investment and credit arm into Dean Witter, Discover & Co.

53. Hyman, *Debtor Nation*, p. 254.

54. Ibid., p. 251.

55. Eric Gould, *The University in a Corporate Culture* (New Haven, CT: Yale University Press, 2003), p. 55.

56. Manning, *Credit Card Nation*, pp. 228–232; Gwendolyn Bounds, "The Great Money Hunt," *Wall Street Journal*, November 29, 2004.

57. Geisst, *Beggar Thy Neighbor*, p. 217.

58. Mandell, *Credit Card Industry*, pp. xix, 72, 78.

59. Nocera, *Piece of the Action*, p. 196; Mandell, *Credit Card Industry*, pp. 77–78.

60. Nocera, *Piece of the Action*, p. 195.

61. Geisst, *Collateral Damaged*, p. 105.

62. Hyman, *Debtor Nation*, p. 257.

63. Mandell, *Credit Card Industry*, pp. 78–79.

64. Nocera, *Piece of the Action*, pp. 147, 304; Geisst, *Beggar Thy Neighbor*, p. 224.

65. Of the states with interest-rate ceilings, South Dakota and Ohio had the highest (24 percent), and Arkansas had the lowest (10 percent). Nocera, *Piece of the Action*, p. 193.

66. Manning, "Credit and Debt in the Age of Influence," p. 8.

67. Hyman, *Debtor Nation*, pp. 246–247.

68. Garon, *Beyond Our Means*, p. 347.

69. Nocera, *Piece of the Action*, p. 392.

70. Geisst, *Collateral Damaged*, p. 29.

71. Garon, *Beyond Our Means*, p. 347; David Sparks Evans, *Paying with Plastic: The Digital Revolution in Buying and Borrowing* (Cambridge, MA: MIT Press, 2005), p. 89.

72. Hearings Before the Committee on Banking, Housing, and Urban Affairs, U.S. Senate, "Nomination of Alan Greenspan," 106th Congress, Second Session (January 26, 2000) (Alan Greenspan, nominee for chair of the Federal Reserve).

73. Ebonya Washington, "The Impact of Banking and Fringe Banking Regulations on the Number of Unbanked Americans," *The Journal of Human Resources* 41, no. 1 (Winter 2006): pp. 106–137.

74. See FundingUniverse.com for profiles of these companies. For a discussion of fringe lending generally, see Manning, *Credit Card Nation*, chap. 7.

75. Consumer Federation of America, "States Grant Payday Lenders a Safe Harbor from Usury Laws," press release, September 7, 1999, www.consumerfed.org /pdfs/safeharpr.pdf.

76. Manning, "Credit and Debt in the Age of Influence," p. 6.

77. In the early twentieth century, it was known as "salary buying," where lenders made loans to workers in exchange for their weekly paychecks. The lenders imposed a fee of around 10–20 percent of the paycheck, but they skirted the usury laws by claiming to provide a service rather than a loan. Geisst, *Collateral Damaged,* p. 51.

78. Erik Eckholm, "Seductively Easy, 'Payday Loans' Often Snowball," *New York Times,* December 23, 2006.

79. David Leonhardt, "TV's, DVD's: All Yours, But First Do the Math," *New York Times,* December 16, 2001.

80. "Rent-to-Own Stores Becoming a Consumer Issue," *New York Times,* February 15, 1993; Leonhardt, "TV's, DVD's."

81. Federal Trade Commission, Bureau of Economics Staff Report, *Survey of Rent-to-Own Customers* (April 2000), p. ES-2.

82. Wendy A. Woloson, *In Hock: Pawning in America from Independence through the Great Depression* (Chicago: University of Chicago Press, 2010), pp. 186, 189.

83. Robert A. Kagan, "The Routinization of Debt Collection: An Essay on Social Change and Conflict in the Courts," *Law and Society Review* 18, no. 3 (1984): 323–372, pp. 351–352n25. For a different view, see Gunnar Trumbull, *Strength in Numbers: The Political Power of Weak Interests* (Cambridge: Cambridge University Press, 2012).

84. Garon, *Beyond Our Means,* pp. 366–367, 370.

85. Geisst, *Collateral Damaged,* pp. 24–25.

86. Mandell, *Credit Card Industry,* p. 90.

87. Richard K. Green and Susan M. Wachter, "The American Mortgage in Historical and International Context," *Journal of Economic Perspectives* 19, no. 4 (Fall 2005): 93–114. The 2000 household debt figure is from Board of Governors of the Federal Reserve System, *Financial Accounts of the United States: Flow of Funds, Balance Sheets, and Integrated Macroeconomic Accounts, Historical Annual Tables, 1995–2004,* www.federalreserve.gov/releases/z1/current/annuals/a1995-2004.pdf.

88. Mishkin and Eakins, "The Savings and Loan Crisis and Its Aftermath," in *Financial Markets and Institutions,* app. 1, chap. 11, pp. 44–45.

89. Garon, *Beyond Our Means,* pp. 343–344.

90. Mishkin and Eakins, "The Savings and Loan Crisis," pp. 44–45.

91. Lewis, *Liar's Poker,* pp. 103–108, 114.

92. Mishkin and Eakins, "The Savings and Loan Crisis," pp. 44–47. For an explanation of why the S&L regulatory agencies historically have been weak, see Federal Deposit Insurance Corporation, "An Examination of the Banking Crises of the 1980s and Early 1990s," in *History of the Eighties: Lessons for the Future* (1997), chap. 4.

93. Mishkin and Eakins, "The Savings and Loan Crisis," p. 49.

94. Calomiris and Haber, *Fragile by Design,* p. 200; Geisst, *Collateral Damaged,* p. 129.

95. Hyman, *Debtor Nation,* pp. 223–239.

96. Geisst, *Collateral Damaged,* pp. 124–125. The other issuers of agency bonds include the Student Loan Marketing Association (SLMA, or "Sallie Mae"), the

Farmers Home Administration, the Federal Housing Administration, the VA, and the Federal Land Banks. Beginning in 1970, Ginnie Mae issued a security that was more like a bond than a pass-through, but inadequate volume caused the agency to stop offering them after a few years. Hyman, *Debtor Nation*, pp. 228–229.

97. "Only a third of commercial banks, in 1984, resold mortgages to the secondary markets. But those that did sell, sold nearly all—90 to 100 percent—of their mortgages." Ibid., pp. 236–237.

98. Lewis, *Liar's Poker*, pp. 81, 86–87.

99. The Senate Banking Committee reported in 2000 that banks had paid fees and contributions to the activist groups of some $9.5 billion. Another study found that "by 2008, banks had undertaken $2.78 trillion dollars in CRA [Community Reinvestment Act] commitments that they would not have undertaken otherwise." Calomiris and Haber, *Fragile by Design*, pp. 18, 222, 224, 231–232.

100. Geisst, *Collateral Damaged*, p. 136. See also Michael S. Carliner, "Development of Federal Homeownership 'Policy,' " *Housing Policy Debate* 9, no. 2 (1998): 299–321.

101. President Bill Clinton, "Remarks on the National Homeownership Strategy," June 5, 1995, http://www.presidency.ucsb.edu/?pid=51448; Suzanne Kapner, "Sunset Boulevard: US Housing," *Financial Times*, August 17, 2010.

102. Calomiris and Haber, *Fragile by Design*, p. 245.

103. Ibid., pp. 231–232, 236, 260–261.

104. Harold James, *The Creation and Destruction of Value: The Globalization Cycle* (Cambridge, MA: Harvard University Press, 2009), p. 152.

105. Calomiris and Haber, *Fragile by Design*, pp. 233, 237–239, 246–248.

106. Louise Story, "Home Equity Frenzy Was a Bank Ad Come True," *New York Times*, August 15, 2008.

107. Hyman, *Debtor Nation*, p. 237.

108. Geisst, *Collateral Damaged*, pp. 9, 75–76, 138. The swelling of ARMs was a result of a 1980 law that abolished interest-rate ceilings. ARMs became even more popular when Fannie Mae and Freddie Mac began buying them.

109. This section relies on Lawrence Gladieux, "Federal Student Aid Policy: A History and an Assessment," in *Financing Postsecondary Education: The Federal Role. Proceedings of the National Conference on the Best Ways for the Federal Government to Help Students and Families Finance Postsecondary Education* (Washington, DC: Brookings Institution, 1995); and Roger L. Geiger and Donald E. Heller, "Financial Trends in Higher Education: The United States," Penn State Center for the Study of Higher Education, Working Paper Series, no. 6 (January 2011).

110. Geisst, *Collateral Damaged*, p. 104.

111. Manning, *Credit Card Nation*, pp. 166–170; Jessica Silver Greenberg, "Majoring in Credit-Card Debt," *Businessweek*, September 4, 2007; Eric Gould, *The University in a Corporate Culture* (New Haven, CT: Yale University Press, 2003), pp. 54–55.

112. Mishkin and Eakins, *Financial Markets and Institutions*, p. 585.

113. The trend continued even when the high-inflation environment of the late 1970s and early 1980s made it harder for corporations to issue bonds because many

investors demanded shorter maturities of five to ten years. Homer and Sylla, *History of Interest Rates*, pp. 332–333.

114. Geisst, *Beggar Thy Neighbor,* p. 215; Geisst, *Collateral Damaged,* pp. 69–70.

115. Michael C. Jensen and William H. Meckling, "The Theory of the Firm: Managerial Behavior, Agency Costs and Ownership Structure," *Journal of Financial Economics* 3 (October 1976): 305–360.

116. Bryan Burrough and John Helyar, *Barbarians at the Gate: The Fall of RJR Nabisco* (New York: HarperCollins, 1990), pp. 5, 101.

117. George P. Baker and George David Smith, *The New Financial Capitalists: Kohlberg Kravis Roberts and the Creation of Corporate Value* (Cambridge: Cambridge University Press, 1999), pp. 61–76.

118. Burrough and Helyar, *Barbarians at the Gate,* p. 139.

119. However, Ross Johnson may have done the LBO to prevent the loss of his perks and any constraints on his free-spending ways. Ibid., pp. 4, 89.

120. Allen Kaufman and Ernest J. Englander, "Kohlberg Kravis Roberts & Co. and the Restructuring of American Capitalism," *Business History Review* 67, no. 1 (Spring 1993): 52–97, pp. 54–61.

121. Burrough and Helyar, *Barbarians at the Gate,* p. 130.

122. "Commercial banks held about 30 percent of the equity capital in KKR's 1982 fund, a figure that remained unchanged for the 1984, 1986, and 1987 funds." Kaufman and Englander, "Kohlberg Kravis Roberts & Co.," pp. 71, 80.

123. Burrough and Helyar, *Barbarians at the Gate,* p. 139.

124. Geisst, *Beggar Thy Neighbor,* p. 262. For a best-selling account of Michael Milken and Drexel that covers the period up to the late 1980s, see Connie Bruck, *The Predators' Ball: The Inside Story of Drexel Burnham and the Rise of the Junk Bond Raiders* (New York: Penguin, 1988).

125. Subordinated debts were riskier, so the lenders demanded higher interest rates. Kaufman and Englander, "Kohlberg Kravis Roberts & Co.," pp. 64, 69, 71–72, 75–76, 78.

126. Most pension funds, now the major source of KKR money, were banned from or shunned hostile takeovers. Burrough and Helyar, *Barbarians at the Gate,* p. 151.

127. Ibid., p. 139.

128. Kaufman and Englander, "Kohlberg Kravis Roberts & Co.," pp. 83–84.

129. Alan D. Morrison and William J. Wilhelm, Jr., *Investment Banking: Institutions, Politics and Law* (Oxford: Oxford University Press, 2007), pp. 261–262.

130. Patrick A. Gaughan, *Mergers, Acquisitions, and Corporate Restructurings* (John Wiley, 2010), pp. 345–346.

131. Mishkin and Eakins, *Financial Markets and Institutions,* p. 333.

132. Burrough and Helyar, *Barbarians at the Gate,* pp. 108, 150, 156.

133. Ibid., pp. 139–141.

134. Lewis, *Liar's Poker,* pp. 219–221.

135. Norman Jewison, dir., *Other People's Money,* starring Danny DeVito and Gregory Peck (Warner Bros., 1991), film.

136. Kaufman and Englander, "Kohlberg Kravis Roberts & Co.," pp. 85, 87.

137. "Leveraged buyouts had peaked in numbers (381) in 1988 and in value ($70 billion by some measures) in 1989." Baker and Smith, *New Financial Capitalists,* pp. 41, 147.

138. Kaufman and Englander, "Kohlberg Kravis Roberts & Co.," p. 89.

139. Mishkin and Eakins, *Financial Markets and Institutions,* p. 333; Jennie Russell Kasindorf, "What to Make of Mike," *Fortune,* September 30, 1996, pp. 80–105.

140. Gaughan, *Mergers, Acquisitions, and Corporate Restructurings,* p. 346.

141. Amendments in 1984 shifted the authority to appoint the judges from the president to the court of appeals. See "History of the Federal Judiciary," Federal Judicial Center, www.fjc.gov/history/home.nsf; Geisst, *Beggar Thy Neighbor,* p. 223.

142. David Skeel, *Debt's Dominion: A History of Bankruptcy Law in America* (Princeton, NJ: Princeton University Press, 2001), pp. 192–193, 242–243.

143. Ibid., pp. 190–191; Bradley Hansen, "Bankruptcy Law in the United States," EH.net Encyclopedia, ed. Robert Whaples, August 14, 2001, http://eh.net /encyclopedia/article/hansen.bankruptcy.law.us.

144. Skeel, *Debt's Dominion,* pp. 187–188, 192, 196–198, and chap. 7 generally.

145. Hansen, "Bankruptcy Law in the United States."

146. Skeel, *Debt's Dominion,* pp. 190, 202.

147. Manning, "Credit and Debt in the Age of Influence," p. 12.

148. Thomas Bak, John Golmant, and James Woods, "A Comparison of the Effects of the 1978 and 2005 Bankruptcy Filing Rates," *Emory Bankruptcy Developments Journal* 25, no. 1 (2008): 11–38, pp. 16–17.

149. Two important works argue that most bankruptcy filers come from middle-class households that have fallen on hard times. Teresa A. Sullivan, Elizabeth Warren, and Jay Lawrence Westbrook, *As We Forgive Our Debtors: Bankruptcy and Consumer Credit in America* (New York: Oxford University Press, 1989); Teresa A. Sullivan, Elizabeth Warren, Jay Lawrence Westbrook, *The Fragile Middle Class: Americans in Debt* (New Haven, CT: Yale University Press, 2000).

150. Morrison and Wilhelm, *Investment Banking,* pp. 254–255; Charles J. Tabb, "The History of the Bankruptcy Laws in the United States," *American Bankruptcy Institute Law Review* 3 (1995): 5–51, p. 35.

151. Much of this section relies on Skeel, *Debt's Dominion.* See esp. pp. 176–177, 181–183, 206, 214, 217–218, 221, 224–225, 229, 236–237.

152. Hunt, "Development and Regulation of Consumer Credit Reporting." Experian was formerly part of the conglomerate TRW.

153. "ACB membership declined from a peak of around 2,200 in 1965 to only about 500" in the early 2000s. Hunt, "Development and Regulation of Consumer Credit Reporting," p. 11; Robert M. Hunt, "A Century of Consumer Credit Reporting in America," Federal Reserve Bank of Philadelphia, Working Paper Series, no. 05–13 (June 2005), p. 16.

154. Tullio Japelli and Marco Pagano, "Information Sharing, Lending and Defaults: Cross-Country Evidence," *Journal of Banking and Finance* 26 (2002): 2017–2045, p. 2026.

155. Loretta J. Mester, "What's the Point of Credit Scoring?" *Business Review*, Federal Reserve Bank of Philadelphia (September/October 1997): 3–16.

156. Akos Rona-Tas and Stefanie Hiss, "The Role of Ratings in the Subprime Mortgage Crisis: The Art of Corporate and the Science of Consumer Credit Rating," in *Markets on Trial: The Economic Sociology of the U.S. Financial Crisis; Part A, Research in the Sociology of Organizations,* vol. 30, ed. Michael Lounsbury and Paul M. Hirsch (Bingley, UK: Emerald Group, 2010), pp. 115–155.

157. Martha Poon, "Scorecards as Devices for Consumer Credit: The Case of Fair, Isaac & Company Incorporated," *Sociological Review,* special issue, 55, issue supplement s2 (October 2007): 284–306, pp. 294–297.

158. Hunt, "Development and Regulation of Consumer Credit Reporting," p. 11.

159. Poon, "Scorecards as Devices for Consumer Credit," pp. 298–300.

160. Ibid., pp. 298–300.

161. Martha Poon, "From New Deal Institutions to Capital Markets: Commercial Consumer Risk Scores and the Making of Subprime Finance," *Accounting, Organizations and Society* 34 (2009): 654–674, pp. 662–664.

162. Ibid., pp. 656, 658.

163. Robert M. Hunt, "The Development and Regulation of Consumer Credit Reporting in America," Federal Reserve of Philadelphia, Working Paper Series, no. 02–21 (November 2002), p. 16

164. Hunt, "Century of Consumer Credit Reporting," pp. 31–32; Robert B. Avery, Paul S. Calem, and Glenn B. Canner, "An Overview of Consumer Data and Credit Reporting," *Federal Reserve Bulletin* (February 2003): 47–73.

165. Kenneth Lipartito, "Mediating Reputation: Credit Reporting Systems in American History," *Business History Review* 87, no. 4 (Winter 2013): 655–677; Hyman, *Debtor Nation*, pp. 214–217.

166. Twentieth Century Fund, Task Force on Municipal Bond Ratings, *The Rating Game* (Millwood, NY: Kraus Reprint Co., 1977 [1974]).

167. David Stimpson (with Christopher Mahoney), "Moody's: The First Hundred Years," Moody's Investors Service, Inc., 2008, unpublished manuscript, pp. 122–124, 138–140. See also Richard Sylla, "An Historical Primer on the Business of Credit Ratings," in *Ratings, Rating Agencies and the Global Financial System,* ed. Richard M. Levich, Giovanni Mainoni, and Carmen M. Rienhart (Boston: Kluwer Academic Publishers, 2002).

168. Timothy J. Sinclair, *The New Masters of Capital: American Bond Rating Agencies and the Politics of Creditworthiness* (Ithaca, NY: Cornell University Press, 2005), pp. 42–46.

169. Stimpson and Mahoney, "Moody's," pp. 140–146. Fitch launched Euro-Ratings Ltd. in London in 1986 to meet the need for a European rating agency, but this failed in 1989.

170. Ibid., pp. 145, 187–194, 208–209.

171. David Steigerwald, "Did the Protestant Ethic Disappear? The Virtue of Thrift on the Cusp of Postwar Affluence," *Enterprise and Society* 9, no. 4 (December 2008): 788–815.

172. This trend holds whether "savings" is defined as including only the "portion of personal income that is left over after personal current taxes and outlays for personal consumption expenditures," or as also including defined benefit pension plans. Marshall B. Reinsdorf, "Alternative Measures of Personal Saving," *Survey of Current Business* 87, no. 2 (February 2007): 7–13; Garon, *Beyond Our Means*, p. 3.

173. Watkins, "Corporate Power and the Evolution of Consumer Credit," p. 910.

174. "The Turning Point," *The Economist*, September 22, 2007.

175. Peter R. Earling, *Whom to Trust: A Practical Treatise on Mercantile Credits* (Chicago: Rand, McNally & Co., 1890).

176. George Anders, *Merchants of Debt: KKR and the Mortgaging of American Business* (New York: Basic Books, 1992).

Postscript

1. Stephen Labaton, "Agency '04 Rule Let Banks Pile Up New Debt," *New York Times*, October 3, 2008. The SEC ended the program in 2008.

2. "Fear and Loathing, and a Hint of Hope—Securitisation," *The Economist*, February 16, 2008. See also Alan M. Taylor, "The Great Leveraging," NBER, Working Paper Series, no. 18290 (August 2012), pp. 1, 11–12.

3. "Fixing Finance," *The Economist*, January 24, 2009.

4. Sheldon Garon, *Beyond Our Means: Why America Spends while the World Saves* (Princeton, NJ: Princeton University Press, 2011), pp. 350–351.

5. Originally, TARP had earmarked $700 billion for the toxic assets, but in 2010 this was reduced to $475 billion. As of October 2014, the federal government had spent over $600 billion bailing out banks, AIG, auto companies, and the GSEs. It has been repaid more than one-half of the loan and has made a profit overall, mostly through dividends earned. "Bailout Tracker," Pro Publica, 2015, http://projects.propublica.org/bailout/main/summary.

6. Lowell R. Ricketts and Christopher J. Waller, "The Rise and (Eventual) Fall in the Fed's Balance Sheet," *Regional Economist* (January 2014).

7. Raghuram G. Rajan, *Fault Lines: How Hidden Fractures Still Threaten the World Economy* (Princeton, NJ: Princeton University Press, 2010), p. 151.

8. The Third Basel Accord, agreed in 2010–2011 and scheduled to be introduced beginning in 2013, was meant to address the inadequacies in bank reserves that were revealed by the financial crisis. One influential criticism of the Basel Accords argues that banks should be forced to rely more heavily on equity rather than debt. Anat Admati and Martin Hellwig, *The Bankers' New Clothes: What's Wrong with Banking and What to Do about It* (Princeton, NJ: Princeton University Press, 2013).

9. *The Economist*, June 26, 2010.

10. "Debt and Deleveraging: The Global Credit Bubble and Its Economic Consequences," McKinsey Global Institute (January 2010).

11. "The Turning Point," *The Economist*, September 22, 2007. The 70 percent figure is from the Bureau of Economic Analysis.

12. "Fear and Loathing."

13. Martha Poon, "From New Deal Institutions to Capital Markets: Commercial Consumer Risk Scores and the Making of Subprime Finance," *Accounting, Organizations and Society* 34 (2009): 654–674, pp. 669–672. Even in April 2013, nearly five years after the crisis hit, a congressional committee on financial services noted that "roughly 90 percent of all residential mortgage originations are securitised into government-backed [bonds]." The government was guaranteeing almost all new mortgage bonds. The evidence suggested that had the government withdrawn its guarantees, house prices would have fallen by another 25 percent. Gillian Tett, *Financial Times,* April 26, 2013.

14. Michael Lewis, *The Big Short: Inside the Doomsday Machine* (London: Penguin, 2011 [2010]), p. 165; Charles Calomiris and Stephen Haber, *Fragile by Design: The Political Origins of Banking Crises and Scarce Credit* (Princeton, NJ: Princeton University Press, 2014), p. 261. In addition to mortgage loans, which make up CMOs, CDOs can be backed by assets such as credit card, automobile, student, and other loans.

15. Calomiris and Haber, *Fragile by Design,* pp. 207, 243, 256.

16. The investment bank J.P. Morgan invented the credit default swap in the 1990s. Frederic S. Mishkin and Stanley Eakins, *Financial Markets and Institutions* (Essex, UK: Pearson Education Ltd., 2012), p. 333; Lewis, *Big Short,* p. 70.

17. John Kay, "Arbitrage Wastes the Talents of Finance's Finest Minds," *Financial Times,* August 26, 2014.

18. Lewis, *Big Short,* pp. 31, 76–78.

19. Mishkin and Eakins, *Financial Markets and Institutions,* pp. 334, 569–571.

20. Henry Paulson, *On the Brink: Inside the Race to Stop the Collapse of the Global Financial System* (New York: Business Plus, 2010), p. 394.

21. Rajan, *Fault Lines,* pp. 142–143, 149.

22. Calomiris and Haber, *Fragile by Design,* pp. 271–272.

23. *Financial Times,* color supplement, October 26–27, 2013, pp. 27–28.

24. Thomas K. McCraw, *The Founders and Finance: How Hamilton, Gallatin, and Other Immigrants Forged a New Economy* (Cambridge, MA: Harvard University Press, 2012), p. 351.

25. Edward L. Glaeser, "A Nation of Gamblers: Real Estate Speculation and American History," NBER, Working Paper Series, no. 18825 (February 2013).

26. Samuel H. Williamson, "What Was the U.S. GDP Then?" MeasuringWorth, 2014, www.measuringworth.org/usgdp.

27. Alan Greenspan, *The Map and the Territory 2.0: Risk, Human Nature and the Future of Forecasting* (London: Penguin, 2014). Greenspan admitted that "animal spirits" play a bigger role in bubbles than had been apparent to him at the time. He recommended raising the capital requirements for financial institutions but cautioned against overregulation.

ACKNOWLEDGMENTS

Edward Balleisen, Richard John, Thomas McCraw, Ken Okamura, Silvana Siddali, Daniel Wadhwani, Mark Wilson, and several anonymous readers commented on early drafts of this manuscript. Audiences and seminar participants at the Harvard Business School, University of Georgia, University of Glasgow, Saïd Business School, and the Business History Conference guided me with their questions and suggestions. The Oxford University Centre for Corporate Reputation provided a congenial and stimulating work environment. Linda Cornell organized the graphics, tables, and permissions with great care and competence. Walter Friedman suggested the initial topic and advised me during all stages of writing. As always, Charles Wilson championed this project from the beginning and served as my ideal reader. To all of them, I give my heartfelt thanks.

INDEX

Accounts receivable, 88, 90, 97, 157–159, 160, 170; credit card, 185, 186, 214; factors and, 232, 233; failure to collect, 160; in 1780s, 240n60; in nineteenth century, 259n79

Adjustment bureaus, 90, 115, 162

AIG (American International Group, Inc.), 219, 222–223

American Association of Small Loan Brokers, 110, 130

American Bankers Association, 138, 188

American Express, 145, 146, 186

Asset-backed securities, 176, 180–181, 214, 217, 221

Associated Credit Bureaus (ACB), 118, 165

Bailouts, 194, 216, 219, 225, 267n13

Balleisen, Edward, 69, 73

Banking Act (1933), 179

Bankruptcy, 31–38, 69–75, 110–115, 162–164 182, 206–209; Chapter 7, 207; Chapter 11, 208, 218; Chapter 13, 207; clause in U.S. Constitution, 34–35; Code, 163–164, 206, 208; corporate, 163–164, 175; and equity receivership, 112–113, 164; exemptions, 72, 73–74, 111, 113; of farmers, 103; involuntary, 31, 42, 71, 114, 163; lawyers, 115, 206, 208;

national laws, 44, 73, 86, 90, 96–97, 110, 111, 113–115, 162–164; prepackaged, 209; of railroads, 90, 96–97, 111–113, 163; referees, 115; in South, 111; voluntary, 71, 73, 74, 78, 111, 114–115, 163

Bank for International Settlements (BIS), 178, 219

Bank of America, 88, 131, 145–146, 159, 187, 272n114

Bank of England, 9, 20, 37, 41, 52, 53

Bank of North America, 19, 20, 22, 36, 42, 47

Bank of the United States (BUS), 49, 61, 85; as central bank, 50, 53; and foreign investors, 55, 56; Albert Gallatin and, 57–58; Alexander Hamilton and, 40; as issuer of currency, 23; Andrew Jackson and, 7, 8, 9, 51; Thomas Jefferson and, 41–42, 49; privileges of, 7

Bank of United States, 125, 132

Bank One, 181, 186

Banks: amount of credit from, 49–50, 159; branches, 10, 83–84, 86, 178; credit departments of, 89; deposits, 5, 6, 47, 82, 87, 88, 98, 110, 125, 127, 140, 151, 175, 176, 182, 231, 248n51, 256n18, 276n189, 280n17; failure of, 60, 125, 127, 179, 248n42; land, 20, 102, 150;

293

Thrift, 138, 139
Tolman, Daniel H., 109, 185
TransUnion, 165, 209, 210, 215
Trotter, Nathan, 60–61, 63–64, 65
Troubled Asset Relief Program (TARP, 2008), 219
Truth in Lending Act (1968), 148, 198
TRW Credit Data, 165

Uniform Small Loan Law, 109, 130
Union Trust Co. v. Illinois Midland Co. (1886), 113
United States Steel Corporation, 95–96
Universal Air Travel Plan, 144
Universal Credit Corporation, 135
U.S. Census of 1890, 97–98, 99, 110
U.S. Treasuries, 5, 40, 175, 181, 198, 219, 230
Usurer's Grip, 109
Usury: adjustable-rate mortgages and, 197; antebellum era, 50, 64–65; Jeremy Bentham on, 30; colonial period, 30; as consumer protection, 31; credit cards and, 187; in Europe, 28–30; finance

companies and, 136; reform of, 105, 107, 109, 129, 130, 170; Adam Smith on, 30, 77

Van Buren, Martin, 52, 55
Veterans Administration (VA), 151, 153, 154, 155
Volcker, Paul, 177, 183

Wall Street (film), 205
Walter E. Heller and Company, 158–159
War of Independence, 3, 20, 22, 34, 39, 40
Watkins, J. B. (J. B. Watkins Land Company), 100–101, 102
Webster, Daniel, 7, 58, 73
Wells, Oscar, 138
Whigs, 7–9, 51, 58, 72, 73, 78
Whyte, William, 122, 143
Williams v. U.S. Fidelity (1915), 162
Willing, Thomas, 47
Workingmen's Loan Association, 106, 118
World War I, 88, 156, 167
World War II, 122, 140–142, 219